This book offers a comprehensive, readable, and authoritative introduction to the study of Shakespeare, by means of nineteen newly commissioned essays. An international team of prominent scholars provides a broadly cultural approach to the chief literary, performative, and historical aspects of Shakespeare's work. They bring the latest scholarship to bear on traditional subjects of Shakespeare studies, such as biography, the transmission of the texts, the main dramatic and poetic genres, the stage in Shakespeare's time, and the history of criticism and performance. In addition, authors engage with more recently defined topics: gender and sexuality, Shakespeare on film, the presence of foreigners in Shakespeare's England, and his impact on other cultures. Helpful reference features include chronologies of the life and works, illustrations, detailed reading lists, and a bibliographical essay.

D1010351

THE CAMBRIDGE
COMPANION TO
SHAKESPEARE

CAMBRIDGE COMPANIONS TO LITERATURE

CAMBRIDGE COMPANIONS TO CULTURE

THE CAMBRIDGE
COMPANION TO

SHAKESPEARE

EDITED BY
MARGRETA DE GRAZIA
University of Pennsylvania

AND

STANLEY WELLS
The Shakespeare Birthplace Trust

CAMBRIDGE
UNIVERSITY PRESS

PUBLISHED BY THE PRESS SYNDICATE OF THE UNIVERSITY OF CAMBRIDGE
The Pitt Building, Trumpington Street, Cambridge, United Kingdom

CAMBRIDGE UNIVERSITY PRESS
The Edinburgh Building, Cambridge CB2 2RU, UK
40 West 20th Street, New York NY 10011–4211, USA
477 Williamstown Road, Port Melbourne, VIC 3207, Australia
Ruiz de Alarcón 13, 28014 Madrid, Spain
Dock House, The Waterfront, Cape Town 8001, South Africa

http://www.cambridge.org

First published 2001
Reprinted 2002 (twice)

Printed in the United Kingdom at the University Press, Cambridge

Typeface 10/12 pt Ehrhardt MT   *System* QuarkXPress™   [SE]

A catalogue record for this book is available from the British Library

Library of Congress Cataloguing in Publication data

The Cambridge Companion to Shakespeare / edited by Margreta de Grazia and Stanley Wells.
p.   cm. – (Cambridge Companions to Literature)
Includes bibliographical references and index.
ISBN 0 521 65094 1 – ISBN 0 521 65881 0 (pbk.)
1. Shakespeare, William, 1564–1616 – Handbooks, manuals, etc.   I. Title: Companion to
Shakespeare.   II. De Grazia, Margreta.   III. Wells, Stanley W., 1930–   IV. Series.

PR2894.C33   2001
822.3'3 – dc21   00-063002

ISBN 0 521 65094 1 hardback
ISBN 0 521 65881 0 paperback

CONTENTS

ILLUSTRATIONS

Illustrations reproduced courtesy of: The Huntington Library (1 and 8); Leslie du Sautoy Read (2); Universiteitsbibliotheek, Utrecht (3); Donald Cooper (4); The Lennox-Boyd Theatre Collection, with thanks to the Honourable Christopher Lennox-Boyd (6); The Raymond Mander and Joe Mitchenson Theatre Collection (7); the Picture Library, the Victoria and Albert Museum (9); the Shakespeare Centre Library (10, 11, 12, 13 and 14).

CONTRIBUTORS

John H. Astington, University of Toronto
Leonard Barkan, New York University
Anne Barton, University of Cambridge
Margreta de Grazia, University of Pennsylvania
Michael Dobson, Roehampton Institute London
Hugh Grady, Beaver College, Pennsylvania
Peter Holland, The Shakespeare Institute, University of Birmingham
Ernst Honigmann, University of Newcastle-upon-Tyne
Russell Jackson, The Shakespeare Institute, University of Birmingham
David Scott Kastan, Columbia University
Dennis Kennedy, Trinity College, Dublin
John Kerrigan, University of Cambridge
Ania Loomba, University of Illinois, Urbana–Champaign
Dieter Mehl, University of Bonn
Barbara Mowat, The Folger Shakespeare Library
Lois Potter, University of Delaware
Susan Snyder, Swarthmore College, Pennsylvania
Valerie Traub, University of Michigan
R. S. White, University of Western Australia

PREFACE

This is the fourth Shakespeare Companion to be published by Cambridge University Press. The first, entitled *A Companion to Shakespeare Studies* and edited jointly by Harley Granville-Barker and G. B. Harrison, appeared in 1934; all the contributors were British with the possible exception of T. S. Eliot, who contributed a survey of criticism from Dryden to Coleridge. Subsequent volumes bear witness, in their contributors and their contents, to shifts in intellectual emphasis, especially in relation to performance, and to the increasing internationalism of Shakespeare studies. In 1971 appeared *A New Companion to Shakespeare Studies*, edited by the Anglo-American team of Kenneth Muir and S. Schoenbaum. Ten of the contributors were American, eight British. Each of these volumes had a single essay on Shakespeare in performance since his own time. This was followed in 1986 by *The Cambridge Companion to Shakespeare Studies* edited by Stanley Wells, which included revised versions of two of the essays from the previous volumes. This time there were nine British, six American, one French, one New Zealand, one Canadian, and one German contributor; three essays were devoted to post-Shakespearian performance.

The present volume, made up entirely of new essays, has (give and take a certain amount of transmigration) nine American, six British, one Canadian, one Indian, one Australian, and one German contributor. Like its predecessors, it attempts to respond to changes in emphasis in Shakespeare studies. Under the sway of new historicism and cultural materialism, the mainly formalist orientation previously characterizing the field has given way to a broadly historical or cultural approach. Textual studies, once the sole domain of editors and bibliographers, have become of pressing general concern, largely in response to the multiple-text controversy. Questions of gender and sexuality in both the plays and the Sonnets have produced new historical materials and newly inflected readings. In addition, criticism has increasingly acknowledged in Shakespeare's plays the presence of persons and populations from beyond the confines of England. This interest in other cultures is also reflected in the stress given to Shakespeare's importance to other nations and histories, particularly colonial and post-colonial. So, too, Shakespearian performance on both stage and film has become more globally oriented. And recent technology has transformed the way Shakespeare is now being experienced both on the page and on the screen. The basic materials appearing in the 1986 volume – on Shakespeare's life, for example, the transmission of the text, and the history of both criticism and pro-duction – are still available. Though discussions of the plays and poems are inte-gral to most of the essays, we have chosen to put a greater emphasis on context. Our aim is to offer readers an expansive historical, cultural, and global context which will enhance the enduring but ever-changing value and force of Shakespeare's works.

Each chapter has its own selective reading list. Readers wishing to continue to keep abreast of current developments in Shakespearian scholarship and criticism may do so through the regular review articles in *Shakespeare Survey*, published annually by Cambridge University Press. Quotations from Shakespeare in this volume are from the Oxford *Complete Works* (1986, etc.), General Editors Stanley Wells and Gary Taylor, and act, scene, and line references are to the reprint of that text in the *Norton Shakespeare* (1998), General Editor Stephen Greenblatt. Quotations from works of Shakespeare's contemporaries are normally modern-ized.

M. de G.
S. W.

26 April 1564	baptized in Stratford-upon-Avon
28 November 1582	marriage licence issued for William Shakespeare and Anne Hathaway
26 May 1583	baptism of Susanna, their daughter
2 February 1585	baptism of Hamnet and Judith, their twin son and daughter
1592	Robert Greene refers to Shakespeare as an 'upstart crow'
1593	publication of *Venus and Adonis*
1594	publication of *The Rape of Lucrece*
15 March 1595	Shakespeare named as joint payee of the Lord Chamberlain's Men, founded in 1594
11 August 1596	burial of Hamnet Shakespeare in Stratford-upon-Avon
October 1596	draft of the grants of arms to John, Shakespeare's father
4 May 1597	Shakespeare buys New Place, Stratford-upon-Avon
1598	Shakespeare listed as one of the 'principal comedians' in Jonson's *Every Man in his Humour*
–	mention of Shakespeare in Francis Meres's *Palladis Tamia*
1599	building of the Globe
8 September 1601	burial of John Shakespeare in Stratford-upon-Avon
2 February 1602	John Manningham notes performance of *Twelfth Night* at the Middle Temple
1 May 1602	Shakespeare pays £320 for land in Old Stratford
1603	Shakespeare named among the 'principal tragedians' in Jonson's *Sejanus*
May 1603	Shakespeare named in documents conferring the title of the King's Men on their company
24 July 1605	Shakespeare pays £440 for an interest on the tithes in Stratford
5 June 1607	Susanna Shakespeare marries John Hall
1608	the King's Men take over the indoor Blackfriars theatre
9 September 1608	burial of Mary, Shakespeare's mother, in Stratford

1609	publication of the Sonnets
1612	Shakespeare testifies in the Belott–Mountjoy case
10 March 1613	Shakespeare buys the Blackfriars Gatehouse
1613	Globe burns down during a performance of *All is True* (*Henry VIII*)
September 1614	Shakespeare involved in enclosure disputes in Stratford
10 February 1616	Judith Shakespeare marries Thomas Quiney
25 March 1616	Shakespeare's will drawn up in Stratford
25 April 1616	Shakespeare buried in Stratford (the monument records that he died on 23 April)
8 August 1623	burial of Anne Shakespeare in Stratford
1623	publication of the First Folio
16 July 1649	burial of Susanna Hall in Stratford
9 February 1662	burial of Judith Quiney in Stratford
1670	death of Shakespeare's last direct descendant, his grand-daughter Elizabeth, who married Thomas Nash in 1626 and John (later Sir John) Bernard in 1649

A CONJECTURAL CHRONOLOGY OF SHAKESPEARE'S WORKS

It is particularly difficult to establish the dates of composition and the relative chronology of the early works, up to those named by Francis Meres in his *Palladis Tamia* of 1598. The following table is based on the 'Canon and Chronology' section in *William Shakespeare: A Textual Companion*, by Stanley Wells and Gary Taylor, with John Jowett and William Montgomery (1987), where more detailed information and discussion may be found.

The Two Gentlemen of Verona	1590–1
The Taming of the Shrew	1590–1
The First Part of the Contention (Henry VI, Part Two)	1591
Richard Duke of York (Henry VI, Part Three)	1591
Henry VI, Part One	1592
Titus Andronicus	1592
Richard III	1592–3
Venus and Adonis	1592–3
The Rape of Lucrece	1593–4
The Comedy of Errors	1594
Love's Labour's Lost	1594–5
Richard II	1595
Romeo and Juliet	1595
A Midsummer Night's Dream	1595
King John	1596
The Merchant of Venice	1596–7
Henry IV, Part One	1596–7
The Merry Wives of Windsor	1597–8
Henry IV, Part Two	1597–8
Much Ado About Nothing	1598
Henry V	1598–9
Julius Caesar	1599
As You Like It	1599–1600
Hamlet	1600–1
Twelfth Night	1600–1
Troilus and Cressida	1602

I

ERNST HONIGMANN

Shakespeare's life

SEVEN years after Shakespeare's death his former 'fellows' or colleagues published the first collected edition of his plays, the great Folio of 1623, 'only to keep the memory of so worthy a friend and fellow alive as was our Shakespeare'. *Our* Shakespeare! The phrase, which has re-echoed down the centuries, was probably in use before his death in 1616. In Spain, a contemporary recorded, Lope de Vega 'is accounted of . . . as in England we should of our Will Shakespeare'. This was how one referred to a classic ('our Virgil', 'our Spenser'), more commonly after his death, and Shakespeare was seen as a classic in his lifetime. The anonymous writer of a preface to *Troilus and Cressida* (1609) said so quite explicitly: the play deserves a commentary 'as well as the best comedy in Terence or Plautus'.

The friends who published the Folio loved and admired the man as well as his works. Ben Jonson contributed a poem 'to the memory of my beloved, the author, Mr. William Shakespeare', and later wrote, 'I loved the man and do honour his memory, on this side idolatry, as much as any.' He was gentle Shakespeare, sweet Shakespeare, good Will, friendly Shakespeare – that, at least, seems to have been the majority verdict. A minority saw him in a less agreeable light.

Born in 1564 in provincial Stratford-upon-Avon, he was the eldest surviving child of John and Mary Shakespeare. John is thought to have been the son of Richard, a husbandman in Snitterfield (four miles from Stratford) who held lands as a tenant of Robert Arden, gentleman. Arden's daughter, Mary, inherited fifty acres when her father died in 1556, and not long after married John Shakespeare. John and Mary therefore belonged to different social levels; John, like his son William, proved to be 'upwardly mobile'.

John Shakespeare is first heard of in Stratford in 1552, when he was fined one shilling for building an unauthorized dunghill or muck-heap in Henley Street. (In Stratford, as in London, excrement and other refuse must have been a familiar sight in public streets.) We assume that John already lived in this street, in the house now known as his son's birthplace. He worked as a glover and whittawer (a curer and whitener of skins), but he also became 'a considerable dealer in wool' (Nicholas Rowe, in his *Life* of Shakespeare, 1709, confirmed by recently discovered records), he sold barley and timber, and he bought houses, including the one adjoining his house in Henley Street. In addition to his probably complex business dealings he participated in civic affairs and rose from minor duties to hold office as chamberlain, member of the town council, alderman, and, in 1568, high bailiff (we would say 'mayor'). He signed official documents with his mark, which may mean that he could not write, though this does not necessarily follow. Whether or not he was illiterate he must have had a good head for business since he was asked to take charge of civic accounts. Is it not likely, though, that Shakespeare's parents were both remarkable people?

Having prospered for some twenty years, John ran into difficulties in the late 1570s. He was let off paying his weekly 4d. for poor relief; he failed to attend council meetings, and consequently was deprived of his alderman's gown (1586); he mortgaged part of his wife's inheritance. It could be that he only pretended to be poor and withdrew from council business for religious reasons – if, like many others, he became a 'recusant' when Queen Elizabeth succeeded Mary in 1558, i.e. he refused to give up the 'Old Faith', Roman Catholicism. Recusants were persecuted more vigorously just when John Shakespeare's difficulties started and were fined for non-attendance at church, and his name appears in a list of non-attenders: apparently he alleged that he stayed away because he feared that he might be arrested for debt. Nevertheless he continued to own houses in Stratford; in 1580, summoned to appear in court at Westminster, he was fined £40 (equivalent to a schoolmaster's salary for two years) for non-appearance. The court, we are told, would not have imposed such a fine if John was believed unable to pay. Did his fortunes really decline, or did he withdraw from the council because, as a recusant, he did not wish to take part in punishing other Catholics? The evidence is not clear.

John Shakespeare died in 1601, and Mary in 1608. We are granted one glimpse of John some fifty years after his death. 'Sir John Mennis saw once his old father in his shop – a merry-cheeked old man that said "Will was a good honest fellow, but he durst have cracked a jest with him at any time."' Who durst – father or son? If the son, this suggests that he sometimes made jests out of season, which is confirmed by other early anecdotes.[1]

John and Mary sent their son to 'a free school' (Rowe), probably the King's New School at Stratford. Here he learned Latin grammar, read Aesop's *Fables*, then moved on to the usual classics: Ovid's *Metamorphoses* (frequently quoted or alluded to in his later writings), Plautus (whose *Menaechmi* and *Amphitruo* supplied the plot for *The Comedy of Errors*), Terence, Virgil, Cicero, and no doubt many others. English and modern European literature and history were not taught at this time. The successive masters at his school, Oxford graduates, several of whom were Catholics or had Catholic connections, were paid £20 a year plus housing. Ben Jonson later wrote disparagingly of Shakespeare's 'small Latin and less Greek': by Jonson's own standards this may have been fair comment, yet Shakespeare probably read Latin as easily as most graduates 'with Honours in Latin' today. It was once thought that he was ignorant of Greek tragedy; not so, it is now said, he knew some Greek tragedies, either in the original or in Seneca's adaptations.

If, as was usual, Shakespeare left school at fifteen or sixteen, what did he do next? According to Rowe, his father 'could give him no better education than his own employment', while a Mr Dowdall (1693) thought that he was 'bound apprentice to a butcher'. John Aubrey heard from the son of one of Shakespeare's colleagues that 'he understood Latin pretty well, for he had been in his younger years a schoolmaster in the country'. Another theory takes us north, to Lancashire, where a wealthy Catholic esquire, Alexander Hoghton, recommended William 'Shakeshafte' to his neighbour, Sir Thomas Hesketh, and at the same time bequeathed him his 'instruments belonging to musics and all manner of play clothes' (August 1581). Was Shakeshafte a player, and could he have been Shakespeare? Could he have worked as an assistant 'schoolmaster in the country' for Hoghton? (The performance of plays by boys was recommended by forward-looking schoolmasters). If so, it would imply that at this date Shakespeare was also a Catholic.

From Hoghton and Hesketh he could have transferred to the service of Lord Strange, a more important Lancashire magnate in whose company, reconstituted as the Lord Chamberlain's Men, we find Shakespeare in 1594. Lord Strange was also suspected of Catholic sympathies.

The curious forms that names could take puzzle us again when, on 27 November 1582, the Bishop of Worcester issued a licence for the marriage of 'Willelmum Shaxpere et Annam Whateley de Temple Grafton'. The next day a bond was signed to protect the bishop, in case the marriage of William 'Shagspere' and Anne 'Hathwey' led to legal proceedings, since William was a minor and Anne was pregnant. Some think that 'Whateley' was a misreading of Hathaway, others that Shakespeare, aged 18, would have preferred not to marry Anne Hathaway, aged 26. It must be added that names – like spelling – could wobble at this time. Shakespeare is 'Shaxberd' in the Revels accounts of 1604–5, Christopher Marlowe also appears as 'Morley' and 'Marlin'.

Anne Hathaway, probably the eldest daughter of Richard Hathaway, a husbandman in Shottery, lost her father in September 1581 and nine months later gave birth to her first child, Susanna (baptized 26 May 1583). On 2 February 1585 the twins Hamnet and Judith were baptized (Hamnet being a variant form of Hamlet); doubtless their godparents were Hamnet and Judith Sadler, family friends.

After 1585 William and Anne produced no more children (unusual in those days: William's parents had eight children over a period of twenty-two years). It may have been shortly thereafter that he left home for a career in the theatre. We first hear of him as an actor and dramatist in 1592, from a rival dramatist who believed that he suffered neglect because of Shakespeare's great popularity. In his *Groat's Worth of Wit* Robert Greene addressed three 'gentlemen, his quondam acquaintance, that spend their wits in making plays' (Marlowe, Peele, Nashe) and denounced 'an upstart crow, beautified with our feathers, that with his "Tiger's heart wrapped in a player's hide" supposes he is as well able to bombast out [i.e. write] a blank verse as the best of you: and, being an absolute Johannes fac totum, is in his own conceit the only Shake-scene in a country'. The pun in Shake-scene and ridicule of a line from *3 Henry VI* ('O tiger's heart wrapped in a woman's hide') leave us in no doubt as to Greene's target. He sneered at an upstart actor who dared to compete with his betters, gentlemen dramatists who had been to university (Shakespeare had not), one who thought his bombastic blank verse superior to theirs, and who threatened to put them all out of business.

Greene, I think, continued his attack in *Groat's Worth of Wit* with an allusion to the fable of the ant and the grasshopper. The grasshopper enjoyed himself in the summer, the ant toiled to prepare for winter. When winter arrived, the grasshopper 'went for succour to the ant his old acquaintance, to whom he had scarce discovered his estate but the waspish little worm made this reply, "Pack hence," quoth he, "thou idle lazy worm . . ."' The grasshopper died, and, concluded Greene, 'like him, myself: like me, shall all that trust to friends or time's inconstancy'. Can we doubt that the busy ant, pursuing two separate careers as actor and writer, drove himself hard? 'Weary with toil I haste me to my bed' (Sonnet 27).

Greene picked on the line from *3 Henry VI* to accuse gentle Shakespeare of having a 'tiger's heart', a charge apparently repeated in 'the waspish little worm'. If we accept that Greene had Shake-scene in mind as the relentless ant, the circumstances become clearer, from Greene's point of view. Shakespeare, we may hope, would have told a different tale. Henry Chettle, who had prepared Greene's pamphlet for the press, apologized: various gentlemen vouched for Shakespeare's 'uprightness of dealing, which argues his honesty, and his facetious [polished; witty] grace in writing, that approves [confirms] his art'. Greene's public attack must have pained Shakespeare, and it is not impossible that he reflected on it in Sonnet 112:

> Your love and pity doth th'impression fill
> Which vulgar scandal stamped upon my brow;
> For what care I who calls me well or ill,
> So you o'ergreen my bad, my good allow? (1–4)

At least one other contemporary, it seems, thought like Greene about Shakespeare. In the anonymous pamphlet *Ratsey's Ghost* (1605) a player is advised to go to London and 'play Hamlet' for a wager. 'There thou shalt learn to be frugal . . . and to feed upon all men, to let none feed upon thee; to make thy hand a stranger to thy pocket . . . and when thou feelest thy purse well lined, buy thee some place or lordship in the country . . .' The player answers that he will do so, 'for I have heard indeed of some that have gone to London very meanly, and have come in time to be exceeding wealthy'. The allusions (Hamlet, New Place – see p. 6 – and going to London) point to Shakespeare rather than Edward Alleyn, the only other player rich enough to buy a 'place' in the country, for Alleyn was a Londoner born and could not 'go to London' at the start of his career.

Greene's fable may help us with another unsolved problem. When did Shakespeare begin his theatrical career? The grasshopper calls the ant 'old acquaintance', which supports the view that he had been around in the theatrical world for some years, i.e. had made an 'early start' (1586 or 1587), not a 'late start' (1590). The late start is still widely supported, yet there are good reasons for the early start which, if correct, could mean that Marlowe (also born in 1564) was not Shakespeare's predecessor as a playwright, as stated in older textbooks, but his exact contemporary.

We next hear of Shakespeare in 1593 and 1594. He dedicated his *Venus and Adonis* and *The Rape of Lucrece* to the young Earl of Southampton (born 1572), the 1593 dedication being couched in formal language ('I know not how I shall offend in dedicating my unpolished lines to your lordship . . .'). The later one indicates that Southampton responded positively.

> The love I dedicate to your Lordship is without end, whereof this pamphlet without beginning is but a superfluous moiety. The warrant I have of your honourable disposition, not the worth of my untutored lines, makes it assured of acceptance. What I have done is yours, what I have to do is yours being part in all I have, devoted yours.

We assume that Shakespeare wrote these poems because plague caused the closing of London's theatres, from the summer of 1592 to the spring of 1594, and he was cut off from his normal income. He and his colleagues, now the Lord Chamberlain's Men, resumed acting in 1594, and performed twice at court in the Christmas season. Three of their leaders signed a receipt for £20 – Richard Burbage, William Kempe, and Shakespeare. Burbage was a gifted tragic actor, Kempe an outstanding clown, and Shakespeare – ? The receipt proves that by 1594 he had won a prominent place in his company. Indeed, Greene – identifying no other actor – implied that Shakespeare helped to lead his fellows as early as 1592, perhaps as their business manager.

Shakespeare's business acumen must have been quite exceptional. In the course of time, as he prospered, he took on new responsibilities, with four distinct roles in his company: (1) 'sharer', one of ten or so owners of the company's assets (play-books, play clothes, properties); (2) 'house-holder', one of the owners or lease-holders of the Globe and Blackfriars theatres; (3) dramatist; (4) actor. Other dramatists were paid from £6 to £12 per play, prices that were clearly negotiable. Shakespeare must have known that his plays were his company's most precious asset, and might have demanded much more than others. He seems to have written, on average, two plays a year until 1602 or so, and thereafter one a year, and this could have been his major contribution.

Dramatists rehearsed their plays with the actors; we hear that Shakespeare 'instructed' them, and Jonson may have glanced at this practice in his memorial poem:

> Shine forth, thou star of poets, and with rage
> Or influence chide or cheer the drooping stage. (77–8)

Hamlet cheers the players when they arrive in Elsinore (2.2.405 ff.) and later warns them against overacting (3.2.1 ff.). The voice of Shakespeare himself?

He 'did act exceedingly well', according to Aubrey. James Wright (1699) heard otherwise – he was 'a much better poet than player'. 'The top of his perfor-mance', said Rowe, 'was the ghost in his own *Hamlet*.' He is also believed to have played Adam in *As You Like It*. It seems likely that he took supporting roles; after 1603 he dropped out of his company's actor-lists, and perhaps felt that he could use his time more profitably in other ways. I imagine that by 1603 he was in a position to do more or less as he wished in his company. He remained with the Chamberlain's Men (known as the King's Men from 1603) for the rest of his working life, writing all told more than three dozen plays.

The order in which he wrote the plays is now pretty well agreed. Yet 'inter-nal' or stylistic evidence and 'external' evidence (references to plays in dateable documents, or references in plays to historical events) give us very few firm dates for individual plays. For example, the allusion to the War of the Theatres in *Hamlet* (2.2.326 ff.) could have been a later insertion in the Folio text or a cut in the second quarto; if *The Troublesome Reign of King John* was a derivative play based on *King John* and not the source of Shakespeare's play, the dates of most of the early plays would have to be changed. Fortunately Francis Meres pub-lished, in 1598, a list of twelve of Shakespeare's plays (including one called *Love's Labour's Won*), an important event for two reasons. He supplied the date by which these plays must have been written, and he named their author. Only some of the twelve had been published before 1598, and they had been issued anonymously.

Until at least 1603 Shakespeare devoted most of his time to the theatre. Nevertheless he had begun to invest heavily in property in Stratford. In 1597 he bought a three-storey house called New Place, the second largest in the town; in 1602 he added 107 acres (43 ha) of arable land and 20 acres (8 ha) of pasture in Old Stratford, paying £320 in cash, an even bigger purchase, and, later in the same year, he bought the copyhold title to a cottage and garden facing the garden of New Place; in 1605 he paid £440 for a lease of tithes in neighbouring villages (this alone yielded an income of £60 p.a.). And he had other business interests: in 1597 he was possessed of 80 bushels of corn and malt (as a speculation?); some years later he sued Philip Rogers for a debt of 20 bushels of malt; in 1608 he sued John Addenbrooke, gent., for a debt of £6. In 1598 a Stratford man, Richard Quiney, wrote to Shakespeare to ask for a loan of £30. The tone of the letter and its financial implications are interesting.

Loving countryman, I am bold of you as of a friend, craving your help with £30 upon Mr Bushell's and my security or Mr Mitton's with me . . . You shall friend me much in helping me out of all the debts I owe in London, I thank God, and much quiet my mind . . . You shall neither lose credit nor money by me, the Lord willing . . . and if we bargain farther you shall be the paymaster yourself . . . The Lord be with you and with us all, amen. [Addressed] Haste. To my loving good friend and countryman, Mr Wm. 'Shackespere' deliver these.

The tone is civilized and gentlemanly; the financial implications are spelt out in a letter from Abraham Sturley to Quiney, recommending caution. Sturley had heard 'that our countryman, Mr Wm. Shak., would procure us money, which I will like of as I shall hear when and where and how'. He warned that the conditions of the loan would be crucial, implying that 'Mr Wm. Shak.' might drive a hard bargain. Like his father, John, who had lent large sums (£80, £100) at the illegal rate of 20 per cent, William seems to have had a sideline as a money-lender, while at the same time Shylock thrilled audiences in London. (The financial manager of a rival acting company, the Admiral's Men, kept a thriving pawn-shop; his accounts have survived.)

How much was Shakespeare helped as a businessman by his parents? It has recently emerged that his father was not only capable of raising very large sums before he experienced those mysterious difficulties in the 1570s and 1580s, he was also accused of illegal wool-dealing (buying 200 tods of wool, or 5,600 pounds, with another purchaser and 100 tods on his own). It is sometimes said that William must have helped to finance his father's application for a coat of arms in 1596 (for which there is no evidence whatsoever. On the contrary: the heralds had noted that John 'hath lands and tenements of good wealth, and substance £500'). Is it perhaps more significant that William began to invest large sums in 1602, eight months after his father died, amounting to something not far removed from £500? I think it quite possible that his parents helped him financially at the start of his career, and even that his mother acted as his business manager in Stratford after 1601, and that her illness and death (in 1608) compelled him to spend more time at home, at least for a while.

Shakespeare's last known investment, the purchase of the Blackfriars Gate-house in London in 1613 (for £140) has been described as a 'speculation rather than for use as a dwelling. He had by then retired to Stratford' – yet in the same year he helped to write two or three plays (*Henry VIII*, *The Two Noble Kinsmen*, the lost *Cardenio*), so he did not think of himself as retired. The Gatehouse, close to the Blackfriars theatre, would have been a convenient London home; aged 49, he could not know that he had only three more years to live.

He had his will redrafted on 25 March 1616. Word must have reached him that his new son-in-law, Thomas Quiney (he had married Judith in February), was due to confess to 'carnal copulation' in the parish church the next day, 26 March. Shakespeare inserted new clauses to protect his daughter against her feckless husband. For example, he bequeathed a sum of £150 to Judith, provided that 'such husband as she shall at the end of . . . three years be married unto . . . do sufficiently assure unto her and the issue of her body lands answerable to [i.e. as valuable as] the portion by this my will given' – an unlikely eventuality. And if Judith lived for three years, the sum of £150 was to be spent for her benefit by the executors, but 'not to be paid unto her so long as she shall be married'. Clearly Shakespeare had no confidence in Thomas Quiney. A tiger's heart wrapped in a father's hide!

He also left bequests to many others, including his only surviving sibling, his sister Joan. She, married to a hatter, was to retain tenancy of the house in which she lived for the yearly peppercorn rent of 12d., and she was to have £50, which the executors were to pay to her or to her sons (i.e. not to her husband). Shakespeare, evidently a very sick man who could only just sign his name, also deleted a bequest to Richard Tyler, who was still alive, and there are other signs of his displeasure. It is in this context that we have to place the single reference to Anne Hathaway – 'Item, I give unto my wife my second-best bed with the furniture' (hangings, coverlets, bed-linen). Had he provided for Anne before he made his will, as some have supposed? Wills of the period often made this explicit. We do not know. There are various signs, however, that he was not a happy husband: the possibility of a shot-gun wedding in 1582; the fact that Anne had no more children after 1585; Aubrey's report that 'he was wont to go into Warwickshire once a year'; stories that link Shakespeare with other women, including the dark lady of the Sonnets; the fact that in purchasing the Gatehouse he brought in three trustees, which had the effect of barring his widow from any right to the property; the curt reference to 'my wife' in the will (testators generally said 'my loving wife'), and the fact that she was not asked to be an executor. He named his daughter Susanna and her husband, Dr John Hall, as his executors, and Susanna as his principal heir (his son, Hamnet, had died in 1596).

Greene (1592) and *Ratsey's Ghost* (1605) reveal Shakespeare as seen by his enemies; his will (1616) confirms that he had a stern, unyielding side. Our only rounded picture of Shakespeare the man is found in his Sonnets – one so extraordinary that many biographers prefer not to take it seriously (see also chapter 5, Shakespeare's Poems, by John Kerrigan). Here he depicts himself as abnormally vulnerable and emotional, often almost unable to control his emotions, whether high or low, and inclined to withdraw from difficult confrontations. He seems to have written many of the Sonnets to explain feelings that he could not express face to face. He adores a 'lovely boy' or young man, probably a nobleman's son, he dotes on a dark lady, and both betray him. He is too forgiving to the young man and knows it (Sonnets 35, 40–2, 70), and, some will say, spiteful to the dark lady (137). Nevertheless he also addresses sharp words to the young man ('thou dost common grow', 'Lilies that fester smell far worse than weeds', 69, 94), and can write tenderly to the dark lady (128). Being Shakespeare, he sees the ridiculousness of his own position (143). The Sonnets, of course, must not be read as 'straight' autobiography – yet why dismiss them as too extraordinary to be credible? Shakespeare was not an 'ordinary' or 'normal' man.

The publisher dedicated the Sonnets 'To the only begetter [inspirer?] of these ensuing sonnets, Mr W. H.', I assume without Shakespeare's permission. Whether or not the poet's love for the young man was homosexual (this is much debated), it might certainly be thought so, which – in view of the penalties against homosexual acts – would be dangerous. Mentioned by Francis Meres in 1598 as Shakespeare's 'sugared sonnets among his private friends', these superb poems remained unpublished for at least eleven years, with the exception of two that appeared in the pirated *Passionate Pilgrim* (1599), and, just as surprisingly, were not reissued between 1609 and 1640. This suggests, I think, that they were thought to be 'compromising'.

Several identifications of the young man have been proposed, including Henry Wriothesley, the Earl of Southampton (W. H. transposed?). Recent biographers have favoured William Herbert, later the Earl of Pembroke and dedicatee of the First Folio, in my view correctly. This W. H., born in 1580, was for many years a generous patron of Ben Jonson, and there are grounds for thinking Jonson the 'rival poet' of the Sonnets, who caused Shakespeare much grief (e.g. Sonnets 78–86). The rival competed for the young man's patronage: he paraded his learning, putting Shakespeare in the shade, he was proud, a polished poet, a flatterer, so overbearing that Shakespeare preferred not to engage with him (and felt that this needed an explanation):

> My tongue-tied muse in manners holds her still
> While comments of your praise, richly compiled,
> Reserve thy character with golden quill
> And precious phrase by all the muses filed.
> I think good thoughts whilst other[s] write good words,
> And like unlettered clerk still cry 'Amen'
> To every hymn that able spirit affords
> In polished form of well-refinèd pen.
> Hearing you praised I say ''Tis so, 'tis true,'
> And to the most of praise add something more;
> But that is in my thought . . . (85.1–11)

A 'tongue-tied' Shakespeare? Other sonnets present the same evasive, introverted personality (e.g. 23, 80, 83, 86, 128, 140) and yet early allusions refer to his unabashed quickness in repartee (cf. p. 2). So, too, early allusions depict him as a boon companion, whereas Aubrey recorded that 'he was not a company keeper, lived in Shoreditch, wouldn't be debauched, and if invited to [be debauched?], wrote he was in pain'. Contradictions? Why, though, expect a rigidly consistent Shakespeare? Do we not feel close to him in both Hamlet and Falstaff?

Shakespeare and Jonson perhaps tippled together in taverns, and had a relationship of sorts for many years. Jonson repeatedly criticized Shakespeare and his plays, and on at least one occasion gentle Shakespeare may have retaliated. In the third Cambridge Parnassus play (1601?) Will Kempe says 'O that Ben Jonson is a pestilent fellow, he brought up Horace giving the poets a pill [in *Poetaster*], but our fellow Shakespeare hath given him a purge that made him beray [foul] his credit [i.e. shit himself].' Jonson was Shakespeare's only major and persistent critic. He was jealous, and could not bear to praise the 'sweet swan of Avon' until after his great rival's death.

In the present century we have learned much about his friends and associates, less about Shakespeare. An American, C. W. Wallace, discovered law-suits that give us vivid pictures of Richard Burbage and his father and, even more important, the Belott–Mountjoy suit of 1612. Stephen Belott had served as apprentice to Mountjoy, a French Huguenot, and had married his master's daughter in 1604. Shakespeare, then a lodger in Mountjoy's house, deposed that he had known the parties for ten years or so, and that he was asked to persuade Belott to marry Mary Mountjoy. He recalled that Mountjoy promised to give a 'portion' with Mary, 'but what certain portion he remembereth not'. A diplomatic loss of memory? He signed his deposition, one of only six surviving signatures. It is sometimes transliterated as 'Willĩm Shakp' but, as C. J. Sisson pointed out to me almost fifty years ago, it ends with a penman's flourish and should read 'Willm Shak.' Compare 'Mr Wm. Shak.' (p. 7 above).

The discoveries of Leslie Hotson, a Canadian, match Wallace's in importance. After *The Death of Christopher Marlowe* (1925) he published, in *Shakespeare versus Shallow* (1931), documents involving various persons close to the theatrical world. Francis Langley, the owner of the Swan theatre, claimed 'sureties of the peace' (i.e. the protection of the law) against William Gardiner, a Southwark JP, and William Wayte; Wayte then claimed 'sureties' against William 'Shakspere', Langley, Dorothy Soer, and Anne Lee (1596). Hotson argued that Gardiner and Wayte were lampooned as Justice Shallow and Slender in *The Merry Wives of Windsor*. His most exciting detective-work followed in *I, William Shakespeare* (1937), an account of Thomas Russell, Esq., a friend named as overseer (assistant to the executors) in Shakespeare's will. Russell owned an estate at Alderminster, four miles from Stratford, and was the stepfather of Sir Dudley and Leonard Digges. Sir Dudley probably gave Shakespeare access to William Strachey's unpublished letter to the Council of the Virginia Company, describing a shipwreck in the Bermudas: this suggested details for *The Tempest*. Leonard Digges, born in 1588, young enough to be Shakespeare's son, contributed verses to the First Folio and a longer memorial poem printed later (1640). He revered Shakespeare the man and the 'fire and feeling' of his plays.

> Be sure, our Shakespeare, thou canst never die,
> But, crowned with laurel, live eternally.

Again, *our* Shakespeare!

Many stories circulated in Shakespeare's lifetime and after his death from less well-informed sources – the 'Shakespeare mythos'. They portrayed him as a poacher, a hard drinker, a lover, and of course a master at repartee. There may well be some truth in some of these anecdotes, or are they too good to be true? John Manningham recorded one in his diary in 1602. When Burbage played Richard III, a woman in the audience made an assignation with him

> to come that night unto her by the name of [i.e. using as password] Richard the Third. Shakespeare, overhearing their conclusion [arrangement], went before, was entertained and at his game ere Burbage came. Then message being brought that Richard the Third was at the door, Shakespeare caused return to be made that William the Conqueror was before Richard the Third.

A story more in character with the ethos of the plays, though not of the Sonnets, we owe to Sir Nicholas L'Estrange (mid-seventeenth century).

> Shakespeare was godfather to one of Ben Jonson's children, and after the christening, being in a deep study, Jonson came to cheer him up and asked him why he was so melancholy. 'No, faith, Ben,' says he, 'not I. But I have been considering a great while what should be the fittest gift for me to bestow upon my godchild, and I have resolved at last.' 'I prythee what?' says he. 'I'faith, Ben, I'll e'en give him a dozen good latten spoons, and thou shalt translate them.'

Notice two puns. Translate could mean 'transform'; godfathers usually gave silver spoons, latten being a cheap alloy. Here Shakespeare appears to smile at Jonson's condescending view of his rival's small Latin and less Greek.

Shakespeare died on 23 April 1616, his widow on 6 August 1623. Their daughters outlived them – Susanna till July 1649, Judith till February 1662. Judith's three sons died without issue; Susanna's only child, Elizabeth, was married twice, first to Thomas Nash, and after his death to John (later Sir John) Bernard. Elizabeth died childless: with her death in 1670 the descent from Shakespeare became extinct.

The story of Shakespeare's life includes many unsolved puzzles, explained differently by different biographers. My account will displease traditionalists on many points – John Shakespeare's 'difficulties', William's possible sojourn in Lancashire, his marriage, the relentless ant, his carefulness with money, the 'early start' of his writing career, his will, his relationship with his wife, his personality as revealed in the Sonnets, his possible homosexuality, his religion. I have discussed these matters elsewhere, at greater length.[2] Of course, I agree with traditionalists more often than I disagree.

'He was indeed honest', Jonson summed up after Shakespeare's death, 'and of an open and free nature; had an excellent fancy, brave notions and gentle expressions.' Like so many other allusions, this one needs to be translated into modern English. Jonson probably meant 'He was indeed an honourable man, and of an unreserved and spontaneous nature; had an excelling imagination, fine ideas and admirable ways of expressing himself.'[3]

Notes

1. The best example is Shakespeare's alleged extempore epitaph for his Stratford friend, John Combe, 'an old gentleman noted thereabouts for his wealth and usury' (Rowe): 'Ten in the hundred lies here engraved, / 'Tis a hundred to ten, his soul is not saved. / If anyone ask who lies in this tomb / "O ho!" quoth the devil, "'tis my John-a-Combe!"'
2. It should be noted that these puzzles in Shakespeare's life remain unsolved: I mention interesting possibilities, but do not regard them as certainties. And it does not follow that, if Shakespeare was brought up as a Catholic (a possibility), the plays we know were written by a Catholic. Many Catholics became Protestants in his lifetime, including John Donne and Ben Jonson. See my *Shakespeare's Impact on his Contemporaries* (London: Macmillan, 1982) for Greene and Shakespeare, Jonson and Shakespeare, Shakespeare's personality, the 'early start'; *Shakespeare: The 'Lost Years'* (Manchester University Press, 1985, revised edn 1998) for Shakespeare's father, Shakespeare in Lancashire, his religion; *Myriad-minded Shakespeare: Essays on the Tragedies, Problem Comedies and Shakespeare the Man*, 2nd edn (London: Macmillan, 1998) for Shakespeare's personality, his will, his marriage. Also my essay 'The First Performances of Shakespeare's Sonnets' in *Shakespeare Performed: Essays in Honor of R. A. Foakes*, ed. Grace Ioppolo (Newark: University of Delaware Press, 2000) for 'Mr W. H.' and the rival poet.
3. All contemporaries of Shakespeare and later commentators cited in this chapter can be identified through the indexes of E. K. Chambers, Park Honan, and Samuel Schoenbaum (see below).

Reading list

Chambers, E. K., *William Shakespeare: A Study of Facts and Problems*, 2 vols. (Oxford: Clarendon Press, 1930).
Fripp, E. I., *Shakespeare, Man and Artist*, 2 vols. (Oxford University Press, 1938).
Honan, Park, *Shakespeare A Life* (Oxford University Press, 1998).
Schoenbaum, Samuel, *William Shakespeare: A Documentary Life* (Oxford: Clarendon Press, 1975).

2

BARBARA A. MOWAT

The reproduction of Shakespeare's texts

There are today many conflicting accounts of the origins of Shakespeare's texts and of their subsequent reproduction. Such has not always been the case. For much of the twentieth century, for instance, editors and textual critics accepted and depended upon a single larger story, and most agreed that the few remaining still-contested details would soon be resolved and absorbed into this larger narrative. Today, instead of seeing such resolution, one is hard pressed to find any part of the story that is not in contention.

Editors and textual critics agree that the extant texts of the plays originated in manuscripts that are lost; and they agree that the plays were first printed in the late sixteenth and early seventeenth centuries, some plays in individual quartos, some in the 1623 Folio, and some in both quarto and Folio.[1] When, however, one looks for consensus beyond these very basic statements, one finds only problems and questions. What, for example, was the provenance of the manuscripts that reached print? Can we, in fact, determine the provenance from an examination of the early printed texts? How many Shakespeare plays were printed in quarto? (Do we count, for example, *The Taming of A Shrew*?) Can the quartos be divided into 'good' texts and 'bad' texts, with the 'bad' having come into print through the memorial reconstruction of actors, or does every quarto instead represent a more or less different Shakespearian version of the play? When a play was printed first in quarto and again in the Folio, and when the printings (both seemingly Shakespearian) contain words and passages that differ widely from each other, how do we explain the differences and how do we construct an edition of that play which reproduces 'Shakespeare's text'?

Some of these are not, of course, new questions. Eighteenth-century scholar-editors, who had little knowledge about early modern dramatic manuscripts (many non-Shakespearian examples of which are still extant) and who knew far less than scholars today about the pre-Folio quartos, asked similar questions. But such questions were central neither to their debates nor to their reproduction of the texts. Their theories centred instead on the Folio. They had inherited from the seventeenth century the fourth edition of William Shakespeare's *Comedies, Histories, and Tragedies*, published in 1685 – 'the last of the series of the great folios', as A. W. Pollard calls this volume, one which 'marks the completion of the task of the printer-editors of Shakespeare's own century'[2] – and initially, at least, they saw their work in terms of rectifying the damage to Shakespeare's texts as represented in this Fourth Folio.

While it is true that these early editors had inherited not only the Fourth Folio but all 'four large folios [of 1623, 1632, 1663, and 1685], in addition to upwards of seventy quarto editions of single plays' (Pollard, p. 164), copies of the earlier Folios and the quartos were quite rare, and the work of the eighteenth-century editors was coloured by the fact that their access to this rare material was limited. (Even in the nineteenth century, the problem continued. James Boswell, writing in 1821, defended his publication of collations of early printed texts on these grounds: 'The earlier copies are of rare occurrence, and can only be procured by a fortunate chance, or at an immoderate price; [though] it by no means follows, that those alone who have access to those expensive rarities, are capable of using what they contain.')[3] Before the eighteenth century ended, the superiority of the First Folio over the other Folios had been established, as had the necessity for obtaining and consulting the early quartos, but for most of the century editorial theorizing about the reproduction of Shakespeare's texts centred on the Folios, in large part because of a statement about the Folio and quarto texts included by Heminges and Condell in the Folio frontmatter, a statement whose significance to the history of textual criticism of Shakespeare can hardly be overestimated.

In the absence of the manuscripts and given the apparent authority of Heminges and Condell as contemporaries and fellow-actors with Shakespeare, their claims about Shakespeare's texts provided a kind of touchstone, though a changing one, for editors and textual critics from Pope (1721) to Pollard (1909). Heminges and Condell claimed that what they printed in the Folio were Shakespeare's 'True Original Copies', his plays 'as he conceived them', and that previous [i.e. quarto] printings represented 'stolen, . . . surreptitious, . . . maimed, . . . [and] deformed' texts.[4] Such language said clearly to early editors that the quartos were not to be taken seriously as texts and that editorial focus must be on the Folio, despite its obviously faulty printing and despite the playhouse 'Mutilations' of the manuscripts Heminges and Condell had provided the printers.[5]

Fortunately for the future of Shakespeare's plays, the early editors, while never claiming any authority for the quartos, did not therefore dismiss them, but from the beginning mined them for interesting variants and for passages not included in the Folio. Their editorial practices were based in the (unexamined) theory that early printings should be edited in the same way as were classical manuscripts. As R. B. McKerrow said in 1933,

> it simply never occurred to men like Pope, Theobald, and Capell that the Shakespeare quartos were not in the same position with respect to the author's original text as the classical manuscripts were, in that they did not represent ends of separate lines of descent from it, but in most cases successive members of a single line.

If the eighteenth-century editors had reflected, he says,

> they would have seen that if we want Shakespeare's original text the only place where we have any chance of finding it is in a quarto or folio which is at the head of a line of descent, and that if descendants of such a quarto or folio have different readings from their ancestor, those readings must be either accidental corruptions or deliberate alterations by compositors or proof-readers, and can in no case have an authority superior to, or even as great as, the readings of the text from which they differ.[6]

McKerrow's thesis about eighteenth-century editorial theory and practice was exemplified and articulated by Lewis Theobald, perhaps the first great Shakespeare editor. Theobald describes his work as comparable to that of editors of classical manuscripts and prides himself on adopting their 'Method of cure' for corrupt texts. 'Our Author', he writes in his 1733 preface, 'has lain under the Disadvantage of having his Errors propagated and multiplied by Time: because, for near a Century, his Works were republish'd from the faulty Copies without the assistance of any intelligent Editor: which has been the Case likewise of many a *Classic* Writer.' Because 'Shakespeare's case has in a great Measure resembl'd that of a corrupt *Classic* . . . the Method of cure was likewise to bear a Resemblance.' Emboldened by 'the success [with which] this cure has been effected on ancient writers', Theobald 'ventur'd on a Labour, that is the first Assay of the kind on any modern Author whatsover' – i.e. the 'Restoring to the Publick their greatest Poet in his Original Purity' (p. xxxviii).

This editorial 'Restoring' proceeded as if all early printings of a play – including the later Folios and later printings of the quartos – carried potential authority. For editors of classical manuscripts in the eighteenth century, such a procedure was proper: any given manuscript recension that survived into the eighteenth century might be considered as representing a distinct manuscript line, and each of its variants was therefore worthy of consideration in the reconstruction of the text.[7] It now seems self-evident that the editing of printed books must proceed by first establishing the relationship among the early printed texts and that it must recognize that 'variants' in a reprint of an edition are probably the result of printing-house error. The inference that follows from that recognition – one that eighteenth-century editors did not make until the 1760s – is that, for Shakespeare's texts, 'readings in a late text which differed from those of an earlier one from which it had itself been printed could not possibly be of any authority' (McKerrow, p. 29). Samuel Johnson understood this principle in theory, but he continued to edit as if he did not quite accept it, and even so canny an editor as Capell wrote in his 'Introduction' that, while he tried to follow the oldest printing of a given Shakespeare text, it often 'became proper and necessary to look into the other old editions, and to select from thence whatever improves the Author'.[8]

The fact that eighteenth-century editors treated the early printings as if they might all have some authority can now be perceived, as it was by McKerrow, as the central problem in their editing of Shakespeare's plays. But the happy corollary of this understanding of the texts is that it led these editors to search out, collect, and eventually collate the otherwise despised quartos – which in turn led to discoveries about the quartos and about their relationship to the Folio that transformed editorial thinking about the reproduction of Shakespeare's texts. In the meantime the editors took as their base text the Folio (for many decades the Fourth Folio) and saw their work as the 'Restoration of the genuine Reading', as Theobald put it. They disagreed violently with each other about their editing practices – Pope degraded to the bottom of the page passages that he suspected of being playhouse additions or corruptions, a practice that Theobald mocked (Pope, he writes, has attacked Shakespeare 'like an unhandy *Slaughterman*; and not lopp'd off the *Errors*, but the *Poet*' (p. xxxv)), while Theobald searched for and proposed better readings to replace the Folio text's 'Depravations', and thus earned a place of infamy in Pope's *Dunciad*. But until the 1760s, editors shared a single larger view of the Shakespeare text, its origins and its pre-eighteenth-century reproduction. Briefly, they agreed that Shakespeare's texts were to be sought for in the Folio (though, in their view, scandalously printed there from manuscripts mutilated by actor–editors). They further agreed that the 'Pieces which stole singly into the World in our Author's Lifetime' – i.e. the quartos – were 'printed from piece-meal Parts surreptitiously obtain'd from the Theatres, uncorrect, and without the Poet's Knowledge' (Theobald, p. xxxviii), and thus, while worth culling for variants, otherwise of little interest.

This theory of the Shakespeare text, premised on the belief that only the Folio texts were worthy of serious consideration as deriving from Shakespeare's hand, collapsed in the 1760s with the discovery that a number of Folio texts had, in fact, been printed from the much maligned quartos. Edward Capell, in the Introduction to his 1767–8 *Mr. William Shakespeare his Comedies, Histories, and Tragedies,* cites instances and lays out evidence that makes a shambles of earlier editorial consensus. Capell first quotes the Heminges and Condell claim mentioned above: 'where before you were abused with diverse stolen and surreptitious copies, maimed, and deformed by the frauds and stealths of injurious impostors, that exposed them: even those are now offered to your view cured, and perfect of their limbs; and all the rest, absolute in their numbers, as he conceived them.' Capell then writes:

> Who now does not feel himself inclin'd to expect an accurate and good performance in the edition of these prefacers? But alas, it is nothing less: for (if we except the six spurious [quartos], whose places were then supply'd by true and genuine copies) the editions of plays preceding the folio, are the very basis of those we have there; which are either printed from those editions, or from the copies which they made use of.

Along with the 'six spurious quartos' which were not used in the Folio printing, Capell also excepts quartos of plays in which 'there are. . . great variations' between the quarto and Folio texts. But he finds in nine plays

> an almost strict conformity between the [quarto and Folio] impressions . . . the faults and errors of the quarto's are all preserv'd in the folio, and others added to them; and what difference there is, is generally for the worse on the side of the folio editors; which should give us but faint hopes of meeting with greater accuracy in the plays which they first publish'd. (pp. 5–6)

Edmond Malone's 1790 edition echoes Capell (without citing him) and then goes on to state the proper editorial inference. He lists fifteen plays 'printed in quarto antecedent to the first complete collection', and notes that, with regard to thirteen of them, 'instead of printing these plays from a manuscript, the editors of the folio, to save labour, or from some other motive, printed the greater part of them from the very copies which they represented as maimed and imperfect'. He then states: 'Thus therefore the first folio, as far as the plays above numerated, labours under the disadvantage of being at least a second, and in some cases a third, edition of these quartos . . . [which] were in general the basis on which the folio editors built, and are entitled to our particular attention and examination as *first* editions.'[9]

Malone also sets out principles for the proper editing of printed texts. Capell had suggested in a brief remark how he as an editor had chosen for each play the proper text to edit: 'the printed copies are all that is left to guide us . . . our first business then, was – to examine their merit, and see on which side the scale of goodness preponderated; which we have generally found, to be on that of the most ancient' (p. 21). Malone provides not a personal statement but an editorial principle:

> It is well known to those who are conversant with the business of the press, that (unless when the author corrects and revises his own works,) as editions of books are multiplied, their errors are multiplied also; and that consequently every such edition is more or less correct, as it approaches nearer to or is more distant from the first. (p. xiii)

While the relationship between Capell and Malone was in its way as fraught as that between Pope and Theobald, the two editors in effect developed between them a new theory of Shakespeare editing, one in which no early printing is seen as offering access to Shakespeare's mind and hand – his 'True Original Copies' having been exposed as, to their thinking, tainted quartos and dubiously chosen manuscripts – and in which the early printing history of Shakespeare's texts is a central concern. In the Capell–Malone textual world, the editor, while continuing to select variants from among the early printed texts, often gives preference to the quarto text over its Folio counterpart and always edits the first-printed text whenever reprinting can be established. The Shakespeare text itself, under the pressure of this new paradigm, changed rather dramatically. Capell in effect began an almost new editorial line, moving away from the Fourth Folio, basing many texts on a given play's quarto printing, and using the First (rather than the Fourth) Folio when a play was first printed there or when, in the case of a play with distinct quarto and Folio printings, he deemed the Folio text the better of the two. The importance of Capell's edition can be judged from the words of G. Blakemore Evans in his essay on 'Shakespeare's Text' in the 1997 *Riverside Shakespeare*: 'A measure of Capell's importance may perhaps be seen in the fact that his name appears more frequently in the Textual Notes to the present edition than that of any later editor.'[10] When Malone constructed his edition in 1790, he incorporated much of Capell's text, and it was this text that continued to be largely reproduced throughout the nineteenth century. One can even argue, as does Evans, that the theory developed by Capell and Malone and the text constructed primarily by Capell and adopted by Malone provided a matrix for Shakespeare editing that extended from the late eighteenth through the early twentieth century, culminating in the 1860s in 'the great Cambridge *Shakespeare*, edited by W. G. Clark and W. A. Wright . . . a text that was to remain . . . the standard for the [following] fifty years' (Evans, p. 62).[11]

To contextualize properly the shift in editorial theory and practice that occurred in the 1760s, as well as the one that occurred in the early twentieth century, it is surprisingly helpful to turn to the insights and language of Thomas Kuhn's influential *The Structure of Scientific Revolutions*. While Kuhn's work centres on *scientific* revolutions – those moments, that is, when the espoused beliefs of a given scientific community undergo a radical change that alters the basic assumptions and practices of that community – Kuhn's description of the forces that lead to such revolutions and of the subsequent shifts in what he named 'paradigms' provides a remarkably fruitful context for examining the history of the Shakespeare editorial community. In Kuhn's language, the 1760s 'revolution' in the theory and practice of editing Shakespeare's texts was a change brought about through 'novelties of fact'.[12] The new fact discovered (one assumes by Capell)[13] was that a basic premise of then-current editorial theory – that the Folio texts were original authorial manuscripts that replaced mutilated quarto printings – was demonstrably false. This discovery toppled the previous paradigm and enabled Capell and Malone between them to establish a new paradigm and a new text, both of which stood unchallenged for almost one hundred and fifty years. The next 'revolution', when it came in the early twentieth century, came – in Kuhn's terms – through a 'novelty of theory'. New facts were, of course, involved – 'facts' about the registering of manuscripts in the Stationers' Register, facts about the correct dating of the Pavier quartos that encouraged scholars to believe that the printed quartos could yield the careful bibliographer yet more secrets about their history.[14] But the major, transformational shift in thinking about the

Shakespeare texts was a simple reinterpretation of the Heminges and Condell attack on the quartos.

The credit for this critical reinterpretation belongs to Alfred W. Pollard, who in 1909 broached the question of whether 'all the Shakespeare quartos [were, through Heminges and Condell's words] tainted more or less indiscriminately with piracy and surreptitiousness, or whether it is possible to distinguish between some quartos and others' (p. 64). This question, he notes, is 'of the highest importance for any valuation of the text of the Folio', since if Heminges and Condell condemned as 'maimed' and 'stolen' the very quartos that they then gave to the printers as copy, 'we have no proof of the exercise of any editorial care' for any text in the Folio, and the resulting 'bibliographical pessimism' that extended from Capell and Malone into the early twentieth century was doubtless justified. Pollard answered his own question with the comforting pronouncement that Heminges and Condell had simply been misunderstood and that their reference to 'piratical editions' was only to what Pollard named 'bad quartos' – namely, the quartos of *Henry V*, *Merry Wives*, and *Pericles*, and the first quartos of *Hamlet* and *Romeo and Juliet*, none of which had been used in the printing of the Folio. To these five, he wrote,

> the epithets 'stolne and surreptitious' may be applied with any desirable amount of scorn and contempt . . . But they should surely not be applied to any other [of the quartos]. Moreover, we can read our First Folio . . . with all the more confidence because we need no longer believe that its editors in their preface were publicly casting stones at earlier editions which they were privately using . . . in constructing their own text. (p. 80)

A reviewer of Pollard's *Shakespeare Folios and Quartos* wrote in the *Liverpool Courier* for 24 December 1909: 'For the first time we now possess a lucid and rational account of how Shakespeare's plays came to be printed both separately and collectively.' W. W. Greg's response to Pollard was just as enthusiastic. Pollard's book, Greg wrote in 1955, released scholars 'from the quagmire of nineteenth-century despondency' about the early printed texts, a despondency that had resulted from a 'mistaken interpretation of what Heminges and Condell had said'. In Greg's words, 'Pollard raised the banner of revolt against two centuries of pessimism, and linked the correct interpretation [of Heminges and Condell's words] with a fresh insistence on and definition of the distinction between what he named the "good" and the "bad" quartos.' While acknowledging that 'Pollard further linked this distinction with certain views on the subject of copyright that have not stood the test of recent criticism', Greg made the more central point that Pollard's 'main thesis . . . no serious critic now disputes'.[15]

Greg's enthusiasm about Pollard's overturning of the reigning paradigm is understandable. Pollard's reinterpretation restored Heminges and Condell to a position of honesty and trustworthiness and removed the stain from most of the quartos and from the Folio text in general. Again to quote Greg:

> those quartos that [Heminges and Condell] reprinted without material alteration contained texts that they knew to be in at least substantial agreement with the originals; and if they showed this discrimination in their use of the quartos, it is only reasonable to suppose that they were equally careful in their selection of the manuscripts from which a majority of the plays in the Folio were printed. (p. 89)

Pollard had led Shakespeare scholars not only out of the 'quagmire of nine-teenth-century despondency' but also out of a 'jungle of disbelief', affording in the process a 'great stimulus to research' (Greg, pp. 83, 92).

Pollard's new theory and the research it spawned quickly toppled the old par-adigm, but the new one was not fully established until the 1930s, after consider-able work by Greg, J. Dover Wilson, E. K. Chambers, and others, and after the publication of R. B. McKerrow's crucial essay on 'The Elizabethan Printer and Dramatic Manuscripts'.[16] Central to the bibliographical work of the intervening years was the finding and analysing of a sample of Shakespeare's (supposed) handwriting in three pages of the 'Book of Sir Thomas More', a project that pro-vided seeming evidence about Shakespeare's spelling and handwriting and that drew attention to extant dramatic documents and the untidy state in which this one, at least, existed.[17] With McKerrow's 1931 essay and its conclusion that the 'good' texts of Shakespeare must, logically, have been printed directly from Shakespeare's own 'rough draft much corrected and never put in order for the press', a new paradigm, 'new bibliography', was essentially in place. Its central tenet was (and is) that most of the early printed texts of Shakespeare's plays are 'good' texts, printed either directly from Shakespeare's holographs or from transcriptions of them made for use in the theatre or for publication or reading; the remaining handful of 'bad' texts can be viewed as anomalies or curiosities, in no way deriving from the author's own draft and thus of little concern to an editor seeking to establish an authentic Shakespeare text. A corollary is that the bibliographer can determine the nature of the copy behind each early printing, and that such a determination is the essential step that must be taken before a Shakespeare play can be properly edited.

The several decades of editing, bibliographical research, and textual criticism that followed the establishment of the new paradigm were remarkably fruitful. One of the functions served by a paradigm, as Kuhn points out, is to 'set the problem to be solved' by the community (p. 27). Under the aegis of new bibliog-raphy, textual critics and bibliographers were set the problem of evolving 'a more scientific and logically rigorous method to govern the critical choice of alternatives in respect to the words of the [Shakespeare] text'.[18] Editors and scholars alike were swept up in an optimistic commitment to the task of discovering what Shakespeare wrote. Editing in terms of authorial intention became, for Shakespeare editors, the norm and, under the rubric of copy-text editing, spread throughout the world of scholarly editing of literary texts. Among Shakespearians, hopes flourished that a definitive text of Shakespeare's works, grounded in scientific application of bibliographical principles, would soon be established.

Again to quote Kuhn: 'one of the things a . . . community acquires with a paradigm is a criterion for choosing problems that, while the paradigm is taken for granted, can be assumed to have solutions' (p. 37). Once Pollard had separated the 'good' texts from the 'bad' and McKerrow had argued persuasively that many of Shakespeare's 'good' texts must have been printed directly from his working manuscripts, the next new bibliographical problem was that of identifying those 'good' texts that traced directly to such manuscripts and those which traced instead to altered or derivative manuscripts – to theatre documents and scribal transcripts, that is. This crucial problem was tackled by W. W. Greg, who, building on McKerrow's work, constructed a manuscript type he named authorial 'foul papers', identifiable in a printed dramatic text through variant speech prefixes, indefinite or vague entrance directions, and other such indications of the author still at work. Greg set this kind of manuscript against theatre 'promptbooks', identifiable through regularized speech prefixes, careful entrance directions (which listed properties, specified the number of minor characters entering, etc.), and other consistencies not present in 'foul papers' texts.[19]

Using Greg's markers, textual critics separated Shakespeare's plays according to their manuscript derivations, and applied to the largest group of texts – the 'foul papers' texts – the information gathered from the three 'Shakespeare' pages in the *More* manuscript. To the plays printed from 'prompt-books' – the next-largest group – they applied assumed information about bookkeepers and how they prepared performance play-books; and to the small group of plays printed from scribal transcripts they applied information about the scribal habits of such known figures as the professional scribe Ralph Crane. For all of the texts, whatever their provenance, the crucial problem set by the paradigm centred on what happened to the manuscript in the printing house – and specifically what happened at the hands of individual compositors. George Walton Williams, writing in 1971, spoke for the paradigm when he foresaw the day when the results of compositor study would allow editors to 'reconstruct the original spellings used by Shakespeare and so to reconstitute, as it were, the lost manuscript of Shakespeare himself . . . This hypothetical, recovered or reconstituted manuscript will be the finally definitive text of Shakespeare, in Shakespeare's own spelling.'[20] Fredson Bowers had earlier described the work of compositor studies as 'stripping the veil of print from the texts', thereby recovering 'a number of the characteristics of the manuscript that was given to the printer. From such evidence', he wrote, 'one may eventually determine, not impressionistically as at present but scientifically, which were Shakespeare's own papers and which copies by perhaps identifiable scribes like Ralph Crane.' Once such a determination was made, editors would have it in their power to produce the 'ultimately authoritative' edition. (Bowers, 'Today's Shakespeare Texts', pp. 58–9).

Despite this strongly optimistic tone, several plays continued to present almost intractable problems. For at least four plays, the disturbing fact emerged that their 'bad' quarto printings could not be ignored. 'Maimed' quartos – believed by most to be the product of abridged performance versions as reported by actors – had been found to have been somehow implicated in the Folio print-ing of *2 Henry VI*, *3 Henry VI*, and *Henry V*; and the quarto of *Richard III*, known to have been used (in one or more of its later reprints) in the printing of the Folio text and for years classified as an authoritative text, was reclassified as a memorially reconstructed 'bad quarto'. Determining precisely what Shakespeare wrote for these four plays – and especially for *Richard III* – thus involved the editor in balancing the errors likely to have been introduced by the faulty memories of the actors against the errors likely to have been introduced by the Folio (and quarto) compositors (Bowers, 'Shakespeare's Text', pp. 84–5).

The situation with five additional plays – *Troilus and Cressida*, *2 Henry IV*, *Hamlet*, *Othello*, and *King Lear* – was more complicated yet. Each of these plays was seen as existing in two substantive versions, each version printed from one of two relatively 'good' manuscripts (perhaps a 'foul papers' manuscript and a 'promptbook') or one version printed from such a manuscript and the other from that 'good' printing annotated with reference to another 'good' manuscript. For each of these plays, the editor must select one version as 'most authoritative' – closest, that is, to the author's 'foul papers' – and then, having determined the exact derivation of each version, the errors likely to have been introduced into each by the author's carelessness, the scribe, the playhouse bookkeeper, and/or the compositors, use his or her editorial judgement in selecting the 'Shakespearian' word or line at every point where the two texts differ (Bowers, 'Shakespeare's Text', esp. pp. 82–3). As Greg warned, because of the 'circum-stances of transmission . . . and the accidents to which the text may have been exposed', Shakespeare's exact words, his 'intention' regarding the text, might not at every point be realized in 'the generally more authoritative edition' (*Editorial Problem*, pp. xxxv, xxix, xxxvi); hence the need for editorial judgement in select-ing the words that were Shakespeare's own. And the need for judgement went beyond the individual word. As Greg pointed out, 'many lines of a play as the author wrote it may not appear at all in what is generally the most authoritative edition, and it follows that the copy-text may on occasion need supplementing from another substantive edition', though the editor must 'admit into the text those [additional passages] only which . . . appear to have come from the pen of the author and to have formed part of his finished design' (pp. xxxvi–xxxvii).

The difficulty of determining Shakespeare's 'finished design' behind plays extant in two quite different texts created one fault-line in the massive structure of the new bibliographical paradigm, and it was at this weak point that pressure was first applied. In 1965 E. A. J. Honigmann suggested that the theory of a single authorial manuscript might be inappropriate;[21] by 1980, that suggestion had become a widespread attack on one of the paradigm's central bases. This

attack, from a 'novelty of theory' proposed by several scholars almost simultaneously, urged that a given Shakespeare play might well have existed in more than
one authorially sanctioned version. Stanley Wells recognized immediately the
paradigm-threatening implications of the new theory, noting in 1983 both the
'*zeitgeist* . . . at work' in developing the theory and the fact that 'acceptance of its
implications requires a mental adjustment that may prove painful'.[22] Scholars
working out the new theory focused initially on the two significantly different
texts of *King Lear*, but *Troilus and Cressida*, *Hamlet*, and *Othello* were then almost
immediately presented as exemplars not of single authorial scripts but of printings of separate versions, each authoritative, each with its own integrity.

The attack on the new bibliographical paradigm spread to another vulnerable
point when the theory of multiple versions of Shakespeare's plays was extended
to include plays printed in 'bad quartos'. Pollard's basic distinction, so freeing to
Greg, McKerrow, Wilson, and their followers, and so central to the paradigm,
was now held to be invalid and void, and the performability and authority of the
quarto printings of *Henry V*, *The Merry Wives of Windsor*, and their fellows were
proclaimed and defended.[23]

Simultaneously, and again following on Honigmann's 1965 suggestion,
Stephen Orgel attacked the paradigm at yet another vulnerable point: namely,
the centrality of the author to editorial theory. In 1981 he wrote:

> Modern scientific bibliography began with the assumption that certain basic
> textual questions were capable of correct answers: that by developing rules of evi-
> dence and refining techniques of description and comparison the relation of edi-
> tions of a work to each other and to the author's manuscript could be understood,
> and that an accurate text could thereby be produced. Behind these assumptions
> lies an even more basic one: that the correct text is the author's manuscript . . .
> We assume, in short, that the authority of a text derives from the author.

This central assumption, he argued, is simply not true of Shakespeare or his
fellow dramatists. Because Shakespeare wrote texts for performance, because
such texts were collaborative, were in effect commissioned and owned by the
company (not the scriptwriter), and were inevitably always under revision, 'the
very notion of "the author's original manuscript" is . . . a figment' and new bibliographical 'emphasis on the author' is 'anachronistic'. Orgel's conclusion is
that 'we know nothing about Shakespeare's original text', and that 'what scientific bibliography has taught us more clearly than anything else is that at the heart
of our texts lies a hard core of uncertainty'.[24]

While Orgel's challenge draws on factual information about the workings of
theatre companies in Shakespeare's day, the thrust is theoretical and potentially
devastating to the new bibliographical paradigm. A different attack, one perhaps
even more threatening, is from 'novelties of fact'. Beginning in the mid-1980s,
William B. Long and Paul Werstine have been arguing that Greg, in setting up
his types of dramatic manuscripts – 'foul papers', 'prompt-books', and scribal

transcripts – in effect misrepresented extant early modern dramatic manuscripts. Because such documents are so rare and so difficult of access, few textual critics could check Greg's representation of the manuscripts' characteristics. Long, Werstine, and others have now carefully examined the documents, and they warn us that the signs that Greg taught textual critics and editors to use in determining the classification of a Shakespeare text in terms of its (hypothetical) manuscript copy simply do not match the characteristics of extant manuscripts.[25] In the first place, as Werstine argues, Greg's 'foul papers' manuscript – which, according to Greg, 'contained the text substantially in the form the author intended it to assume though in a shape too untidy to be used by the prompter' (*Editorial Problem*, p. 31) – is not represented by any extant dramatic manuscript. Further, and more important, the variations in speech headings and the indefinite entrance directions, which Greg isolated as clear signs of 'foul papers' manuscript copy, can be found equally readily in theatrical and scribal manuscripts. The bookkeeper, according to Long, in fact made very few changes to extant authorial or scribal manuscripts, and so-called 'prompt-books' are thus in no way regularized, as Greg had claimed they were (Long, 'Precious Few', p. 417).

The implications of this attack from 'novelties of fact' are huge: namely, there is no way to tell from an early printed text of a Shakespeare play whether it was printed from Shakespeare's holograph or from a play-book. When the force of this attack is joined by such other 'novelties of fact' as newly revised information about how printing houses actually functioned,[26] hardly a 'fact' supporting New Bibliographical assumptions remains standing. This does not mean, though, that the paradigm has lost its hold. Major recent editions of Shakespeare's plays continue to describe their textual principles and practices in determinedly new bibliographical terms. The Oxford *William Shakespeare: The Complete Works* sets itself apart from the more clearly paradigmatic editions by accepting the theory that Shakespeare revised his plays and by choosing to print the version (imagined) closest to the theatre rather than the one closest to Shakespeare's original manuscript. But even in the Oxford edition, the editors' method of determining the provenance of the versions is firmly grounded in Greg's 'foul papers'/'promptbook' categories and characteristics, and the editors' decision to print the performance version seems grounded in part in their belief that the performance version is a Shakespearian revision. (As Michael Bristol put it, 'If there are now two *King Lear*s where before there was only one, that is because both *King Lear*s have been authorized by Shakespeare.')[27] Ironically, then, the Oxford editors, in choosing the performance text to print, choose the text that represents the author's 'final intentions', thus placing themselves comfortably within the paradigm.

Thus, even in the Oxford edition and despite the challenges to the factual bases of new bibliographical theory, the paradigm maintains its hold on the reproduction of Shakespeare's texts. To understand this puzzling state of affairs, it is helpful to turn again to Kuhn, who points out the enormity of what is involved in overturning an established paradigm, which is never renounced simply because members of the community uncover 'severe and prolonged anomalies' nor even when the community begins to 'lose faith and then to consider alternatives': 'Once it has achieved the status of paradigm, a scientific theory is declared invalid only if an alternate candidate is available to take its place. The decision to reject one paradigm is always simultaneously the decision to accept another' (p. 77).

In the truly scientific world that Kuhn describes, the only way out of such a crisis as that in which the field of Shakespeare textual criticism currently finds itself would be the establishment of a new paradigm. Since ours is an intellectual rather than an experimental/scientific community, and since the 'world' we study and theorize about is composed not of the material universe but of a set of printed texts, Kuhn's description of paradigm shifts may be far less predictive than it is for, say, modern physics. Note that, despite today's conflicting accounts of the origins of the texts and their subsequent reproductions, editions continue to pour out of the presses and, increasingly, out of computer databases. Many scholars who have most cogently challenged the new bibliographical paradigm are themselves engaged in editing Shakespeare's texts. And new theories about the origins of the plays (Orgel's and Goldberg's theories of the text as an anthology of possible performances; Dutton's theory of Shakespeare's 'literary' text as opposed to the playhouse performance text; Trousdale's theory about the completely indeterminate text)[28] bring not only the (perhaps discouraging) need for 'reconstruction of prior theory and the reevaluation of prior fact', (Kuhn, p. 7) but also intellectual excitement and a new sense of possibilities.

In tracing the broad outlines of the critical and editorial community's response to the printing and reproduction of Shakespeare's texts, I have ignored at every stage a host of forces impinging on that reproduction and have passed over in silence the multitude of fascinating details that make vivid the larger story. In the latter half of the nineteenth century, for example (to take one brief period from this four-hundred-year history), to tell the story of the reproduction of the texts one would need to consider the impact of positivism and its offshoot, the canonization of literary secular saints (Shakespeare pre-eminent among them); one would want to tell about the founding of the Shakspere Society, its fascination with metrical tests, and its odd spawning of disintegrationism; one would describe the explosion in kinds and types of editions – the family editions (Bowdler's, in particular), Furness's New Variorum editions, elaborate pictorial editions, facsimile editions. (A book editor in the 1864 issue of the *Athenaeum* wrote, 'Another, – and another, – the volumes come like Banquo's children, never pausing, never promising to pause. A week that does not bring us a new edition seems to lack a characteristic feature.')[29] One would linger over the editorial ramifications of John Payne Collier's claims to have found a 1632 Folio annotated in a seventeenth-century hand.[30] And one would address the fact that publication in books is not the only (perhaps not the primary) route of 'reproduction' of

Shakespeare's texts, and would therefore give a parallel account of stage productions, promptbooks, directors, actresses, actors, theatres.

Every half century, perhaps every decade, offers its own version of this controlling philosophical and social context, with its own special fascinations[31] – nor can the story of Shakespeare's texts be fully told or understood without placing the editors, textual critics, and editions in these larger contexts. But for the purposes of this brief survey, the story of the succeeding communities of editors and scholars – their shared commitment to the texts; their absorption of new facts, new theories; their struggles to make sense of the all-too-sparse evidence – provides its own interest. Further, it gives us a way of looking dispassionately at the present moment in Shakespeare textual studies and of looking with hope towards a future in which a new paradigm may be established (one based perhaps in intertextual theory, or in community acceptance of some theory already proposed), or in which the new bibliography may find a way to explain and absorb the factual and theoretical challenges to its hegemony, or in which editing may flourish in the absence of any accepted paradigm. It is possible to see the present editorial moment as a disturbing one, but its unruly state can also be seen as holding considerable excitement and promise.

Notes

1. The terms 'quarto' and 'folio' are printers' designations for the formats of books, folios being made up of sheets of paper folded only once, quartos of sheets of paper folded twice. Quartos are therefore small books, much like today's paperback editions of individual plays; the 1623 Folio is a large volume containing thirty-six plays in double columns.
2. Alfred W. Pollard, *Shakespeare Folios and Quartos: A Study in the Bibliography of Shakespeare's Plays, 1594–1685* (London: Methuen, 1909), p. 164.
3. James Boswell, *The Plays and Poems of William Shakspeare, with the corrections and illustrations of various commentators* . . . [London: 1821], I, xiv.
4. *Mr. William Shakespeares Comedies, Histories, & Tragedies* (London: 1623), Title page [A1], 'To the great Variety of Readers', A3.
5. Lewis Theobald, *The Works of Shakespeare: In Seven Volumes* (London: Bettesworth, Hitch, Tonson . . . 1733), p. xxxviii.
6. Ronald B. McKerrow, 'The Treatment of Shakespeare's Text by his Earlier Editors, 1709–1768'. Annual Shakespeare Lecture of the British Academy. Read 26 April 1933. From the *Proceedings of the British Academy*, vol. 19, no. 20, p. 21.
7. It was not until the nineteenth century that Karl Lachmann established a 'genealogical' approach to the editing of classical manuscripts, thus transforming manuscript editing.
8. Edward Capell, *Mr William Shakespeare his Comedies, Histories and Tragedies* (London: for J. & R. Tonson, [1768]), I, p. 21.
9. *The Plays and Poems of William Shakespeare in 10 Volumes* (London: H. Baldwin, 1790), I, xii–xiii.
10. *The Riverside Shakespeare*, 2nd edn (Boston: Houghton Mifflin, 1997), p. 62.
11. The Cambridge *Shakespeare* appeared between 1863 and 1866, with an important revision by Wright in 1891–3 and a one-volume version (the Globe edition) appearing in 1864.

12. Thomas S. Kuhn, *The Structure of Scientific Revolutions*, 2nd edn, enlarged (University of Chicago Press, 1970), p. 52.

13. Samuel Johnson, in his 1765 edition, lists among the pre-Folio editions of *Richard II*: '4to for *Matthew Law*, 1615, from which the first Folio was printed' (*The Plays of William Shakespear* (London: Tonson, 1765), IV, [2]). It is thus possible that Johnson should be credited with the discovery that Folio texts were set from quarto copy, though if so Johnson seems not to have made much of this discovery.

14. See Fredson Bowers, 'Shakespeare's Text and the Bibliographical Method', *Studies in Bibliography* 6 (1954), 71–91, esp. pp. 71–2. See also Paul Werstine, 'Shakespeare', in *Scholarly Editing: A Guide to Research*, ed. D. C. Greetham (New York: MLA, 1995), pp. 253–82, esp. p. 265.

15. *The Shakespeare First Folio: Its Bibliographical and Textual History* (Oxford: Clarendon Press, 1955), pp. 83, 92, 88.

16. *The Library*, 4th series, 12: 3 (1931) 253–75, esp. p. 275. As Greg wrote in 1955, 'it was R. B. McKerrow who in 1931, in what has been described as "One of the most illuminating bibliographical papers ever written", first brought the author's draft into the forefront of the critical picture' (p. 96).

17. Alfred W. Pollard, W. W. Greg, E. Maunde Thompson, J. Dover Wilson, and R. W. Chambers, *Shakespeare's Hand in the Play of Sir Thomas More* (Cambridge University Press, 1923).

18. See Fredson Bowers, 'Today's Shakespeare Texts, and Tomorrow's', *Studies in Bibliography* 19 (1966), 39–65, esp. p. 58.

19. *The Editorial Problem in Shakespeare* (Oxford: Clarendon Press, 1942), pp. 22–48.

20. 'On Editing Shakespeare: *Annus Mirabilis*', *Medieval and Renaissance Studies* 5 (Chapel Hill: University of North Carolina Press, 1971), 61–79, esp. p. 73.

21. *The Stability of Shakespeare's Text* (London: Edward Arnold, 1965).

22. 'The Once and Future *King Lear*', in *The Division of the Kingdoms: Shakespeare's Two Versions of King Lear*, ed. Gary Taylor and Michael Warren (Oxford: Clarendon Press, 1983), pp. 1–22, esp. pp. 17, 20.

23. See, e.g., Steven Urkowitz, '"Well-sayd Olde Mole": Burying Three *Hamlet*s in Modern Editions', in *Shakespeare Study Today*, ed. Georgianna Ziegler (New York: AMS Press, 1986), pp. 37–70; see also Laurie E. Maguire, *Shakespearean Suspect Texts: The 'Bad' Quartos and Their Contexts* (Cambridge University Press, 1996.)

24. 'What is a Text?' *Research Opportunities in Renaissance Drama* 24 (1981), 3–6, esp. p. 3.

25. William B. Long, '"A Bed for Woodstock": a Warning for the Unwary', *Medieval and Renaissance Drama in England* 2 (1985), 91–118; Paul Werstine, 'Narratives about Printed Shakespeare Texts: "Foul Papers" and "Bad" Quartos', *Shakespeare Quarterly* 41 (1990), 65–86. See also Werstine, 'Plays in Manuscript', in *A New History of Early English Drama*, ed. John D. Cox and David Scott Kastan (New York: Columbia University Press, 1997), pp. 481–97, and Long, '"Precious Few": English Manuscript Playbooks', in *A Companion to Shakespeare*, ed. David Scott Kastan (Oxford: Blackwell, 1999), pp. 414–33.

26. See, e.g., D. F. McKenzie, 'Printers of the Mind: Some Notes on Bibliographical Theories and Printing-House Practices', *Studies in Bibliography* 22 (1969), 1–75; Peter W. M. Blayney, *The Texts of 'King Lear' and Their Origins*, vol. I, *Nicholas Okes and the First Quarto* (Cambridge University Press, 1982) and 'Introduction to the Second Edition', *The Norton Facsimile of the First Folio of Shakespeare* (New York: W. W. Norton, 1996), pp. xxvii–xxxvii.

27. *Shakespeare's America / America's Shakespeare* (London: Routledge, 1990), p. 113.

28. See Stephen Orgel, 'The Authentic Shakespeare', *Representations* 21 (1988), 1–26; Jonathan Goldberg, '"What? In a Names That Which We Call a Rose": the Desired

Texts of *Romeo and Juliet'*, in *Crisis in Editing: Texts of the English Renaissance*, ed. Randall McLeod (New York: AMS Press, 1988), pp. 173–202; Richard Dutton, 'The Birth of the Author', in *Texts and Cultural Change in Early Modern England*, ed. Cedric C. Brown and Arthur F. Marotti (New York: St Martin's Press, 1997), pp. 153–78; and Marion Trousdale, 'Diachronic and synchronic: Critical Bibliography and the Acting of Plays', in *Shakespeare: Text, Language, Criticism: Essays in Honour of Marvin Spevack*, ed. Bernhard Fabian and Kurt Tetzeli von Rosador (Hildesheim: Olms, 1987), pp. 304–14.

29. On the canonization of literary saints, see Tricia Lootens, 'Saint Shakespeare and the "Body" of the Text: Legends and "Emendatory Criticism"', in *Lost Saints: Silence, Gender, and Victorian Literary Canonization* (Charlottesville: University Press of Virginia, 1996), pp. 15–22. On disintegrationism, see Hugh Grady, *The Modernist Shakespeare: Critical Texts in a Material World* (Oxford: Clarendon Press, 1991), pp. 43–51. (Grady draws on Kuhn's concepts of paradigms to describe the 'modern' and the 'modernist' periods, using the term much more broadly than it is used by Kuhn or in this essay.) The *Athenaeum* citation is from 24 December 1864, p. 863. I am grateful to Georgianna Ziegler for this reference.

30. See J. Payne Collier, *Notes and Emendations to the text of Shakespeare's Plays from Early Manuscript Corrections in a copy of the Folio, 1632, in the possession of J. Payne Collier* . . . (London: Whittaker, 1853). See also J. O. Halliwell, *Observations on Some of the Manuscript Emendations of the Text of Shakespeare, and Are they Copyright?* (London: John Russell Smith, 1853); N. E. S. A. Hamilton, *An Inquiry into the Genuineness of the Manuscript Corrections in Mr. J. Payne Collier's Annotated Shakspere, Folio, 1632, and of certain Shaksperian Documents likewise published by Mr. Collier* (London: Richard Bentley, 1860).

31. For the eighteenth century, for example, see Margreta de Grazia, *Shakespeare Verbatim: The Reproduction of Authenticity and the Apparatus of 1790* (Oxford: Clarendon Press, 1991); Colin Franklin, *Shakespeare Domesticated: The Eighteenth-century Editions* (Aldershot: Scolar Press, 1991); Joanna Gondris, ed., *Reading Readings: Essays on Shakespeare Editing in the Eighteenth Century* (Madison: Fairleigh Dickinson University Press, 1998); Nichol Smith, *Shakespeare in the Eighteenth Century* (Oxford: Clarendon Press, 1928); Marcus Walsh, *Shakespeare, Milton, and Eighteenth-century Literary Editing* (Cambridge University Press, 1997); and Simon Jarvis, *Scholars and Gentlemen: Shakespearian and Textual Criticism and Representations of Scholarly Labour, 1725–1765* (Oxford: Clarendon Press, 1995). Jarvis helpfully recommends Kuhn's concept of paradigm shifts as a way of reading the work of eighteenth-century editors in a non-condemnatory way.

Reading list

Blayney, Peter W. M., *The First Folio of Shakespeare* (Hanover: Folger, 1991).

de Grazia, Margreta, *Shakespeare Verbatim: The Reproduction of Authenticity and the Apparatus of 1790* (Oxford: Clarendon Press, 1991).

de Grazia, Margreta and Peter Stallybrass, 'The Materiality of the Shakespearean Text', *Shakespeare Quarterly* 44 (1993), 255–83.

Dutton, Richard, 'The Birth of the Author', in *Texts and Cultural Change in Early Modern England*, ed. Cedric C. Brown and Arthur F. Marotti (New York: St Martin's Press, 1997), pp. 153–78.

Goldberg, Jonathan, '"What? In a Names That Which We Call a Rose": the Desired Texts of *Romeo and Juliet'*, in *Crisis in Editing: Texts of the English Renaissance*, ed. Randall McLeod (New York: AMS Press, 1988), pp. 173–202.

Grady, Hugh, *The Modernist Shakespeare: Critical Texts in a Material World* (Oxford: Clarendon Press, 1991).

Jarvis, Simon, *Scholars and Gentlemen. Shakespearian and Textual Criticism and Representations of Scholarly Labour, 1725–1765* (Oxford: Clarendon Press, 1995).

Long, William B., '"A Bed for Woodstock": a Warning for the Unwary', *Medieval and Renaissance Drama in England* 2 (1985), 91–118 .

'"Precious Few": English Manuscript Playbooks', in *A Companion to Shakespeare*, ed. David Scott Kastan (Oxford: Blackwell, 1999), pp. 414–33.

Lootens, Tricia, 'Saint Shakespeare and the "Body" of the Text: Legends and "Emendatory Criticism"' in *Lost Saints: Silence, Gender, and Victorian Literary Canonization* (Charlottesville: University Press of Virginia, 1996), pp. 15–22.

Maguire, Laurie E., *Shakespearian Suspect Texts: The 'Bad' Quartos and Their Contexts.* (Cambridge University Press, 1996).

Mowat, Barbara A., 'The Form of *Hamlet*'s Fortunes', *Renaissance Drama* 19 (1988), 97–126.

'Nicholas Rowe and the Twentieth-century Shakespeare Text', *Shakespeare and Cultural Traditions*, ed. Tetsuo Kishi, Roger Pringle, and Stanley Wells (University of Delaware Press, 1994), pp. 314–22.

Orgel, Stephen, 'What is a Text?', *Research Opportunities in Renaissance Drama* 24 (1981), 3–6.

'The Authentic Shakespeare', *Representations* 21 (1988), 1–26.

Trousdale, Marion, 'Diachronic and Synchronic: Critical Bibliography and the Acting of Plays', in *Shakespeare: Text, Language, Criticism: Essays in Honour of Marvin Spevack*, ed. Bernhard Fabian and Kurt Tetzeli von Rosador (Hildesheim: Olms, 1987), pp. 304–14.

Walsh, Marcus, *Shakespeare, Milton, and Eighteenth-century Literary Editing* (Cambridge University Press, 1997).

Wells, Stanley, Gary Taylor, *et al.*, *William Shakespeare: A Textual Companion* (Oxford: Clarendon Press, 1988).

Werstine, Paul, 'Shakespeare', in *Scholarly Editing: A Guide to Research*, ed. D. C. Greetham (New York: MLA, 1995), pp. 253–82.

'Narratives about Printed Shakespeare Texts: "Foul Papers" and "Bad" Quartos', *Shakespeare Quarterly* 41 (1990), 65–86.

'Plays in Manuscript', in *A New History of Early English Drama*, ed. John D. Cox and David Scott Kastan (New York: Columbia University Press, 1997), pp. 481–97.

3

LEONARD BARKAN

What did Shakespeare read?

WARWICKSHIRE illiterate; supplier of story-lines to the groundlings; Renaissance polymath. You show me your Shakespeare, and I'll show you a hypothesis about the size and character of his library. We have no hard facts about Shakespeare the reader: no personal documents, no inventories, no annotated volumes with his bookplate. And though his dramatic characters often turn up with books in their hands (sometimes merely *pretending* to read them), we have no neatly autobiographical equivalent of the opening moment in Sir Philip Sidney's *Astrophil and Stella*, where the struggling poet consults pages from his predecessors' work. The impossibility of answering the question only adds to its allure, promising to tell us both who Shakespeare was and how he wrote. Do we see the collected works as the product of an uncanny alchemy of sophistication and complexity performed by a provincial with moderate education and limited book-learning? Are they the output of an extraordinarily hard-working crafts-man who had a knack for taking what was mostly second-rate contemporary writing and transforming its superficial excitements into more profound forms of high sensation? Or should we accept the proposition that the plays and poems represent a full engagement in the high culture of early modern Europe? In these responses to the matter of Shakespeare's reading one can trace both the history of his reputation and the changing fashions of his critics.

Of all these possibilities, Shakespeare the unlettered country boy deserves most immediate attention because it is the place where both biography and crit-icism begin. The famous lines on the subject, from the poem that introduces the First Folio, possess every kind of precedence and authority:

> Soul of the age!
> The applause, delight, the wonder of our stage!
> My Shakespeare, rise: I will not lodge thee by
> Chaucer or Spenser, or bid Beaumont lie
> A little further, to make thee a room;
> Thou art a monument without a tomb,
> And art alive still while thy book doth live,
> And we have wits to read, and praise to give . . .
> For if I thought my judgement were of years,
> I should commit thee surely with thy peers:

> And tell how far thou didst our Lyly outshine,
> Or sporting Kyd, or Marlowe's mighty line.
> And though thou hadst small Latin, and less Greek[1] . . .

Ben Jonson, as ever greatest of collaborators and most problematic of friends, is so masterful an epigrammatist that this last concessive clause will inspire centuries of lore concerning what Shakespeare read. His motives are complex, to say the least, and the very fact that the phrase gets wrenched out of context will only serve to intensify the mixed messages. Jonson is writing a traditional poem of praise and not, at least on the face of it, giving Shakespeare a grade in classics. Rather he begins with a simple paradox, appropriate to issuing the 'Complete Works' seven years after their author's demise: the man is dead, the works live on. In the lines quoted above, Shakespeare is awarded his enduring place within the English Dead Poets' Society; then the subject shifts to his competition with the ancients. The proposition – and it must trouble Jonson, of all people – is that an English writer might enter the company of immortals whom he does not know how to read.

Not that Jonson is being altogether ingenuous. He is himself by auto-proclamation the most learned of authors who descended into the popular world of the theatre. And the classical form of his praise reminds us that there are other writers with large Latin and more Greek. But ancient languages and literatures may not be the ultimate issue here. Jonson's project is to make us understand that Shakespeare is a poet of nature first and of art second; and even if one strand of humanism from the Renaissance to Alexander Pope will declare that Homer and nature are the same, we inevitably inherit a Shakespeare who achieved his magic while being a mediocre reader of the ancients.

Whether that estimate is true or not, there is, alternatively, a large part of Shakespeare's library which Jonson would never have advertised in his eulogy, that enormous body of writings which has been collected under the rubric 'Sources of Shakespeare's Plays'. While some of this material is itself Latin and Greek, this part of Shakespeare's reading has tended to be quite segregated from the canon that Jonson had in mind. However well or badly we imagine Shakespeare knew them, the authors implied in the Folio poem are learned humanist forebears who shed lustre on any modern writer operating under their influence; and that influence itself is understood as operating via a complex set of intellectual mediations. Shakespeare's 'sources', on the other hand, are likelier to be minor figures, sometimes contemporary, often appearing in a sort of *Reader's Digest* form of publication; and this influence, far from being construed as subtle or cerebral, expresses itself as instrumental, opportunistic, or even plagiarizing. The two kinds of reading generally refer to different moments in Shakespeare's life, i.e. his schooling in Stratford v. his daily work as the provider of some two scripts a year to a busy London theatrical company. They have also experienced quite separate fortunes in criticism. The classical predecessors, as we have seen, are launched in the very earliest texts promulgating Shakespeare, while in later times they contribute to philosophical and theoretical approaches to the plays. The sources begin to be of interest only in the eighteenth century, when they are often treated as signs of Shakespeare's lack of originality; subsequently, they fuelled whole industries of pedantic attempts to nail down a precise point of origin for his every text.

Our purpose here will be to consider all of this as one related body of material, to declare that 'what Shakespeare read' consists of a lifetime of experience with text, both that which he found in pre-existing books and that which he composed. In opening up the space between the reading and the writing, our topic turns out to be the most old-fashioned and the most new-fashioned of critical subject matters, resting upon all the scholastic analyses of Shakespeare's grammar school or his sources, while it raises those modern epistemological doubts that have clustered around source, influence, individual authorship, and the ownership of language.

We have no personal information about Shakespeare's education and therefore no direct sense of the texts he studied as a child. It is, however, reasonable to assume that he attended the King's New School in Stratford-upon-Avon; and, since there is abundant documentation concerning many primary and grammar schools throughout England at that time, it is not difficult to reconstruct both a list of texts and a sense of educational techniques. Pupils began with their ABC's and early on worked to master English by reading religious texts like simple catechisms and the Psalms. As early as the age of six or seven, 'grammar school' would begin, which, of course, meant Latin grammar.

Here we can postulate a plausible book-list for the Stratford boy. William Lily's Latin Grammar, first compiled near the beginning of the sixteenth century and still in use two hundred and fifty years later, was the universal foundation. The first part, written in English and known as the *Shorte Introduction* (or, more colloquially, the *Accidence*), took the student through the rudiments of grammar and inflection. In the second part, called the *Brevissima Institutio*, instruction was itself in Latin, covering morphology, syntax, figures of speech, and prosody. During these same early grades pupils were being put through texts of simple maxims in readily construable Latin. The *Sententiae pueriles* of Leonhardus Culmannus, which first appeared in the 1540s, consisted of a graded sequence of truisms, beginning with two words, then progressing to three, and so on. Of even wider usage was the *Disticha moralia* ascribed to Cato; here, too, the emphasis is on enduring verities appropriate to schoolboys, including exhortations to assiduousness, sexual morality, heroism, and acceptance of death. Similar again, both for its aphoristic quality and for its anthology form, was the notably influential Latin version of Æsop's *Fables*, also read in the first years of instruction.

The next phase of Latin readings included another classical-style compendium, the *Zodiacus Vitae* of Palingenio (written c. 1528, also popular in its

English translation by Barnabe Googe, first published in the 1560s), a twelve-book poetic farrago full of proverbial lore but including some substantial materials from antique culture relating to astronomy, metaphysics, and natural philosophy. Also at this time the schoolboy Shakespeare would have been presented with the first instances of what we would recognize as literature. Not that they are necessarily the most auspicious names. The first, Terence, formed one of the bases for Latin instruction all over Europe because his dialogue was thought to give the fullest impression of the way classical Latin was actually spoken; but lest we picture the infant proto-playwright mapping out his career as he construes the *Eunuch*, it should be pointed out that there is small trace of Terence in Shakespeare and far more of Plautus, who was decidedly less popular in the schools. The other threshold literary figure was Battista Spagnuoli (1447–1513), author of a set of eclogues entitled the *Bucolica*. The vast popularity of Mantuan, as he was always called, remains a historical mystery: whatever the reason, for the later Renaissance he was the supreme master of the bucolic mode, heir to his countryman Virgil (and sometimes thought to be superior to him), the official first teacher of poetics and cradle of pastoralism.

All this was generally mastered by the age of twelve: small Latin indeed. In the Upper School, the reading list covered most of the canonical Latin corpus. Some of these authors, like Ovid, will count for more in Shakespeare's works than they did in the curricula; others, like Virgil, less. For the most part, however, the allusiveness of Shakespeare's language (and of the culture in which he lived) is so universal that it is difficult to superimpose school reading upon playwriting with precision. Poets such as Horace, Juvenal, and Persius certainly stuck in the dramatist's mind, though they hardly seem to be foundational; the same could be said of the leading prose writers in the curriculum, such as Sallust and Cæsar. Indeed, Shakespeare's relation to the high literary canon in Latin seems so personal, so different from a replication of assigned reading, that we might suppose him a dropout somewhere in his early teen years.

But that would be a mistake, given a quite different subset of schoolboy classical readings. To us the above great names represent the inevitable summit of ancient Latinity. But in an early modern education such as Shakespeare's, the progression is not from language to literature but from grammar to rhetoric. Thus the real focus of reading in the middle and upper school years – and here Shakespeare's studious familiarity is beyond dispute – is on that body of texts devoted to oratory. The foundational work is the *Ad Herennium*, then attributed to Cicero, which offered a complete structural account of diction, speech, argument, and style. In combination with the *Topics* of Cicero (an authentic work) and, for the upper forms, the *Institutio oratoriae* of Quintilian, this body of school texts not only introduced pupils to the advanced study of language but also formed the basis for all the study of logic that found its origins in Aristotle and its dissemination in every facet of intellectual and public life. Any account of law or medicine, of political theory or natural history, of ethics or metaphysics –

indeed, literary criticism itself, so far as it exists in this period – can be traced to systems of thought and expression that are inculcated by this reading list in advanced rhetoric.

I use the term 'reading list' precisely in its limiting sense. From beginning grammar to the classicizing language of all the professions, we should note *how* as well as *what* the student was reading. Pupils were learning another language almost from the time they began school, but the two languages were construed in fundamentally different ways. It is almost as true in Shakespeare's time as in Dante's that grammar is a property of Latin and not of the vernacular. It follows that the study of classical language is *structural*; in other words, we hear only about mastering grammar and syntax and never about mastering vocabulary. Both the early presence of an alternative language and the bias toward a systemic linguistics produce a consciousness of language as a thing in itself and not just as a frictionless instrument. But the mechanics of the learning process leave even more tangible marks. From the very beginnings of instruction, the method appears to have been question and answer: that is, language as a school subject is performed as a dramatic conversation. Once the basic patterns have been explored through these verbal exchanges, text itself takes the form of *sententia*. The first Latin readings in the curriculum, as we have seen, are collections of maxims; further, students were led through them in such a manner that the achievement of correct Latin was signalled by their finding of the appropriate verbatim *sententia*, like 'amor vincit omnia' or 'comparatio omnis odiosa est', thus identifying correct language and abiding truth as one and the same package.

None of this centres on the practice of translation. That activity – rather curiously, given modern method – is focused upon the rendering of English into Latin rather than the reverse. The texts most commonly chosen are themselves revealing: collections of English *sententiae*, whose correct rendering presumably recapitulates their classical origins; or, certain books from the (already translated) Bible, especially Psalms, Proverbs, or the apocryphal Ecclesiasticus, which, once again, can be readily rendered in the form of pithy sayings. Thus pupils are creating their own new Latin out of familiar English. As time goes on, however, they are doing something more. The summit of translation activity in the schoolroom, propounded by Roger Ascham and based on Cicero, required the pupil to go back and forth from a Latin text to an English translation to a reinvented Latin and so on until perfect competence was achieved. This remarkable exercise enforces complex relations between replication and originality: students keep inventing as they travel across the language barrier until they achieve a text that is at once their own voice and the re-creation of a pre-existing model. What begins as a make-work exercise involving elementary school Latin will culminate in a more complicated relation to the major canonical writers of classical prose and poetry.

If translation was the capstone for grammar, then original composition formed the principal activity for the more advanced training in rhetoric. The first steps in this direction were oral, even dramatic: pupils and master held question-and-answer conversations in Latin. But soon reading and writing are closely intertwined. At the most basic level, they strung together *sententiae* into 'themes', thus moving out from the proverbial lore of their reading into slightly more expanded sententiousness. With the more advanced readings, like the *Ad Herennium* or Ovid's *Heroides*, they began to compose epistles in prose or verse; finally they were expected to produce full-blown orations. All these educational processes consist of creative composition emerging from a set of readings that are at once theoretical and exemplary, offering both precept and prototype. Here the work depended on post-classical workbooks emerging out of Cicero and Quintilian, including the *Epitome* of Susenbrotus and the *Progymnasmata* of Aphthonius. More than their loftier predecessors, these texts were used interactively: they directed pupils essentially to place themselves in hypothetical or imaginative situations, sometimes historical, sometimes mythological, and to create their own Latin text. The resulting exercises were inevitably full of tropes, self-conscious about their status as discourse, and – most important of all – they amounted to dramatic impersonations. So, to descend to a perhaps simplistic historical comparison, while we have for decades taught college students to express their own selves and are rewarded with a fundamentally solipsistic public discourse, Renaissance education taught its upper grammar school students to impersonate other voices, and they were rewarded with a flowering of public oratory and theatre.

Finally, there is one other major author – the only modern – whose influence shaped the process of an English sixteenth-century education. In a series of texts on education, including the *Institutio hominis Christiani*, the *De ratione studii*, and the *Institutio principis Christiani*, and in a set of close personal relations with John Colet, Dean of St Paul's, Erasmus had laid out nearly all the principles of modern education. It is Erasmus who gives official status to the logical line that goes back towards Cicero and Aristotle and forward towards Descartes – that is, a set of stable and coordinated relations between truth and language. It is Erasmus who establishes the canon of classical authors suitable for instruction, and it is he who enforces the heuristic and moral value of the *sententia* in reading-matter (it was his edition of Cato that was widely used in school), while also relegating purely sententious, often spuriously classical, works to a secondary position in favour of a moralistic literary criticism applied to major writers. It is Erasmus who shows the way to students, both in his *De conscribendis epistolis* and in his *Colloquies*, in the first demonstrating how to place letter-writing in a dramatic context and in the second offering the fullest modern example of humanistic discussion in multiple voices written in fine classical Latin. Then, at the highpoint of grammar-school education, came his famous *De Copia*, which offered both precept and example in the composition of language that was elegant, highly figured, and capable of almost infinite variation. Whether Shakespeare read Erasmus or not, he certainly had an Erasmian education.

The marks of all these processes and influences are written everywhere in Shakespeare's text. A simple census of all the Latin that appears in the playtexts reveals how many of the phrases are traditional maxims, traceable to early education. Often they are taken specifically from Lily's Latin Grammar, as for instance Sir Andrew's 'Not to be abed after midnight is to be up betimes, and *diliculo surgere* [to rise at dawn], thou knowest' (*Twelfth Night*, 2.3.1–2) or Tranio's 'If love have touched you, naught remains but so – / *Redime te captum quam queas minimo* [Ransom yourself from captivity at the lowest possible price]' (*Shrew*, 1.1.155–6), which is actually misquoted just as it is in Lily's Latin Grammar; indeed, when Horace's oft-repeated 'Integer vitae [The man upright in life]' is cited in *Titus Andronicus* (4.2.20), Chiron actually says, 'I read it in the grammar long ago.' Whether vernacular or classical, Shakespeare's usage is deeply imbued with *sententiae*; and some of the most famous of his riffs on traditional expressions, like 'All the world's a stage' or 'We are such stuff as dreams are made on', derive from Latin tags learned in school. Even Shakespeare's Bible shows evidence of his classical training: the books he most commonly cites are just the same Psalms, Proverbs, and Ecclesiasticus that he translated into Latin as a schoolboy.

On a number of occasions Shakespeare actually stages primary education. In *The Taming of the Shrew*, Lucentio, impersonating a Latin tutor to gain access to Bianca, follows the schoolroom practice of construing, or translating. His text is from the first book of Ovid's *Heroides*; but, given his amorous purposes, the translation he offers is, to say the least, idiosyncratic: '"*Hic ibat*", as I told you before – "*Simois*", I am Lucentio – "*hic est*", son unto Vincentio of Pisa – "*Sigeia tellus*", disguised thus to get your love . . .' (3.1.31–3). Bianca, herself no mean pupil, returns the translation exercise, as students were expected to do: '"*Hic ibat Simois*", I know you not – "*hic est Sigeia tellus*", I trust you not . . .' (3.1.40–1). (Her translation at least has the virtue of keeping the Latin clauses logically together. For the record, the lines actually mean, 'Here flowed the Simois, here lies the Sigeian land.') *The Merry Wives of Windsor* includes a whole scene explicitly taken from instruction in Lily's Grammar, referred to as the 'accidence'. Here the construing is misconstrued not by deliberate deception, but by the ignorance of the (female) onlookers, who turn innocent Latin into off-colour English, and by the mediocre performance of the pupil, William, in response to his Welsh schoolmaster, Evans. He does reasonably well with the basics, such as *hic, hæc, hoc*, but he comes aground in the more advanced translation practice:

Evans. What is '*lapis*', William?
William. A stone.
Evans. And what is a 'stone', William?
William. A pebble.
Evans. No, it is '*lapis*'. I pray you remember in your prain.
William. '*Lapis*'.   (4.1.26–31)

William fails at the Cicero–Ascham translation method, i.e. Latin to English and back to Latin.

Love's Labour's Lost is above all Shakespeare's monument to the problems of grammar and rhetoric; there is hardly a scene that does not contain exercises in semantics or translation or else larger theories of language. Critical to the whole enterprise is the trio of (pseudo-) learned characters: Don Armado, the new-style wit; Nathaniel, the half-educated priest; and, of special interest here, Holofernes the classically trained schoolmaster. More pedant than pedagogue, Holofernes speaks in a perpetual construing from Latin to English; he cites numerous schoolbook *sententiae*; he quotes and comments on Mantuan as well as Ovid; he lords it over his fellow-'scholars'; he offers time-honoured and conservative views on English orthography.

Just how deeply these forms of reading and learning penetrated Shakespeare's invention may be observed most fully in a scene where no actual schoolmaster appears. It is an exchange between Touchstone and William in *As You Like It*:

Touchstone. . . . Is thy name William?
William. William, sir.
Touchstone. A fair name. Wast born i' th' forest here?
William. Ay, sir, I thank God.
Touchstone. Thank God – a good answer . . . You do love this maid?
William. I do, sir.
Touchstone. Give me your hand. Art thou learned?
William. No, sir.
Touchstone. Then learn this of me: to have is to have. For it is a figure in rhetoric that drink, being poured out of a cup into a glass, by filling the one doth empty the other. For all your writers do consent that *ipse* is he. Now you are not *ipse*, for I am he.
William. Which he, sir?
Touchstone. He, sir, that must marry this woman. Therefore, you clown, abandon – which is in the vulgar, leave – the society – which in the boorish is company – of this female – which in the common is woman; which together is, abandon the society of this female, or, clown, thou perishest; or, to thy better understanding, diest; or, to wit, I kill thee, make thee away, translate thy life into death, thy liberty into bondage. I will deal in poison with thee, or in bastinado, or in steel. I will bandy with thee in faction, I will o'errun thee with policy; I will kill thee a hundred and fifty ways.   (5.1.19–52)

The learned fool treats his hapless interlocutor to an almost complete performance of the grammar-school education that an Arden rustic cannot have experienced for real. First, catechism; then, the central proposition of dialectic, which lies at the heart of the relations among grammar, rhetoric, and logic, transmitted in terms of 'ipse' and 'cups' via Cicero and Quintilian[2]; then, the practice of construing from one language to another, in this case, from Lofty to Bumpkin;

finally, as a graduation exercise, an invention in the spirit of Erasmus' *De copia*, except that where the original merely offered multiple ways of *saying* something (specifically, 'Thank you for your letter'), Touchstone's diverse formulations provide multiple ways of *doing* something, i.e. murdering William by elegant variation.

Whether the grammar-school curriculum surfaces in the voice of the pedant or the parodist, it tells us something. For one thing, these textual materials nearly always betray an awareness that people speak many languages: Evans's instruction in *The Merry Wives of Windsor* is confusing less because of the Latin than because he is rendering both languages via Welsh; Touchstone affects to accommodate the language of the country; and the would-be lovers in *The Taming of the Shrew* are attempting to invent private languages. Further, all these appearances of early curricula delineate a world that is inescapably alternative to that of real (i.e. theatrical, or lived) experience. The texts of grammar, rhetoric, and literature, when rendered *as* texts, are in a profound sense bracketed – as are, of course, the characters who import them. Brilliant or foolish, these individuals speak of that which is external, unlived, or, at best, exemplary rather than real; and even when the characters are not marginal, like Hamlet when he appears to be citing Juvenal ('the satirical slave says here that old men have grey beards . . .' (2.2.196–7)), their reading forms part of a textual alternative to actual experience.

Still, if the real issue is how such reading might be assimilated, it is best to understand Holofernes and Touchstone as polar opposites. The schoolmaster, it must be remembered, has great ambitions as a poet, producing, first, a laboured alliterative epigram on the hunting of the deer and then the (blessedly) fragmented pageant of the Worthies. Like his own creator, in other words, he travels the distance between old reading and new writing. Just how catastrophic this travel may be is demonstrated by his own literary criticism of one of the play's competing poets, the sonneteering Biron:

> for the elegancy, facility, and golden cadence of poesy – *caret* [i.e. is lacking]. Ovidius Naso was the man. And why, indeed 'Naso' but for smelling out the odoriferous flowers of fancy, the jerks of invention? *Imitari* is nothing. So doth the hound his master, the ape his keeper, the tired horse his rider. (4.2.114–18)

The irony is, of course, that Holofernes imagines himself to be on the side of invention over imitation when his poetry is agonizingly, almost regurgitatingly, derivative from the books that he inculcates and the pedantic languages that he speaks. The further irony is that true invention can emerge only from a properly understood practice of imitation. Young William Page may move pointlessly from *lapis* to *stone* and back to *lapis*. But that same system of instruction also allows for the alien, bracketed, frequently ancient, and always garbled prior text to become one's own voice, indeed, to define what that voice is. Such an achievement – the pun must be forgiven, since it is Shakespeare's – is the touch-stone of the real poet.

A man is sitting in London around 1600 in the middle of a personal library whose catalogue corresponds precisely to the 'Sources of Shakespeare's Plays': what can we say about his reading taste? Voracious; more middle-brow than high-brow; heterodox; philosophically not of the avant-garde; anglo-centric in certain ways, generally having to do with past and present public institutions, yet at the same time revealing a considerable fondness for continental story-telling. He is something of a history buff – in that field, his holdings range from the learned to the ephemeral. Theatre, represented a bit sparsely by comparison, is both classic and contemporary, with a sprinkling of university closet drama. There is a certain taste for current events, especially at the level of political intrigue and life-styles of the rich and famous: these are often to be found in the pamphlet collec-tion. As for high-brow literature, you are more likely to find a few well-thumbed volumes than a complete catalogue of the major works.

But let us name the names. As for the serious favourites, Ovid and Plutarch are visible everywhere, and Seneca is only a little less prominent. For classical history, apart from Plutarch, Livy was most often studied, but it is noteworthy that the real source may have been the *Epitome* of Livy written by Florus in the second century AD. Other historians seem to have been consulted only for spe-cific projects: Scotland, Denmark, and Turkey (this last for *Othello*) occasioned specialized research, while *Julius Cæsar* appears to have required a lot of supple-mentary reading, including Tacitus, Appian, and perhaps Sallust and Suetonius.

Among Shakespeare's sources in his own language, the largest share belongs to the chroniclers who furnished material for the history plays. The compendia that he read most exhaustively were Edward Hall's *Union of the two Noble and Illustre Famelies of Lancastre and Yorke* (1548), the *Chronicles* of Raphael Holinshed (1578, 1587), and John Stow's *Chronicles of England* (1580) and *Annales of England* (1592). Together, these offered the dramatist not only the raw data, both dynastic and anecdotal, but also the methodologies of history-writing and the special politics of the Tudor ascendancy. Of a different kind, but persis-tently influential, are such literary works as the didactic *Mirror for Magistrates* (1559) and Samuel Daniel's poetic *First Fowre Bookes of the Civile Wars* (1595), while yet another approach to the materials comes from the strenuous polemics for the Protestant cause offered by John Foxe in his *Acts and Monuments*, known as the *Booke of Martyrs* (first published in English, 1563). Figures of exceptional cultural fascination, including King John, Richard III, Henry V, and Falstaff had generated their own specialized source materials.

On what we would consider the more literary side, Shakespeare's English-lan-guage reading list tended to be similar to ours. So far as the fourteenth-century masters are concerned, Chaucer is writ large in *A Midsummer Night's Dream* and

Troilus and Cressida, while John Gower makes his mark both at the very beginning of the dramatist's career (*Comedy of Errors*) and the very end (*Pericles*). The two greatest non-dramatic masterpieces of Shakespeare's own age, Sir Philip Sidney's *Arcadia* and Edmund Spenser's *Faerie Queene*, find their way into comic, historic, and tragic works, with *King Lear* embracing elements of both.

Shakespeare's tastes were not exclusively highbrow, however. Among the works of prose fiction, Barnaby Riche's *Apolonius and Silla* (1581), Robert Greene's *Pandosto* (1588), and Thomas Lodge's *Rosalynde* (1590) might be forgotten today were they not the principal sources for *Twelfth Night*, *The Winter's Tale*, and *As You Like It*, but they prove to be lively works in their own right that vindicate Shakespeare's dependence on them. John Lyly's *Euphues* (1579), whose mix of wit and eros and pedantry swept through Elizabethan literate culture, can be detected in the language of every overwrought lover in the comedies. So far as theatrical literature is concerned, Shakespeare's tastes are decidedly popular. While Marlowe and Jonson exercise some influence, it appears that Anon. is virtually his favourite dramatist, as witness his careful reading of *The Troublesome Reign of King John* (1591), or the complex ways in which *The Rare Triumphes of Love and Fortune* (1589) and *Mucedorus* (first version, 1598) are woven into the plots of the late romances.

Lists of titles like these need to be grounded in a larger sense of the contemporary intellectual climate, particularly as regards book-making and book-reading. At the level of European culture in general, two factors must not be forgotten: first, the continental Renaissance, now more than a century old, had stimulated an enormous opening-up in the category of literature, both that which was revived from the past and that which was being newly produced; second, the invention and growth of printing continued to disseminate the material objects of reading in greater quantity and to a wider audience. England, besides feeling these effects, was by the later sixteenth century in the grip of a quite self-conscious drive to found and promote a national – or even nationalist – literary culture, the evidence of which is not only such highly visible careers as those of, say, Spenser and Ralegh, but also a flood of literary rivalries and disputes which generated a great deal of ink and rendered book-making itself a matter of public interest. Indeed, these sometimes became the actual stuff of drama, as is clear from the frequent appearance of names like Gabriel Harvey, Thomas Nashe, Robert Greene, and George Chapman in the explanatory notes to Elizabethan playtexts.

Two other matters bear even more directly on Shakespeare's sources as a body of text. From the 1560s onwards, a gigantic industry of translation revolutionizes what it is possible for the English to read. Though the dramatist's familiarity with passages in the original is often demonstrable, Shakespeare's plays would scarcely have been possible without: Hoby's Castiglione (1561), Adlington's Apuleius (1566), Golding's Ovid (1567), North's Plutarch (1579), Harington's

Ariosto (1591), Chapman's Homer (1598, in part), Holland's Livy (1600), Fairfax's Tasso (1600), and Florio's Montaigne (1603). To say that is, of course, to return to 'small Latin and less Greek': as a reader, Shakespeare was pretty much like most of us who have a reasonable command of a foreign language. Faced with the bulk of something like the *Orlando Furioso*, we would still prefer a reliable trot; and the chances of our experiencing the whole work and of going back to it in the original are vastly increased by the existence of a good translation. The translations cited above are, for the most part, better than good: they are brilliantly imaginative, if not always accurate by our standards, and some of them, particularly those in prose, helped create a new literary English. As Shakespearian reading, these works function in a variety of ways, ranging from idle perusal, to direct use as source, to material for minute verbal plagiarism. All the while they were putting him in touch with contemporary and past masterpieces, as well as with the phenomenon of multiple languages in the same space.

The other book-making circumstance, while related to the matter of translation, is much harder to pin down. The hypothetical Shakespearian source-library is notably rich in a kind of volume whose origins go back to the Middle Ages but whose international career is very much alive and well in the sixteenth century, namely, the compendium of stories. At the canonical peak of the genre is Boccaccio's *Decameron* (itself a Shakespearian source, relevant to *All's Well*, *Cymbeline*, and *Merry Wives*); other such texts include the *Gesta Romanorum*, which dates back to the thirteenth century, *Il Novellino* by Masuccio of Salerno (1476), the *Novelle* of Bandello (1554), *Il Pecorone* of Giovanni Fiorentino (1558), and *Gli Hecatommithi* of Giraldi Cinthio (1565), plus related versions in other languages including *Histoires tragiques* by Pierre Boaistuau (1559) and by François de Belleforest (1564), Geoffrey Fenton's *Certaine Tragicall Discourses* (1567), and William Painter's *Palace of Pleasure* (1567). Collectively, this body of material touches upon a remarkable range of Shakespearian texts – not only, as one might expect, tales of fantasy and love such as *Merchant*, *Pericles*, and *Cymbeline* but also those set in very different universes like *Merry Wives*, *Titus Andronicus*, *Timon of Athens*, and even *Hamlet*.

These collections of narratives in part represent an early modern codification (in some cases fabrication) of folktales; in their vast overlapping interrelations we can witness a whole field – call it literary bumper cars – where stories are made and remade via translation, imitation, elaboration, parody, and recombination. If, for instance, one follows the source trail of *Romeo and Juliet* or *Othello*, where there is a proximate originary work (Arthur Brooke's *Tragicall Historye of Romeus and Juliet* and Cinthio's *Hecatommithi*) but behind it a tangle of versions coming out of Bandello and his inheritors, one is struck by the difficulty of pinning down Shakespeare's specific route of derivation, especially given questions concerning his familiarity with languages. But more than that, one notices that this range of material made available to the dramatist a kind of postgraduate course in comparative structural narratology. And even if these anthologies appear to be 'literature lite', they also remind us that some of Shakespeare's most prestigious source books, including the *Metamorphoses* and Plutarch's *Lives*, are themselves structured in the form of composite and detachable parts that invite comparison.

Now, having listed all these points of origin, ancient and modern, lofty and popular, we must ask the slightly ingenuous question, did Shakespeare really *read* his sources? As I have suggested earlier, it is clear enough that he read his school-texts quite independently of instrumentalizing them for some new piece of writing. It is also clear that there is a body of important works of such universal presence within early modern civilization – one might borrow Foucault's desig-nation of 'transdiscursive', by which he refers to Marx and Freud – that they are present everywhere in the formation of the plays via some deep acculturation. One can hardly imagine, for instance, the erotic ideals of the Sonnets without Plato, or the politics of Milan and Naples in *The Tempest* without Machiavelli, or the transports of love, whether straight or parodied, from *Love's Labour's Lost* to *Antony and Cleopatra*, without Petrarch. Likewise, without the Bible we could not begin to account for turns of phrase like Hamlet's 'There's a special provi-dence in the fall of a sparrow' (5.2.157–8), or Bottom's 'The eye of man hath not heard, the ear of man hath not seen . . .' (*Dream* 4.1.204–5), or, indeed, the very title *Measure for Measure*, with its multiple reverberations from the Sermon on the Mount. All of these books, in whatever form and by whatever necessary intermediaries – he *read*.

But centuries of source study, applying itself to Bandello, or the anonymous playtexts, or even the canonical classics which form the basis of the dramatic plots, have suggested that Shakespeare did not so much read these works as cut and paste them – that is, he opportunistically stole what he needed, ignored the rest, and sublimed everything. These assumptions are well worth questioning. To put the matter in its simplest terms, authors generally can discover something in another book only once they have read that book independently of its precise future usefulness. Shakespeare, in other words, might have consulted Richard Knolles's *Generall Historie of the Turkes* when he had already worked out the circumstances of *Othello*, but he is less likely to have dreamed up a tale about a Moor marrying a Venetian lady and then gone to a first reading of Cinthio's *Hecatommithi*, 3.7, either accidentally or in the foreknowledge that he would find what he needed there. And by whatever chronology of consultation, exported material remains touched with its own original context. The source book, whether it is *The Faerie Queene* or *The Three Ladies of London*, enters a compli-cated calculus of inspiration for any author under its influence.

These abstract principles become concrete when we follow some quite specific paths of Shakespearian sourcing. In a set of interesting articles, Martin Mueller has shown how certain stories, while providing the main point of origin for a single play, also haunt the dramatist's imagination repeatedly and throughout his career. Bandello's tale of Fenicia and Timbreo includes all the main events of the

Claudio and Hero plot in *Much Ado*, but elements in this story continue to generate important moments in later plays, including *Othello*, *Cymbeline*, and *The Winter's Tale*, where Shakespeare seems to be trying to do different things – generally less rational and more magical – with the Bandello source. Plutarch's *Life of Brutus* is a primary source for *Julius Caesar*, but the relation between Brutus and his wife Portia weaves itself through a set of variations on the conduct of married life in *The Merchant of Venice*, *1 Henry IV*, and *Macbeth* (as well as *Lucrece*). In an equally persistent way, *The True Chronicle Historie of King Leir*, before it reaches its fullest expression, has already helped shape the way Shakespeare represents the state of nature in *As You Like It*, assassination in *Richard III* and *Hamlet*, and the competition among suitors in *The Merchant of Venice*.

Some of the associations Mueller draws may be tenuous, but he makes a strong case that most of Shakespeare's favourite sources were known to him by the time he was in his twenties. (Interestingly, the notable exceptions are narratives drawn from current events, like the case of Cordell Annesley, which provided materials for *Lear*, and the writings about Virginia voyages that formed a basis for *The Tempest*.) In Mueller's words, 'It should therefore be a fundamental axiom of source criticism to observe the consequences of the fact that Shakespeare's readings jostled each other in his memory and settled in a complex web of memory pathways long before they became sources for plays he intended to write.'[3] In effect, source study becomes not the map for a uni-directional pathway but a means to trace the reciprocal relation between distinctive features in Shakespeare's creative imagination and a library of texts which are themselves subject to revisionary reading and adaptation in light of that imagination.

If, for instance, we imagine a cluster of narrative elements including nobly born wives who are entangled for good or ill with their husbands' public lives (e.g. Lucrece, two Portias, Lady Percy, Desdemona, Lady Macbeth, Hermione), calumniated women presumed dead but merely sleeping (e.g. Hero, Hermione, Innogen, and – stretching the point a little – Desdemona), and fathers and daughters (too numerous to list), not only do we refer to the plots of half the plays but we also map out a very broad field of source relation that goes back to a relatively small number of originary texts. To literalize the process: Shakespeare finds the stories that replicate his personal obsessions; the stories give those obsessions certain shapes; he in turn re-shapes them by producing ever-varying adaptations; in the end he becomes a reader of, and source for, himself.

When Polonius asks Hamlet what he is reading, the Prince replies, 'Words, words, words' (2.2.192). It's a joke from Hamlet's antic disposition, and a good one, since both Renaissance and modern psychology can readily picture madmen as losing the thread of sequential discourse and focusing instead on syntactically disconnected verbal units. For the purposes of literary criticism, however, such madness may be prerequisite. To identify Shakespeare's reading only by the larger structures derived from a classical education or the plots derived from pre-existing narratives is to neglect the independent power of the word. This is not the place to rehearse all the by now familiar arguments from structuralism and post-structuralism concerning the 'death of the author'. Suffice it to say that both the structures of language and, more to the point, all the ambient vocabularies at a given historical or cultural moment contribute to the composition of any piece of writing as much as do the consciously manipulated materials traditionally classed as intellectual underpinnings or sources.

This kind of reading, for which Roland Barthes's felicitous term is the *déjà lu*, concerns us not just out of universal theoretical correctness but because Shakespeare proves to have been a kind of language sponge, a picker-up of specialized lexicons from every conceivable stratum of his society. In this field it would be impossible to give a full account of Shakespeare's library, or indeed of all the sequences of imagery and allusion in the plays that testify to his skills at absorption. Perhaps the clearest index to this phenomenon is the response of scholars who have attempted to account for this verbal adeptness by imagining a Shakespeare who was not so much a linguistic polymath as a real practising multi-professional. Shakespeare has been, over the centuries, a lawyer, a doctor, a thief, a theologian, a Catholic, a Protestant, a duellist, a military man, a falconer, a keeper of hounds – all because he had mastered their respective languages.

Let us permit one quite respectable instance to stand for this kind of argument in general. A. F. Falconer argues that the opening scene of *The Tempest* is in every detail nautically correct. Expressions like 'take in the topsail' and 'lay her a-hold' do not represent mere colourful sea-talk but the perfectly phrased set of orders designed to save the ship under the given conditions of wind, shore, and ocean. From which Falconer concludes that Shakespeare 'could not have come by this knowledge from books'.[4] That may be true: there is no surviving sixteenth-century text in which all of these locutions are neatly laid out, and it is possible that the man who lived his whole life many days' arduous travel from the sea had managed to do some apprentice work aboard a sailing vessel, preferably among tars who had colourful tales to tell of the Bermuda triangle. But it is more likely – and the same would go for many other first-hand vocabularies – that Shakespeare derived this knowledge from a combination of reading, listening, and loving the play of language.

Perhaps it is Shakespeare's own fascination with books – or some attempt to exorcise that fascination – that turns so many of his characters into readers. Most of the time when book-learning enters the dramatic scene, as the example of *Love's Labour's Lost* has already suggested, it is in opposition to real experience. Love in particular seems to keep little company with reading. Some amorous bookmen are hopeless: Slender reveals his ineptitude as a lover by regretting that he has not brought Tottel's *Miscellany* to help him woo Anne Page (*Merry Wives* 1.1.165); nor do we entertain higher hopes for Malvolio's prospects with Olivia when he determines to 'read politic authors' (*Twelfth Night* 2.5.141). But when

Juliet tells Romeo that he kisses by the book (1.5.107), or when Rosalind-Ganymede reports on an uncle who read out lectures against love (*As You Like It* 3.2.312), or when Lysander reports the lesson of all those tales and histories that 'The course of true love never did run smooth' (*Dream* 1.1.134), the place of reading appears more complicated. It is not so much a contradiction of experience as a necessary first step along the way.

And that dynamic points finally to Shakespeare's two greatest dramatic scenes of reading, one from the beginning of his career, the other from the end. The raped, mutilated, and silenced Lavinia of *Titus Andronicus*, in an attempt to reveal the horrors of her own experience, can do nothing but point to a book in which the story of Tereus, Procne, and Philomela has pre-written the miserable sequence of events. The precision of the parallel – although Shakespeare's version is more horrific – enables both the characters and the audience to read experience as though it were a book and read the book as though it were experience. Prospero's book, which he prizes above his dukedom, is both the sign and the substance of his magical power. When, at the end of the play, he drowns it 'deeper than did ever plummet sound' (*Tempest* 5.1.56), he and all those who have survived the shipwreck are returned to Europe, to politics, to life, death, and marriage – in short, to the fullness of natural experience. Lavinia's volume is quite explicitly Ovid's *Metamorphoses*, and while Prospero's is less directly identifiable, it is signalled by an incantation that comes almost verbatim from the same work. When Shakespeare's characters have their fullest experience of reading, they turn to Shakespeare's favourite source.

Notes

1. Citation is to *Ben Jonson*, ed. Ian Donaldson (Oxford University Press, 1985), p. 454.
2. See T. W. Baldwin, *William Shakspere's Small Latine and Lesse Greeke* (Urbana: University of Illinois Press, 1944), II, 116–20.
3. Martin Mueller, 'From Leir to Lear', *Philological Quarterly* 73 (1994), 197.
4. A. F. Falconer, *Shakespeare and the Sea* (New York: F. Ungar, 1964), p. 39.

Reading list

Baldwin, T. W., *William Shakspere's Petty School* (Urbana: University of Illinois Press, 1943).
    William Shakspere's Small Latine and Lesse Greeke (Urbana: University of Illinois Press, 1944).
Barkan, Leonard, *The Gods Made Flesh: Metamorphosis and the Pursuit of Paganism* (New Haven: Yale University Press, 1986).
Barthes, Roland, 'The Death of the Author', in *Image Music Text*, trans. S. Heath (New York: Hill and Wang, 1977).
Bullough, Geoffrey, ed., *Narrative and Dramatic Sources of Shakespeare*, 8 vols. (London: Routledge and Kegan Paul, 1957–75).
Donaldson, E. Talbot, *The Swan at the Well: Shakespeare Reading Chaucer* (New Haven: Yale University Press, 1985).

Foucault, Michel, 'What is an Author?' in *Language, Counter-Memory, Practice*, trans. D. F. Bouchard and S. Simon (Ithaca, N.Y.: Cornell University Press, 1977).

Halpern, Richard, *The Poetics of Primitive Accumulation: English Renaissance Culture and the Genealogy of Capital* (Ithaca, N.Y.: Cornell University Press, 1991).

Jardine, Lisa, and Anthony Grafton, *From Humanism to the Humanities: The Institutionalizing of the Liberal Arts in Fifteenth- and Sixteenth-Century Europe* (London: Duckworth, 1986).

Lennox, Charlotte Ramsay, *Shakespear Illustrated: or, the Novels and Histories, on which the Plays of Shakespear Are Founded* (New York: AMS Press, 1973 (first published in 1753–4)).

Lynch, Stephen J., *Shakespearean Intertextuality: Studies in Selected Sources and Plays* (Westport, Conn.: Greenwood Press, 1998).

Mueller, Martin, 'From Leir to Lear', *Philological Quarterly* 73 (1994), 195–217.

'*Hamlet* and the World of Ancient Tragedy', *Arion* 5 (1997), 22–45.

'Plutarch's "Life of Brutus" and the Play of Its Repetitions in Shakespearean Drama', *Renaissance Drama*, n.s. 22 (1991), 47–93.

Muir, Kenneth, *The Sources of Shakespeare's Plays* (New Haven: Yale University Press, 1978).

Orme, Nicholas, *Education and Society in Medieval and Renaissance England* (London: Hambledon Press, 1989).

Patterson, Annabel, *Reading Holinshed's Chronicles* (University of Chicago Press, 1994).

Salingar, Leo, *Shakespeare and the Traditions of Comedy* (London: Cambridge University Press, 1974).

Whitaker, Virgil K., *Shakespeare's Use of Learning: An Inquiry into the Growth of His Mind and Art* (San Marino, Calif.: Huntington Library, 1953).

4

MARGRETA DE GRAZIA

Shakespeare and the craft of language

W HEN Richard II banishes the nobleman Thomas Mowbray for life, it is not the loss of family, friends, property, or even country that Mowbray laments. It is the loss of language, or rather of *his* language, the language into which he was born: 'The language I have learnt these forty years, my native English, now I must forgo' (*Richard II* 1.3.153–4). Mowbray's anticipation of the loss – 'so deep a maim' (150) – turns banishment into as severe a penalty as execution: 'What is thy sentence then but speechless death, / Which robs my tongue from breathing native breath?' (166–7). To deprive a man of his language is to deprive him of life itself, for speaking is as necessary to life as breathing. As we learn later when his banishment is repealed, Mowbray does not long survive this death sentence. After having lived out his days in a venture requiring no English, crusading in the Holy Land against 'black pagans, Turks, and Saracens' (4.1.86), he retires to Venice and dies.

Mowbray's poignant response to banishment reminds us that the English of Shakespeare's plays was hardly the universal language it would one day become. On the stage of Shakespeare's Globe, however, English was spoken worldwide. Whether the plays take place in the ancient world of Ephesus, Rome, and Egypt, or in the modern world of Venice, Vienna, and Elsinore, the common tongue is English. In *Pericles*, Gower apologizes for the play's assignment of the same language to the numerous countries of the Levant visited by Pericles, 'To use one language in each sev'ral clime' (18.6). *The Tempest* mocks the same convention when two Neapolitans marvel to hear English spoken on the remote isle on which they find themselves stranded. 'My language!' (1.2.432) exclaims Ferdinand upon first hearing Miranda speak; 'Where the devil should he learn our language?' (2.2.63–4) puzzles Stefano when he first hears Caliban cry out. The joke, of course, is that the Neapolitans are themselves speaking not the Italian of their homeland but the English of Shakespeare's theatre. And yet, in fact, this language was then spoken in only a tiny fraction of the world, on one island, or rather the south-east part of that island, where it was hardly yet stable or centralized.

If there was any language in the early modern period with a claim to universality it was Latin. It was the language of scholarly and official exchange that served to unite the nations of Europe long after the fall of the Roman Empire. In

England, although the Protestant Church service after the Reformation was conducted in English, Latin remained the language of learning, in both the grammar schools and universities. Shakespeare, at the grammar school he attended in Stratford, would have learned to read and write (and even speak) not English but Latin, in lessons requiring translation and declension not unlike those recited by his dim namesake William in *The Merry Wives of Windsor* (4.1); (see also chapter 3, What Did Shakespeare Read?, by Leonard Barkan). Latin could be taught in the schools because unlike English it had been regulated by a grammar, codified by dictionaries, and fixed by uniform spelling. In addition, the language had been refined and polished through a vast corpus of erudite and literary works.

It may have been precisely because Latin was a dead language, no longer native to any nation or peoples, that it served Christendom so well. Yet in the sixteenth century, a burgeoning nationalism pressed the major countries of Europe to develop their own vernaculars. In England, as well as in Italy, France, Spain, and Portugal, a mounting sense of national identity led to attempts to perfect a distinct vernacular capable of rivalling Latin as the language of learned and civil exchange. During the Reformation, England had a special incentive to do so. No project was more important to the Reformation than the translation of the Vulgate, the Latin version of the Bible, into the vernacular tongues. And yet English, especially through the first half of the century, was regarded as rough, rude, even barbaric, lacking both the expressive range and eloquence of the Latin standard. Unlike the European Romance tongues, English had been cut off from imperial Rome by the Viking occupation; for several centuries what we now call Old English, the Germanic language of the northern conquerors, had prevailed. It was not until England was again invaded, this time by the French-speaking Normans, that the native tongue came back into contact with Latin. After 1066, what is now identified as Middle English emerged, distinguished from Old English by two major developments: the infiltration of Latinate French words and the loss of heavy Germanic inflections, the endings of words that indicated their grammatical function.

In the sixteenth century, Latinate words continued to enlarge English vocabulary and new syntactic structures served in the place of lost inflections. The process continued over many centuries, but it was much accelerated by the nationalist imperative to make the vernacular as rich and versatile as Latin. During the time Shakespeare was writing, the process occurred with little regulation. There was no academy to supervise its development, as there was in Italy and would soon be in France. There were no dictionaries to define every word of the language, and prescribe spelling, pronunciation, etymology, function, and meaning. Nor were there any grammars setting the rules by which sentences were to be constructed. Dictionaries and grammars were thought necessary only for classical and foreign tongues. Shakespeare, in short, was writing before English had been standardized. For both words and sentences, 1600 was a time of innovation and experimentation. It proved a linguistic climate favourable to

Shakespeare's genius. The vitality and diversity that continue to attract and dazzle us four hundred years later were stimulated by the distinctive feature of language in his time: its openness to lexical enrichment and syntactic flexibility.

We tend to overlook the fact that four centuries separate Shakespeare's English from our own because we generally read his works in modernized editions rather than in the early quartos or Folio. In our editions, spelling and punctuation have been emended to meet modern standards. Only occasionally will an obsolete word remind us that English has undergone change. We no longer ask for 'eisel' if we want vinegar or 'sack' when we want sherry. Sometimes it is not only the word that has fallen into disuse, but the very thing it named. This is particularly true of fashion: women no longer wear 'chopines' or 'farthingales' or even 'ruffs'. Metaphors often elude us because they assume familiarity with activities now defunct: bears are not baited, nor are petards hoisted. Even spontaneous interjections can be dated: 'alack!' (for sorrow), 'fie!' (for disgust), or 'pish!' (for impatience). In some instances, scholarly research has failed to discover the meaning of certain words: some are in slang or dialect, but not all (are the 'scamels' Caliban retrieved from the rocks in the Folio the same as the 'seamews' of the modern edition (*Tempest* 2.2.164)? What does Petruccio intend when he four times pronounces 'soud' (*Shrew* 4.1.123)?) But it is familiar words which are more likely to lead astray. For example, the grave-digger and his companion in *Hamlet* are designated 'clowns' (5.1) less because they are funny than because they are peasants. The 'weeds' Viola lacks at the end of *Twelfth Night* are not uncultivated plants but her own clothing (5.1.248). The 'bravery' Paroles demonstrates is ostentation with no trace of courage. Other common words are misleading because they have lost an earlier ambiguity. Take 'let'. When Hamlet, having been beckoned by his father's ghost, says to his companions, 'I'll make a ghost of him that *lets* me' (*Hamlet* 1.4.62), he is threatening to kill not anyone who *allows* him to follow the ghost, but rather anyone who *hinders* him. Other words, too, seem to have done a semantic about-face. 'Anon' if used today would mean 'soon' rather than 'at once' as it clearly must when Prince Hal harries the tapster Francis (*1 Henry IV* 2.5.23–73). To call a man 'fellow' would suggest comradery not disdain, as it does when Kent insults Oswald (*Lear* 2.2.11);[1] Othello's 'excellent wretch' strikes us as an odd term of endearment for Desdemona (*Othello* 3.3.92); so, too, does Lear's 'poor fool' for the dead Cordelia (*Lear* 5.3.304).

These isolated differences at the level of the word are easily cleared away by the editorial glosses which have been accumulating around Shakespeare's texts since the early eighteenth century. If we turn to virtually any passage of the early texts, however, the linguistic changes separating us from Shakespeare appear more pervasive. Looking, for example, at Mowbray's response to banishment in the 1597 quarto of *Richard II*, we might be struck by the irregular capitalization, punctuation, spelling, and diction. Except for 'English' none of the nouns should be capitalized. Apostrophes should be inserted to mark both possessives and

> *Mowb.* A heauy fentence, my moft foueraigne Liege,
> And all vnlookt for from your Highneffe mouth,
> A deerer merit not fo deepe a maime,
> As to be caft forth in the common ayre
> Haue I deferued at your Highneffe hands:
> The language I haue learnt thefe forty yeeres,
> My natiue Englifh now I muft forgo,
> And now my tongues vfe is to me, no more
> Than an vnftringed violl or a harpe,
> Or like a cunning inftrument cafde vp,
> Or being open, put into his hands
> That knowes no touch to tune the harmonie:
> within my mouth you haue engaold my tongue,
> Doubly portcullift with my teeth and lippes,
> And dull vnfeeling barren ignorance
> Is made my Gaoler to attend on me:
> I am too olde to fawne vpon a nurfe,
> Too far in yeeres to be a pupill now,
> What is thy fentence but fpeechleffe death?
> Which robbes my tongue from breathing natiue breath,

1   A page from the 1597 quarto of *Richard II*. Mowbray's speech.

elision. There are no full stops; a single question mark pops up at the end, one line too soon; commas appear at the end of almost every verse line. Superfluous suffixes abound (-*e*, -*es*, -*de*, -*t*) and unconventional spellings ('ayre', 'yeeres', 'pupill'). Forms of address are inconsistent: Mowbray switches his form of address to Richard from 'your'/'you' to 'thy'. 'Violl' is close enough to modern violin, but 'cunning' seems wrongly applied to an instrument; and even those familiar with fortresses might puzzle over both the spelling of portcullis and its use as a verb. It is not that this passage has escaped proofing: its anomalies are typical of printed texts before standardization, modernization, and editing.

If we turn back to our modern editions, we appreciate the degree to which editing has facilitated our reading. The page looks clean, almost transparently so; the crude disuniformities of the early texts have been removed so that our reading can pass unencumbered to the realm of signification. Yet a return to the material marks of the early texts is instructive precisely because they there retain their opacity, requiring us to look *at* them rather than see *through* them. They remind us of something modernized texts tend to conceal: language is a material medium to be experienced like the rest of the material world through the senses.[2]

Spoken words issue from the mouth *as sound* and are received by ear; written words are produced by the hand *as marks* and taken in by eye.

It is because poetry works with the material stuff of language that it is so often in this period considered a craft or skill as well as an art. Indeed in the early modern period there was no clear distinction between art and craft; the word *art* was similar to the Greek term *techne* and could designate both the arts of language and the mechanical arts. It is not surprising, therefore, to find Socrates in Plato's dialogue *Cratylus* discussing the right use of language through analogies taken from the crafts of weaving, carpentry, and metalworking. In the first full-scale treatise on poetic criticism printed in England (*The Art of English Poesy*, 1589), George Puttenham repeatedly refers to poetry as a craft, trade, or skill and compares it to joinery and tailoring. Even Sir Philip Sidney, in his more idealized account, derives the word *poet* from the Greek *poiein*, 'to make'. As an artisan applies his skill to his raw materials in order to produce an artifact (a garment, a table, a kettle), so the poet applies his technique to language to produce a poetic work. In the case of the playwright, the artisanal affiliation is even more apparent. The suffix *-wright* (maker) inducts him into the company of shipwrights, cartwrights, and wheelwrights. This is not to deny the role of poetic genius, but rather to link it to an ability to wield the linguistic materials at hand.

Among Shakespeare's working materials, the smallest sense-making unit was the word. It has been estimated that Shakespeare had at his command upwards of 25,000 words, considerably more than any other writer of English. On the basis of the *Oxford English Dictionary*'s entries of first uses since 1100, some scholars have credited Shakespeare with the invention of a surprisingly high percentage of the many thousand words that entered English during his lifetime. Many are sceptical of such attributions, however, noting that the *OED* gives not the first use of a term, but the first known recorded use. Moreover, for reasons that will become apparent in the course of this essay, it is hard to determine what distinguishes a new word from a variant. Considerable liberties could be taken with morphology, the phonetic and graphic form of words, before dictionaries set their boundaries. The size and shape of words were routinely changed, indeed rhetorical handbooks of the time recommend the lengthening, shortening, and alteration of words, primarily for the sake of variety. Words were available in double forms, so one could choose, for example, between 'betwixt' and 'twixt', 'list' and 'listen'. Their protean quality was considered an asset for the poet. A word could be stretched or contracted depending on what the metre required. For the same reason, the *-ed* ending by which the past participle of most verbs is formed could be silent or pronounced. When Mowbray complains that his tongue will be of no more use to him 'Than an unstring*ed* viol or a harp' (*Richard II* 1.3.156) *-ed* must be pronounced to make up the iambic pentameter; in the line that follows, however, -ed must be silent, 'Or like a cunning instrument cas*ed* up'. So, too, verbs in the third person could end with silent -*s* or syllabic -*eth*;

'The bird of dawning sing*eth* all night long' (*Hamlet* 1.1.141). Words were also shortened by elision: two syllables could contract into one, as in 'o'er', just as two or even three words could slur into one, as in ''tis' or 'i'th'adage' (*Macbeth* 1.7.44). It is only by the strictures of later ages that these variations were deemed affected, archaic, or just plain incorrect.

The same plasticity can be seen in a variety of processes by which the sense of a word was changed by alteration of its size and shape. Shakespeare's language abounds with words which have been transformed by affixation, the addition of prefixes or suffixes. By tacking on one little syllable, the sense of a word could be negated, intensified, or sharpened. *Out* could be put before or after a verb to push its sense over the top. Othello boasts that his service to Venice will '*out*-tongue' the charges against him (*Othello* 1.2.19); Poor Tom boasts that he has '*out*-paramoured the Turk' (*Lear* 3.4.85–6); Hamlet warns against acting that '*out*-Herods Herod' (*Hamlet* 3.2.12). *Out* could also be affixed to the end of a noun, to better target its object: Antigonus is condemned as the 'thrower-*out* of the babe' and Autolycus is almost the 'finder-*out*' of Perdita's identity (*Winter's Tale* 3.3.28, 5.2.109). *All*, too, could be set before or after a word, to enlarge its scope: Lear appeals to the '*all*-shaking thunder' (*Lear* 3.2.6) and Macbeth wishes consequences to be final, 'the be-*all* and the end-*all*' (*Macbeth* 1.7.5). *Over* precedes words to express excess: Macbeth bids his pale messenger to prick his face to '*over*-red thy fear' (*Macbeth* 5.3.15); a messenger compares Laertes' rebellion to an ocean '*over* peering' its banks (*Hamlet* 4.5.95); the bawd Mistress *Over*done has had eight husbands, '*over*done by the last' (*Measure* 2.1.181). If frequency of usage be any indication, *un-* was Shakespeare's favourite prefix. Perhaps he was fascinated by how two letters can negate a word and yet still leave it literally intact. Lady Macbeth calls for the destruction of her womanhood, '*un*sex me here' (*Macbeth* 1.5.39), and berates her husband for being '*un*manned in folly' (3.4.73), and yet the categories of gender remain; Richard II may be'*un*kinged', but the office of kingship lives on (*Richard II* 5.5.37).

In addition to being lengthened and shortened, words, particularly monosyllables, could be conjoined. Compounds were considered particularly suited to English because of its abundant monosyllables; in addition, by using them to enrich the language, importation from ancient and foreign tongues could be avoided. It was to avoid the Latinisms associated with the Roman Church that Sir John Cheke translated the gospel of Matthew by replacing the Latinate diction of previous translations with native Saxon compounds: his substitutions include *uprising* for 'resurrection', *freschman* for 'proselyte', *forsayaiers* for 'prophets'.[3] There was also a movement to challenge the dominance of Latin in the various fields of learning. In *The Art of Reason, rightly termed, Witcraft* (1573), Ralph Lever gave English compounds for the traditional Latin terms of logic or *witcraft*: *endsay* appears for *conclusio*; *foresay* for *premissae*; *naysay* for *negatio*, and *yeasay* for *affirmatio*. Similarly inspired, Puttenham in *The Art of*

English Poesy offered English equivalents, usually compounds, for the classical terms of rhetoric; as we shall see below, many of the figures involved repetition, as his translations make apparent: *epizeuxis* he anglicizes as 'cukoospell', *epana-lepsis* as 'echo sound'.[4] The need for English equivalents for Latin terminology was also met by 'hard word lists', specialized dictionaries which offered syno-nyms for unfamiliar or difficult words like the Latinate abstractions used in law, theology, and medicine.

Shakespeare parodies the use of both Latinisms and compounds in the 'great feast of languages' (5.1.34–5) set out by *Love's Labour's Lost*, primarily through the linguistic excesses of Armado and Holofernes, the former a traveller blamed for importing outlandish and newfangled terms, the latter a pedant charged with affecting learned or 'inkhorn' ones. The two together litter the play with Latinate marvels like 'peregrinate' (5.1.13) and 'festinately' (3.1.4) as well as with new-fired compounds like 'ebon-coloured ink' (1.1.233–4) and 'twice-sod simplicity' (4.2.19). Although the comedy's sober ending seems to turn against such verbal display, Shakespeare never quite renounces it. Consider Antonio's way of saying that he has nowhere to go – 'My determinate voyage is mere extravagancy' (*Twelfth Night* 2.1.9–10); or Troilus' conviction that Cressida is chaste, 'there's no maculation' in her heart (*Troilus* 4.5.63). Indeed, some of Shakespeare's most affecting lines set a Latinism off against a foil of Saxon monosyllables: Cesario's eagerness to 'Halloo your name to the reverberate hills' (*Twelfth Night* 1.5.241); Othello's portentous avowal of love for Desdemona,

> Perdition catch my soul
> But I do love thee, and when I love thee not,
> Chaos is come again. (*Othello* 3.3.91–3)

Shakespeare also uses compounds freely, even while apologizing for not using them, as in Sonnet 76 where he regrets that he has not varied his style by turning 'To new-found methods and compounds strange'. The most explosive compounds occur in colloquial exchanges, often in the form of custom-made insults: Thersites calls Ajax 'mongrel beef-witted lord' (*Troilus* 2.1.11–12) and Timon curses his sycophantic followers, 'trencher-friends', 'cap-and-knee slaves', 'minute-jacks' (*Timon* 3.7.88–9). But their particularity also allows for imaginatively beautiful couplings: 'night-tripping fairy'(*1 Henry IV* 1.1.86), 'cloud-capped towers' (*Tempest* 4.1.152), 'time- bewasted light' (*Richard II* 1.3.214).

The same malleability that we have been tracing at the level of the word can also be observed in longer units. Basic to grammar-school instruction was learn-ing how to vary a statement. Erasmus' widely used treatise *De Copia* (1512) illus-trates the possibilities for linguistic generation with some 150 variations for saying 'I was pleased to receive your letter', and some 200 for saying, 'I will remember you as long as I live.' Schoolboys were expected to learn how to reduce as well as expand material, so that length could be adjusted as the situation required. Shakespeare knew the technique well. Consider Gaunt's description of England in his famous paean:

> This royal throne of kings, this sceptred isle,
> This earth of majesty, this seat of Mars,
> This other Eden, demi-paradise . . . (*Richard II* 2.1.40–2)

He stacks up eighteen nominal phrases before topping them with a delayed predicate, 'Is now leased out' (59). Name-calling offers the perfect occasion for such stockpiles, as demonstrated when Hal mounts insults against that 'huge hill of flesh' Falstaff (*1 Henry IV* 2.5.224–5): 'that trunk of humours, that bolting-hutch of beastliness, that swollen parcel of dropsies . . .', a list that could be extended beyond its nine epithets, or cut back to a single pejorative, 'an old fat man' (408–11). Curses like Timon's or Lear's tend to come in similar volleys. So too does praise, as in Ophelia's encomium on an earlier Hamlet. Like Gaunt's paean to England, it ends up by abruptly bringing down what it had so piled up:

> The courtier's, soldier's, scholar's eye, tongue, sword,
> Th'expectancy and rose of the fair state,
> The glass of fashion and the mould of form,
> Th'observed of all observers quite, quite, down. (*Hamlet* 3.1.150–3)

A modern sensibility may be tempted to discern nuances of meaning among these variations. After all, what is the point of repeating words unless meaning is intensified or developed? But it is the number and variety of such phrases that appear to have been valued. The same practice can be observed in Shakespeare's abundant use of adages. In *Hamlet* proverbs, always complete in themselves, are followed by others rehearsing more or less the same truism. Laertes warns his sister to guard her chastity with a run of no less than five proverbs (1.3.36–44). The same reiteration occurs in the Mousetrap play in which the Player King gives a good dozen proverbs on the difficulty of keeping promises (3.2.169–95). Like words and phrases, these sayings can work as modular units to be inserted or removed as circumstances dictate. What is now regarded as a fault of redundancy would have been thought to add the weight of authority. We can also gauge the practical value of such units. Ready-made, they can be inserted or deleted, depending on theatrical exigencies. In addition, these stockpiles lent themselves to the customary textual practice of recording words, phrases, and adages read in books or heard in conversation. They were jotted in tablebooks (Hamlet carries one) which would in turn provide a handy thesaurus for future utterance.

Thus far we have dealt with verbal units from the word to the axiom without giving thought to syntax. In the linguistic interlude between Germanic inflection and modern English, words possessed syntactic as well as lexical flexibility. With inflected endings on the wane and with grammatical regulations not yet in force, one part of speech could convert to another through a process linguists call *conversion*. Present usage affords numerous examples of the most common kind of conversion, from noun to verb, but the dictionary prevents us from converting *any* noun to a verb. We can say that we were 'fathered', but we cannot say, as Edgar can in comparing his own state to Lear's, 'He childed as I fathered' (*Lear* 3.6.103). Shakespeare was free to convert any noun to a verb, imparting to the verb the semantic specificity normally limited to nouns. Caliban grumbles, 'you *sty* me / In this hard rock' (*Tempest* 1.2.345–6); Coriolanus resolves to ingratiate himself to the plebs, 'I'll *mountebank* their loves' (*Coriolanus* 3.2.132), and Timon curses fellow man, 'Destruction *fang* mankind' (*Timon* 4.3.23). Less frequently, conversion takes place between other parts of speech. Nouns and verbs can both change to adjectives. Examples of the former include the '*pelican* daughters' cursed by Lear (*Lear* 3.4.72), the '*salt* imagination' discovered in Angelo (*Measure* 5.1.393); an example of the latter appears in Macbeth's attempt to inure his '*initiate* fear' (*Macbeth* 3.4.142). Conversely, adjectives can function as both nouns and verbs: Cleopatra dreads being displayed in captivity before 'poor'st *diminutives*' (*Antony* 4.13.37); Roderigo, says Cassio, was instructed to '*Brave* me upon the watch' (*Othello* 5.2.335).

Before standardization, parts of speech had more freedom to shift their grammatical position as well as function. Not infrequently the common word order of subject/verb/object is inverted. The verb often precedes the subject – 'Met I my father' (*Lear* 5.3.188); the object often precedes the verb, 'I such a fellow saw' (4.1.33); and sentences containing both types of inversion are not uncommon: 'That handkerchief / Did an Egyptian to my mother give' (*Othello* 3.4.53–4). In a number of remarkable periodic sentences, the verb is withheld until the very end of the sentence. The delay can be racking, as when Edgar draws out tension leading to his father's death,

> But his flawed heart –
> Alack, too weak the conflict to support! –
> 'Twixt two extremes of passion, joy and grief,
> Burst smilingly. (*Lear* 5.3.195–8)

It can also shock, as when Othello punctuates his sentence and his life with the same 'O bloody period!' (*Othello* 5.2.366). Modifiers – adjectives, adverbs, participial phrases – need not be placed close to what they modify. Sometimes the subject they modify is not stated at all. When the ghost reports to Hamlet, ''Tis given out that, *sleeping in mine orchard* / A serpent stung me' (*Hamlet* 1.5.35–6), we would fault his use of a dangling participle in the italicized phrase: no subject is present for the adjectival phrase to modify. Primary verbs are often distant from their auxiliaries, as in the Duke's recommendation of words over violence, 'Your gentleness *shall* force / More than your force *move* us to gentleness' (*As You Like It* 2.7.101–2). Because there were fewer prepositions and conjunctions, and less subordination and co-ordination, the relation of clauses to one another is not always clear. For example, in Gratiano's ironic sneer, 'The Hebrew will turn Christian; he grows kind' (*Merchant* 2.1.174), we are left to infer the relation of the two clauses. Punctuation, concerned more with delivery than grammatical relations, offers little help. Consider the exiled Mowbray's final words in the 1597 quarto:

> Farewell (my Liege) now no way can I stray,
> *Save back to England* all the world's my way.

The italicized phrase could restrict either the clause before or after it; a modern editor will assign it to one or the other, but Shakespeare had it both ways.

The lexical and syntactic flexibility available to Shakespeare did not outlast him by long. In the seventeenth century, several dictionaries were printed with an increasing number of entries beyond the specialized vocabularies of the 'hard word' lists, and by the eighteenth century everyday words were also included. At the same time, grammars began to appear which at first merely apply the rules of Latin grammar to English, but then codify rules specifically for English. In 1665, the Royal Society impanelled a committee of poets and philosophers to oversee the improvement of the language. Its aims were indicative of the new linguistic tide, condemning all 'amplifications, digressions, and swellings of style', and prescribing as ideals 'brevity and purity'.[5] In addition it called for an economy of expression altogether antithetical to the repetitive practices we have been tracing: 'so many *things* almost in an equal number of *words*'. Shakespeare did not fare well under the new regime. Indeed the literature of the Elizabethan age in general was deemed 'barbaric' and in need of rehabilitation and refinement. It is in this age that Shakespeare's plays were rewritten for the stage according to new linguistic as well as literary criteria; and soon after began the massive editorial labour of 'correcting' what had come to be judged Shakespeare's errors, excesses, and irregularities.

In this new cultural climate, there was one feature of Shakespeare's style that repeatedly came under critical fire: wordplay. The pun in particular was repeatedly singled out as a 'fault' or 'vice' of Shakespeare and his age. In retrospect, we can understand why this prominent Shakespearian feature proved such an irritant to succeeding ages. The pun is unruly, working in violation of both dictionary and grammar.[6] Take, for example, Hamlet's famous pun on sun/son. When the newly crowned king asks him, 'How is it that the clouds still hang on you?', Hamlet responds by extending Claudius' meteorological metaphor, 'Not so, my lord, I am too much i'th'*sun*' (*Hamlet* 1.2.66–7). Hamlet, because he is literally standing before (perhaps even beneath) the newly ascendent sovereign *sun*, cannot be under the clouds. At the same time, the word *son* springs from *sun*, recalling Hamlet's status as descendant of the recently deceased king. The *sun/son* pun conjoins two words now held apart by separate entries in the dictionary. In addition, grammar now disallows the homophonic overlap: 'i'th'*son*' is ungrammatical. A material property of language – sound – operates without regard for the linguistic rules; one shared sound triggers two senses at once and intimates a semantic relation, in this case the monarchical association of celestial *sun* and lineal *son*.

Of course, before the rules governing usage were codified there was nothing transgressive about this kind of activity. Such homophonic overlapping is encouraged by the flexible state of the language before standardization. Needless to say, the overlap is not always meaningful. Comic puns are funny precisely because they are senseless: we laugh when Antipholus asks for a crow to bash down the door and his servant responds by nattering on about fowls and feathers (*Errors* 3.1.81–5). But there are other puns which tap into expansive networks of cultural meaning. Shakespeare frequently activates puns on *heir*, a key word in the many plays that concern patrilineal succession: after the tempest, Ariel assures Prospero that 'Not a *hair* perished' in the company that included Ferdinand, Prospero's designated *heir* (*Tempest* 1.2.218). Similarly punning reverberates around *knot* when virginity is at issue: Bertram's note to his mother announces his vow never to consummate his marriage to Helena: 'I have wedded her, *not* bedded her, and sworn to make the "*not*" eternal' (*All's Well* 3.2.21).[7] Another semantic cluster is released around discussions of any of the many senses of *will*, ranging from the testamentary document to the faculty of choice to sexual desire and even the organs of that desire, both male and female; in Sonnets 136 and 137, Shakespeare draws his own proper name into the network.

In describing the lexical and syntactic movement open to Shakespeare, we must be careful not to conclude what is in any case impossible: that Shakespeare wrote without regulative norms. The presence of norms is confirmed whenever we laugh at a character's misuse of a word (malapropism) or breach of grammatical usage (solecism), for our amusement at deviations presupposes a sense of proper usage. Quite predictably, it is the unlearned who 'mistake the word' (*Two Gentlemen* 3.1.277), and predictably, too, the word often derives from the learned Latin. Often one abstraction is confused with its opposite, a particular problem when questions of right and wrong are in the balance, as they are for the constables Dogberry and Elbow. Dogberry arrests two '*auspicious* persons' (*Much Ado* 3.5.41), is indignant that his office and age have not been '*suspect*[ed]' (4.2.67–8), and would see justice in condemning a villain to 'everlasting *redemption*' (50–1). Elbow arraigns 'two notorious *benefactors*' (*Measure* 2.1.47), testifies that a whorehouse is *respected* while denying that his wife 'was ever *respected*' (2.1.151). It is Mistress Quickly, however, who is the supreme malapropist, and her numerous verbal blunders run through the three Henry plays as well as *The Merry Wives of Windsor*. More often than not, she mistakes an abstract Latinate term for a like-sounding familiar and concrete one. She hears 'nouns' as wounds (*Merry Wives* 4.1.20), 'incarnate' as carnation (*Henry V* 2.3.29), and charges Falstaff with being a 'honeysuckle' instead of a homicidal villain (*2 Henry IV* 2.1.44). If Latinisms confuse, Latin itself utterly confounds. When she overhears the parson drilling William on his Latin lessons, she mistakes grammatical Latin terms for bawdy English sound-alikes, and concludes that the parson has been teaching the youth the use not of the genitive case but of Jenny's genital case, quizzing him on the ins-and-outs 'hick and hack' (*Merry Wives* 4.1.57) of copulation rather than the basics (the *hic* and *haec*) of declension.

There is a similarity between how the illiterate Mistress Quickly hears Latin and how the foreign Princess Catherine speaks English in *Henry V* (3.4). In both cases, sound tends to drift in the direction of the carnal. Catherine's French accent twists the English names of the parts of the body into obscenities, 'the elbow' slips into '*de ilbow*' or dildo (42). To the vagaries of the unschooled and the foreign, should be added those of the non-English: the stereotyped accents of the Irish, Scots, and Welsh, particularly in *Henry V*. Their mispronunciations demarcate the bounds of properly spoken English. It is no accident that all three types of broken English should be heard in *Henry V*, the play concerned with unifying England through the conquest of a foreign power. The conqueror King Harry avoids the speech of the conquered altogether except to speak one flawless sentence in French by which he asserts his possession over his new bride and territory. As both king in this play and prince in the previous two, Henry demonstrates his proficiency in English, mastering various class and regional dialects in securing the supremacy of the King's English that would eventually become the standard.[8]

The 'Hard-handed' artisans or 'rude mechanicals' of *A Midsummer Night's Dream* also mistake words or, more accurately, mis*place* them, when they try their hands at putting on a play (5.1.72). Having 'never laboured in their minds till now' (73), they are not used to working with the linguistic stuff of plays. Their errors pertain less to the form of individual words than to their syntactic relations. They put verbal units in wrong relation to one another. Pyramus links his verbs to the wrong objects, so that he sees what he should hear and vice versa. 'I see a voice. Now will I to the chink / To spy an I can hear my Thisbe's face' (5.1.190–1); Thisbe similarly affixes predicates to the wrong subjects, 'These lily lips / This cherry nose' (317–18). Confusion's masterpiece occurs when Quince the carpenter mispunctuates the prologue he delivers, disordering the syntax in such a way that what was intended as a courteous compliment to the Duke is delivered as a rude insult (108–17). The seams and joints holding the whole together are in the wrong place, so that he ends up producing the literary equivalent of a poorly assembled garment or piece of furniture. One of the Duke's party compares his speech to a 'chain', a frequent emblem for the rightly ordered language of eloquence or rhetoric. But this speech is 'like a tangled chain – nothing impaired, but all disordered' (124–5).

There is a tragic counterpart to this syntactic breakdown. In *The Rape of Lucrece*, the narrator describes how Lucrece's speech was affected by the threat of rape: 'She puts the period often from his place / And midst the sentence so her accent breaks' (565–6). Psychic shock throws syntax into disarray. 'Unshaped use' also characterizes Ophelia's speech in madness, and hearers try to supply the frame it lacks, 'They aim at it / And botch the words up fit to their own thoughts' (*Hamlet* 4.5. 9–10). 'I am cut to the brains' (*Lear* 4.6.187), cries Lear, and his madness at its most acute tears language into syntactic bits and pieces, as when he repels himself with lurid imaginings of his own birthplace, the womb:

> there's hell, there's darkness,
> There's the sulphurous pit, burning, scalding,
> Stench, consumption! Fie, fie, fie! pah! pah! (4.6.124–6).

Connectives similarly disappear when Othello visualizes his wife making love to Cassio, 'Pish! Noses, ears, and lips! Is't possible? Confess? Handkerchief? O devil!' (*Othello* 4.1.40–1), until he collapses in spasms. Jealousy also fractures Leontes' speech: he gives vent to thoughts of his wife's sexual betrayal in syntax so disjointed that some editors have been driven to emend it (*Winter's Tale* 1.2.139–48).[9]

Two types of linguistic deviance, then, testify to the operation of linguistic norms, one morphological, affecting the shape of words, and the other syntactic, affecting how words are joined together. In both cases, sound strays from sense. Comedy's phonetic drift (from homicidal to *honeysuckle*, from elbow to *de ilbow*) results in absurdity; tragedy's syntactic dislocations end in linguistic pieces (Lear's 'pah', Othello's 'pish'). Words turn into mistakes, syntax is pushed to the breaking point. In both cases sound has strayed too far from sense. Before standardization, it is the study of rhetoric that is largely concerned with co-ordinating the audible and the intelligible. Unlike grammar, rhetoric flourished in Shakespeare's day (again, see also chapter 3, What Did Shakespeare Read?, by Leonard Barkan). It was at the core of the school curriculum; students identified and imitated its tropes and figures. Several rhetorical handbooks were in print, some drew examples from English works, and one of them, as we have seen, supplied English equivalents for the classical terms. Like all arts and skills, rhetoric had a purpose: to persuade by striking the ear and affecting the mind.

We have not entirely lost the rhetorical tradition so familiar to Shakespeare. Indeed many rhetorical terms, those pertaining to transformations of sense, continue to provide the mainstay of our critical vocabulary: our uses of irony, hyperbole, understatement, ambiguity, metaphor, and antithesis can be found in any listing of traditional rhetorical tropes. But the terms that pertain to sound are now obsolete. As an important modern authority on rhetoric in Shakespeare's age explains, 'One thing is certain, that every person who had a grammar-school education in Europe between Ovid and Pope knew by heart, familiarly, up to a hundred figures, by their right name.'[10] It can be no accident that the rhetorical figures fell into disuse at the same time that dictionaries and grammars became regulative. For the figures are concerned primarily with empowering words by repeating sounds. A modern sensibility can appreciate the repetition of letters and syllables (alliteration, assonance, rhyme) but the repetition of words is thought to be monotonous and inefficient. Yet rhetoric taught repetition: it provided schemes for organizing language in patterns of reiterative sound.

A glance at a few figures of repetition suggests how rhetoric could structure language through its use of sound, without regard to grammar. For example, the straight repetition of a word, *epizeuxis*, can obviate the need for grammatical links, as in the complete syntactic unit by which Lear expresses the finality of Cordelia's loss: 'Never, never, never, never, never!' (*Lear* 5.3.307). Interrupted repetition, called *ploce*, overtaxes grammar in order to form its own singsong sense, as in Biron's axiom on the futility of study, 'Light, seeking light, doth light of light beguile' (*L.L.L* 1.1.77). Thaisa expresses the resemblance between the young and old Pericles by *anaphora*, a simple repetition at the beginning of two clauses that clinches the likeness without labouring it grammatically:

> Are you not Pericles? *Like him you* spake,
> *Like him you* are. (*Pericles* Scene 22, 52–3)

Anidoplosis, a line which begins by repeating what precedes it, can substitute for a connective; Hamlet, for example, uses this figure to move from death to afterlife:

> To die, *to sleep*.
> *To sleep*, perchance to dream. (*Hamlet* 3.1.66–7).

Antimetabole repeats words but in inverse order, as in Othello's last words, spoken over the dead Desdemona; the rhetorical criss-cross binds the two sentences together so tightly that the lack of a subject in the second is irrelevant.

> I *kissed* thee ere I *killed* thee. No way but this:
> *Killing* myself, to die upon a *kiss*. (*Othello* 5.2.368–9)

In these figures, we see how rhetoric formed patterns of coherence not through intelligible grammatical relations but through acoustic repetition.

The echoic patterns constructed by rhetoric are intended to catch and hold the ear. Emblems of rhetoric in the period literalize this effect: a chain issuing from the mouth of the speaker binds the ears of the listeners and moves them bodily. The legendary forefathers of poetry, Orpheus and Amphion, were also associated with the power to move; the one moved animals, the other stones. 'It is not words that shakes me thus' (4.1.39–40), says Othello of the words Iago has insinuated into his system. But of course they do. They shake him even as he speaks and then throw him to the ground. Prospero's words also possess the power to move: his 'potent art' begins in the commands he voices to Ariel who then performs them, '[t]o'th'syllable' (*Tempest* 5.1.50, 1.2.505). Prospero's breath thus passes to Ariel who is 'but air' and then to other airy spirits to the end of putting air in motion: the tempestuous storm which opens the play by grounding the ship, the 'auspicious gales' (5.1.21, 318) which end the play by wafting it homeward. The same power of breath could be said to move dramatic action itself; what happens on stage, as on Prospero's island, depends on the vocalized vibrations of air, the stops and starts of words spoken by characters. This kinetic power resembled the virtue sixteenth-century poetic treatises called by the Greek term, *energia* – what Sidney defined as 'forcibleness' and Puttenham as 'a strong and virtuous operation'. That our word energy derives from a word once designating a specifically linguistic dynamic suggests the degree to which language in Shakespeare's age was considered a kind of physical resource with the potential to put human bodies into motion. Under the sway of lexicons and grammars, language largely lost this potential, but we still have record in Shakespeare's plays and poems of how productively and effectively it could be exploited.

Notes

1. *King Lear* is quoted throughout from Norton's Conflated Text.
2. Margreta de Grazia and Peter Stallybrass, 'The Materiality of the Shakespearean Text', *Shakespeare Quarterly* 44 (1993), 1–29.
3. Charles Barber, *Early Modern English* (Edinburgh University Press, 1997), pp. 62–3.
4. George Puttenham, *The Arte of English Poesie*, ed. Gladys Doidge Willcock and Alice Walker (Cambridge University Press, 1936), pp. 198–209.
5. Thomas Sprat, *The History of the Royal-Society for the Improving of Natural Knowledge*, ed. Jackson Cope and Harold Whitmore Jones (1667; facs. rpt St Louis, Mo.: Washington University Press, 1958), p. 113.
6. Margreta de Grazia, 'Homonyms Before and After Lexical Standardization', *Shakespeare Jahrbuch*, 127 (1990), 143–56.
7. Patricia Parker, *Shakespeare from the Margins: Language, Culture, Context* (University of Chicago Press, 1996), pp. 199–204.
8. Paula Blank, *Broken English* (London and New York: Routledge, 1996), pp. 14–15.
9. Stephen Orgel, ed., *The Winter's Tale* (Oxford University Press, 1996), pp. 8–9.
10. Brian Vickers, 'Shakespeare's Use of Rhetoric', in *A New Companion to Shakespeare Studies*, ed. Kenneth Muir and S. Schoenbaum (Cambridge University Press, 1971), p. 86.

Reading list

Blake, N. F., *Shakespeare's Language: An Introduction* (New York: St Martin's Press, 1983).
Empson, William, *Seven Types of Ambiguity* (London: Chatto and Windus, 1956).
Erasmus, *On Copia of Words and Ideas*, trans. Donald B. King and H. David Rix (Milwaukee, Wis.: 1963).
Hussey, S. S., *The Literary Language of Shakespeare* (London and New York: Longman, 1982).
Joseph, Sister Miriam, *Shakespeare's Use of the Art of Rhetoric* (New York: Columbia University Press, 1947).
Kermode, Frank, *Shakespeare's Language* (New York: Farrar, Strauss, Giroux, 2000).
Lass, Roger, *The Cambridge History of the English Language*, vol. III (Cambridge University Press, 1999).

Magnusson, Lynne, *Shakespeare and Social Dialogue: Dramatic Language and Elizabeth Letters* (Cambridge University Press, 1999)

Mahood, M. M., *Shakespeare's Wordplay* (London and New York: Methuen, 1957).

Parker, Patricia, *Shakespeare from the Margins: Language Culture, Context* (University of Chicago Press, 1996)

Salmon, Vivian and Burness, Edwina, *A Reader in the Language of Shakespearean Drama* (Amsterdam and Philadelphia: J. Benjamin, 1987).

Sonnino, Lee Ann, *A Handbook of Sixteenth Century Rhetoric* (London: Routledge and Kegan Paul, 1968).

Trousdale, Marion, *Shakespeare and the Rhetoricians* (London: Scolar Press, 1982).

Vickers, Brian, *The Artistry of Shakespeare's Prose* (London: Methuen, 1968).

Classical Rhetoric in English Poetry (London: Macmillan, 1970).

5

JOHN KERRIGAN

Shakespeare's poems

THOUGH Shakespeare was celebrated as a playwright during his lifetime, he seems to have been almost as well known for his narrative and lyrical poems. His short epics *Venus and Adonis* and *The Rape of Lucrece* – apparently written while the theatres were closed by plague in 1592–4 – went through numerous editions and were widely quoted and imitated. By 1598, the commentator Francis Meres was comparing his 'mellifluous and honey-tongued' contemporary to the Roman poet Ovid and picking out for approval 'his sugared sonnets among his private friends'.[1] It is possible that Meres was referring to privately circulated poems which have now been lost, but most scholars believe that he had in mind manuscript versions of the sonnets which Shakespeare wrote and revised over several more years until they (or a selection of them) were printed in 1609 in conjunction with his most intricate long poem, 'A Lover's Complaint'. Meanwhile the corpus of indubitably authorial poems was completed in 1601 with the publication of 'The Phoenix and Turtle' – an allegorically suggestive elegy for a couple of birds, which appeared in Robert Chester's enigmatic *Love's Martyr* alongside lyrics on the same subject by leading poets of the day.

I add the qualifier about authorship because, almost from the outset, the canon of Shakespeare's poems has been blurred. It became so partly because the manuscript milieu in which the 'sugared sonnets' circulated was one in which attributions were often casual, but partly for the contrary reason, that Shakespeare tended to have work by others ascribed to him because of his prestige as a poet. In 1599, for example, the publisher William Jaggard put out a money-making collection called *The Passionate Pilgrim. By W. Shakespeare*. This starts with a pair of sonnets – 'When my love swears that she is made of truth' and 'Two loves I have, of comfort and despair'[2] – which are universally agreed to be Shakespeare's: although more bitter than 'sugared', they are likely to have been among the privately circulated poems alluded to by Meres, and they reappear in variant form in the 1609 *Shakespeare's Sonnets*. But the plausibility of Jaggard's '*By W. Shakespeare*' fades as these sonnets are succeeded first by three poems lifted from *Love's Labour's Lost* and then by an array of lyrics written by Marlowe, Sir Walter Ralegh, Thomas Deloney and others.

It is symptomatic of the conservative eclecticism of scholarly tradition that *The Passionate Pilgrim* was for generations included in collected editions of

Shakespeare. Modern editors no longer admit it as a matter of course, but they still echo Jaggard in mixing canonical with questionable texts. Some of the poems promoted in this way were associated with Shakespeare from an early date and might conceivably be from his pen. Here, for instance, is a gift-poem preserved in a seventeenth-century manuscript and supposedly written for a Stratford schoolmaster to send with a pair of gloves to his mistress:

> The gift is small,
> The will is all:
> Alexander Aspinall

Like the quatrain 'epitaph on John Combe, a noted usurer' ambiguously attributed to Shakespeare in 1634 ('If anyone ask who lies in this tomb, / "O ho!" quoth the devil, "'tis my John-a-Combe"'), this triplet is so slight that it is impossible to form a judgement about its authorship on internal grounds.[3]

Other texts, however, are substantial enough for internal evidence to accumulate. Several recent editions include, for example, a 578-line *Funeral Elegy in Memory of the Late Virtuous Master William Peter* published in 1612 and claimed for 'W.S.' on both the title page and dedication.[4] That this text was not associated with Shakespeare until a few years ago would not rule out the attribution if its linguistic and ideological properties were compatible with the rest of the *œuvre*. Despite some support from computer tests, however, the poem's advocates have been unable to persuade many that its defensive puritanism and pedestrian verse-style are Shakespearian. Such passages as

> As then the loss of one, whose inclination
> Strove to win love in general, is sad,
> So specially his friends, in soft compassion
> Do feel the greatest loss they could have had . . . (507–10)

would do little credit to William Stradling, William Sclater, or the other obscure candidates proposed by scholars for the honour of being 'W.S.' It is almost impossible to think of them being composed by the late-period Shakespeare who wrote *The Winter's Tale* and *The Tempest*.

If *The Passionate Pilgrim* were merely a fraud perpetrated on the Elizabethan public it would be of little interest. Since, however, Jaggard's desire to create a collection which could appear to be '*By W. Shakespeare*' encouraged him or his agents to select verse from the period which looked Shakespearian, his book gives us some insight into the qualities in Shakespeare's poetry which were valued at the time. Above all, that means registering the vogue for witty eroticism generated by *Venus and Adonis*. For the eye-catching, opening section of *The Passionate Pilgrim* includes no fewer than four poems – one known to be by Bartholomew Griffin – in which the subject-matter of that short epic is revisited in the alternate-rhymed fourteen-line sonnet form which Shakespeare was making his own.

Here is the first of those poems:

Sweet Cytherea, sitting by a brook
With young Adonis, lovely, fresh, and green,
Did court the lad with many a lovely look,
Such looks as none could look but beauty's queen.
She told him stories to delight his ear,
She showed him favours to allure his eye;
To win his heart she touched him here and there –
Touches so soft still conquer chastity.
But whether unripe years did want conceit,
Or he refused to take her figured proffer,
The tender nibbler would not touch the bait,
But smile and jest at every gentle offer.
　　　Then fell she on her back, fair queen and toward:
　　　He rose and ran away – ah, fool too froward![5]

This gives us in a nutshell the opening phase of the story which *Venus and Adonis* develops from Ovid (none of the *Passionate Pilgrim* sonnets cares to deal with the tragic end of the tale, where Adonis is killed by a boar and transformed into a flower). As in the narrative poem, the hero of the sonnet is not the sturdy young man of the *Metamorphoses* but a tender lad, an immature tiddler, just as Venus is a seductress given to fondling and telling tales rather than the vigorous figure who, in Ovid, joins Adonis in hunting.

Struck by such connections, the great eighteenth-century scholar Edmond Malone thought the *Passionate Pilgrim* sonnets on this topic early works by Shakespeare, 'when he first conceived the idea of writing a poem on the subject of Venus and Adonis'.[6] This view may well have been shared by Elizabethan readers of Jaggard's book, and to that extent the sonnets can be taken as part of the 'Shakespeare' matrix. But modern commentators have edged them away from the canon by emphasizing the appearance of a version of one of them in Griffin's *Fidessa* (1596); and the poems' paucity of figurative language, together with a certain obviousness in their humour, do make it more likely that 'Sweet Cytherea . . .' is the work of Griffin emulating Shakespeare's sexual playfulness and deft way with broad comedy. That would explain why the couplet of the sonnet seems to recall in shorthand the touchingly farcical passage in Shakespeare where Venus pulls Adonis to the ground on top of her, where he wriggles and pleads to be free, and ends up running away (589–816).

While the Venus and Adonis sonnets are testimony to the pleasure that Shakespeare's contemporaries took in his powers as a story-teller, and, in partic-ular, in his ability to extract piquant situations from classical legend, other texts from the period show them enjoying at least as much his command of praise and persuasion. In the *Parnassus* plays performed at St John's College, Cambridge, between about 1598 and 1601, for instance, the aspiring writer Ingenioso and the doltish Gullio are equally taken with this aspect of *Venus and Adonis*. Invited to produce a sample of Shakespearian verse, Ingenioso launches into an imitation

then a parody of the poem's highly imaged rhetoric. Gullio, more feebly, prac-
tises courting his mistress by reciting (and somewhat garbling) Shakespeare's
entire second stanza:

> Thrice fairer than my self, thus I began,
> The god's fair riches, sweet above compare,
> Stain to all Nymphs, more lovely than a man,
> More white and red than doves and roses are:
> Nature that made thee, with herself had strife,
> Saith that the world hath ending with thy life.[7]

It is integral to the comedy here that Gullio debases his source by normalizing
what it inverts. 'More lovely than a man' is bathetic when said to a mistress, but
in the narrative poem, where it is spoken by Venus to a sexually indifferent
Adonis, it mimics conventional courtship to unconventional ends. The whole
opening sequence in Shakespeare ambiguates the young man's beauty, lending
his laddish charms a girlish allure, and in the process it renders problematic the
traditional rhetoric of love, as the goddess adapts complimentary formulae more
usually applied to women by men. This is typical of the way Shakespeare's poems
both test and revitalize erotic language. In many of the Sonnets, for example, the
addressee is a 'lovely boy' admired by the male poet, so that routine-sounding
expressions of attraction are tinged with a homoeroticism almost unique in the
period. In *The Rape of Lucrece*, as disconcertingly, stock praises of the 'white and
red' in the heroine's cheeks are shown to be complicit with voyeurism and sexual
violence. And in 'A Lover's Complaint' the rhetoric of compliment and comparison proves dangerously superficial, and inextricable from lying.

Though Shakespeare's Venus starts with praise, she quickly realizes its ineffi-
cacy. Adonis wants to go hunting, and to hang out with his friends; he doesn't
care to be told that his complexion is redder than roses and whiter than the
plumage of doves. Nor is he moved when Venus advances arguments also heard
in the early sonnets, that fairest creatures have a duty to reproduce and that they
can, by breeding, defeat death (163–74). All this serves to heighten the comedy
of male reluctance, but Shakespeare characteristically generates a complicating
degree of sympathy for Adonis. Venus is likened early on to 'an empty eagle,
sharp by fast . . . devouring all in haste' as she kisses Adonis' face (55–7), and
frustration makes her so importunate that her embraces eventually threaten to
merge the poem with *The Rape of Lucrece*:

> With blindfold fury she begins to forage.
> Her face doth reek and smoke, her blood doth boil,
> And careless lust stirs up a desperate courage,
> > Planting oblivion, beating reason back,
> > Forgetting shame's pure blush and honour's wrack. (554–8)

In Ovid's *Metamorphoses* narratives are interwoven and punctuated with illustrative fables. The legend of Venus and Adonis, for instance – itself one of several

embedded in Orpheus' lament for the dead Eurydice – is interrupted by an account of how Atalanta lost a race with one of her suitors by stopping to pick up golden apples. This method of story-telling is followed in the Elizabethan genre of erotic narrative poetry to which *Venus and Adonis* belongs. In Thomas Lodge's *Scylla's Metamorphosis* (1589), for example, which is generally taken to be the first work of its kind, the tale of how Glaucus was rejected by Scylla, and how Scylla (smitten by Cupid) was in turn rejected by Glaucus, is bracketed by a narrative which presents the poet as a grief-stricken lover, weeping beside the Thames. More inventively, Marlowe, in *Hero and Leander* (pub. 1598), adds a tale about Hermes' love for a shepherdess, his theft of nectar from heaven, and Cupid's part in the plot, to explain why the Fates refused to bless Hero and her lover with lasting happiness.

Venus and Adonis is influenced by this tradition, but the sub-stories which interrupt it owe little to classical myth. When Venus' arguments in favour of breeding are rebuffed, she is given fresh encouragement by the arrival of a 'breeding jennet, lusty, young, and proud' which so excites Adonis' stallion that he breaks his tether and pursues the mare. Careless of his master's cries, he courts the flirty jennet, and shows, when discouraged, all the moodiness of a human lover. In the end the horses gallop off to the woods together, where nature takes its course (259–324). Later, as she tries to discourage Adonis from hunting the boar, Venus urges him to pursue 'the timorous flying hare'. In six remarkable stanzas she tells the story of a hunt: the uncoupling of the hounds, the zigzag course which 'poor Wat' takes in the hope of shaking off his tormenters, and the sad state of 'the dew-bedabbled wretch' as he weakens and declines into misery (673–708).

These episodes are of a piece with Shakespeare's larger plan to translate the events of classical legend into a rural setting which resembles his native Warwickshire. But their function in the poem is tied up with a set of questions about the relationship between the human and the bestial which preoccupied Shakespeare more deeply than has usually been recognized, through *Hamlet* to *King Lear* and beyond. Keith Thomas has shown that, in the early modern period, a received account of the natural world as full of emblems and analogies of the human condition was giving way to a more scientific, detached understanding. Attitudes to animals were correspondingly in flux: while most people were persuaded by Genesis that man had dominion over the beasts, which had been created to serve his needs, some felt that the well-being of horses or hares was a matter for humane concern. The essayist Montaigne, for instance, whose work would influence Shakespeare in the late 1590s, declared: 'If I see but a chicken's neck pulled off or a pig sticked, I cannot choose but grieve; and I cannot well endure a silly dew-bedabbled hare to groan when she is seized upon by the hounds.'[8]

The narrative of the jennet and the courser is ambiguated by these evolving attitudes. Traditionally, in art and literature, a riderless horse who throws off his

bridle and roams is interpreted as an emblem of ungoverned passion, of dangerously unsocialized behaviour, but Venus takes the episode as demonstrating the
naturally ennobling power of affection and the rightness of seizing pleasure
(385–408). She may be right to believe that the horses show what it is natural for
humans as well as animals to do, but the courtship of the beasts is so sophisticated in its play of moods and described so anthropomorphically that it is impossible for the reader to resolve with any certainty relations between the natural and
the cultural. The narrative about Wat is equally thought-provoking, because the
more Venus becomes caught up in her story the more distressing she makes the
hare's predicament, until she subverts her purpose in telling the tale to Adonis
and makes coursing after Wat seem less attractive than hunting the boar – a
quarry that at least has a sporting chance of injuring its persecutors. Though
Shakespeare was not the first poet to express sympathy for hunted animals, it
would be plausible to read *Venus and Adonis* at this point as an advanced polemic
against blood-sports.

All this is far removed from the claustrophobic world of *The Rape of Lucrece*.
Shakespeare's Venus woos Adonis in open countryside, and the poem is laced
with images of birds, flowers, and wild beasts. The protagonists carry into the
poem something of their significance in classical myth as figures of regenerative
nature. Tarquin and his victim, by contrast, inhabit a closed environment of fab-
ricated objects and political duplicity. Events are set in train in a tent, near the
besieged city of Ardea, where Collatine rashly boasts of his wife's beauty and
virtue. When Tarquin visits Lucrece, the domestic geography is marked out in
darkened corridors and chambers. He unbolts doors, crosses thresholds, and
finds her in a shrouded bed. The closest the poem can offer to the alternative perspectives provided in *Venus and Adonis* by the jennet and the hare episodes comes
when Lucrece, after the rape, scrutinizes a tapestry or wall-painting on the
subject of the fall of Troy (another besieged city) and interprets it in the light of
her new awareness of the discrepancy between how people appear and the wickedness of their intentions.

Those contrasts between the poems are as clear as their common interest in
more or less aberrant sexuality, but they also share, more subtly, a fascination
with the operations of language, especially in extreme states of eloquent power-
lessness and inarticulacy. This preoccupation is not unusual in early
Shakespeare: among the comedies, *Love's Labour's Lost* is exercised by linguistic superabundance and silence, while *Titus Andronicus*, among the tragedies, is
a showcase for flights of eloquence and for afflicted or inflicted dumbness. In
Venus and Adonis and *Lucrece*, however, there is even greater scope than in the
theatre (where audiences tire) for exploring the paradoxes of solitary loquacity,
while the presence of narrators in the poems allows for nuanced distinctions
between what is heard and what is not, because a poem can shade direct into
indirect speech more readily than a play, and can use the indirect free style to
insinuate into a narrator's voice enough of the vocabulary and values of the char-

acters to create shifts of sympathy which bring in train difficult questions of judgement.

Speech in *Venus and Adonis* runs the gamut from bickering to desolate lament, and its distribution between protagonists crucially shapes the reader's responses. We find it hard to empathize with Adonis, for instance, during the dozens of opening stanzas in which he is denied significant utterance. When he attempts to speak, Venus stops his lips (46–7), and his words are suppressed by the narrator as well as by the goddess of love: 'He saith she is immodest, blames her miss; / What follows more she murders with a kiss' (53–4; cf. 47–8). It's true that his initial burst of direct speech, one hundred and thirty lines later, sounds abruptly petulant: 'And now Adonis, with a lazy sprite . . . cries, "Fie, no more of love! / The sun doth burn my face; I must remove"' (181–6). But his eloquence proves formidable in his defences of chastity (523–36, 769–810), where he points out his 'unripe years', and complains that Venus stands for 'sweating lust' not love. These speeches are unlikely to persuade readers that Venus is simply wrong to argue for pleasure and procreation, but they balance the poem by introducing elements of a debate structure.

The heroine of *The Rape of Lucrece* is even slower to be heard. When Tarquin, arriving at Collatine's mansion, 'stories to her ears her husband's fame' (106), she responds with the taciturnity of an ideal Elizabethan wife: 'Her joy with heaved-up hand she doth express, / And wordless so greets heaven for his success' (111–12). Arguments against the rape are initially put by the rapist, not by Lucrece (190–280), and when he enters her chamber, her voice is not directly heard ('she with vehement prayers urgeth still / Under what colour he commits this ill' (475–6)). Only after Tarquin has threatened that, if she resists him, he will murder a slave and put his corpse in bed next to her, then tell the world that he found them together, does Lucrece break into direct speech; and even then her protests and pleas are prefaced by an account of how imperfectly she articulates:

> She puts the period often from his place,
>   And midst the sentence so her accent breaks
>   That twice she doth begin ere once she speaks. (565–7)

Once she warms up, however, Lucrece proves so relentlessly eloquent that her assailant is moved to silence her by wrapping her mouth in the bedclothes. Elizabethan readers had an appetite for lengthy laments, but the complaint against Time and Opportunity which Lucrece utters on Tarquin's departure is by any measure remarkable. Roused by the dawn chorus, she then calls upon Philomel – who was (according to Ovid) transformed into a nightingale after her rape by Tereus – to join her in a duet of grief. The onward sweep of her plaint, which continues for hundreds of lines, is sustained by Shakespeare's resourceful management of rhyme. In *Venus and Adonis* he had combined melodiousness with epigrammatic point by using a rhyme-scheme that moved smoothly from a quatrain into a couplet: *ababcc*. The additional rhyme in the *Lucrece* stanza (*ababbcc*) makes for amplitude, creating an internal pause and fulness; but the intricacy of the scheme can also express perplexity, as the heroine's experience of betrayal fills her with questions about life and brings her into 'disputation with each thing she views' (1101). Especially in her second great monologue, in front of the tapestry or wall-painting of Troy, Lucrece is forensic and fretful.

Between these sections falls an episode which painfully brings home how Lucrece's sense of the world has been changed. Summoning her maid, she calls for pen and ink, writes a letter to Collatine, and hands it to a servant for delivery. These simple actions tangle her in a web of fears about transparency. Before the rape she was innocent about the rhetoric of appearances. As the narrator says of the welcome she gives to Tarquin:

> she that never coped with stranger eyes
> Could pick no meaning from their parling looks,
> Nor read the subtle shining secrecies
> Writ in the glassy margins of such books. (99–102)

After the assault, she is morbidly sensitive to the potential visibility of her violation. Even writing the letter becomes a torment as she gauges how much or how little she needs to say to persuade Collatine to come to her without disclosing what has happened. When the homely groom called to carry this message proves bashful and blushes, she imagines that 'he blushed to see her shame' (1338–44).

This encounter leads neatly into the sequence where Lucrece deciphers the picture of the fall of Troy because there, too, she is concerned with the legibility of motives and experiences. Scanning the faces of Hecuba and Sinon, she identifies grief and hypocritical evil respectively. The former elicits her tears, but the calm demeanour of Sinon, betrayer of Troy to the Greeks, puts her in mind of Tarquin – whose action as a rapist is figured in the poem as the sacking of a city – and she tears at his image with her nails. If the rape has given her a crying need to find sisters in suffering (Philomel, Hecuba) it also incites her to hermeneutic suspicion:[9] to look for 'the subtle shining secrecies' that can be read in faces. The preoccupation with speech in *Venus and Adonis* is developed in *The Rape of Lucrece* into an acute awareness of the reading as well as the production of visible and audible signs.

To some extent this follows from the poem's emphasis on honour and shame. Shakespeare's Romans are frequently led by those criteria, but Lucrece is their victim: the very importance that she attaches to reputation saps her ability to face scrutiny, and convinces her that 'The light will show charactered in my brow / The story of sweet chastity's decay' (807–8). Construing herself in the honour-code as bringing shame upon her husband, and therefore as wronging him, she gives a Roman twist to the psychology by which rape victims blame themselves for the crime. She seeks to wipe away dishonour by stabbing herself in front of Collatine and her kinsmen, and urging them to revenge. This is not, however, the only possible reaction to her plight. An alternative view, which St Augustine famously espoused, and which was available to Shakespeare's readers from the Christian beliefs in which they were steeped, would hold that, since Lucrece's soul and will were untainted by the rape, she had nothing to punish in herself. The problem is then the suicide, held by Christians to be a sin: if she killed herself on account of the rape, did she do so because she had secretly desired it?

Shakespeare does nothing to suggest this (though covert desire is imported into even such a sympathetic version of the legend as Benjamin Britten's opera – based on a libretto by Eric Crozier – *The Rape of Lucretia*). He does, however, compound the problem by the way he constructs the narrator's perspective. In the passage about the letter and the groom, for instance, the poet speaks of Lucrece's 'disgrace' as well as her 'shame' (1320, 1344), and more obliquely of her 'guilt' (1342). By installing such traces of the heroine's self-judgement in the narrative voice, Shakespeare goes further towards endorsing her values than might be expected. And when she stabs herself, we are told that her blood divides into two streams, one 'pure and red' and the other 'black, and that false Tarquin-stained' (1742–3). Is this merely a conceit, or is the poet saying that Lucrece has been polluted by the rape? With such irresolutions in play, it is easy to sympathize with the view that *The Rape of Lucrece* fails to transcend its double debt to classical and Christian traditions.[10]

Venus and Adonis and *Lucrece* seem to have been conceived of as a pair, if not from the outset then at least from the moment when Shakespeare dedicated the former (as he would the latter) to Henry Wriothesley, Earl of Southampton, and promised 'to take advantage of all idle hours till I have honoured you with some graver labour'. The two poems can be fruitfully read in conjunction, both because they share themes and because they are cleverly contrasted to display the young poet's range. To some extent the early sonnets can also be connected with the narratives: they share a fascination with praise, procreation, the natural world, Time, and mortality, and their virtuosic handling of an *ababcdcdefefgg* rhyme-scheme grows out of Shakespeare's experiments with the quatrain-plus-couplet stanza in *Venus and Adonis*. How far the Sonnets share the same origin or occasion as the longer poems is, however, a matter of controversy. The attractive and literate Earl of Southampton, who was nineteen when *Venus and Adonis* was published, seems a likely model for the Adonis-like youth who is encouraged to marry in the opening group of poems, and who is usually taken to be the addressee of the entire run of one hundred and twenty-six sonnets which precede the set of twenty-eight more or less focused on a dark-complexioned, black-haired woman. When the Sonnets appeared in 1609 they were introduced by a dedication which included Southampton's initials in reverse:

> TO.THE.ONLIE.BEGETTER.OF.
> THESE.INSVING.SONNETS.
> Mᴿ.W.H. ALL.HAPPINESSE. . . .

Does 'W.H.' codedly allude to Henry Wriothesley or refer to Shakespeare's later patron, William Herbert, Earl of Pembroke (dedicatee of the First Folio in 1623)? Do the initials point to someone more obscure and now unidentifiable, or are they a random invention of the publisher, designed to suggest quite falsely to a potential purchaser that the poems tell a scandalous story from life?

How those questions are (part guessingly) answered will have large implications for the way the Sonnets are read as a whole, yet the answers will also be shaped by the experience of grappling with particular poems. In the seventeenth and eighteenth centuries, most people encountered the Sonnets in a text established by John Benson's 1640 edition of the *Poems*, which ran sonnets together to make them look like Caroline verse epistles, and intermixed them with material taken from *The Passionate Pilgrim*. In this setting individual sonnets could not receive the close scrutiny which they began to get from such Romantic-period admirers as John Keats, and which they have enjoyed at the hands of twentieth-century readers more or less influenced by literary formalism – from Robert Graves and Laura Riding's analysis of Sonnet 129 in 1926[11] to Helen Vendler's 1997 study of all hundred and fifty-four poems.[12] The modern tradition of interpreting each sonnet as a self-contained artifact has undoubtedly generated a fuller appreciation of Shakespeare's achievement, but it has tended to undervalue those trains of meaning which run between the sonnets as they interact with one another and unevenly imply a narrative of courtship, infatuation, poetic rivalry, and sexual disgust. Nor does a formalist approach do justice to the social dimension implicit in the way numbers of the poems present themselves (as gifts, as messages, as requests for patronage).[13] Just as with the plays, a range of critical approaches seems to be necessary if the multi-dimensional greatness of the Sonnets is to be grasped.

It has sometimes seemed odd to readers that the opening sonnets on procreation should give way with so little justification to poems about the capacity of poetry to immortalize the young man. One reason for the smooth transition is that Shakespeare drew his arguments in favour of breeding from a model letter by Erasmus which he encountered in Thomas Wilson's *Arte of Rhetorique* (1553, rev. 1560) – a venue calculated to remind the poet that the arts of literary imitation and of reproducing likenesses have traditionally been compared to the resemblance which nature frames between a father and his son. The somewhat tepid incitements to procreate which make up the early sonnets could modulate readily, for an Elizabethan, into arguments about poetry as *imitatio*.[14] Locally, in Sonnets 15–19, that means a shift in subject-matter from the 'lines of life' which mark genealogical charts to the 'lines' of verse on a page which are fathered by the young man's beauty. More largely, it means that the later sonnets about literary derivativeness, such as 130 about the 'dark lady' ('My mistress' eyes are nothing like the sun') and the series about the rival poet or poets who seduce the youth with praise (78–86), are not – or at least not only – the product of events in a background narrative but the evolution of a set of concerns prepared early on.

There is no doubt, however, that surprise is as typical of the experience of reading the Sonnets as is the pleasure of thematic development. And nowhere is Shakespeare more challenging than in the poem which follows the procreation group:

> A woman's face with nature's own hand painted
> Hast thou, the master-mistress of my passion;
> A woman's gentle heart, but not acquainted
> With shifting change as is false women's fashion;
> An eye more bright than theirs, less false in rolling,
> Gilding the object whereupon it gazeth;
> A man in hue, all hues in his controlling,
> Which steals men's eyes and women's souls amazeth.
> And for a woman wert thou first created,
> Till nature as she wrought thee fell a-doting,
> And by addition me of thee defeated
> By adding one thing to my purpose nothing.
>> But since she pricked thee out for women's pleasure,
>> Mine be thy love and thy love's use their treasure.

Sonnet 20 has been admired for its light-footed myth-making, its lively feminine rhyming, its fertile wordplay; but it has also provoked outrage and whitewashing among the homophobic. Should 'one thing to my purpose nothing' be read as proof that the poet has no interest in the young man's prick, and, by extension, his male sexuality? Or is its statement to that effect calculated to seem disingenuous given the homoerotic tonality of the rest of the sonnet? Or does the phrase, taken with the couplet, more boldly insinuate that the poet finds the young man's prick (if not the zero-ring of his anus) as attractive as other men do the 'nothing' – the vaginal 'o' – quibblingly located between a woman's legs in some Elizabethan poetry and drama?

Recent work on homosexuality in early modern England has gone far towards elucidating what is unorthodox and what merely conventional in the Sonnets[15] – to such an extent that, in a revisionist essay, it has been suggested that, historically understood, the real 'scandal' of these poems does not lie in the homoeroticism which they share with certain passages in Spenser and Richard Barnfield but in the blackness of the woman found almost repulsively attractive in Sonnets 127–52.[16] Whatever the validity of that analysis, feminist critics are right to insist on the nastiness of the misogyny which these later-numbered poems conjure and sometimes deal in, without collapsing into. The non-Shakespearian phrase 'dark lady' may describe well enough the seductive musician who plays the virginals in Sonnet 128, but the poet uses harsher epithets after the woman and the young man betray him sexually (Sonnets 40–2, 133–4). If the youth continues in some moods to be 'all' to the poet (e.g. 109), the lady is reduced to the all-open promiscuity of her vagina – what Sonnet 137 calls 'the bay where all men ride . . . the wide world's common place'.

Certainly it is the sonnets to the 'lovely boy' that come closest to demonstrating the devotion that Shakespeare lauds in the lyric that he contributed to *Love's Martyr*. Robert Chester's mélange of complaint, dialogue, and verse encyclopaedia (lore about beasts, flowers, and gemstones), interrupted by Arthurian narrative and rounded off with 'Diverse Poetical Essays on . . . the Turtle and Phoenix',[17] is one of the hardest books to make sense of in Elizabethan literature. But Shakespeare took some interest in what his 'Phoenix and Turtle' was part of, if only in retrospect,[18] and he became engaged enough in his commission to make the 1601 poem one of the most closely worked he ever wrote. Indeed it has probably attracted such a high proportion of contextual readings (the phoenix as Queen Elizabeth, the turtle as her rebellious favourite, the Earl of Essex, or the English people)[19] because it concentrates so intently on the question explored by many of the Sonnets – what, then, is love? – that it strips away the circumstantial bearings which interpretation tends to appeal to, and renders its subject metaphysical:

> Here the anthem doth commence:
> Love and constancy is dead,
> Phoenix and the turtle fled
> In a mutual flame from hence.
>
> So they loved as love in twain
> Had the essence but in one,
> Two distincts, division none.
> Number there in love was slain . . . (21–8)

The late-numbered sonnets to the youth, which are also generally thought to be (as Jacobean texts) the latest in date of composition,[20] sometimes strike a relatedly metaphysical note; but they do not abstract their absolutes. The frequently quoted Sonnet 116, for instance – 'Let me not to the marriage of true minds / Admit impediments' – by starting from a negative, an implicit rebuttal, alerts the reader to a view of love more tempered and compromised than it espouses. As complexly, Sonnet 124 defines the absoluteness of devotion by appropriating for it, and trumping, the idea of a politic life:

> If my dear love were but the child of state
> It might for fortune's bastard be unfathered,
> As subject to time's love or to time's hate,
> Weeds among weeds or flowers with flowers gathered.
> No, it was builded far from accident;
> It suffers not in smiling pomp, nor falls
> Under the blow of thrallèd discontent
> Whereto th'inviting time our fashion calls.
> It fears not policy, that heretic
> Which works on leases of short-numbered hours,
> But all alone stands hugely politic,

> That it nor grows with heat nor drowns with showers.
>   To this I witness call the fools of time,
>   Which died for goodness, who have lived for crime.

In Sonnet 55 Shakespeare had confidently asserted the power of poetry to outlast marble and gilded monuments. By 64–5 he is, more cautiously, inclined to hope that, despite Time's destruction of brass and stone, his love will keep his verse alive. Now, in 124, the claims for poetry are humbly dropped and love itself is credited with monumental constancy. The paradox is that, to sustain these claims, the poem demonstrates the shortness of its verbal half-life by using as a foil to the permanence of love a topicality which must always have been ambiguous and which is now opaque. Editors properly speculate as to the identity of 'the fools of time' – Mary Queen of Scots? Essex? the Gunpowder plotters? – but the poem takes its dialogue between the eternal and the contingent into the shadows of history.

If constancy in 124 achieves by these means something of the value claimed for it in 'The Phoenix and Turtle' there are many other sonnets in which it paradoxically proves a recipe for turbulence. This is a process explored throughout the volume in which the Sonnets were published, in poems to the dark-favoured mistress as well as to the young man, and, at the end of the book, in 'A Lover's Complaint' – that superbly involved long poem in which a woman abandoned by a beautiful youth is overheard in a pastoral landscape telling a venerable herdsman how she was seduced. Scholars have shown that the ensemble of sonnets, anacreontic verse (in Sonnets 153–4) and complaint which makes up the 1609 quarto would have been recognized by contemporaries as following a standard pattern, and that they would have read different parts of the book together.[21] The same arrangement structures, for instance, the collection which Shakespeare arguably learned most from: Samuel Daniel's *Delia* (1592), a sequence of fifty sonnets, followed by an anacreontic ode and 'The Complaint of Rosamond'. There has also been extensive work on 'A Lover's Complaint' itself, validating its authorship, dating it to *c.*1602–5, and demonstrating how skilfully it synthesizes elements of medieval and Renaissance love-lament with features derived from that widely read collection of historical verse-narratives, *A Mirror for Magistrates* (1559).[22] Yet this poem has received only a fraction of the critical attention lavished on the Sonnets which precede it.

The turbulence which can afflict devotion seems to inscribe the very setting in which the events of 'A Lover's Complaint' take place:

> From off a hill whose concave womb re-worded
> A plaintful story from a sist'ring vale,
> My spirits t'attend this double voice accorded,
> And down I laid to list the sad-tuned tale;
> Ere long espied a fickle maid full pale,
> Tearing of papers, breaking rings a-twain,
> Storming her world with sorrow's wind and rain. (1–7)

This is the landscape of hysteria (a womb in a hillside) as well as of echo and covertness. The poem starts with a warning that what we are going to hear (including the plaintful words of the male lover who seduced the maid) will be inflected by her distraction as well as by the poet who reports what the echoes allow him to discern. The text is a recessive artifact with several levels of rewording, but it is too emotionally fraught to be experienced as an intellectual puzzle. Whatever 'fickle' can mean to the poet or the reader before 'the sad-tuned tale' is heard, it emphasizes the psychological instability which makes the maid deal so passionately with the love tokens in her hands.

Following the conventions of complaint, the framework so carefully established in Shakespeare's opening stanzas falls away as the maid's speech takes over the poem. The herdsman who leaves off grazing his cattle in order to sit beside her and listen does not strike up a dialogue. No doubt his presence encourages the maid to investigate and explain her grief instead of merely deploring its potency, and the terms used of him ('reverend man' and 'father') have strong enough religious overtones to reinforce the impression that the way she tells her tale is both confessional and morally defensive. But the overwhelming effect is of a speaker attempting to climb out of emotional nets which entangle her the more firmly the more she struggles to escape. The dynamics of complaint prove so self-sustaining that the poem does not reach a conclusion. A text in this genre typically ends with a return to its introductory framework, giving the speaker an opportunity to urge the poet–narrator not to repeat his or her mistakes, or allowing a moral to be drawn from the speaker's intransigence. 'A Lover's Complaint', however, refuses to simplify in that way: excluding the poet–narrator, forgetting the herdsman, it ends with an ecstatic declaration by the maid of how the youth could seduce her all over again.

Though lexically and syntactically more adventurous than Shakespeare's earlier poems – to the point, at times, of mannerism – 'A Lover's Complaint' is recognizably their successor. Like *The Rape of Lucrece*, it uses the inwovenness of rhyme royal (*ababbcc*) to communicate an abused woman's perplexity. Like Adonis and the young man of the Sonnets, the poem's 'maiden-tongued' seducer (99–100) has an attractively girlish charm. His faithlessness is bound up, moreover, with that fluency in praise and persuasion which Shakespeare attributes to Venus, hints at in Tarquin, and admires yet dislikes in the rival poets of the Sonnets. Not just eloquent in himself (120–6), he trades in the rhetoric of others when he flatteringly hands over to the maid the signifying jewels, locks of hair, and 'deep-brained sonnets' (197–217) which his previous conquests gave him when seeking his attentions. The poem is too realistic about the susceptibility of women to the physical beauty of men to claim that the maid was seduced by language alone, but it remains a mark of Shakespeare's self-consciousness as a poet that he should be alert to the power of his medium to work for ill.

By 1640, when Benson produced his recast version of the Sonnets and 'A Lover's Complaint' in *Poems*, *Venus and Adonis* had been through at least sixteen editions and *The Rape of Lucrece* eight. While the narrative poems found an immediate readership, the Sonnets seem to have fallen on stony ears. After the Romantic period this situation was reversed. Hazlitt's denunciation of *Venus and Adonis* and *Lucrece* as 'like a couple of ice houses . . . about as hard, as glittering, and as cold'[23] set the tone for a period in which they were slighted as rhetorical machines and the Sonnets increasingly admired as intimate accounts of Shakespeare's own experience, or at least as revelations of his thoughts about the great themes of human existence – love, jealousy, the passage of time, death. Only in the last few decades have a greater frankness about the peculiarities of human sexuality, and a post-modern taste for camp wit and decorative artifice, helped advance the claims of *Venus and Adonis*, *The Rape of Lucrece*, and, at last, 'A Lover's Complaint'. Sensibilities are never permanent, but it is good that, for now, readers seem open to the full range of Shakespeare's poetic achievement.

Notes

1. *Palladis Tamia. Wit's Treasury* (1598), fols. 281ᵛ–2ʳ (modernized).
2. Quoting the text in *The Poems*, ed. John Roe, New Cambridge Shakespeare (Cambridge University Press, 1992).
3. Except where indicated quotations from Shakespeare and poems attributed to him, including *A Funeral Elegy*, ed. Donald W. Foster, are taken from *The Norton Shakespeare*.
4. *The Complete Works of Shakespeare*, ed. David Bevington, 4th edn (New York and Harlow: Longman, 1997); *The Riverside Shakespeare*, ed. G. Blakemore Evans, 2nd edn (Boston: Houghton Mifflin, 1997); *Norton Shakespeare*.
5. *Passionate Pilgrim* 4, in *Poems*, ed. Roe.
6. Quoted in *Poems*, ed. Roe, p. 241.
7. Excerpted from *The Return from Parnassus, Part 1* (c. 1599), III.i, in *Norton Shakespeare*, p. 3325, and modernized here.
8. Keith Thomas, *Man and the Natural World: Changing Attitudes in England 1500–1800* (London: Allen Lane, 1983), esp. sect. IV, quoting Montaigne (in Florio's Elizabethan translation) on p. 173.
9. Cf. John Kerrigan, 'Keats and *Lucrece*', *Shakespeare Survey* 41 (1989), 103–18.
10. See e.g. Ian Donaldson, *The Rapes of Lucretia: A Myth and its Transformations* (Oxford: Clarendon Press, 1982), ch. 3.
11. 'William Shakespeare and E. E. Cummings: a Study in Original Punctuation and Spelling', accessibly excerpted in *Shakespeare: The Sonnets. A Casebook*, ed. Peter Jones (London: Macmillan, 1977).
12. *The Art of Shakespeare's Sonnets* (Cambridge, Mass.: Belknap Press (Harvard University Press), 1997).
13. See e.g. John Barrell, 'Editing Out: the Discourse of Patronage and Shakespeare's Twenty-Ninth Sonnet', in *Poetry, Language and Politics* (Manchester University Press, 1988), pp. 18–45, and Arthur F. Marotti, 'Shakespeare's Sonnets as Literary Property', in *Soliciting Interpretation: Literary Theory and Seventeenth-Century English Poetry*, ed. Elizabeth D. Harvey and Katharine Eisaman Maus (University of Chicago Press, 1990), pp. 143–73.
14. Cf. John Kerrigan, 'Between Michelangelo and Petrarch: Shakespeare's Sonnets of

Art', in *Surprised by Scenes: Essays in Honour of Professor Yasunari Takahashi*, ed. Yasumari Takada (Tokyo: Kenkyusha, 1994), pp. 142–63, esp. pp. 150–6.

15. The best survey is Bruce R. Smith, *Homosexual Desire in Shakespeare's England: A Cultural Poetics* (University of Chicago Press, 1991).

16. Margreta de Grazia, 'The Scandal of Shakespeare's Sonnets', *Shakespeare Survey* 47 (1994), 35–49.

17. *Love's Martyr: Or, Rosalin's Complaint* (1601), z1r (modernized).

18. 'The Epistle of Lucius Tiberius the Roman Lieutenant, to Arthur King of Britanny' (H2r–3r) and the orations which follow must count among the minor sources for *Cymbeline*.

19. There is a valuable summary in *Poems*, ed. Roe, pp. 41–9.

20. See A. Kent Hieatt, Charles W. Hieatt and Anne Lake Prescott, 'When Did Shakespeare Write *Sonnets* 1609?', *Studies in Philology* 88 (1991), 69–109.

21. Katherine Duncan-Jones, 'Was the 1609 *Shake-speares Sonnets* Really Unauthorized?', *Review of English Studies* n.s. 34 (1983), 151–71 and pp. 165–71, *The Sonnets and A Lover's Complaint*, ed. John Kerrigan, New Penguin Shakespeare (Harmondsworth: Penguin, 1986), pp. 13–14.

22. MacDonald P. Jackson, *Shakespeare's 'A Lover's Complaint': Its Date and Authenticity*, University of Auckland Bulletin 72, English Series 13 (1965), *Motives of Woe: Shakespeare and 'Female Complaint'. A Critical Anthology*, ed. John Kerrigan (Oxford: Clarendon Press, 1991).

23. *The Characters of Shakespeare's Plays* [1817], intro. Sir Arthur Quiller-Couch (London: Oxford University Press, 1955), p. 272.

Reading list

Barroll, Leeds, *et al.*, 'Forum: A Funeral Elegy *by W.S.*', *Shakespeare Studies* 25 (1997), 91–237.

Booth, Stephen, *An Essay on Shakespeare's Sonnets* (New Haven: Yale University Press, 1969).

Donaldson, Ian, *The Rapes of Lucretia: A Myth and its Transformations* (Oxford: Clarendon Press, 1982).

Dubrow, Heather, *Captive Victors: Shakespeare's Narrative Poems and Sonnets* (Ithaca, N.Y.: Cornell University Press, 1987).

Duncan-Jones, Katherine, 'Was the 1609 *Shake-speares Sonnets* Really Unauthorized?', *Review of English Studies* n.s. 34 (1983), 151–71.

Jackson, Macdonald P., *Shakespeare's 'A Lover's Complaint': Its Date and Authenticity*, University of Auckland Bulletin 72, English Series 13 (1965).

Jones, Peter, ed., *Shakespeare: The Sonnets. A Casebook* (London: Macmillan, 1977).

Kerrigan, John, ed., *Motives of Woe: Shakespeare and 'Female Complaint'. A Critical Anthology* (Oxford: Clarendon Press, 1991).

Keach, William, *Elizabethan Erotic Narratives: Irony and Pathos in the Ovidian Poetry of Shakespeare, Marlowe, and their Contemporaries* (New Brunswick: Rutgers University Press, 1977).

Pequigney, Joseph, *Such Is My Love: A Study of Shakespeare's Sonnets* (University of Chicago Press, 1985).

Shakespeare, William, *The Sonnets*, ed. Hyder Edward Rollins, New Variorum Shakespeare, 2 vols. (Philadelphia: Lippincott, 1944).

Shakespeare's Sonnets, ed. Stephen Booth (New Haven: Yale University Press, 1977).

The Sonnets and A Lover's Complaint, ed. John Kerrigan, New Penguin Shakespeare (Harmondsworth: Penguin, 1986).

Sonnets, ed. G. Blakemore Evans, New Cambridge Shakespeare (Cambridge University Press, 1996).

The Poems, ed. John Roe, New Cambridge Shakespeare (Cambridge University Press, 1992).

Shakespeare's Sonnets, ed. Katherine Duncan-Jones, Arden Shakespeare (Walton-on-Thames: Nelson, 1997).

Smith, Bruce R., *Homosexual Desire in Shakespeare's England: A Cultural Poetics* (University of Chicago Press, 1991).

Vendler, Helen, *The Art of Shakespeare's Sonnets* (Cambridge, Mass.: Belknap Press (Harvard University Press), 1997).

6

SUSAN SNYDER

The genres of Shakespeare's plays

PRESENTING the dramatic works of Shakespeare in the Folio of 1623, John Heminges and Henry Condell categorized them in the table of contents under 'Comedies', 'Histories', and 'Tragedies'. What may strike us now as a conventional grouping was not so at the time: in the most obvious precedent for such a collection, the 1616 *Works* of Ben Jonson, the plays were arranged chronologically. The organizational principle they chose, which is featured as well in the title of the collection – *Mr. William Shakespeares Comedies, Histories, & Tragedies* – invites readers of Shakespeare's plays to read in the light of genre, apprehending family resemblances within each group as well as individual distinctions.

For that matter, the individual nature of any work of art is hard to grasp without some sense of the genre to which it belongs – its 'kind', in the language of Shakespeare's day. The genres or kinds can be seen, in Rosalie Colie's words, 'as tiny subcultures with their own habits, habitats, and structures of ideas as well as their own forms'.[1] In recognizing such habits as clowns and wordplay for comedy, and such habitats as royal courts and battlefields for histories and tragedy, we construct a notion of a play's *modus operandi* that in turn conditions our reactions as dialogue and action unfold. A sense of the norms of genre guides us through that unfolding: prompting sympathy or detachment, highlighting the significance of what we witness, and raising expectations about what is to come. The author may also at times invoke generic codes in order to play against them, refusing to fulfil the expectations he has aroused and thus pointing us in a marked new direction. This contra-use of genre may be overt, as when Shakespeare at the end of *Love's Labour's Lost* denies, or at least postpones, the traditional comic ending of multiple marriages and has one of the thwarted bridegrooms complain, 'Our wooing doth not end like an old play' (*L.L.L.* 5.2.851). It may be more subtle and pervasive, as when *The Tempest* reshapes the makings of revenge tragedy into reconciliation[2] or *Romeo and Juliet* abruptly derails promises of a comedic conclusion with the deaths of Mercutio and Tybalt and destroys young lovers and all in the subsequent wreck.

Of the three Folio genres, two – comedy and tragedy – were part of traditions stretching back to classical times, traditions which in England encompassed native elements as well. The history play, though its place alongside the other two was established by the early seventeenth century, had come forth much more recently, in the English popular theatre of the late 1580s and 1590s. One effect of the three-genre grouping chosen by Heminges and Condell for their late colleague's plays was perhaps to remind readers of the central role played by Shakespeare himself in developing, or even originating, the Elizabethan history play.

However long familiar, the genres of comedy and tragedy were usually theorized during this period in a reductive, schematic way. While Aristotle's thoughts on tragedy received extensive Renaissance commentary, especially on the Continent, the dominant influences on dramatic genre theory were not the *Poetics* but certain later codifications of generic difference: 'De tragoedia et comoedia', made up of two late fourth-century essays by the grammarians Donatus and Evanthius and widely circulated in editions of the plays of Terence used in Renaissance schools and universities, and a similar treatise by another early grammarian, Diomedes. Conflating their several pronouncements produces a series of rudimentary oppositions between the comic and the tragic. Comedies take their plots from fiction, tragedies from history. Comedy involves men of middling estate; its perils are small-scale, its outcomes peaceful. In tragedy, 'omnia contra', the persons and issues are exalted and they end unhappily. Comedy, beginning in turmoil but ending in harmony, celebrates life; but tragedy's course from prosperity to calamity expresses rejection of life.[3] English Renaissance writers when addressing dramatic genre repeat these schematic oppositions again and again without doing much to advance or refine them. The notion of drama, particularly comedy, as ethical instructor was especially useful to writers trying to defend the English stage against the persistent attacks of moralists (for example Thomas Lodge in his *Reply to Gosson* and Thomas Heywood in *An Apology for Actors*), and to Sir Philip Sidney defending imaginative literature in general in *An Apology for Poetry*.

Sidney advances in support of comedy the definition then ascribed to Cicero: by imitating 'the common errors of our life' and inviting reactions of scorn and ridicule, comedy teaches us what not to do.[4] In fact, this works better as a debating point than as a gloss on actual comedies of the 1580s when Sidney was writing, or on those Shakespeare wrote in the following two decades. Indeed, by deploring the recalcitrance of 'naughty play-makers and stage-keepers' even while praising comedy's proper social aim, Sidney himself tacitly recognizes a large gap between theory and practice. Farces and romantic fantasies hardly mirrored everyday life, and the driving impulse of most comedies was not to punish error but to entertain. Nor is there any evidence supporting Sidney's parallel didactic claim for tragedy, that watching the downfall of unjust rulers made kings fear to be tyrants. Other aspects of the grammarians' generic paradigms, however, can in spite of their limitations be more usefully pursued in the actual dramatic practice of those Elizabethan plays that have survived (many were never printed, or no copy now exists), which in turn may fill out those laconic formulas and uncover their implications.

What is implied by the most basic distinction of all, that comedy ends happily and tragedy unhappily? Since all plots involve threats and dangers, the assumption is that while in tragedies these threats are fulfilled, in comedies they may be evaded. Evanthius characterizes the dangers of comedy as small in scale compared to those of tragedy, but Shakespeare's comic protagonists regularly face alienation, abandonment, and death. What makes the difference is not less serious perils but the operation of a kind of 'evitability' principle whereby shifts and stratagems and sheer good luck break the chain of causality that seemed headed for certain catastrophe. Portia finds a hole in Venetian law through which Antonio may escape without paying his pound of flesh (*The Merchant of Venice*); Dogberry's watchmen accidentally uncover the villainy of Don John and deliver Hero from disgrace and death (*Much Ado about Nothing*). Reality itself, seemingly fixed, turns out in the comic world to be both mutable and malleable. In *As You Like It* a chance meeting with a hermit results in the sudden conversion of the tyrant Duke Frederick, who then easily gives back the throne he usurped from his brother; Oberon's magic redirects Demetrius' love from Hermia to Helena so that the lovers of *A Midsummer Night's Dream* may be tidily paired. In tragedy, on the other hand, the causal chain unwinds inexorably towards destruction, cutting off alternative possibilities of escape or potential new beginnings. In *King Lear* the army led by Cordelia that seemed to promise deliverance is defeated; and in a final shocking blow even the refounded relationship of father and daughter is cut off by Cordelia's murder. In *Antony and Cleopatra*, Antony is cornered in Egypt, loses his last battle, and can find himself again only by dying.

Even though Shakespeare occasionally drew a tragic plot from fiction, the premise that tragedies are based on the givens of history or established legend and comedies on fictional events the writer can mould as he wishes has its own internal logic. The chain of cause and consequence is more usual in lived experience than magical transformation. Actual lives, no matter how rich in power and achievement, always end in the final defeat of death, and tragedies, whether they end in death or not (Shakespeare's always do), have the same fated quality of what has already happened and cannot be changed or evaded. In its unerring movement towards that inevitable conclusion, tragedy enacts the cadential rhythm of every human existence, even while it protests against that inevitable end in its countermovement of expanding heroic self-realization.

The insistence of tragic formulas on events of great magnitude and persons of exalted estate accords with life thus felt from the inside, the unique self and its never-to-be-repeated life. (Shakespeare's Othello, Antony, and Titus Andronicus are indispensable military commanders, Julius Caesar and the men who kill him are central to the leadership of Rome; even Romeo and Juliet are the focal points of a social division that threatens to destroy a whole city.) But life may also be apprehended, by different minds or by the same minds in different circumstances, in a more social way: as something common and ongoing, the community weathering upheavals and vicissitudes by finding new ways to adapt and regroup. The clever devices that untie comic knots enact this real sense of continuity and new opportunity even while they remould hard facts into the image of our wish. Comedy's more ordinary characters, who evade death and disgrace and move on to marry and procreate, assert against the personal orientation of tragedy a sense of life as an endless stream in which we participate but are not the whole story.

From an intertextual perspective, Elizabethan tragedy grows, like any other form, out of roots in earlier literature. Classical drama provided one source, although the work of the great Greek tragedians in Shakespeare's time was known, if at all, mainly to the learned in the occasional Latin translation. Euripides was more admired than Aeschylus or Sophocles, and also more available in Latin versions; individual plays of his have been claimed as models for the rhythm of *Titus Andronicus*, 'suffering to an intolerable pitch, followed by the relief of aggressive action' and for the pervasive disillusionment of *Troilus and Cressida* with its self-divided characters and unstable values.[5] Better known and more revered than any Greek was the Roman tragedian Seneca. The models his plays provided for high passionate rhetoric, structured by repetition and opposition, probably assisted Renaissance writers, including Shakespeare, on their way to mature tragic verse. On the other hand, Seneca may have been credited with too much influence in other areas: the comic dramatist Terence is the more likely model for five-act structure, and the complaining ghost was already omnipresent in the narrative tragedies generally labelled *de casibus* after Boccaccio's archetypal collection detailing the falls of the mighty, *De casibus virorum illustrium*. Boccaccio's work was translated at one remove by Lydgate in his fifteenth-century *Falls of Princes* and later imitated in a popular compilation, *The Mirror for Magistrates*, which was first issued in 1574 and republished several times, with substantial additions, through 1610. In the *Mirror*, figures from English and Roman history narrate in the first person their greatness and fall, providing numerous models for individual tragedies – Richard II, Duke Humphrey of Gloucester, Locrine, Julius Caesar, and so on – and cumulatively a sense of the instability of worldly greatness. That sense also pervades Seneca's dramas and, from a different perspective, the equally well-known narratives of mutability in Ovid's *Metamorphoses*. Another cumulative effect of the *Mirror* narratives has potential relevance for the sense of blurred responsibility in most of Shakespeare's tragedies, where personal failings and external circumstances operate in a mysterious conjunction to bring down the hero. The *Mirror* collection as a whole creates a similar ambiguity, with some figures attributing their falls to personal flaws and crimes while others blame fortune, the instability of this fallen world.

The native medieval drama offered no direct model for tragedy, but certain features of it point towards the tragic: especially the Passion of Christ in the mystery plays, a single life and death freighted with significance; and in the morality plays the deployment of personified virtues and vices to explore internal conflict. After the Reformation, a new theological emphasis on reprobation made tragic shaping a possibility in Protestant moralities such as *Enough is as Good as a Feast* (1560s) and *The Conflict of Conscience* (1570s). At the same time a few early attempts at tragedy began appearing. Some were classical in orientation, such as Sackville and Norton's *Gorboduc* (1562) and Gascoigne's *Jocaste* (1566), performed at the universities and Inns of Court, and some more popular, such as *Horestes* (1567) and *Cambises* (1569/70), which mingled high and low estates and leavened the tragic events with a large dose of comedy. These plays, although variously wooden, flat, and incoherent, nevertheless gesture towards a serious secular drama. Norman Rabkin has found promise of the more golden future in the very confusions that make *Gorboduc* and *Cambises* individually unsatisfactory as works of art: the ambivalences that cloud any clear moral message in them thus open the way to tragic complexities as some neat causality inside a single moral system could not.[6]

In any case, the golden future was not long in coming. The 1580s saw the beginnings of true tragic shape and style in two successful dramas of the commercial stage: *The Spanish Tragedy* (?1587) and *Tamburlaine* (1587–8). In the first, by Thomas Kyd, the central premise of revenge is complicated by questions about the relation of such individual justice to social and divine law. *The Spanish Tragedy* also keeps blurring the line between theatricality and life, so that events presented as plays become all too real, and courses of action apparently individually willed are shown to be a fated script. The second, by Christopher Marlowe, opened up new horizons with its soaring verse and grand heroic vision. Both plays eschew the reductive moralizing that had short-circuited any tragic effect in earlier proto-tragic poems and dramas, *Tamburlaine* instead celebrating heroic virtù and *The Spanish Tragedy* underlining its ironies of concept and perspective. The next notable developer of tragic possibility was Shakespeare himself, in the 1590s and the early 1600s.

No single formula informs Shakespeare's tragedies. The decisive tragic act may be variously placed, as early as the first scene in the case of *King Lear*, which then traces out in the rest of the action the ramifications of Lear's giving up power and dividing the kingdom, or as late as the last scene in the case of *Othello*, where the emphasis is rather on the complicated internal and external forces that push the Moor to murder the wife he loves. In the tragedies of the 1590s Shakespeare's focus shifts from heroic suffering in *Titus Andronicus* to social and generational tension in *Romeo and Juliet* to the clash between personal integrity and political imperative in *Julius Caesar*. When he later returns to some of these areas of tragic conflict – the dialectic of personal and political in *Coriolanus*, generational dynamics and monumental suffering in *King Lear* – the result in each case is a different tragic vision. If they are linked by any distinctive feature, it is the structuring of events to mark the limits of the hero's power by moving him from his sphere of established mastery into a situation demanding another, perhaps diametrically opposed, kind of effectiveness. Othello and Coriolanus must leave the straightforward hostilities of war for the covert rivalries of peace-time society; Brutus and Hamlet, the amplitude of uncommitted speculation for a realm of action that calls for decisive deeds. More voluntarily, Macbeth goes from an honourable subordination to a royal power he cannot wield righteously, and Lear in the other direction, from supreme authority to dependence.

In 1598, Francis Meres in his *Palladis Tamia* noted the pre-eminence 'among the Latins' of Plautus for comedy and Seneca for tragedy, and praised Shakespeare as 'among the English the most excellent in both kinds'. That Meres lists along with *Titus Andronicus* and *Romeo and Juliet* as examples of Shakespeare's tragedies four plays later classed in the Folio as histories – not only the tragically shaped *Richard II* and *Richard III* but *King John* and *Henry IV* as well – suggests the instability of generic labelling at the time and the fluid mingling of kinds. Meres may also have had some difficulty in getting his total of Shakespearian tragedies up to six in order to balance the six comedies he has just listed: *The Two Gentlemen of Verona, The Comedy of Errors, Love's Labour's Lost, A Midsummer Night's Dream, The Merchant of Venice*, and the problematic *Love's Labour's Won*, which refers either to a lost play or to one now known under another name. While Shakespeare's great tragic period, the decade from 1599 to 1607 or 1608, was still to come, Meres had no trouble finding successful comedies to list. Indeed, if modern chronologies are correct, he could have added others: *The Taming of the Shrew, The Merry Wives of Windsor, Much Ado About Nothing*. After something like ten years writing for the public stage, Shakespeare's credentials in comedy were well established.

The tradition of comedy that Shakespeare inherited and developed was as mixed as that of tragedy but considerably richer in examples. The classical models were Plautus, as Meres notes, and Terence, whose influence on structure and character in Elizabethan comedies is more observable than that of Seneca in the early tragedies. The plots of Plautus and Terence work out of tight spots through deceptions and mistakings to a gratifying conclusion in recovery of lost children, exposure of impostors, and removal of impediments to youthful male desire. But English comedy also had deep roots in popular festivals, characterized variously by song and dance, disguising, ritual abuse, and the mocking or up-ending of authority under the chaotic rule of temporary kings or queens. Tied as they were to the round of the agricultural year, the festivals celebrated fertility through individual sexual coupling as well as communal rites. In both their elaborate pretences involving disguise and their usual conclusion in the mating of the young, festive practices merged easily with the classical comedy plot. The clowning spirit infiltrated serious medieval drama, to enliven the Flood story with Noah's shrewish wife and even the Nativity with the chicanery of Mak the sheep-stealer, and to leaven the moralities' action of fateful moral choice with the antics of the Vice. Like tragedy, comedy was fed from non-dramatic sources as well, ballads and romance narratives such as *Amadis de Gaule* and Heliodorus' *Aethiopian History*, that presented strenuous quests and much-tried loves in a climate of wonders.

Romance, classical structure, and festive elements had already begun to come together in drama when Shakespeare began writing, in such school and university plays as *Ralph Roister Doister* (1552) and *Gammer Gurton's Needle* (1553) and later in John Lyly's fantasies written for the boys' companies and comedies of the adult popular theatre by George Peele and Robert Greene (1580s and 1590s). While the school plays feature clowning, romance elements come into their own with such comedies as *The Old Wife's Tale* (Peele) and *Friar Bacon and Friar Bungay* (Greene).

Courtship is the staple activity in the comic drama of Shakespeare and his Elizabethan contemporaries, driving the main plot or, less often, a subplot (as when Antipholus of Syracuse woos Luciana around the edges of a welter of mistaken identities in *The Comedy of Errors*). While these plays pursue love wholeheartedly, they are equally energetic in negating death. Like their carnivalesque antecedents marked by burlesque funerals and resurrections, they invoke the end of life only to avoid it, undo it, distance it, laugh it off. Only the most minor characters in them actually die. Quite a few, like Hero in *Much Ado About Nothing*, are believed to be dead, only to reappear in due course among the living in a triumph of 'evitability' and wish-fulfilment. The same bent to reshape reality can be seen in the many controller-figures who haunt these comedies, working their transformations through magic, like Friar Bacon (*Friar Bacon and Friar Bungay*, *John of Bordeaux*) and Oberon (*A Midsummer Night's Dream*), or through their own ingenuity like Petruccio (*The Taming of A Shrew / The Shrew*). The frequent disguisers and deceivers belong with this group in that they manipulate others through their superior knowledge. Their stratagems, indispensable for the dramatic structure, generate both complications and resolutions. While such manipulators are typically male, like the hero of *Mucedorus* and the suitors in *Fair Em*, Shakespeare fostered his own tradition of women who control events in their plays – sometimes aided by disguise in the manner of Portia in *The Merchant of Venice* or Rosalind in *As You Like It*, sometimes relying on sheer force of wit and wisdom, as do the ladies in *Love's Labour's Lost* and the wives in *The Merry Wives of Windsor*. Not all his comedies work this way, and in a few, such as *The Two Gentlemen of Verona* and *Twelfth Night*, male disguise confers on the heroine only knowledge, without the power to alter events. Nevertheless, Shakespeare's 'women on top' speciality has its own relevance to the comic mode, which rejoices, like the seasonal festivals that animate it, in temporarily placing servants over masters and women over men, dislocating the hierarchies sanctioned by its society only to reassert them at the play's end.

Another decided preference is for the plural. Plotting is typically multiple, including frames and inductions as well as subsidiary actions, and tone often varies accordingly. Refined love-longings are set off by the more physical preoccupations of servants and clowns, intent like the slaves of Roman comedy on getting dinner and avoiding danger. The resulting suggestion of alternative realities was most fully developed by Shakespeare in his repeated comic device of contrasting worlds: court and forest in *A Midsummer Night's Dream* and *As You Like It*, Venice and Belmont in *The Merchant of Venice*. The point is not to choose fluidity and anarchy over strict social and hierarchical codes, or the law of love over the law of property, but to include both, adjusting one to the other in a new, productive balance. Comic inclusiveness thus reinforces 'evitability', achieving a broader view that sees around the impasse. In encouraging alternative meanings, it also underlies the verbal play for which comedy always has room. Fools and lovers alike bandy words with delight, derailing or ignoring the forward thrust of the action for the local pleasures of pun and clever insult. In such verbal acrobatics, and in larger complications of action, the principle of 'dilation' expounded by Patricia Parker finds its place in comic structure – to a great degree *generates* that structure. Its devices, derived from rhetoric, of repetition, doubling, preposterous reversal, amplification, and multiplication of words and errors structure comedy's dramatic time from beginning to conclusion, indeed function largely to defer that conclusion.[7]

From a different point of view, Alexander Leggatt also sees comic inclusiveness as antithetical to closure, pointing out that since comedy regularly contradicts itself by incorporating opposite perspectives – for example mocking marriage while working to bring marriages about – it naturally mocks itself as well, undermining its own practices.[8] 'Our wooing doth not end like an old play' is part of the very convention it flouts.

The history play lacks such clear generic markers. The 1623 Folio lists Shakespeare's histories between the comedies and the tragedies, ordered by historical chronology: *King John*, *Richard II*, the two parts of *Henry IV*, and *Henry V* come before the three parts of *Henry VI* and *Richard III*, which were written earlier, with *Henry VIII* coming last. Even in Shakespeare's time, it was easier to recognize the history play than to define it. In the anonymous play *A Warning for Fair Women*, which brings on stage all three genres personified, tragedy is associated with high passion and violent deaths and comedy with wit and the lesser passions of lovers, but the only clue to history's nature is her drum and ensign, suggesting war. Some years later, in his defence of the theatre, Heywood proposes that the deeds of worthies constitute the core of the history play, held up for emulation and, in the case of the English histories, patriotic pride.[9] These pointers are relevant as far as they go, implying concentration on public affairs as characteristic of the history play, battle as a central action, and a nationalist flavour to the proceedings.

The dramatic practice of Shakespeare and his fellow playwrights suggests a more specific focus in the dynastic politics of recent English history, the later Plantagenets and, after the death of Elizabeth I in 1603, the Tudors. Shakespeare's Plantagenet plays and his later *Henry VIII* were accompanied by others in the same areas such as the anonymous *Troublesome Reign of King John* and *Woodstock*, Marlowe's *Edward II*, Heywood's *1* and *2 Edward IV*, the anonymous *True*

Tragedy of Richard III, and the later *Sir Thomas Wyatt* by Dekker and Webster and *If You Know Not Me, You Know Nobody*, by Heywood. If a basis in recent national events was felt to define the genre, we can understand why Heminges and Condell would exclude from their middle category Shakespeare's plays based on Britain's remote/legendary past (*King Lear*, *Cymbeline*), as well as those based on Roman history. Plays in the latter group, such as *Julius Caesar* and *Antony and Cleopatra*, have in common with the English histories a pervasive concern with tensions between public and private values, a preoccupation with power and its conflicted passage from one ruler to another, and (except for *Antony*) a marginalizing of the sexual relations so central to some tragedies and almost all comedies. What they lack is Englishness, and in making that definitive for their history category, Heminges and Condell imply a particular relationship between these plays and their English readers.

That relationship, the special meaning of the English past for the English present, was both general and specific. The history play arose at a time when the sense of nationhood was crystallizing in England as in other European states, part of a heightened interest in earlier times that took in chronicles, ballads, and pamphlets as well. Elizabethans looked to events and figures from those times – not only kings and their battles but country squires, folk heroes, and common soldiers with their different activities and perspectives – to anchor the corporate English identity they were newly defining. In a more focused way, playwrights might dramatize through the Plantagenets current political forces both conservative and radical. Certainly some issues of the history plays were current concerns as well: religious factionalism threatened Elizabethan society as well as that of the Wars of the Roses, powerful nobles still challenged central monarchic rule, and conflicts over the succession to the throne had particular resonance in a land ruled by an aging childless queen.

Conceived and valued in these terms, the history play was tied more closely than the other two genres to what actually happened, or was understood to have happened, and accepted artificial structuring less readily than the more openly fictive comedy and tragedy.[10] Formally it inclines towards the episodic, and its endings, though frequently signalled by the death of the eponymous king, nevertheless offer more provisional closure than the other genres, with a new ruler succeeding and the life of the nation continuing. Perhaps because of this openended, *in medias res* quality, critics of the histories have sought a larger framework in which to comprehend them. Such formulations of an overarching structure owe something to the 'Tudor myth' perceived by E. M. W. Tillyard in Plantagenet history: innocence lost with the deposition of Richard II, rebellion and unrest culminating in military losses abroad and increasingly savage fighting at home until Richard III gathers all wickedness into himself and is cast out by the redemptive figure of Henry Tudor. The lost ideal order is usually located in the reign of Edward III; or, looking only at Shakespeare's histories and bearing

in mind the composition of the Henry VI–Richard III group before the historically earlier Richard II–Henry V group, one may with Phyllis Rackin see Henry
V himself as the 'lost heroic presence that the entire historical project is designed
to recover' – gone and mourned in the first tetralogy, not even fully present in
much of the second, often absent or play-acting, and even in his own play ambiguously presented.[11] In any case, behind the various versions of mythic loss and
renewal is the ur-myth that structured human history on the medieval stage, the
fall and redemption of man. Even this perspective, however, cannot completely
enclose history's open-endedness in full recovery, for history still goes on: the
loss of Eden is an accomplished fact, but final redemption, on the individual level
at least, is only a hope for the future.

    If elements in the history play kept it from full adherence to the conventional
organizations of either tragedy or comedy, it nevertheless drew freely on both
genres for devices large and small. The common pattern tracing the reign of a
king, who rises to and wields great power and then loses all in defeat and death,
accommodated easily to tragic shaping, all the more so since so many of the major
figures of the history plays had already undergone such treatment in the *Mirror*
narratives. Single-figure trajectories determine structure in such Shakespearian
histories as *Richard II* and *Richard III*, and strongly condition it in others, such
as *Henry VI*. In these *Henry VI* plays, however, the falls of Talbot, Humphrey
of Gloucester, and Richard of York are single elements in more various designs,
which include also the bizarre career of Joan of Arc, the Duchess of Gloucester's
dabbling in sorcery, the love affair of Margaret and Suffolk, and the waxing and
waning fortunes of the pathetic Henry. Already sharing with comedy its concern
with a whole society, the history play in such instances borrows comic practices
as well, the multiplying of actions and even in some cases the actions themselves
– the duchess's spirit-raising, Suffolk's winning Margaret for himself instead of
his master, the king going incognito among common folk, as Henry V later does
on the eve of Agincourt – all were familiar from the comic drama, especially what
Anne Barton has called the 'comical history', which deploys historical personages such as James IV and William the Conqueror in romance actions.[12] The
Henry IV plays are perhaps structurally closest to comedy, with plots based in
different social and ideological worlds commenting on one another by contrast
and ironic analogy rather than feeding into one line of action. If there is a structure peculiar to the political play, not shared by tragedy or comedy, it may be that
described by Geoffrey Bullough in the *Henry VI* plays, which also characterizes
the political tragedy *Julius Caesar*: 'a wavelike motion' as figures become significant power-players, then are challenged and downed by others who in turn are
overthrown.[13]

    The sense of ongoing motion implicit in successive waves suggests how the
histories also differ from the comedies and tragedies in their apprehension of
time and their mode of closure. Tragic time is relentlessly linear, irreversible, all

too short. Death is the end towards which Renaissance tragedies move, an end rendered all the more final for the individual when the Reformation swept away the doctrine of purgatory and the practice of intercession for the dead. The real impending defeat facing the hero in secular drama, however, is not damnation but what Michael Neill has called 'the horror of indistinction', which is paradoxically 'the supreme occasion for exhibitions of individual distinction', the stance that we recognize as heroic.[14] Comic time is elastic, even reversible. The right person arrives on the scene just in time to ward off catastrophe: Valentine to rescue Sylvia in *Two Gentlemen*, the missing twins in both *Comedy of Errors* and *Twelfth Night* to save Egeon and Viola. Death itself is not final. In their conclusions comedies invoke a new phase of life rather than the absolute end, but the solution of the comic dilemma, accompanied by comeuppances for the obstructive figures and multiple pairings-off for the marriageable, gives a sense of closure nevertheless. Projections beyond the immediate comic stasis are rare. The histories, however, habitually look before and after. *1 Henry VI*, for example, begins by mourning for the dead Henry V and celebrating his deeds, and ends with the projected marriage of Henry VI to Margaret not yet achieved and her adulterous affair with Suffolk already prepared for. Even the hero–king's triumphs in *Henry V* are dimmed by the epilogue's forward look to Henry's early death and the contested rule of his successor that would lead to loss of territories in France and civil war in England. Whether the provisional closure is ominous like this one, or problematic, as at the end of *Richard II* when the new Henry IV vows to lead a crusade to the Holy Land to do penance for his part in the murder of his predecessor, or hopeful, as in *Henry VIII* when Cranmer prophesies over the infant Elizabeth the greatness of her future reign, the history play moves not towards completion but into ongoing time.

   While the plays overall confirm the generic divisions laid out by the Folio table of contents, it is clear even from my brief review that there was considerable commerce between those subcultures of comedy, history, and tragedy. For one thing, the stories audiences liked, romances in particular, did not necessarily accord neatly with tragic or comic paradigms.[15] For another, viewers liked variety in their theatrical entertainment. The mixture of kings and clowns, hornpipes and funerals, that Sidney deplored in his *Apology* went back to the medieval drama and would continue long after Sidney's death. Several of the Folio designations are problematic. May we not consider *Richard II* and *Richard III* as tragedies, labelled as such in their quarto publications and the latter even in its Folio heading, praised as such by Meres, and certainly akin to the other tragedies in their single-figure, rise-and-fall structure? Do the Roman plays, especially *Julius Caesar* and *Coriolanus*, not have as much in common with the histories' preoccupation with struggles for power and issues of state as with the tragedies' more personal emphasis? Source material seems to have determined placement in both these instances, English as opposed to Roman history. Does source material also account for a more notable anomaly, *Cymbeline* listed among the tragedies? Comedic in structure and concluding in happy reconciliation rather than death, *Cymbeline* is nevertheless based on the same body of legendary British history that lies behind Fletcher's *Tragedy of Bonduca* and Shakespeare's own *King Lear*. *Troilus and Cressida*, which Heminges and Condell placed with the tragedies but earlier was promoted as a comedy in the printer's advertisement to the 1609 quarto, presents another generic puzzle, compounded for readers of the Folio because the copy was apparently cleared for publication so late in the printing process that the play is placed ambiguously between the histories and tragedies, with a separate set of signatures unconnected to either sequence, and is omitted entirely from the table of contents. Should we see it as a tragedy (so designated in its Folio heading and running titles) because, like *Cymbeline*, it is based on legendary history? And indeed, unlike *Cymbeline*, has a heroic war as its framework and ends with the death of a major warrior? Or should we accept the 1609 label of comedy because the play systematically deflates those towering figures and debunks their idealized causes? The question is still with us three centuries later: in the first two generations after World War II, editions of Shakespeare's complete works that organize the plays generically usually place *Troilus* with the tragedies, but recently it appears more often among the comedies.

Both *Troilus* and *Cymbeline* are best seen as generic experiments, in the context of changes in theatrical fashion as the seventeenth century began. The history play in its later manifestations (*Edward IV*, *Jane Shore*) was veering into romance and folk comedy. In comedy, the new prominence of the boys' companies fostered a taste for modes that made use of the child actors' wit and quickness but made fewer demands on them in the way of emotional depth: the satiric comedy in which Jonson and Marston led the way and the city comedy exemplified by Middleton – its scene bourgeois, competitive, money-driven London, its staple action trickery. Shakespeare did not pursue the citizen comedy line – *The Merry Wives of Windsor* has an English setting and middle-class characters who perpetrate various deceptions but money is hardly central and the play is too genially romantic to foreshadow the harsher tone of Middleton and the 'Ho' plays. *Troilus*, however, in its pervasive spirit of detached parody, is somewhat akin to the 'comical satires' written for the boy actors.

More recent critics, whether viewing *Troilus* as ironic tragedy or as satiric comedy, have largely followed the lead of the late nineteenth-century critic F. S. Boas in grouping it with two other Shakespeare plays of the early 1600s, *Measure for Measure* and *All's Well That Ends Well*.[16] These 'problem plays' (Boas's label gestured at social-issue drama in the manner of Ibsen while reformulating the problems in ethical terms) share a grittiness not apparent in Shakespeare's earlier comedy, addressing deep-rooted perversions in both individuals and societies resistant to the magico-metamorphic strategies that heretofore had produced satisfying comic conclusions. The harsh imperatives of class division and rampant sexual appetite invoked by these experimental plays push uneasily against the fairy-tale devices that move their plots forward and supposedly resolve them.

As for *Cymbeline*, though this crowded play incorporates some tragic features, it has deeper affinities with two other late plays, *The Winter's Tale* and *The Tempest*, and with another not included in the First Folio but usually ascribed at least in part to Shakespeare, *Pericles*. The plays in this mode were responding in some degree to recent developments on the theatre scene, the popularity of masques at court and the availability of a new indoor acting space at Blackfriars, more intimate than the Globe. Often designated as romances – another nineteenth-century category, this one devised by Edward Dowden[17] – they may be thought of either as a subset of comedy in that they achieve a final harmony, or as a merger of tragedy and comedy in that this reconciliatory phase comes only after prolonged evil and suffering. If they are part of the same generic adventure that produced *Measure for Measure* and *All's Well that Ends Well*, Shakespeare now finds a way of holding in solution the diversity of tone and action whose clash made those earlier Jacobean comedies problematic, returning to the romantic narratives he had drawn on in some earlier comedies but with additional emphasis on the peculiar features of the romance mode. His plots in these late plays are episodic in structure and vastly extended in time and space. The larger view that results generates a perception of time different from that in earlier comedy as well as that in the histories and the tragedies: whether or not actually personified as in *The Winter's Tale*, time is shown as shaped and patterned, its past disorder made meaningful by present retributions or fulfilments. This evolving larger vision creates a certain distance between audience and stage action which is increased by the conscious fictionality of that action, its improbabilities and miraculous turns of event, including manifestations of the divine, and by the recurrent narrator figures like Gower in *Pericles* and Time in *The Winter's Tale* who 'tell' the drama at key points.[18] In terms of Marianne Moore's celebrated definition of poetry,[19] Shakespeare in the romances accentuates the imaginary quality of his gardens in order to contain very real toads. It is in that realness, that grounding of extreme emotions and actions in a comprehensible internal psychology, that Shakespeare's last plays diverge most markedly from the contemporary tragicomedies of Beaumont and Fletcher which they resemble in surface characteristics.

Generic traditions in Shakespeare's time, often blending and always evolving, nevertheless served as guides: to playwrights in developing their material, to audiences and readers in understanding the plays they produced. In addition to the internal genre indicators discussed in this chapter, spectators at the theatres were directed in their reactions by the look of the stage itself, hung with black for a tragedy and perhaps with some other colour for non-tragic drama.[20] In Shakespeare's hands, genre conventions provided shape rather than limitation, in musical terms a kind of ground on which – and sometimes against which – he played the individual descant of each play.

Notes

1. Rosalie L.Colie, *The Resources of Kind: Genre-Theory in the Renaissance*, ed. Barbara K. Lewalski (Berkeley: University of California Press, 1973), p. 116.
2. Michael Neill, 'Remembrance and Revenge: *Hamlet, Macbeth*, and *The Tempest*', in *Jonson and Shakespeare*, ed. Ian Donaldson (Atlantic Highlands, N.J.: Humanities Press, 1983), pp. 45–9.
3. Donatus, Evanthius, and Diomedes are summarized in Madeleine Doran, *Endeavors of Art: A Study of Form in Elizabethan Drama* (Madison: University of Wisconsin Press, 1954), pp. 105–9, and Marvin T. Herrick, *Comic Theory in the Sixteenth Century* (Urbana: University of Illinois Press, 1960), pp. 56–7; a translation and analysis of the Donatus–Evanthius treatise by S. Georgia Nugent appears in *Shakespearean Comedy*, ed. Maurice Charney (New York: New York Literary Forum, 1980), pp. 259–80.
4. Sir Philip Sidney, *An Apology for Poetry; or, The Defence of Poetry*, ed. Geoffrey Shepherd (Edinburgh: Nelson, 1965), p. 117. Subsequent references are also to this page.
5. On *Titus*, see Emrys Jones, *The Origins of Shakespeare* (Oxford: Clarendon Press, 1977) p. 98 (discussion, pp. 85–107); on *Troilus*, see Margaret J. Arnold, '"Monsters in Love's Train": Euripides and Shakespeare's *Troilus and Cressida*', *Comparative Drama* 18 (1984), 38–53.
6. Norman Rabkin, 'Stumbling toward Tragedy', in *Shakespeare's 'Rough Magic': Renaissance Essays in Honor of C. L. Barber*, ed. Peter Erickson and Coppélia Kahn (Newark: University of Delaware Press, 1985), pp. 28–49.
7. Patricia Parker, *Literary Fat Ladies: Rhetoric, Gender, Property* (London and New York: Methuen, 1987), chs. 2 and 5.
8. Alexander Leggatt, *English Stage Comedy 1490–1990: Five Centuries of a Genre* (London and New York: Routledge, 1998), ch. 7, esp. pp. 146–9.
9. *A Warning for Fair Women*, Tudor Facsimile Texts (New York: AMS Press, 1970), Induction, A2–A3; Thomas Heywood, *An Apology for Actors* (1612), B3–B4.
10. G. K. Hunter, 'Truth and Art in History Plays', *Shakespeare Survey* 42 (Cambridge University Press, 1989), 15–24.
11. Phyllis Rackin, *Stages of History: Shakespeare's English Chronicles* (Ithaca, N.Y.: Cornell University Press, 1990), pp. 29–30.
12. Anne Barton, 'The King Disguised: Shakespeare's *Henry V* and the Comical History', in *The Triple Bond: Plays, Mainly Shakespearean, in Performance*, ed. Joseph G. Price (University Park: Pennsylvania State University, 1975), pp. 92–117.
13. Geoffrey Bullough, *Narrative and Dramatic Sources of Shakespeare*, vol. III (London: Routledge and Kegan Paul, 1960), p. 168.
14. Michael Neill, *Issues of Death: Mortality and Identity in English Renaissance Tragedy* (Oxford: Clarendon Press, 1997), pp. 33–4, 51–88.
15. G. K. Hunter, *English Drama 1586–1642: The Age of Shakespeare*, Oxford History of English Literature, vol. VI (Oxford: Clarendon Press, 1997), p. 93.
16. F. S. Boas, *Shakspere and his Predecessors* (London: J. Murray, 1896), ch. 13. Boas's inclusion of *Hamlet* in this category was not adopted by most later critics.
17. *Shakspere: A Critical Study of his Mind and Art* (New York and London: Harper and Bros, 1899), pp. x–xi.
18. On distancing, fictionality, and narrativity in the last plays, see Barbara A. Mowat, *The Dramaturgy of Shakespeare's Romances* (Athens: University of Georgia Press, 1976), chs. 2 and 3.
19. Moore's 'Poetry' in its first version (1935) calls poets to present 'imaginary gardens

with real toads in them', in *Selected Poems*, with an introduction by T. S. Eliot (New York: Macmillan Company, 1935).

20. For black hangings marking tragedy, see the opening line of *1 Henry VI* and *A Warning for Fair Women*, Induction, A3. The New Cambridge Shakespeare editor Michael Hattaway speculates that another colour may have indicated comedy: *The First Part of King Henry the Sixth* (Cambridge University Press, 1990), p. 24.

Reading list

Barber, C. L., *Shakespeare's Festive Comedy: A Study of Dramatic Form and its Relation to Social Custom* (Princeton University Press, 1959).

Colie, Rosalie L., *The Resources of Kind: Genre-Theory in the Renaissance*, ed. Barbara K. Lewalski (Berkeley: University of California Press, 1973).

Danson, Lawrence, *Shakespeare's Dramatic Genres* (Oxford University Press, 2000).

Doran, Madeleine, *Endeavors of Art: A Study of Form in Elizabethan Drama* (Madison: University of Wisconsin Press, 1954).

Frye, Northrop, *Anatomy of Criticism: Four Essays* (Princeton University Press, 1957).

Leggatt, Alexander, *English Stage Comedy 1490–1990: Five Centuries of a Genre* (London and New York: Routledge, 1998).

Mowat, Barbara A., *The Dramaturgy of Shakespeare's Romances* (Athens: University of Georgia Press, 1976).

Neill, Michael, *Issues of Death: Mortality and Identity in English Renaissance Tragedy* (Oxford: Clarendon Press, 1997).

Orgel, Stephen, 'Shakespeare and the Kinds of Drama', *Critical Inquiry* 6 (1979).

Rackin, Phyllis, *Stages of History: Shakespeare's English Chronicles* (Ithaca, N.Y.: Cornell University Press, 1990).

Snyder, Susan, *The Comic Matrix of Shakespeare's Tragedies* (Princeton University Press, 1979).

Wheeler, Richard P., *Shakespeare's Development and the Problem Comedies: Turn and Counterturn* (Berkeley: University of California Press, 1981).

7

JOHN H. ASTINGTON

Playhouses, players, and playgoers in Shakespeare's time

Playhouses

SHAKESPEARE had more predecessors as an Elizabethan actor than he did as an Elizabethan dramatist. Theatrical culture was thriving well before the performance of the famous plays we read today, which date from the 1580s and thereafter. Yet in the year of Shakespeare's birth, 1564, the Bishop of London wrote to the Secretary of State, Sir William Cecil, to complain about players performing in London every day, doubly concerned about the spread of plague likely from the assembly of large groups of people gathered as audiences and the ungodly character of plays and theatres. His letter speaks of 'the houses where they play their lewd interludes'. We know little of where Londoners were watching plays in 1564, but three years later a special stage and auditorium were built in Stepney for a show which was not ungodly at all: it was described as the story of Samson. The Red Lion playhouse, to give it the title of the farmhouse or inn where it was built, lay about three-quarters of a mile (0.9 km) east of the city walls. It had a large platform stage – 30 feet by 40 (9 m by 12 m) – and galleries for the audience to sit and watch the play. It seems that the important features of the best-known Elizabethan playhouse, the Globe, opened in 1599, were established in theatre buildings more than thirty years earlier.

Possibly the Red Lion was not built for the long term – we hear no more of it after the year in which it was put up – but its investors tried again, more successfully, in the following decade. John Brayne, the brother-in-law of the player and entrepreneur James Burbage, had financed the Red Lion; in 1576 the two men together launched the venture of the playhouse called simply the Theatre. This building evidently was a success: it lasted for twenty-three years, and was demolished only to rise again in a different location as the framework of the Globe. It was therefore of the same size and general character as the Globe: a 'round' playhouse (actually polygonal, as the ring of galleries was made up of angled bays built with straight timber), with an open yard in its centre, in which part of the audience stood to watch the play, and a large platform stage projecting from one side of the enclosing three storeys of galleries, where the rest of the audience might sit, for higher prices. The Theatre stood in Shoreditch, to the north of the city walls beyond Bishopsgate; it was soon joined by a neighbouring building of

99

2   Overhead view of the remains of the Rose playhouse, 1989

a similar character, the Curtain, built in 1577. These two playhouses were still operating when Shakespeare arrived in London, and he probably acted in both buildings.

Seventeenth-century views of London show a series of playhouses on the south bank of the river Thames, in Southwark, opposite St Paul's Cathedral. The Globe stood in that area, and today stands there again. The first of this group of playhouses was the Rose, built by the theatrical entrepreneur Philip Henslowe in 1587, and subsequently extended in 1592. Since its foundations were uncovered in 1989 (see plate 2) it has been the sixteenth-century theatre building for which we have the fullest range of information, since the archaeological remains can be read together with the surviving records about the theatre's productions, written down by Henslowe. The Rose was rather smaller than the Theatre and the Globe; the diameter of these theatres has been calculated at about 100 feet (30.5 m), a dimension followed in the new Bankside Globe. The diameter of the roughly circular plan of the Rose was about three-quarters that size, so that the interior dimensions of the theatre were considerably smaller, and its largest audiences, with the house packed, perhaps reached two thousand people; the Globe, by contrast, held about three thousand at its fullest.

Perhaps the most interesting discovery at the site of the Rose was that of the foundations of two stages, the second a consequence of the extension of one side of the theatre in 1592, when the stage was moved back. Both versions of the stage had roughly the same size and form, considerably smaller than the platform of the Red Lion, and not in the shape of a regular rectangle: about 36 feet (11 m) wide at midpoint, the sides tapered to the front. At the rear the angles of the galleries defined its limits, so the entire platform was trapezoidal, and its maximum depth was about 17 feet (5m). This was the stage on which Marlowe's plays were first presented, as well as several of Shakespeare's earliest plays, the *Henry VI* series and *Titus Andronicus* among them; Shakespeare himself probably acted in the theatre in the early 1590s.

Following the archaeological finds at the Rose site a small part of the Globe's foundations was also uncovered, later in 1989; one angle of the galleries and what appears to have been the base of a stair turret demonstrate that the theatre was constructed in a manner similar to the Rose. Unfortunately, too much of the foundation lies under remaining buildings to excavate more at the present, so that the exact dimensions of the Globe's plan are yet to be discovered. Several other kinds of evidence have traditionally been used to interpret the appearance and character of the Globe. Soon after its opening in 1596 the Swan playhouse was attended by a Dutch visitor, who made a sketch of the interior. A contemporary copy of this drawing and the accompanying notes survives, and was rediscovered in Utrecht rather more than a hundred years ago (see plate 3). The theatre is very awkwardly drawn, but it is the only 'eye-witness' view of the interior of a large Elizabethan playhouse we know of today. It shows a large platform-stage with doors and a balcony at the rear, a stage roof carried on elaborate pillars rising from the stage, a playhouse flag and a trumpeter announcing a performance, and a yard and three-storey ring of gallery seating surrounding the performing area: all these features must resemble conditions at the Globe. A further indication that the Globe's stage was large is that in 1600 it was used as a model in a contract for a new theatre – the Fortune – to replace the aging Rose, which perhaps had proved too small to be profitable. At the Fortune the platform stage was to be a little over forty feet (12m) wide, and approaching 30 feet (9m) in depth.

In planning the new Globe, opened in 1996, dimensions were calculated from the meticulous views of the old theatre made by the Czech artist Wenzel Hollar just before it disappeared from the London landscape. What Hollar saw from the tower of Southwark Cathedral, his viewpoint for a panorama of the whole of London, was the *second* Globe, built in 1613 to replace its predecessor, burnt down in a fire which began during a performance of Shakespeare and Fletcher's play *Henry VIII*. But in 1613 the new theatre rose on the old foundations – part of which were found in 1989 – and hence was the same size; indeed it was the same size as the Theatre, the frame of which had been used to build the first Globe. So although the latter theatre had a career of only fourteen years, for almost seventy years a building of similar size and general character was to be found in London. The Globe we can visit today, to the north-west of the original site, is modelled on the first theatre of that name. It is not a replica of its predecessor, but a reconstruction based on the best knowledge available at the end of the twentieth century. The character of the stage has been formed by the Swan drawing. Visitors may be impressed by the sheer size of the yard, which it would

3   Copy by Aernout van Buchel of a drawing of the Swan playhouse by Jan de Witt, 1596.

4   *As You Like It* at Shakespeare's Globe theatre, 1998.

take many standing audience members to fill, and of the stage, almost twice as wide as it is deep (44 feet (13 m) by 24 feet (7 m)). Moving around the angles and levels of the galleries gives one many different views of the stage and the performers; where one sits or stands can considerably alter what one sees. The surroundings of the stage are colourful, and decorated with many visual details based on surviving sixteenth-century painted decoration. Eyes used to the plainness and neutrality of modern theatre buildings will find such elaboration rather surprising.

The Globe was only one kind of Elizabethan playhouse; in 1608 Shakespeare's company moved into a second theatre which had been in the possession of the Burbage family since before the Globe was built: the Blackfriars playhouse. The theatre took its name from the old precinct in which it stood, an extensive group of medieval buildings originally belonging to the Dominican friars, to the south and west of St Paul's Cathedral, on the slope of Ludgate Hill. The playhouse was set up within the old frater (refectory), a large hall with stone walls and gothic windows. Unlike the Globe, then, the Blackfriars was an entirely enclosed theatre, without the benefit of natural light from the sky above, but also without the consequent disadvantages of bad weather: wet and cold conditions would have reduced business at theatres like the Globe.

We know that the Blackfriars was considerably smaller than the Globe, and had a smaller stage; the entire space James Burbage had acquired was 44 feet (13 m) wide by 66 feet (20 m) long, within which both stage and auditorium were accommodated. The best estimate of the size of an audience in such a space is about six hundred people. The result was no doubt a more intimate theatre, although the darker conditions perhaps made actors' faces harder to see. The theatre was lit by candles and torches, although plays continued to be performed there in the afternoon, as they were in the outdoor theatres. The Blackfriars proved a success, and although the actors continued to use both theatres, moving their plays from one to the other, the smaller indoor space was to emerge as the leading playhouse of London in the years following Shakespeare's death.

The enclosed theatre, illuminated by stage lighting, was not a new discovery in 1608. A distinct playhouse had been set up in another part of the Blackfriars buildings in 1576, the year in which the Theatre was built. Medieval players had as commonly played indoors, in halls and large chambers, as they had in uncovered spaces. In the years before playhouses were built in London actors performed in spaces temporarily adapted for theatrical use, and during Shakespeare's lifetime they continued to do so, either when they were commissioned to entertain for special occasions or when they embarked on their regular tours of the English provinces. Some of the most important people of the realm saw plays not in the playhouses but in their own great houses and palaces. *Othello* was presented before King James, for example, in November 1604 within the Banqueting House at Whitehall, a large rectangular hall quite unlike the Globe. The performance was at night, and was lit by a great array of chandeliers hanging over the entire auditorium and stage. Even the legal society of the Middle Temple called the actors to perform before them in their own hall, where *Twelfth Night* was presented in February 1602. When the actors visited provincial cities or towns – Norwich, Leicester, and Bristol, among many other places – they may have performed in theatrical spaces set up outdoors in inn yards, or within enclosed guildhalls and town halls. Temporary theatres, of a variety of sizes, shapes, and character, constitute a further category of Shakespearian playing space.

Shakespeare's working life as an actor, then, would have made him well aware that his plays had to be capable of adaptation to larger or smaller stages, and more or less elaborate facilities. All theatres of the period, indoors or outdoors, permanent or temporary, had to be provided with two essential features: a stage, on which the actors moved and spoke, and abutting it a tiring house, or backstage space, separated from the stage by a wall or curtain, through which entries and exits were made. (The tiring house was so called because it was there that the actors dressed, or [at]tired themselves; changing costumes was an important matter, as we shall see.) These two simple physical elements accommodated most of the action of most of Shakespeare's plays. We know that a raised balcony is needed in *Romeo and Juliet* (2.1; 3.5), and a trap for the graveyard scene in *Hamlet* (5.1), but such special scenes are very infrequent compared with those simply involving the movement of actors on, around, and off the platform stage.

In temporary theatres temporary tiring houses are likely to have been made of hanging cloth; in the playhouses a structural wall stood at the upstage limits. The drawing of the Swan shows two large double doors set laterally in this wall; the new Globe has three entries, a central opening having been added to the Swan design. Such a central door certainly existed in contemporary playhouses: a drawing of an indoor theatre by the architect and designer Inigo Jones shows a tiring house with three doors, arranged as at the Globe, while the theatre he built for King Charles I at Whitehall Palace in 1630 had *five* doors, centred symmetrically on a larger stage entry. Probably the polygonal tiring-house wall at the Rose was also provided with a central door in addition to entries on either side of it. Entries with doors, like those at the Swan and the new Globe, were and are used practically when required – knocked on from within the tiring house, in *Macbeth* (2.2–2.3), or locked, in *Richard II* (5.3).

The Swan drawing shows the position of the acting station above the stage, on the second storey of the tiring house, reached by stairs from backstage. Not only did this serve for Juliet's bedroom, but also Cleopatra's monument, and the walls of cities in the history plays. The drawing also shows a structural feature with theatrical consequences: the large pillars holding up the stage roof which protected both the actors and the painted timber of the stage from the weather. The pillars affect both stage traffic and sightlines, and they proved to be one of the major concerns of modern actors when the new Globe opened for an experimental season in 1995. Indoor theatres, whether playhouses or temporary spaces, did not require them; if the stage at the Blackfriars was smaller, the entire area was practical and visible.

Players

How Shakespeare became an actor we do not know. He was not born into a theatrical family, as many actors were: the leading star of his company, Richard Burbage, was the son of James, also an actor, as well as playhouse-builder and entrepreneur. Nor was Shakespeare born in London, the birthplace of many actors, and the centre of operations for all the prominent playing companies. Although he probably began acting with other companies, we know that by 1594, when he was thirty, Shakespeare had joined a newly formed group of players called the Chamberlain's Men – officially they were the servants of Sir Henry Carey, Lord Hunsdon, the Lord Chamberlain of Queen Elizabeth's court. Such patronage was a necessary condition of Elizabethan theatre business. Actors had a well-defined cultural position, but their status was problematic in a society which ranked its members either by their inherited wealth or by their trades. Although actors banded together in companies, shared profits, and trained apprentices, their 'product' was not in the form of material goods, and they never organized themselves into a guild, the traditional trade body that gave its members mutual support and social standing. The contemporary answer was for groups of actors nominally to enter the service of a prominent nobleman; while they had to answer to his authority their connection to him gave them social position and protection, and they were otherwise free to run their playing company as a business, acting in public for profit. To be servants of Lord Hunsdon, however, offered rather more, in that the Lord Chamberlain supervised entertainments at court: to play before the queen was both prestigious and profitable.

The Chamberlain's Men prospered, and shortly became one of the two leading companies of London – the other was the Admiral's Men, led by the great actor Edward Alleyn. In 1603 the new monarch, King James, gave his own patronage to Shakespeare's company, and they took the title of the King's Men. The success of Shakespeare's plays in the theatre contributed to the prominence of the company, but otherwise we can infer that the individual actors formed close working bonds. The personnel of the company changed somewhat over the years of Shakespeare's membership in it, but it retained a core of colleagues who remained with it throughout their working lives. One of the bonds was financial: Elizabethan and Jacobean actors shared investments (in payments for plays, costumes, and so forth) and the consequent risks and profits. Sharers, so called, constituted the financial management of the company, and together made decisions on all the business involved in presenting plays. As permanent members of the company they played the leading roles in productions, and hired other actors and stage staff as they were needed. Shakespeare's company included a second group of investor–actors called householders, who owned part of the two theatres the company eventually acquired. All other acting companies rented the theatres in which they played, in the form of a proportion of the daily box-office paid to the owner. Within Shakespeare's company ownership provided considerable profit to those, like Shakespeare himself, who held a stake in the buildings, as well as forming a further bond among its leading partners.

Profit apart, working conditions dictated that players commit themselves one to another. Some signed formal contracts about their duties and obligations, but comradeship and mutual responsibility – team spirit – must have been more binding than any piece of paper. Players were required to work very hard indeed, under conditions quite different from those in the theatre today. The earliest surviving list of Shakespeare's company gives the actors who performed Ben Jonson's *Every Man in his Humour* in 1598: there are ten names, including Shakespeare's, although their parts are not specified. The play has sixteen speaking parts, as well as a number of walk-on mute roles. Three of the sixteen are female characters, which would have been played by the boy apprentices who traditionally took women's parts. So either three more adult actors would have to have been hired to cast the play, or – as we know commonly was the case – three of the actors doubled roles. *Every Man in his Humour* is relatively undemanding in this respect. Shakespeare's own *Julius Caesar* was acted at the Globe in the following year, 1599, when it was seen by a Swiss visitor, Thomas Platter, who described it as having 'about fifteen characters [*personen*]'. There are more than twice that number of speaking parts in the play, so Platter's estimate is likely to be of the number of players: the ten actors involved in Jonson's play, two boys playing the roles of Calphurnia and Portia, and a number of journeyman actors hired to swell the scenes of crowds and armies. Even so, those actors not playing the parts of leading characters who appear through much of the play – Caesar, Mark Antony, Brutus, and Cassius – would have been required to take more than one part. Many actors would have had to cope not only with learning different sets of lines, but timing their costume changes within the tiring house, so as to present physically differentiated characters on the stage.

The learning of lines was a constant task. To satisfy a public which went to the theatre relatively regularly the actors needed to present new productions at suitably frequent intervals, as the film industry does today. Unlike modern films or plays, however, new plays were not presented in a run of several weeks; after the première a play might not be performed again until the following week, becoming part of a circulating repertory which kept a number of plays in performance during the playing season. If that season lasted from late summer to the following spring, thirty or more distinct plays might be performed by the company. It was therefore possible for those from out of town to go to the same playhouse five days in a row and not see the same play twice. At the start of a season new plays might be introduced every second week, but once playing was under way actors had to learn and rehearse any new material while performing a constantly changing repertory each day in the afternoon; reviving old plays that had not been performed for some months or years would also have required some preparation time. The working day was therefore a long one, and at any given time during a season a player would have to have been prepared to perform in nine or ten plays, knowing the lines for perhaps two or three roles in each play. Shakespeare wrote many of his plays while maintaining such a schedule.

The theatre season in London had a variable length, and in some years the players hardly performed at all: 1603, for example. When Queen Elizabeth died in March the playhouses were closed as a sign of mourning; shortly thereafter there was a virulent plague outbreak, and the theatres remained closed for almost a full year. Epidemics enforced idleness on Shakespeare and his fellows; the fleas which caused bubonic plague were always present in large communities and under certain conditions they spread infection for which there was no known cure, and which frequently led to a painful death. The civic authorities did understand that large assemblies spread the disease, however, and playhouses were regularly closed when the weekly number of deaths from plague rose above a certain figure; often this occurred in the summer. The large playing companies therefore calculated the time they devoted to touring as usually falling in some part of the summer months. It was also easier to travel in the summer, when unpaved roads were drier. Acting companies visited many cities and towns throughout England; although there were no playhouses in Norwich, Coventry, and Gloucester the players performed their plays there before the local townspeople. In *Hamlet* Shakespeare dramatizes the visit of a group of touring players, who put on one of their pieces, slightly altered, in a palace hall. *Hamlet* itself travelled the country, however, and was seen in other places outside London: the first printed edition of the play (1603) announced that it had been acted in both Oxford and Cambridge, 'and elsewhere'.

The most elusive of all questions about Shakespeare's company is also the one to to which we should most like to have the answer: How did they play *Hamlet*? Even today describing the effect of acting is an impressionistic endeavour, as we realize if we read a number of different newspaper reviews of a play we happen to have seen, or indeed if after the show we compare our own reactions with those of friends. We can readily imagine that Elizabethan performances of Shakespeare's plays were different from those we see today, perhaps assuming that modern productions are more 'natural' in their effect than what we might take to be the rather 'formal', possibly rather declamatory style of performance in 1600. Both the terms I place in quotation marks are notoriously vague, however, and especially are culturally and temporally determined. What we find 'natural' in acting now would not have been considered so fifty years ago; current films will look odd and stagey in some years' time. Acting styles were changing in Shakespeare's day also, probably more rapidly than today. The rhetorical brio appropriate to delivering the grandiloquent lines of Marlowe and Kyd was the subject of mockery ten years later. Ensign Pistol, in *2 Henry IV*, is in love with the sweeping gestures, both verbal and physical, of a theatrical style that by 1598 could be counted on to look and sound amusingly out of date.

A further point follows from this one. To a degree, the style of a text determined the style of the playing, and still does so. Moreover, many Shakespeare texts have a great range of styles, and the acting must adjust itself accordingly. Romeo may be rather ridiculous in his first moody affectation of love, fast and funny with Mercutio, but must register the intensity of the lyricism once he sees Juliet, and in the famous balcony scene that follows.

Elizabethan actors no doubt dealt with the rhythms of dramatic verse more readily than their modern counterparts, since poetry was a chief medium of the contemporary theatre, as it no longer is. Players would have known a great many more poetic lines, as we have seen, when they learnt the parts for a new play. In a theatre where words were so important a strong and supple voice must have been one of the first requirements of an actor, and it is not surprising that the companies made up entirely of boy players, popular in the earlier Elizabethan period and again around the turn of the century, were connected with choirs: the Children of the Chapel were treble singers of church music for the queen, and Paul's Boys sang in the choir of St Paul's Cathedral. A naturally strong voice which had been trained, then, might lead one to a career on the stage. But the visual effect of the player was just as important. Contemporary manuals of oratory stress that effective speakers should exercise 'the three Vs': *vox, vultus, vita* (voice, facial expression, and literally 'life' – animation, we might say). In a passage from *Love's Labour's Lost* the all-important combination of speech and bodily gesture becomes 'the two As', as Boyet describes the efforts of the lords of Navarre to train the page Mote in a speech of praise he is to address to the French ladies:

Action and accent did they teach him there.
'Thus must thou speak', and 'thus thy body bear'. (5.2.99–100)

The word 'action' is also crucial to the most famous dramatic discussion of contemporary acting, Hamlet's comments to the players (*Hamlet* 3.2). Although some modern commentators have suggested that Shakespeare's fellows had a coded repertoire of hand and arm gestures with specific meanings, Hamlet tells the players not to 'saw the air too much' with their hands, and modern experience in the new Globe shows that small gestures and facial expressions can be seen quite well at a distance. It is also clear that, as on the modern stage and screen, the face was expected to be the actor's chief visual medium of communication, in both comedy and tragedy. The leading early comedian Richard Tarlton, who died in 1588, had a famous gag of sticking his head out from the tiring-house entry, and peering bemusedly at the audience, to great delight. And an elegy written after the death of the great Richard Burbage in 1619 speaks of his acting the part of a lover 'with so true an eye', allowing the audience to read the emotional register of the character through his gaze.

When Burbage played a lover the object of his affections would have been performed by a boy, perhaps his own apprentice, wearing a wig and a woman's dress. This convention was certainly the most formal characteristic of Shakespearian playing in that it employed a frankly theatrical representation of reality, and it is hard today to imagine that Elizabethan and Jacobean performances of female roles could have matched those of modern actresses in power and subtlety. One cannot argue the defence very far, having no evidence, but there are two points to remember in considering the difference between Shakespeare's stage and our own. First, audiences in Shakespeare's day were used to the convention, and didn't think twice about it, other than when comparing the relative skill of individual performers in the parts, or when they were reminded about it by the play itself (as they are, for example, in *The Two Gentlemen of Verona* (4.4.101–70), perhaps Shakespeare's very first play). Second, although the boys were formally apprentices they were evidently very skilled, or they would not have been entrusted with some of the longest and most taxing parts in Shakespeare's plays: Juliet, Viola, Lady Macbeth, and Cleopatra. At any given time a company must have sought to keep two or three boy players at the peak of their power; it is rare that a play calls on more than that number of principal female roles. Hamlet jokes that puberty and a breaking voice would put an end to a boy's career in female parts, but evidence from later in the seventeenth century suggests that some specialists in such roles could continue playing them into their twenties, presumably training their voices to retain a higher register.

The women's gowns worn by the boy players formed part of the acting company's stock of costumes, on which a good deal of money was spent. It is an overstatement to call Shakespeare's stage 'bare', since it was colourfully painted and decorated with hanging cloths, but it remained largely unchanged from scene to scene, with the exception of moments when essential large properties were carried on to the stage: Desdemona's bed at the end of *Othello*, for example. Otherwise visual dynamism and variety were given to the theatrical space by the movement of the colourfully and richly dressed actors across its expanse. An inventory made by Edward Alleyn about 1598 lists costumes made of velvet, damask, silk, and cloth of gold, trimmed with fur and metallic lace. All these materials were expensive, and the tailors' work to make them up added considerably to the cost of costumes. A black velvet gown made for the role of Anne Frankford at the première of *A Woman Killed with Kindness* (Rose, 1603) cost six pounds thirteen shillings, more than the six pounds Thomas Heywood was paid for writing the play. Costumes for new plays were, given such expenses, a mixture of new and old, drawn from the wardrobe stock. Certain generic costumes were endlessly reused, no doubt: Friar Lawrence's robe in *Romeo and Juliet* would have been worn again by Friar Francis in *Much Ado*, a few years later. Special costumes marked special characters: Shylock draws attention to his 'Jewish gaberdine'. As for the function of costumes in marking a historical period, the Elizabethan approach was probably rather eclectic, following Renaissance graphic representation in that respect: in sixteenth-century paintings figures from remote classical or biblical history might be dressed in contemporary fashions and fabrics, and be set in contemporary townscapes. The medieval wars fought on the Elizabethan stage in the chronicle and history plays were represented, Ben Jonson scathingly said, by 'three rusty swords'. He was exaggerating, but the armour on stage at the Globe for the battle of Agincourt is far more likely to have been Elizabethan than 'correct' early fifteenth-century pieces. The Globe's theatrical armour, in fact, probably reappeared in a wide range of fictional contexts. Shakespeare and his contemporaries knew a certain amount about the archaeology of Roman costumes, but the players are unlikely to have made more than occasional indications of classical style in the costumes for the Roman plays. In the text of *Julius Caesar*, indeed, the conspirators in Act 2 are described as wearing hats and cloaks like Elizabethan gentlemen. A surviving sketch of characters from *Titus Andronicus* shows a mixture of contemporary and conventionally 'antique' clothing, while Tamora is dressed as a timeless fairy-tale queen, in a long dress and a crown.[1]

The attention which the players sought from their audiences through such display also attracted criticism. The preacher John Stockwood in 1578 lamented the decay of public morality in a city where theatres were more popular than churches: 'Will not a filthy play with the blast of a trumpet sooner call thither a thousand, than an hour's tolling of a bell bring to the sermon a hundred?' Such religious opposition to the players can easily be called 'Puritan', but by no means all Puritans, if by that term we mean those people in favour of more radical Protestant reform of the English Church, were opposed to playgoing. The rhetoric which excoriated plays and players as sources of immorality and uncleanness was something of a 'hellfire' tradition, partly inherited from the early Church fathers' attacks on the immorality of the late Roman theatres, and was an attitude adopted by a religious right wing with varying individual shades of theological character. The players themselves would have been more seriously concerned with the bureaucratic opposition of the civic authorities, who were charged with keeping public peace and order, and were understandably nervous about potentially unruly assemblies of large numbers of people. The Lord Mayor of London regularly requested the Privy Council – the highest executive body of the royal government – to suspend the players' licences and to close down the playhouses. Once again, a certain amount of the rhetoric of such requests was for show: the mayor and aldermen were concerned to protect their prerogative to administer the city themselves, and jurisdiction over a playhouse run by the King's Men, for example, was not entirely a clear matter. In the immediate neighbourhood playhouses were probably more welcome than the official complaints about disorders and affrays might suggest, since they increased what these days would be called the local tax base: merchants could sell goods to the theatregoers, and the players seem generally to have acted as good neighbours, living in the area, and contributing to the funds for the poor of the local parish.

Playgoers

How many thousands went to the playhouses, and how unruly were they, in fact? To answer such questions we have to distinguish different periods in the development of the Elizabethan and Jacobean theatre, since the number and the kinds of playhouses changed over the course of Shakespeare's lifetime, as did the audiences they attracted. Playhouses were built in London because it had a large population, which grew quickly in the seventeenth century. By 1616 there were about a third of a million people living there, from whom the regular playgoers came – those who went to see plays month after month and year after year. In addition, London drew many visitors, both those from abroad, like Thomas Platter, and from other parts of the kingdom on commercial and legal business. Foreign visitors particularly went to the playhouses since they were one of the sights of London: nothing else quite like them was to be found anywhere else in Europe, and the English players had a high reputation.

Between 1590 and 1600 two large playhouses seem to have served to accommodate most playgoers: on days when both the Rose and the Theatre were packed there would have been about five thousand people watching plays. There were other playhouses – the Curtain and the Swan – and at least two inns in the city where plays were occasionally seen, but the normal market would seem to have supported two principal places. Only occasionally would they both have been full, so perhaps between two and three thousand people visited theatres on an average day. To go to the playhouse one would have needed both money and time, of which money was probably more available to many. Plays were shown in the afternoon for a period of two or three hours, and a working day for labourers, apprentices, and journeymen normally lasted from dawn to dusk. Such people would have had to wait for holidays to see plays. In *Pierce Penniless* (1592) Thomas Nashe satirically listed those free in the afternoons as courtiers, legal students from the Inns of Court, and soldiers. He does not mention women, but it is clear that many women from the middle classes and the gentry went to the theatres. Satirical and critical accounts of audiences single out the deviant figures of thieves and prostitutes, who no doubt frequented theatres, though not with the prominence moralistic satires would suggest.

Basic admission to the Curtain playhouse in 1599, Thomas Platter recorded, cost a penny: for that sum one could stand in the yard to watch the play. Seated accommodation cost a penny more, with the very best seats at a total of threepence. To go to the Globe and theatres like it was not especially expensive; prices at the Blackfriars and similar indoor playhouses were always higher – the cheapest admission cost sixpence – with a consequent effect on the social level of the audiences.

That Shakespeare's plays were performed to a socially mixed audience, then, as has often been stated, is broadly true, if we remember that the very highest (a few) and the very lowest (many) would not have been at the Globe. The elite expected that the players would come to them, and the impoverished had no pennies to spare on the theatre. Many contemporary accounts of the behaviour of the audience are, once again, satirical exaggerations. That audiences were excessively noisy, rowdy, or inattentive as a matter of course is hardly to be believed of theatres where much of the playgoers' pleasure was to be derived from listening. In a full theatre, remarks the anonymous writer of the character of 'An Excellent Actor' (1615), 'you will think you see so many lines drawn from the circumference of so many ears, while the actor is the centre'. An audience's approval and disapproval, during the performance and after it, were certainly more freely expressed than in a modern theatre, where audiences are constrained by darkness and a prevailing etiquette of patient quietness, so that the actor at the centre had to control the kind of attention the scene required. 'Tedious' actors, a passage from *Richard II* reminds us, could soon lose an audience's interest (5.2.23–8).

The wide variety of Shakespeare's plays reflects the tastes of the contemporary theatre. Their isolation as complex works of literature may make us forget that the plays were written – and sometimes rewritten – for a market. Shakespeare's genres and subject-matter were designed to fit in with the demands of a playgoing public, and to compete for an audience with material offered by rival playing companies. That his plays proved themselves in the theatre is shown not so much by their appearance in print as by their survival in the repertory of the King's Men after Shakespeare's retirement and death: many were still being acted and still drawing audiences when the theatres were closed in 1642 at the outbreak of the Civil War.

Notes

1. This manuscript drawing, probably by Henry Peacham, is generally not believed to be a representation of Shakespeare's play in performance. The problems of the drawing and the accompanying text are reviewed by R. A. Foakes, *Illustrations of the English Stage 1580–1642* (Stanford University Press, 1985), pp. 48–51. Recently June Schlueter has claimed that the scene in the drawing is that of a German play derived from Shakespeare: see June Schlueter, 'Rereading the Peacham Drawing', *Shakespeare Quarterly* 50 (1999), 171–84.

Reading list

Astington, John H., *English Court Theatre 1558–1642* (Cambridge University Press, 1999).

Barroll, Leeds, *Politics, Plague, and Shakespeare's Theater* (Ithaca, N.Y.: Cornell University Press, 1991).

Beckerman, Bernard, *Shakespeare at the Globe, 1599–1609* (New York: Macmillan, 1962).

Bowsher, Julian, *The Rose Theatre* (London: Museum of London, 1998).

Chambers, E. K., *The Elizabethan Stage*, 4 vols. (Oxford: Clarendon Press, 1923).

Foakes, R. A., 'Playhouses and Players', in *The Cambridge Companion to English Renaissance Drama*, ed. A. R. Braunmuller and Michael Hattaway (Cambridge University Press, 1990), pp. 1–52.

Gurr, Andrew, *Playgoing in Shakespeare's London*, 2nd edn (Cambridge University Press, 1996).

The Shakespearean Stage 1574–1642, 3rd edn (Cambridge University Press, 1992).

Hattaway, Michael, *Elizabethan Popular Theatre* (London: Routledge, 1982).

Hodges, C. Walter, *The Globe Restored*, 2nd edn (London: Oxford University Press, 1968).

Ingram, William, *The Business of Playing* (Ithaca, N.Y.: Cornell University Press, 1992).

Knutson, Roslyn Lander, *The Repertory of Shakespeare's Company* (Fayetteville: University of Arkansas Press, 1991).

Mulryne, J. R. and Margaret Shewring, eds., *Shakespeare's Globe Rebuilt* (Cambridge University Press, 1997).

Orrell, John, *The Quest for Shakespeare's Globe* (Cambridge University Press, 1983).

Somerset, Alan, '"How Chances It They Travel?" Provincial Touring, Playing Places, and the King's Men', *Shakespeare Survey* 47 (1994), 45–60.

Thomson, Peter, *Shakespeare's Professional Career* (Cambridge University Press, 1992).

8

ANNE BARTON

The London scene: City and Court

'In the south suburbs', Antonio tells Sebastian in *Twelfth Night*, 'at the Elephant / Is best to lodge' (3.3. 39–40). Illyria may be a geographically remote and fictitious country. Its capital, where the comedy unfolds, often seems to shadow a more familiar city, and not just because there was, in fact, an Elizabethan inn called the Elephant in the High Street of Southwark, that London suburb south of the Thames in which Shakespeare's Globe playhouse stood. Like London, Illyria's capital is close to the sea, and also to wooded country in which its ruler can be urged to divert himself by hunting deer *par force* – on horseback, with hounds. According to Antonio, Orsino's city is renowned for its 'memorials and the things of fame' (23): churches, private monuments, and public buildings like those John Stow had described with loving care in his great *Survey of London* (1598/1603). It is a mercantile centre too, its foreign trade sufficiently important that the inhabitants of another state will even compensate for booty taken in war in order not to disrupt so beneficial a peacetime 'traffic'. In many streets, as Antonio alerts Sebastian when lending him his purse, pretty but unnecessary things are displayed for sale, 'idle' luxuries likely to attract a tourist's eye. Then, as Sebastian will soon (momentously) discover, there is the Countess Olivia's mansion, the equivalent of those great residences of the nobility (Somerset House, or Leicester House) which lined the Thames from London proper to Westminster, an abode endowed with gardens, a private chapel, and a large, well-staffed household. Orsino's court too, although ducal rather than royal, is similar to the one at Elizabeth's and then James's Whitehall in being a centre not only of fashion but of government.

Behind *Twelfth Night*, Shakespeare's London hovers like a ghost: an outline scarcely visible until you look for it. It can be glimpsed fleetingly in certain of his other comedies as well: at a distance in *The Merry Wives of Windsor*, in Dogberry's instructions to the night watchmen of *Much Ado About Nothing*, and above all in the Vienna of that very urban play, *Measure for Measure*. Like Illyria, Vienna is ruled by a duke. But his court too is located in a kind of bastard city: at once foreign and disconcertingly close to home. Before being pulled down at Angelo's command, Mistress Overdone's house 'of resort' (a euphemism for brothel) was to be found in the suburbs, as were most of London's own. The whole fracas, moreover, in Act 2 about what was or was not done to Mistress

Elbow in the supposed bath-house (another euphemism) Mistress Overdone now runs – the altercation that impels Angelo to fling out of his own court with the exasperated but scarcely very judicial wish that 'you'll find good cause to whip them all' (2.1.125) – is rooted firmly in the London Shakespeare's audience knew: from the stewed prunes on offer in the dish that was not exactly china, and the public room called 'The Bunch of Grapes' whose fire Master Froth prefers in winter, down to Escalus' discovery of a well-known brand of civic turpitude. For seven years, any householder in Elbow's ward who finds himself appointed as local constable in the annual election has evaded the office by paying Elbow to undertake its duties for him.

Shakespeare was not unusual in setting comedies in foreign (or entirely fictional) cities, while deliberately evoking, at least in some of them, a place closer to home. Dekker and Middleton's two-part collaboration, *The Honest Whore* (1604), supposedly takes place in Milan. Apart, however, from being seamed with local, specifically London references (the Bear Garden on Bankside, the apprentices' rallying cry of 'Clubs!', St Paul's Cross, or the painted posts customarily set up outside the doors of high-ranking city officials), Part 1 actually ends in Bedlam – the London hospital for mad people outside Bishopsgate – and Part 2 in a similarly undisguised Bridewell, the house of correction for whores and the 'idle poor' in Farringdon Ward Without. Only in *The Merry Wives of Windsor*, in this as in almost all other respects a special case, did Shakespeare allow himself to be topographically so precise in a comedy. But Windsor is only London's neighbour, not the city itself. He was conspicuous in refusing to participate in that vogue for comedies set quite straightforwardly in London that seems to begin with Dekker's *The Shoemaker's Holiday* of 1599, and runs unabated (indeed, with increasing topographical emphasis on particular London localities such as Covent Garden, Hogsdon, Islington, Marylebone, or the Strand) up to the closing of the theatres in 1642. Virtually every other major dramatist writing during these years produced one or more London comedies: Jonson, Chapman, Marston, Middleton, Dekker, Heywood, Massinger, Beaumont, Fletcher, and Shirley. For Shakespeare, on the other hand, London was a place actually to be staged only in his English histories, where it was separated from the present by a considerable gap of time. He was unusual too among his contemporaries in never supplying a text for the Lord Mayor's Show, the annual progress through London that celebrated the new incumbent's assumption of office, any other civic triumph or procession, or for a masque at court. Yet London was the place in which most of his working life was spent.

The City

The city in which the young Shakespeare arrived, at some indeterminate date in the late 1580s, was in a number of respects unique among the capitals of Europe. The river Thames, flowing through it from west to east, had contributed to what, by the end of the sixteenth century, was already an unrivalled commercial success. London enjoyed an easy access to the sea and to trading ports abroad that was the envy of most foreign capitals, and it exploited its position energetically. In 1586, William Camden looked at the harbour and opined that 'a man would say, that seeth the shipping there, that it is, as it were, a very wood of trees disbranched to make glades and let in light, so shaded it is with masts and sails'.[1] The central portion of the city had also developed a system of government, and an independence from the Crown, without parallel elsewhere. Shakespeare's London was really several overlapping cities, not one. At its heart lay the City proper, a densely populated area only about 2 square miles (5 sq km) in extent, stretching north of the river from the Tower of London in the east to Ludgate, just past St Paul's, at its western extremity. It was possible to walk from one end to the other in about half an hour. This was where civic power lay.

The City's twenty-six wards, divided into one hundred and fifteen parishes, spilled over its boundaries in a few cases (Farringdon Ward Without, or Bridge Ward Without) but basically it was contained within mediaeval walls, established originally by the Romans, but later fortified, and pierced by what in Shakespeare's time had become ten gates. Although officially subject to the Crown, the City was essentially autonomous and, over the space of some five hundred years, during which it had occasionally been forced briefly to relinquish some of its privileges, the monarchy (increasingly dependent upon the City for financial loans) had finally learned not to interfere. It was ruled from the Guildhall by a Lord Mayor elected each year from among the twenty-six aldermen, one from each ward, who constituted the Court of Aldermen, and also by the two hundred and twelve elected members of the Common Council, its membership again distributed among the wards. The City's basis was firmly mercantile, vested in the various guilds, or livery companies, into which the merchant classes – the grocers, the mercers, the goldsmiths, the shoemakers, and so on – had organized themselves hundreds of years before. Founded originally to guarantee standards within a particular trade, to regulate the training of apprentices and to safeguard the interests of their adult members, these fraternities had gradually discovered that by co-operating with each other, and setting up a central adminstration, they could govern the City as a whole – overseeing not only its commercial interests but what they saw as its physical, moral, religious, and social (including hygienic) wellbeing.

The thorn in the flesh of the essentially conservative rulers of the City was what would now be called Greater London: the suburbs steadily expanding outside the walls, and the 'liberties'. These last precincts were mostly extramural as well – but not entirely so. Blackfriars and Whitefriars, former monastic establishments dissolved under Henry VIII, lay within the walls. Both, in Shakespeare's time, housed companies of child actors, with Blackfriars eventually providing an alternative playing place for his own company, the King's Men. Over all these areas the City's jurisdiction was limited, yet it was precisely in them that activities deeply offensive to the aldermen and the Common Council burgeoned, chief among them being prostitution, gambling, bear-baiting, and plays. The situation was exacerbated by the fact that London was experiencing a population explosion. From about 15,000 in 1550, it had leaped by Elizabeth's death in 1603 to an estimated 140,000 within the limits of the City itself, with another 40,000 inhabiting the suburbs. Expansion continued throughout and beyond Shakespeare's lifetime, until by the mid-seventeenth century the whole untidy sprawl would constitute the largest city of Europe. Immigration, from other parts of England and from the continent, was entirely responsible for this increase. (The influx of foreigners, many of them fleeing religious persecution abroad, was not always welcome to the natives, a problem Shakespeare addressed in his contribution to *The Book of Sir Thomas More* (1595).) Thanks to crowded and unsalubrious conditions – above all in the confined space of the City itself – births in the metropolis lagged well behind burials, and not just during periodic outbreaks of plague. Even London's rulers came to find residence outside the walls desirable for themselves, and it was in those areas that most of the late sixteenth and early seventeenth century growth took place. Open fields, where young men had once practised archery and citizens walked to take the air on spring and summer evenings, were inexorably built over – as John Stow never ceased to lament.

Stow's *Survey of London*, compiled when its author was already an old man, is largely the celebration of a city whose antiquity he (like other Elizabethans) enjoyed tracing back – if with a good deal of healthy scepticism – to a legendary past. Even as Rome, Stow points out, dignified itself by claiming the Trojan Aeneas as its founder, so Londoners sometimes entertained Geoffrey of Monmouth's fantasy about 'the town that Brutus sought by dreams' (as Sir Thomas Wyatt put it), this particular Brutus being the lineal descendent of Aeneas. Stow was himself a member of the Merchant Taylors guild, and he dedicated the second edition of his book in 1603 to Robert Lee, then Lord Mayor of the City. He seems to have been acquainted with Ben Jonson, but the *Survey* of 1603 conspicuously refuses to notice particular London playhouses, or those who wrote for them, although a few (disapproving) paragraphs do recognize its bear-baiting arenas, and its stews – including certain brothels in Southwark notoriously under the jurisdiction of the Bishop of Winchester. (Hence Pandarus' snide sexual allusion to the hissing goose or prostitute of Winchester in the epilogue to Shakespeare's *Troilus and Cressida*.) Stow had himself perambulated all twenty-six of the City's wards, street by street, as well as venturing outside them into Westminster, and some of the suburbs and liberties – including Southwark's Bankside. In 1598, he did record the names of the Theatre and the Curtain in Shoreditch, but only to strike them out in 1603. That edition makes no mention of what Ben Jonson later called 'the glory of the Bank' – Shakespeare's Globe – even though foreign visitors noted the theatre as impressive. It may well, for Stow, have been the last straw.

Stow's accounts are faithful to much of the city as it was at the time of his writing, but also seamed with nostalgia for the older, less crowded London of his youth, with greater breathing space around it, and more traditional as well as cohesive in its observances and ways. Characteristically, he was happy to memorialize the long-since abolished London mystery cycles once performed at Clerkenwell and Skinners' Well – no texts survive – while dismissing the great contemporary flowering of Elizabethan drama ('Comedies, Tragedies, Interludes, and Histories, both true and feigned: for the acting wherof certain public places have been erected') in about the same tone and as many words as he devoted to cock-fights and tennis.[2] Stow was typical, in this respect, of London's solid middle class, men who thought apprentices wasted too much valuable working-time watching plays, an activity from which they might, in addition, be seduced into attitudes and vices that were anathema to aldermen and members of the Common Council. In addition, they complained, the basest kind of people congregated in the theatre. They would have been happy to shut them down altogether, if only they could, and did manage to do so (sensibly enough) from time to time during outbreaks of plague.

Stow's London, as travellers from abroad amply testified, was a wealthy and beautiful city – at least on the surface, and in certain parts. It was also, on closer inspection, extremely dirty and a hotbed not only of disease but of chicanery and crime. Even Stow felt obliged to chronicle the efforts of London's mayors over the centuries to do something about its increasingly inadequate sewerage system, through periodic cleansings of London's various ditches and water-courses, clogged with filth. (The City's rulers also attempted, through the appointment of official 'scavengers' in the various parishes, to exercise some control over the kitchen middens, piles of refuse, and what was politely called 'night-soil' that tended, especially in the poorer sections of London, to encumber the streets.) Stow's comment, however, at the end of his section on water-courses and ditches – 'I will so leave it, for I cannot help it' – says it all.[3] It was also true that as the pressure on accommodation increased in the expanding City, tenements tended to be erected whose jutting upper stories effectively blocked out light and air from the thoroughfares below, turning them into unhealthy warrens of infection. This was the other side of Spenser's 'silver streaming Thames', alive with river traffic, its banks gaily ornamented with flowers, and of the London so often personified in civic pageants as a majestic lady, her head crowned with turrets and towers, to be glorified in plays like Heywood's two-part *Edward IV* (1599) and *If You Know Not Me, You Know Nobody* (1604/5) or Dekker's *The Shoemaker's Holiday*.

What Shakespeare himself thought of this city of such glaring contrasts can only be conjectured. It was, as it happened, the only place in England for an aspiring, professional actor/dramatist to be. He made both his fortune and his reputation in the capital – like many other provincial men – but he never moved his family from Stratford to London and, when he retired from the theatre, it was to a rural Warwickshire with which he had never lost touch. He did, towards the end of his life, add a London property to those he had accumulated in or near Stratford – a gatehouse in the Blackfriars area – but it was merely an investment: he seems to have had no intention of occupying it himself. In London, he made do with various rented lodgings, one apparently near Bishopsgate, another with the Mountjoy family, purveyors of head-dresses for ladies in Silver Street, Cripplegate Ward (where he was to become involved in an altercation over the daughter's marriage settlement). He can scarcely have been unaware either of the various plays written to celebrate London, or of all those (including works by his friend Ben Jonson) that dramatized its seamy, criminal side: something also being energetically explored throughout the 1590s in the various rogue and 'cony-catching' pamphlets turned out by Dekker, Nashe, and Shakespeare's old detractor Robert Greene. It was only, however, in his English histories, including *Henry VIII*, where London tended to be unavoidable as (at least) a partial setting that he confronted the city directly, in ways that sometimes permit a glimpse of the metropolis he himself knew, not simply of the mediaeval and early Tudor predecessors recorded in his source material.

Understandably, it is when Shakespeare departs from Holinshed and the other chroniclers and begins to invent freely that his own London sometimes flickers into existence. The carriers at Rochester in *1 Henry IV*, struggling out of bed before dawn in an inn lamentably stingy with its chamber-pots, so that 'we leak in your chimney, and your chamber-lye breeds fleas like a loach' (2.1.19–20), are testimony not only to his own probable acquaintance with inferior hostelries on the road into London, but to the increasing need of the metropolis to provision itself from a considerable distance outside. The second carrier's 'gammon of bacon and two razes of ginger' are to be delivered 'as far as Charing-cross', while the ravenous turkeys (a New World import unknown in England until long after the period of the two tetralogies) in the first carrier's pannier are almost certainly heading for 'the Poultry', a specialized market area between the Stocks and Cheapside.

For the idea that the wild young prince and his cronies visit a tavern in London's Eastcheap, Shakespeare was indebted to the old, anonymous play *The Famous Victories of Henry V* (?1586), and possibly to Stow's *Chronicles* (1580). The place itself, however, as realized in the two parts of *Henry IV*, he clearly fleshed out from a knowledge of similar establishments in the London of his day. (Indeed, the long-standing tradition that Falstaff's tavern is called 'The Boarshead', although this is never explicitly stated in either play, may indicate some ready association contemporaries made between Shakespeare's fictional locale and an existing Eastcheap tavern of that name.) Under the management of a husband and wife team (the Quicklys) in Part 1, it looked initially like a bustling, prosperous place, employing apprentices like young Francis (presumably in training to enter the vintners' guild) and enjoying a large, well-behaved clientele. In Part 2, things have fallen off badly. The Host is dead. His widow has taken over the business – as not infrequently happened in London in Shakespeare's time – but trade has apparently dwindled. A tavern dependent upon Falstaff as a lodger, perpetually in arrears with his payments, and given to entertaining not only his raffish followers Nym and Bardolph but Doll Tearsheet the whore, is in danger of being condemned as a disorderly house. Indeed Mistress Quickly has already been summoned before Master Tisick, the local magistrate deputizing for the alderman of the ward, to answer charges that, although previously well thought-of, she is now 'in an ill name' for the 'swaggering companions' who patronize her establishment. The City officials took a dim view of such places. Apart, however, from the extremely doubtful prospect of one day becoming Lady Falstaff, the Hostess retains something of which she can be proud: Hal, the madcap Prince of Wales, can still pay her an informal visit, linking – in however unorthodox a way – the heart of the City with the Court at Westminster.

Stow (quite properly) treats Westminster in his *Survey* as an entity topographically distinct from the City and from its suburbs and liberties. Yet already, expansion westward from the centre was eroding the old boundary. Later, under James I and Charles I, property developments such as the Duke of Bedford's in Covent Garden, master-minded by Inigo Jones, or the proliferation of fashionable residences along the Strand, were to blur the line of demarcation further, while maintaining the City's venerable independence from royal Westminster. Communication remained close between these two centres of London power, something neatly symbolized in the Lord Mayor's Show, which escorted the new incumbent in state from the Guildhall, just north of Cheapside, to Westminster and back, after he had taken his oath of office, and (crucially) been confirmed in both places. This route significantly resembled the one taken by Elizabeth I on the day before her coronation in 1558, when she went in procession through the City along the great artery of Cheapside to St Paul's and Temple Bar, accepting a Bible and a purse of gold from its representatives along the way. James I's coronation procession in 1604 cannily reinscribed her route, this time with Shakespeare and eight other members of the newly patented King's Men, to whom a royal issue of four and a half yards of red cloth apiece had been made for the occasion, probably somewhere in the throng. (Charles I's high-handed refusal to follow the example of his two predecessors, after the City had put in hand elaborate preparations for the event, can be seen as the beginning of a souring of relations with the Crown that would lead to the City's defection to the Parliamentarian side at the outbreak of the Civil War.)

The London of Shakespeare's English histories before *Henry VIII* is both rooted in its past, as recorded in the chronicles that were his primary source, and shot through with details and allusions reflecting the capital he himself knew. Most striking here is the Chorus that introduces Act 5 of *Henry V*, with its comparison of the great civic welcome that greeted the victor of Agincourt on his return from France with what would happen now should the Earl of Essex come triumphant from Ireland, 'bringing rebellion broached on his sword'. Again,

London would 'pour out her citizens, / The Mayor and all his brethren in best sort'. This was not, of course, to be, but the sense of continuity across the centuries matters nonetheless. It was a continuity reinforced by the antiquity of many of London's landmarks and monuments. 'Julius Caesar's ill-erected Tower', as the Tower of London is mis-described in *Richard II* (in fact it was begun by William the Conqueror), is a sinister and frequent presence in Shakespeare's histories, just as it was in his own London and remains, to some extent, today. Equally familiar to members of his audience were such venerable structures as the old St Paul's, Westminster Palace and Westminster Hall, Westminster Abbey, the Inns of Court, the Guildhall, and Baynard's Castle – not to mention street and place names: Cheapside, Smithfield, Fish Street, Cornhill Street, Eastcheap, or Holborn – all survivors of the late mediaeval London presented in the majority of the histories. Only *King John* stays entirely clear of the metropolis, in terms both of reference and setting.

Whatever he thought of the City's hostility to his own profession, in *Richard III* Shakespeare took some steps to redeem its credit. It is clear in Hall that Edmond Shaa, Lord Mayor of London, proved entirely co-operative at the time the Lord Protector was plotting to seize the crown from his young nephew Edward V: 'upon trust of his own advancement, where he was of a proud heart highly desirous, [he] took on him to frame the city' to Richard and Buckingham's will.[4] Shakespeare's Lord Mayor, by contrast, may be naive – in the end, he is entirely taken in by Richard's charade of religious piety – but there is no suggestion that he is self-seeking or corrupt. Urged by Buckingham in Act 3 to persuade the citizens of the bastardy of Edward IV's children, he simply (to the duke's disgust) summarizes what Buckingham has just said, without adding to it 'any warrant from himself'. The citizens are not impressed. Shakespeare's alterations to his source here are interesting because, without exactly falsifying history, he nonetheless has slanted it so as to make plain that these London citizens are in a very different class from those fickle, impressionable Roman plebeians who throw up their sweaty nightcaps in *Julius Caesar* – or indeed from most, though significantly not all, of Jack Cade's followers in *2 Henry VI*. He had already, in Act 2, scene 3 of *Richard III*, invented an anonymous trio, meeting in the street, who discuss with dignity and considerable political acumen the implications of Edward IV's death for an England once again to be 'governed by a child'. Now, the citizens' 'wilful silence' when urged by Buckingham to cry 'God save King Richard!' has to be explained away by an embarrassed Mayor: 'the people were not used / To be spoke to but by the Recorder' – their own civil magistrate, as opposed to a representative of the Crown (3.7.29–30). The Mayor is, of course, in a tight place, but his excuse brings to the surface something important: the fact that London has to be won over by Westminster, and that its own protocol and governmental hierarchy are things even dukes and kings need to respect.

The Court

It was, however, Westminster, rather than the City, the Court rather than the Guildhall, of which Shakespeare was (necessarily) most aware. Created originally as the royal seat of the Norman kings, Westminster had become by the fifteenth century the centre of administration and government for the country as a whole. In Shakespeare's time, it consisted mainly of a palace – incorporating the great Hall constructed originally by the Conqueror's son William Rufus, nearly 240 feet (73 m) long and 40 (12 m) in height – the Abbey, and various associated buildings and spaces, the most important of which was the comparatively recent, adjacent palace of Whitehall. As York House (under which name it figures in Shakespeare and Fletcher's *Henry VIII*), Whitehall had been built by Wolsey as a lavish residence for himself. After the Cardinal's fall in 1529, it was appropriated and enlarged by Henry, effectively becoming, under him, and his Tudor and Stuart successors, for the greater part of the year, the 'Court'. Much of the monarch's domestic administration, in charge of his Steward, as well as the law courts and Parliament, continued to operate from the old palace complex nearby. Whitehall, however, housed the sovereign's person, in a series of carefully graded spaces extending outward from the intimacy of the Bedchamber and various withdrawing chambers, access to which was denied to all but a select few, to the somewhat more populous but still elite Privy Chamber, the Presence Chamber, where the monarch could sometimes be viewed – by those with any right to be present at court at all – receiving ambassadors and other guests, or dining in state, the Great Chamber, and finally, a Hall. Over all this territory, the Lord Chamberlain held sway.

During holiday seasons, meaning (essentially) Christmas and Shrovetide, plays and masques were put on in the Great Chamber, the Hall, or the Banqueting House, the last a specially designed, freestanding structure within the Whitehall complex. The first, temporary Banqueting House, built under Elizabeth to receive the French commissioners in 1581, was demolished in 1606 by James I, who replaced it with a more impressive but still wooden, galleried structure. This version (which burned to the ground in 1619, to be succeeded by the magnificent Inigo Jones stone building that still exists) is one with which Shakespeare must have been very familiar. He is likely, indeed, to have performed there with other members of his company, not only in plays from the repertory of the King's Men but in court masques, which relied upon professional actors for the speaking parts. As James's own liveried servants, granted their royal patent only a few weeks after he was proclaimed king, Shakespeare's company enjoyed a certain prestige. They had already been fortunate, during the latter part of Elizabeth's reign, in the patronage of George Carey, second Lord Hunsdon, the queen's second cousin and, from 1597, Lord Chamberlain (see also chapter 7, Playhouses, Players, and Playgoers in Shakespeare's Time, by John

Astington). Illness, however, forced Hunsdon to retire from this influential post in 1601, and after the death of the queen it was conferred officially upon someone else. It must have come as a considerable relief to the former Lord Chamberlain's Men, whose patron Hunsdon was now of little use to them, to find themselves so rapidly put under royal protection in the new reign.

Exactly why they were so favoured remains a matter of debate, but neither Shakespeare nor the great actor Richard Burbage is likely to have been the immediate cause. Elizabeth had clearly liked plays and, in 1583, singled out her own royal company, henceforth known as the Queen's Men. Indeed, had it not been for her insistence that plays were necessary for her 'solace' at court, the Privy Council would not have been able so consistently to override the City's objections to the public theatres, places in which (so the convenient fiction went) plays had to be rehearsed before the best of them appeared at court. If the courtier Dudley Carleton is to be believed, James by contrast took 'no extraordinary pleasure in them'.[5] His fit of ill temper during the masque *Pleasure Reconciled to Virtue* (1618) – 'Devil take you all, dance!' – suggests that it was for the dancing, not Jonson's beautifully structured text, that he had come. Shakespeare may have intended *Macbeth* to compliment James as a descendant of Banquo, the Duke's reluctance in *Measure for Measure* to 'stage' himself to the eyes of the populace as a flattering allusion to James's well-known aversion to making large-scale public appearances, and Prospero's renunciation even of 'white' magic at the end of *The Tempest* as a concession to the monarch's uncompromising views about necromancy. Given the choice, James would almost certainly have preferred to be slaughtering stags at Royston rather than sitting through a court performance of *The Winter's Tale*. That the number of theatrical performances recorded at Whitehall, and at Greenwich Palace and Hampton Court, actually increased during James's reign is almost certainly due to the fact that he, unlike Elizabeth, had a family. Queen Anne, Prince Henry, and Prince Charles were theatre-lovers. All three participated at various points in court masques. Anne is even said to have made a one-off appearance at a public playhouse – something neither Elizabeth, James, nor Charles I ever did – and the royal patent issued to the King's Men in 1603 was soon followed in 1604 by the designation (though as yet without patent) of the former Admiral's Men as Prince Henry's servants, and Worcester's Men as Queen Anne's. On a number of occasions, all three companies were to find themselves summoned to entertain a royal audience at court that turned out not to include King James.

There is no evidence – and small likelihood – that Shakespeare ever enjoyed even that approximation to a personal relationship with King James that Jonson seems to have had. Although (along with other members of the King's Men) he was made a Groom of the Chamber in 1604, this 'honour' – also extended to some members of the Queen's company – implied little more than the occasional need at court for extras to augment the native entourage during the visits of important foreign emissaries. It is improbable that James ever had more than the

slightest idea who Shakespeare was, or that this dramatist who never wrote a
court masque, never collaborated with Inigo Jones, and lacked his friend Jonson's
freight of classical learning, succeeded in gaining access to royal chambers
beyond the relatively public ones at Whitehall, let alone converse with the king.
Under Elizabeth, his situation may have been different. Her court, as historians
have established, was more distant, less 'participatory', than that of James – a
consequence, in part, of the fact that she was a woman, surrounded in the most
private rooms of the royal suite almost entirely by other women.[6] The idea that
the queen herself commanded Shakespeare to write *The Merry Wives of Windsor*
(in fourteen days), because she wanted to see a play about Falstaff in love, was
first recorded by John Dennis in 1702. The story may be apocryphal, but its existence points nonetheless to a traditional association of Shakespeare with the
Virgin Queen, more than with her successor, that is underpinned, to some
extent, by the plays themselves.

At the end of *Henry VIII*, Cranmer utters a prophecy about Anne Boleyn's
infant daughter that many people, a decade after Elizabeth's death, thought had
been fulfilled: 'She shall be / . . . A pattern to all princes living with her, / And
all that shall succeed' (5.4.20, 22–3). Tact required Cranmer to look forward to
the reign of King James as well, but he does so both more briefly and in less
hyperbolic terms. The underlying suggestion is that the Stuart reign is to be celebrated as a continuation of Elizabeth's, an affinity that by 1613 was increasingly
open to doubt. Although her last years were less than happy, soured by the Essex
plot, and by what had become a grotesque disparity between reality and the myth
of the eternally beautiful maiden queen, the memory of Elizabeth tended to
shine ever more brightly as the seventeenth century advanced, against mounting
dissatisfaction with the policies and behaviour of James. Shakespeare's own attitude to the two monarchs his theatre company occasionally entertained is, as
usual, hard to discern. It is true, however (although scholars and critics have continually tried to ferret out covert allusions), that James is mentioned explicitly
only once in the plays (in *Henry VIII*) while unmistakably direct references to
Elizabeth occur not only there but in *Henry V*, *A Midsummer Night's Dream*, *The
Merry Wives of Windsor*, and the Sonnets. They are all the more remarkable
given what appears to have been Shakespeare's ingrained reluctance to invoke
living contemporaries.

That Elizabeth is 'the mortal moon [who] hath her eclipse endured' in Sonnet
107 has almost always been acknowledged and, except for a few recalcitrant pro-
ponents of an early date for all the Sonnets, the 'sad augurs [who] mock their own
presage' in the following line taken as a reference to the unexpectedly easy trans-
ference of rule to her Stuart successor. But James himself is oddly depersonal-
ized and shadowy, indeed present in the sonnet only obliquely through glancing
references to the balm used to anoint sovereigns during the coronation ceremony,
and to the 'peace' which, in 1603, had belied premonitions of civil war. As 'our
gracious Empress', Elizabeth figures unequivocally in the Chorus introducing

Act 5 of *Henry V*. Mistress Quickly may briefly play the role of Fairy Queen in the Herne the Hunter episode that concludes *The Merry Wives*; the 'radiant queen' invoked by Pistol in this last act is clearly Elizabeth herself. The play may or may not have been intended to honour Shakespeare's patron the Lord Chamberlain, Lord Hunsdon, shortly before his installation at Windsor as a Knight of the Garter in April 1597. Certainly this hypothesis makes sense of the elaborate instructions to the fairies about the cleaning and scouring of Windsor Castle, including the Garter stalls, that it should be 'Worthy the owner, and the owner it' (5.5.57). Though the passage may serve too, less glamorously, as a reminder that the continual shifting about of the court from one palace to another, not to mention its various summer progresses through the country, are likely to have been less a product of Elizabeth's or James's restlessness than of the periodic need, in a time of primitive sanitation, to clear up the mess inevitably generated by so many people packed under one roof.

All the various attempts to associate the first performance of *A Midsummer Night's Dream* with a specific noble wedding, at which the queen was present, have so far failed. That is also true of efforts to identify the entertainment described by Oberon in the same play (2.1.158), involving a mermaid on a dolphin's back, and an abortive attempt by Cupid to strike the 'fair vestal thronèd by the west' with one of his love arrows, with a particular and real one attended by Elizabeth. There can, however, be no doubt as to the identity of the impervious 'fair vestal' herself. As for Elizabeth's court, traces of it can be identified, heavily disguised, in the course of the action: the ruler's addiction to the chase – like her father Henry VIII, the queen took much pleasure in hunting – even, in the form of the changeling boy, the disputes that often arose about Wards of Court – well-born orphans legally transferred to someone else's protection during their period of minority. Philostrate, 'our usual manager of mirth' (5.1.35), who has carefully previewed all the various entertainments on offer to Theseus and Hippolyta 'on their wedding day at night', and gives the Duke a list of them, is the equivalent of Henry Tilney, the queen's Master of the Revels. An official under the authority of the Lord Chamberlain, it was his job to select suitable plays for performance at court, censor them (when necessary), and arrange for the erection of a temporary stage, and scaffolding for the spectators, in whichever palace chamber had been designated for the performance. In the earlier Tudor court, his equivalent had also, on occasion, provided props and minimal scenery, but by Shakespeare's time the professional actors seem to have been accustomed to bring their own – although not quite in the sense understood by Peter Quince and his company in the troublesome matter of Moonshine and Wall.

The folly and corruption of courts was a favourite theme of Elizabethan and (especially) Jacobean dramatists. Prudence dictated that they firmly dissociate such courts either in time or place from the one at Whitehall. Yet, even before the scandal of the Overbury murder in 1613, which would disastrously implicate King James's favourite Robert Carr, Earl of Somerset, Italy had often looked suspiciously like a dramatic surrogate for somewhere much nearer at hand. Shakespeare, whether writing under Elizabeth or James, took little part in this. In Le Beau, Duke Frederick's foppish courtier in *As You Like It*, Paroles in *All's Well That Ends Well*, whose soul, as Lafeu snappishly remarks, is his clothes, or the water-fly Osric in *Hamlet*, whose affectations both of speech and dress are so mercilessly pilloried by the prince, he did venture a little way into the territory so enthusiastically explored by Jonson, Middleton, Webster, Massinger, Fletcher, and other contemporary dramatists. But only a little way. His courts, as in the early histories, may be riven by faction, and his rulers – Henry VI, Richard III, or Claudius and Lear – are often wicked or inept. From the kind of satiric anatomy of daily life in the Court that other dramatists so frequently indulged in, he seems to have shied away. Indeed, in the late plays, although Antiochus, Cymbeline, and Leontes behave appallingly, their courts tend to be models of fair-minded (and often dissenting) propriety. Nobody believes that Hermione is unfaithful, or trusts Cymbeline's wicked queen. When Prince Florizel discovers that Autolycus is a rogue, he turns him out of his service. As with the city of London in which he lived, Shakespeare seems to have been determined, in his plays, to reflect only sporadically, and at a distance, the two very different Elizabethan and Jacobean courts whose patronage he came to enjoy, and to do all this with a lack of social detail or animosity that was singular in his time.

Notes

1. See the useful collection, *London in the Age of Shakespeare: An Anthology*, ed. Lawrence Manley (London and Sydney: Croom Helm, 1986), p. 35.
2. John Stow, *The Survey of London*, ed. C. L. Kingsford, 2 vols. (Oxford University Press, 1908), I, 93.
3. Stow, *Survey of London*, I, 20.
4. Edward Hall, *The Union of the Two Noble . . . Famelies of Lancastre and Yorke*, in *Narrative and Dramatic Sources of Shakespeare*, ed. Geoffrey Bullough, 8 vols. (London: Routledge, 1957–75), III, 269.
5. Quoted in Leeds Barroll, *Politics, Plague, and Shakespeare's Theater* (Ithaca, N.Y.: Cornell University Press, 1991), p. 27.
6. See David Starkey's Introduction to *The English Court: From the Wars of the Roses to the Civil War*, ed. D. A. L. Starkey (London: Longman, 1987).

Reading list

Archer, I. W., *The Pursuit of Stability: Social Relations in Elizabethan London* (Cambridge University Press, 1991).

Astington, John H., *English Court Theatre 1558–1642* (Cambridge University Press, 1999).

Barroll, Leeds, *Politics, Plague, and Shakespeare's Theater* (Ithaca, N.Y.: Cornell University Press, 1991).

Beier, A. L and R. Finlay, eds., *London 1500–1700: The making of the Metropolis* (London: Longman, 1986).

Bergeron, D. M., *English Civic Pageantry 1558–1642* (London: Edward Arnold, 1971).

Boulton, Jeremy, *Neighbourhood and Society: A London Suburb in the Sixteenth Century* (Cambridge University Press, 1987).

Dillon, Janette, *Theatre, Court and City, 1595–1610: Drama and Social Space in London* (Cambridge Universty Press, 2000).

Foster, F. F., *The Politics of Stability: A Portrait of the Rulers in Elizabethan London* (London: Royal Historical Society, 1977).

Harding, Vanessa, 'Early Modern London 1550–1700', *The London Journal* vol. xx: no. 2 (London: Longman, 1995).

Manley, L., *Literature and Culture in Early Modern London* (Cambridge University Press, 1995).

Manley, L., ed., *London in the Age of Shakespeare: An Anthology* (London and Sydney: Croom Helm, 1986).

Montrose, Louis Adrian, *The Purpose of Playing: Shakespeare and the Cultural Politics of the Elizabethan Theatre* (University of Chicago Press, 1996).

Mullaney, S., *The Place of the Stage: License, Play and Power in Renaissance England* (Chicago and London: University of Chicago Press, 1987).

Paster, Gail Kern, *The Idea of the City in the Age of Shakespeare* (Athens: University of Georgia Press, 1986).

Porter, R., *London: A Social History* (London: Hamish Hamilton, 1994).

Rappaport, S., *Worlds Within Worlds: Structures of Life in Sixteenth Century London* (Cambridge University Press, 1989).

Smith, Bruce R., *The Acoustic World of Early Modern England* (Chicago University Press, 1999).

Smith, D. L., R. Strier and D. Bevington, eds., *The Theatrical City: Culture, Theatre and Politics in London 1576–1649* (Cambridge University Press, 1995).

Starkey, D. A. L., ed., *The English Court: From the Wars of the Roses to the Civil War* (London: Longman, 1987).

Stow, John, *Survey of London* (1598/1603), ed. C. L. Kingsford, 2 vols. (Oxford University Press, 1908, rpt 1968).

9

VALERIE TRAUB

Gender and sexuality in Shakespeare

DURING much of the twentieth century, scholarly interest in the way that issues of gender and sexuality affect the meaning of Shakespeare tended to take a few limited forms. Many critics made note of his witty and intelligent female characters and lauded his depiction of romantic love. Guides to Shakespeare's 'bawdy language' were published to help readers understand his 'dirty' jokes and puns.[1] And rumours of Shakespeare's own homosexuality circulated among readers of the Sonnets. But not until the late 1970s and early 1980s did critics, motivated by the feminist and gay liberation movements, begin a systematic examination of gender and sexuality in the works of 'the patriarchal bard'.[2] Critical conversation since those initial debates has clarified that the aim of a feminist or 'queer' approach is not to find evidence that Shakespeare was sympathetic to the plight of women, or to berate him for being misogynous, or to prove that he was homosexual. Rather, the analysis of gender and sexuality allows us to understand the variety of ways that Shakespeare responded imaginatively to sex, gender, and sexuality as crucial determinants of human identity and political power.

Sex refers to the anatomical and biological distinctions between male and female bodies. Gender refers to those meanings derived from the division of male and female, and thus to the attributes considered appropriate to each: 'masculine' and 'feminine'. Sexuality refers to erotic desires and activities. Whereas anatomical sex is to a large extent 'natural', gender and sexuality exist primarily as constructions of particular societies. What it means to be a woman or a man, or to desire the same or the opposite sex, varies from culture to culture and changes historically. Masculinity, for instance, is typically associated with sexual aggression in our own time, whereas during Shakespeare's life, women were considered to be more lustful than men. And neither gender nor sexuality can be thought of separately from the body, for the body provides the basis for assumptions of gender difference as well as the potential for erotic pleasure.

The beginning of an understanding of gender and sexuality during Shakespeare's life is the patriarchal household. Patriarchy in the late sixteenth century referred to the power of the father over all members of his household – not only his wife and children, but servants or apprentices. The father was likened to the ruler of the realm, and a well-ordered household was supposed to run like a well-ordered state. Early modern culture was resolutely hierarchical, with women, no matter what their wealth or rank, theoretically under the rule of men. Because women generally were believed to be less rational than men, they were deemed to need male protection. Legally, a woman's identity was subsumed under that of her male protector; as a 'feme covert', she had few legal or economic rights. An extreme example of this belief is expressed in *The Taming of the Shrew*, when Petruccio, newly married to Katherine, calls her 'my goods, my chattels. She is my house, / My household-stuff, my field, my barn, / My horse, my ox, my ass, my anything' (3.3.101–3). At the end of the play Katherine appears to acquiesce, as she instructs other women – whether seriously or ironically – to welcome their subservience:

> Thy husband is thy lord, thy life, thy keeper,
> Thy head, thy sovereign, one that cares for thee,
> And for thy maintenance commits his body
> To painful labour both by sea and land,
> To watch the night in storms, the day in cold,
> Whilst thou liest warm at home, secure and safe,
> And craves no other tribute at thy hands
> But love, fair looks, and true obedience,
> Too little payment for so great a debt. (5.2.150–8)

Employing the analogy of household and kingdom, Katherine enjoins other women to accept their 'natural' inferiority. This position of inferiority required women to strive for four virtues: obedience, chastity, silence, and piety. Yet, the existence of the notion of a shrew or scold – as embodied in rebellious characters like Katherine – suggests that not all women obeyed or kept silent. 'Shrew' links female insubordination to unruly female speech, and speech was one of women's most powerful weapons. The force of female speech is borne out in *Othello*, when the 'shrewish' Emilia points to Iago as the cause of Desdemona's murder, and in *The Winter's Tale*, where Paulina continually reminds Leontes of his guilt, and thereby brings about his repentance.

Condemning women as shrews or scolds was a useful tactic for men wary of losing their authority. So too was calling a woman a whore. 'Loose in body and tongue' was a common condemnation, linking female erotic transgression to gossip and scolding. Erotic transgression referred not only to adultery (extramarital sexual intercourse) and fornication (premarital sexual intercourse), but any erotic behaviour that lacked the sanction of father and church. Chastity – defined as virginity for an unmarried woman, and monogamous fidelity for a married woman – was, after a woman's economic position, the most important determinant of her social status. As Laertes warns his sister Ophelia about Hamlet's amorous intentions:

> Then weigh what loss your honour may sustain
> If with too credent ear you list his songs,
> Or lose your heart, or your chaste treasure open

To his unmastered importunity.
Fear it, Ophelia, fear it, my dear sister,
And keep within the rear of your affection,
Out of the shot and danger of desire. (1.3.29–35)

A woman's 'chaste treasure' likewise is the focus of *Much Ado About Nothing*, where the 'nothing' of the title is the reputation Hero loses after being wrongly accused by her betrothed, Claudio, of infidelity. Hero swoons, is taken for dead, and indeed, is metaphorically dead until resurrected by the restoration of her chaste reputation.

While some elite, usually urban, women benefited from the expansion of humanist education in the sixteenth century, and one exceptional woman, Queen Elizabeth I, ruled the realm, the majority of women found their access to the public sphere decreasing, as the economic roles they played in the late medieval period contracted. Recurrent inflation, land shortages, high population growth, and widespread migration and poverty combined to create a 'crisis of order', during which, if 'patriarchy could no longer be taken for granted', it nonetheless developed new, and in some cases quite subtle, tactics for enforcing the subordi-nation of women.[3] Although the Protestant belief in the spiritual equality of men and women accorded some women greater spiritual dignity and power, and fos-tered as well a more 'companionate' and affectionate mode of marriage, these gains did not translate into economic, political, or social equality.[4]

The ideology of chastity, constraints against female speech, and women's con-finement within the domestic household are summed up by the phrase 'the body enclosed', which refers simultaneously to a woman's closed genitals, closed mouth, and her enclosure within the home.[5] 'The body enclosed' encapsulates the prescriptive power of patriarchal doctrine; however, it fails to capture the ways that women asserted their desires and will – their agency – within such ideological constraints. Early modern England was a culture of contradictions, with official ideology often challenged by actual social practice. Competing ver-sions of masculinity and femininity vied for dominance, in a social contestation that is recorded by Shakespeare's plays. The rate of premarital pregnancy was relatively high – and is represented dramatically by the pregnant Juliet of *Measure for Measure*. Women often held considerable power within their own households, overseeing the labour and education of their children and servants – as does Hermione in *The Winter's Tale*. Women did venture out in public, as Shakespeare's own theatre audience, which included women of all social classes, attests. They also held productive roles in the early modern economy – but this is perhaps where Shakespeare is most conservative, for he limits his representa-tion of women's economic labour to that of household servants, tavern-keepers, bawds, and prostitutes. Nonetheless, the pressure of women pushing against patriarchal strictures can be felt throughout Shakespearian drama. When the previously obedient Desdemona frankly proclaims her desire for Othello before the Venetian senate, her father Brabanzio is so astonished that he can only believe her to be bewitched. Nonetheless, she achieves the senate's permission to accompany her newly wed husband to Cyprus.

Because dramatic action in Shakespeare depends on conflict, his plays are more focused on the disruption of the social order – even, in some cases, on a 'world turned upside down' – than on the tranquil reproduction of the household and the state. Dramatic conflict is located within familial, social, and political transitions, particularly in moments of marriage, death, and genealogical succession.[6] Chaos – whether political, domestic, or psychological, and whether experienced as positive or negative – is the basic element through which Shakespeare's protagonists realize their identities. The conclusions of the plays, however, tend to restore the social order. And because chaos is often expressed as an inversion of gender hierarchy, the reconstruction of order tends to reinstate masculine authority.

Traditionally, scholarship has defined Shakespearian comedy as a play that ends in marriage, tragedy as a play that ends in death, and romances as tragedies that end comically (with the restoration of the father's rule and the marriage of his children). Comedies have tended to be viewed as 'romantic' or 'problem', depending on how easily marital closure is attained. In the words of one critic summing up conventional wisdom: 'comedy moves from confusion to order, from ignorance to understanding, from law to liberty, from unhappiness to satisfaction, from separation to union, from barrenness to fertility, from singleness to marriage, from two to one'.[7] But the 'courtship plot' of comedy is not merely a generic convention. Because marriage, reproduction, and inheritance were the basic building-blocks of society, and because gender identity functioned as a central determinant of an individual's social position, the placement of women and men within the hierarchies of the patriarchal household and the negotiation of cultural meanings of masculinity and femininity are animating concerns of each of Shakespeare's genres. (For a discussion of genres, see chapter 6, The Genres of Shakespeare's Plays, by Susan Snyder.)

The importance of gender and sexuality is evident even in the history play, a genre that focuses almost exclusively on the military and political exploits of men. On the one hand, history turns to comedy in the final act of the final play of the Henriad, as the victorious King Henry V 'woos' the French princess Catherine, thereby uniting England and France in a dynastic marriage. But prior to this comic resolution, gender and sexuality crop up as figurative tropes on the battlefield, when a weary if determined Henry attempts to persuade the mayor of the besieged town of Harfleur to open his gates to the invading troops. If not, he vows,

> The gates of mercy shall be all shut up,
> And the fleshed soldier, rough and hard of heart,
> In liberty of bloody hand shall range
> With conscience wide as hell, mowing like grass

Your fresh fair virgins and your flow'ring infants.
What is it then to me if impious war
Arrayed in flames like to the prince of fiends
Do with his smirched complexion all fell feats
Enlinked to waste and desolation?
What is't to me, when you yourselves are cause,
If your pure maidens fall into the hand
Of hot and forcing violation? (*Henry V* 3.3.87–98)

Here, the women of Harfleur are rhetorically central, even though they never appear on stage. Having used the threat of rape to open Harfleur's gates, Henry later recalls the link between cities and virgins, joking amidst marriage negotiations that he 'cannot see many a fair French city for one fair French maid that stands in my way' (5.2.293–4). The French king retorts that his cities have 'turned into a maid – for they are all girdled with maiden walls that war hath never entered' (296–7). The equation between women and cities constructs women as territory to be protected or conquered.

Such analogies demonstrate that gender and sexuality underlie not only Shakespeare's depiction of character, but his use of image and metaphor. Such notions also reveal that gender and sexuality enact social *structures*. Calling Catherine 'our capital demand, comprised / Within the fore-rank of our articles' (5.2.96–7), Henry defines the princess as an object of exchange, as marriage is exposed as a means to further 'homosocial' bonds among men.[8] Through the exchange of women, women's agency is constrained, while male bonds are created and consolidated. Fully cognizant of her place within this system, Catherine answers Henry's proposal, 'wilt thou have me?' with the politically astute, 'Dat is as it shall please de *roi mon père*' (5.2.228–9). That women typically are the possessions to be exchanged is attested by Shakespeare's exploration of one exception: in *All's Well That Ends Well*, when the aristocratic Bertram is offered as a reward to the low-born Helen for curing the ailing king, Bertram reacts with anger and astonishment, and flees without consummating the marriage.

Shakespeare tends to represent marriage as the 'natural' lot of male and female characters. When Benedick, a self-proclaimed confirmed bachelor, begins to succumb to his friends' marriage plans, he does so with the justification, 'The world must be peopled' (*Much Ado* 2.3.213). Conflating biological reproduction with the institution of marriage, Benedick's formulation has the force of a command. For women, the imperative was even stronger. Although Jaques in *As You Like It* versifies the 'seven ages of man', from cradle to soldiering to senility, for women the stages of life are confined to three: 'maid, wife, and widow', with each stage corresponding to woman's marital status. Those characters left outside Shakespeare's marital conclusions tend to be both male and 'alien' in some way – whether because of their temperament, ethnicity, religion, lower rank, or exclusive desire for another man.

Shakespeare's comedies and romances tend to focus on daughters whose age and rank make them desirable spouses for men seeking to improve their social standing. In the absence of a father, beautiful and wealthy heiresses such as Portia in *The Merchant of Venice* and Olivia in *Twelfth Night* temporarily rule over their own households. Their anomalous positions of authority indicate what is at stake in patriarchal marriage: the legitimate succession of the father's genealogy and the productive consolidation of wealth, land, and labour power. Thus, Portia's situation stands for the plight of most women in the marriage market. Albeit expressed in the fairy-tale terms of a choice among three caskets, the play enacts the theoretical dictum that 'the will of a living daughter [is] curbed by the will of a dead father' (*Merchant* 1.2.21–2).

Yet, despite the metaphoric extent of the father's reach, Shakespeare's plays often present his power as limited, with plots exploring the ramifications of the daughter's rejection of his will. The action of such different plays as *A Midsummer Night's Dream* and *Romeo and Juliet* is set in motion when daughters defy their fathers, upholders of a harsh patriarchal law that brooks no challenge to its authority. Hermia and Lysander attempt to escape the 'sharp Athenian law' (*Dream* 1.1.162) – Duke Theseus' edict that Hermia either must marry her father's choice, Demetrius, or be cloistered in a nunnery, or be executed – by fleeing in the dead of night to Lysander's widowed aunt. Although they never make it beyond the woods surrounding Athens, their desires are fulfilled after a night of midsummer madness, when desires run amuck under the influence of Puck's love potion. Juliet's love for the kinsman of her father's enemy propels her into a secret marriage, resulting in the tragic death of both lovers. Despite the differences in comic and tragic outcomes, in both cases Shakespeare comes down firmly on the side of romantic love, even as he presumes the necessity of marriage for everyone and carefully ensures that each character is betrothed to another of similar station and rank.

Nowhere is the focus on daughters more acute than in Shakespeare's romances, where the psychic issues at stake in the father's successful espousal of his daughter are most fully revealed. The daughter of romance is often lost: unknown to her father, Perdita of *The Winter's Tale* grows up in far-off Bohemia, while Marina of *Pericles* is imprisoned in a bawdy house while her disconsolate father wanders the world. Only Miranda of *The Tempest* is safely under her father's control, and Prospero masterfully orchestrates the tempest that will bring her a noble husband and restore his dukedom.

In contrast to the centrality of daughters in the romances and comedies, none of Shakespeare's tragedies or histories presents a woman as primary protagonist. Nonetheless, women – and ideas of femininity – are crucial to the unfolding of both history and tragedy. In the tragedies, women often serve as a source of the male hero's downfall. When daughters fail to comply with their fathers' wishes, when wives appear too independent, tragedy begins. The masculinity of Shakespeare's tragic heroes is paradoxically vulnerable, dependent on women's confirmation and approval. If their masculine self-image is challenged, male characters descend into rage, tyranny, even madness. When Cordelia refuses to comply with her father's demand for a performance of devotion, King Lear's astonishment turns to fury as he impetuously divides his kingdom, banishes Cordelia, and ultimately succumbs to madness. The Fool accurately, if misogynistically, marks the beginning of Lear's descent as the moment when 'thou madest thy daughters thy mother; . . . when thou gavest them the rod, and put'st down thine own breeches . . .' (*Lear* 1.4.149–51).[9] In *The Winter's Tale* Leontes similarly banishes Hermione after convincing himself, on the basis of no evidence, that she is committing adultery with his best friend. Leontes mourns her 'death' for many years, before being released from grief and guilt by the power of forgiveness, the prospect of Perdita's marriage to Polixenes' son, and the 'rebirth' of Hermione as a living statue. Othello succinctly articulates his dependence on Desdemona's love:

> Perdition catch my soul.
> But I do love thee, and when I love thee not,
> Chaos is come again. (3.3.91–3)

Once Iago convinces him of her infidelity, Othello is undeterred from a jealous rage that proves murderous and self-annihilating.

Because men have only women's word for the legitimacy of their children, and because patrilineal authority is necessarily transmitted through women's reproductive bodies, men are represented as particularly susceptible to female deception. Over and over again, women are accused of being something other than what they *seem*. In *Much Ado About Nothing* Claudio curses Hero:

> Out on thee, seeming! I will write against it.
> You seem to me as Dian in her orb,
> As chaste as is the bud ere it be blown.
> But you are more intemperate in your blood
> Than Venus or those pampered animals
> That rage in savage sensuality. (4.1.54–9)

Just as a fantasy of adultery impels tragic action, in the comedies a humorous acknowledgement of cuckoldry often articulates and assuages male anxiety. Cuckold jokes, expressed through images of a deer's horn placed on top of a man's head, imply that every man is a potential cuckold. Whereas Othello opines that 'A hornèd man's a monster and a beast' (4.1.59), a song in *As You Like It* suggests that cuckoldry is man's inevitable fate:

> Take thou no scorn to wear the horn;
> It was a crest ere thou wast born.
> Thy father's father wore it,
> And thy father bore it.
> The horn, the horn, the lusty horn
> Is not a thing to laugh to scorn. (4.2.14–19)

Despite the economic advantages to married life, not all women or men wanted to marry. Adult women who, at any stage in their life, were unmarried composed 20 per cent of the north-west European population.[10] Although Shakespeare tends to represent marriage as the 'natural' beginning of adulthood, Emilia in *The Two Noble Kinsmen* voices her resistance. Proclaiming 'That the true love 'tween maid and maid may be / More than in sex dividual', Emilia agrees when her sister observes that Emilia 'shall never . . . Love any that's called man' (1.3.81–5). Isabella of *Measure for Measure* similarly wants only to be left free to become a nun, but, just as Emilia is married off to the victorious knight Palamon, Isabella is in the final act betrothed to Duke Vincentio – and without a line of dialogue indicating her feelings about the matter. It is hardly coincidental that Isabella is surrounded by prostitutes and bawds, as if her desire to be a 'bride of Christ' must be countered by the most extreme (and in *Measure for Measure*, degraded) form of sexual exploitation.

Yet, for all their degradation, prostitutes are, with the exception of orphaned heiresses, Shakespeare's most independent women, all of them having attained some measure of financial independence. Mistress Quickly and Doll Tearsheet of the Henriad and Mistress Overdone of *Measure for Measure* make enough money selling alcohol and their bodies to oversee their own establishments and command their own servants. As if to offset this autonomy, such women are the object of derision – particularly Mistress Quickly, whose fast and loose use of the English language associates her with other buffoons, such as the Captains Fluellen, Jamy, and Macmorris, whose Welsh, Scottish, and Irish dialects provide much of the humour of *Henry V*.

Quickly's frequent malapropisms imply that women themselves are a disordered or foreign language, metaphorically or literally residing at the borders of the English (or Roman) state. Mortimer's Welsh wife in *1 Henry IV* speaks not a word of English; her father translates her incomprehensible speech for her amorous husband who, in vowing to learn Welsh, allies himself with that which is foreign and, in the terms of the play, unmanly. When, in *Henry V*, Princess Catherine embarks on an English lesson in preparation for her future role as England's queen, she inadvertently slips into bawdy double entendres as she attempts to force her tongue into an English pronunciation of body parts.

Just as female characters are often characterized as foreign, foreign lands are frequently feminized. The threat of an alien femininity is embodied by Cleopatra, the Egyptian queen who seduces and ultimately causes the downfall of one of the most powerful men in the world. Throughout *Antony and Cleopatra*, Egypt is represented as feminine, warm, fertile, and sensuous, while Rome is masculine, cold, sterile, and hard. The erotic mingling of Egypt and Rome results in the hero's death and the destruction of Cleopatra's reign. Conversely, in *Henry V*, Henry looks forward to an erotic congress that will result in the imperialist birth of 'a boy, half-French half-English, that shall go to Constantinople and take the Turk by the beard' (5.2.195–6).

Gendered language is also employed to cajole characters into accepting a national identity, as when Joan la Pucelle appeals to Burgundy's loyalty by imaging France as a wounded breast:

> Look on thy country, look on fertile France,
> And see the cities and the towns defaced
> By wasting ruin of the cruel foe.
> As looks the mother on her lowly babe
> When death doth close his tender-dying eyes,
> See, see the pining malady of France;
> Behold the wounds, the most unnatural wounds,
> Which thou thyself hast given her woeful breast. (*1 Henry VI* 3.7.44–51)

Joan's attempt to compel Burgundy to imagine himself as a mother demonstrates that men as well as women are constructed through cultural ideas of gender.

In the comedies, the most common male identity is that of the lover, a 'feminized' position insofar as it separates men from economic and military pursuits. The role of the male lover is frequently mocked by female characters, as when Rosalind challenges Orlando's qualifications to be considered a true lover; such a man, she jokes, would have 'A lean cheek, which you have not; a blue eye and sunken, which you have not; an unquestionable spirit, which you have not; a beard neglected, which you have not . . . Then your hose should be ungartered, your bonnet unbanded, your sleeve unbuttoned, your shoe untied, and everything about you demonstrating a careless desolation' (*As You Like It* 3.2.338–45).

If Rosalind wittily anatomizes the conventional male lover's disorderly body, mind, and dress, in the histories and tragedies masculine identity is deadly serious. The fate of nations depends on male strength, valour, and rational judgement. The development of the young man into a leader other men will follow is the theme of *1* and *2 Henry IV*, as the 'madcap Prince of Wales' learns to forgo adolescent pastimes, gain the stature and authority to succeed his father, and bring to rest civil strife. Prince Hal's development requires that he hone his rhetorical expertise, prove himself in battle against a rival 'brother', Hotspur, and banish pleasure as embodied by the 'jolly knight', Falstaff. His attainment of all three depends on his ability to manipulate other men's ideas of manhood, as becomes clear in his effort to rouse his weary troops to battle with the promise of a cross-class brotherhood:

> For he today that sheds his blood with me
> Shall be my brother; be he ne'er so vile,
> This day shall gentle his condition.
> And gentlemen in England now abed
> Shall think themselves accursed they were not here,
> And hold their manhoods cheap whiles any speaks
> That fought with us upon Saint Crispin's day. (*Henry V* 4.3.61–7)

The transmission of patriarchal and royal power is almost always a moment of social weakness, exposing a contradiction at the heart of patriarchal society: whereas men rely on one another to support structures of male dominance, they must also be willing to kill one another. In the internecine bloodshed of the histories, rival 'brothers' vie for the crown. But male competition is not only a matter of history or tragedy. *As You Like It* and *The Tempest* depict younger brothers usurping the place of the elder brother legally guaranteed by the laws of primogeniture. The difference is that comedy and romance tend to idealize fatherly authority – Duke Senior benignly governs his fellow forest exiles and Prospero rules omnisciently over his island kingdom – while the histories present political rule as inherently unstable, a matter of unsavoury power ploys.

Manhood, of course, is not only a concern of men. Faced with the dishonour of her kinswoman, Beatrice exclaims, 'O God that I were a man! I would eat [Claudio's] heart in the market place' (*Much Ado* 4.1.303–4). Her sense of masculine honour provokes Benedick to challenge Claudio to a duel. Other women also prod men into acts of violence, such as Lady Macbeth, who goads her husband into committing regicide:

> When you durst do it, then you were a man;
> And to be more than what you were, you would
> Be so much more the man. . . . I have given suck, and know
> How tender 'tis to love the babe that milks me.
> I would, while it was smiling in my face,
> Have plucked my nipple from his boneless gums
> And dashed the brains out, had I so sworn
> As you have done to this. (1.7.49–59)

Proving herself to be the 'better man', Lady Macbeth makes Macbeth feel less than one; and he hardly would have heeded the prophecy of the three 'weird sisters' if not so shamed and spurred on. So too, Goneril berates her husband, Albany, for being a 'Milk-livered man!' (*Lear* 4.2.52), while Volumnia claims her breast to be the physical source of her martial son's manhood: 'Thy valiantness was mine, thou sucked'st it from me' (*Coriolanus*, 3.2.129).

If Volumnia acts as though she wishes she could replace Coriolanus on the battlefield, in the history plays some women do take up arms. In *Henry VI* both Joan and Queen Margaret lead armies, but their power is undermined by the way they are demonized by other characters and by the playwright, who ultimately represents them as witches and shrews. The existence of such 'manly women' places particular pressure on men. As Patroclus says to Achilles, 'A woman impudent and mannish grown / Is not more loathed than an effeminate man / In time of action' (*Troilus* 3.3.210–12). The fear of appearing 'unmanly' motivates Achilles to invite his enemy Ajax to the Grecian camp, leading to a resumption of his involvement in the fighting. Several of Shakespeare's tragic heroes are stricken with a fear of effeminacy. Lear observes of his own rising hysteria, 'O, how this mother swells up toward my heart! / *Hysterica passio*, down, thou climbing sorrow, / Thy element's below!' (2.4.54–6). Insofar as 'Hysterica passio' alludes to a gynaecological ailment – the 'suffocation of the mother', the results of a 'wandering womb' or uterus – Lear imagines himself as a woman whose body is out of control. At the same time, he fights against this self-recognition, imploring, 'touch me with noble anger, / And let not women's weapons, water-drops, / Stain my man's cheeks!' (2.4.271–3). Whereas Lear's images of 'the mother' within reveal a man divided against himself, *Macbeth* enacts a paranoid flight from femininity. Assured that he will die only at the hands of a man 'not born of woman' (5.3.4 and 5.7.3), the hero indulges in a fantasy of male identity uncontaminated by uterine birth.

As *Macbeth*'s reliance on the image of a caesarean birth implies, the body provides an imaginative structure for many of Shakespeare's plays. Furthermore, erotic jokes, puns, and innuendoes pepper the plays with references to breasts, the anus, and genitals, as well as lust and sexual intercourse. Such 'bawdy language' not only contributes to the depiction of character, but exposes the body as a resource for linguistic play. In *The Merchant of Venice* the cry of Shylock over the elopement of his daughter, as narrated by Solanio, forges an uncomfortable, if comic, link between his daughter and his money that depends on bodily tropes:

'My daughter! O, my ducats! O, my daughter!
Fled with a Christian! O, my Christian ducats!
Justice! The law! My ducats and my daughter!
A sealèd bag, two sealèd bags of ducats,
Of double ducats, stol'n from me by my daughter!
And jewels, two stones, two rich and precious stones,
Stol'n by my daughter!' (2.8.15–21)

In addition to the implied equation between his ducats and his daughter, the reference to 'two sealèd bags' and 'two rich and precious stones' (stones being a vernacular term for testicles) forges a further association. Such 'body language' reveals that Jessica's secret marriage, made worse by her theft of money and conversion to Christianity, signifies the loss of Shylock's masculinity.

Access to sexual language and knowledge was not confined to men. Although Katherine finds herself unwillingly engaged in bawdy repartee with Petruccio (2.1.211–59), she nonetheless comprehends his lewd meanings, just as Ophelia understands Hamlet's crude references to her lap (3.2.101–22). Desdemona's servant, Emilia, argues that wives experience the same sexual desires as their husbands:

Let husbands know
Their wives have sense like them. They see, and smell,
And have their palates both for sweet and sour,
As husbands have. What is it that they do
When they change [exchange] us for others? Is it sport?

> I think it is. And doth affection [lust] breed it?
> I think it doth. Is't frailty that thus errs?
> It is so, too. And have not we affections,
> Desires for sport, and frailty, as men have?
> Then let them use [treat] us well, else let them know
> The ills we do, their ills instruct us so. (4.3.91–101)

Emilia's sexual philosophy reeks of the bitterness born of mistreatment; yet, it is nothing like the disgust that pervades the erotic consciousness of some of the male protagonists. Hamlet's contempt for his mother's swift remarriage spirals into revulsion for all female bodies (1.2.129–59), while Lear rants misogynistically against the female genitals:

> But to the girdle do the gods inherit.
> Beneath is all the fiends'; there's hell, there's darkness,
> There's the sulphurous pit, burning, scalding,
> Stench, consumption! (4.6.123–6)

One of the more disturbing implications of the body's metaphoric potential is the way in which racialized images of sexuality serve Shakespeare as a metaphor for the 'unnatural'. Iago exploits this connection when he awakens Brabanzio to the news that 'an old black ram / Is tupping your white ewe' (*Othello* 1.1.88–9), furthering the implication of Othello's bestiality and barbarism with the prediction, 'you'll have your daughter covered with a Barbary horse, you'll have your nephews neigh to you' (1.1.112–14). If Iago's racism is an expression of his own diseased imagination, Shakespeare employs no such distancing techniques in his representation of Caliban, whose attempted rape of Miranda is used to legitimize slavery. Displacing the historical actualities of colonialism, wherein European conquerors raped native women, *The Tempest* justifies Caliban's servitude as the 'natural' position for the creature Prospero calls 'This thing of darkness' (5.1.278).

The body is also a site of disease, and Shakespeare frequently employs venereal disease to figure what is wrong with social and erotic relations. Images of syphilis (called 'the French pox', in a nationalistic displacement of responsibility) crop up whenever prostitution is invoked. Doll Tearsheet dies 'of a malady of France' (*Henry V* 5.1.73) after Falstaff has charged, 'you help to make the diseases, Doll. We catch of you, Doll, we catch of you' (*2 Henry IV*, 2.4.39–41). Syphilis heightens the sense of disgust permeating *Troilus and Cressida*, functioning as a metaphor for the diseased 'body politic', as well as for the contagious transmission of misguided desires throughout the play.

Such a claustrophobic and diseased world, however, is not the whole story of Shakespearian eroticism. A number of plays treat eroticism as the happy consequence of the movement into adulthood. Under the auspices of a pastoral 'green world' – the forest of Arden, the woods outside Athens, the coast of Bohemia – characters experience a temporary release from the strictures of family and the city or court. In this 'world turned upside down', inversions of the usual gender order momentarily expand romantic and social possibilities, as women and men speak freely, commoners mingle with aristocrats, and a 'holiday humour' prevails (*As You Like It* 4.1.59–60).[11] In Arden, Rosalind cheerfully instructs Orlando in the expectations of wives and the proper way to woo. In the Athenian woods, Helena, Hermia, Lysander, and Demetrius experience a dizzying exchange of desires, while the faerie queen Titania is made to fall in love with an ass. If midsummer madness descends into violence, and Oberon's humiliation of Titania offsets the marital happiness of the Athenian lovers, nevertheless, a variety of desires has been explored. The confining of such exploration to a specific geographical location, however, suggests that all such fun is temporary: it is to the city or court – and the social stratification such locales represent – that most of the characters return.

Rosalind, of course, tutors Orlando in the arts of love while disguised as a young man. The vogue for the cross-dressed heroine on the Renaissance stage gave birth to some of Shakespeare's most independent heroines. Viola, Portia, and Julia also don a masculine disguise which grants them freedom of movement and authority. It is while disguised as a law clerk that Portia successfully defeats Shylock in court. And it is while in service to Orsino that Viola discovers her own passion for impersonation and a penchant for falling in love. Despite the fact that adolescent boys and young men performed all female parts in Shakespeare's company, only twice is a male character cross-dressed – and both Flute's theatrical portrayal of Thisbe in *A Midsummer Night's Dream* and Falstaff's unwilling female impersonation in *The Merry Wives of Windsor* make them the comic butt of a joke. Shakespeare depicts male characters as uncomfortable 'descending' into femininity, while female characters enjoy the elevation of status their temporary manhood permits.

Because gender and sexuality are so closely intertwined, inversions of gender identity affect erotic desire as well. When Rosalind cross-dresses, she takes on the name of Ganymede, the Greek boy who was swept to heaven by Jove to serve as his lover and cup-bearer. Thus associated with a central myth of male homoeroticism, Rosalind's relationship to Orlando is imbued with homoerotic desire while she toys with him as Ganymede impersonating Rosalind. Throughout *As You Like It* erotic desires partake of a conditional mode structured by the question, 'What if . . .?' What if I were your Rosalind? What if you were my Orlando? Such erotic contingency is emphasized in the epilogue, when the boy actor playing Rosalind refers to his own impersonation of a woman: 'If I were a woman', he says, 'I would kiss as many of you as had beards that pleased me, complexions that liked me, and breaths that I defied not.' In the context of a play that has thoroughly upset conventional gender divisions, this statement further challenges the binary logic of male *or* female, homosexual *or* heterosexual.

In fact, the division between homosexual and heterosexual was not evident in Renaissance England. Nor, in contrast to our own time, were erotic desires and practices generally linked to a sense of personal identity, as the modern terms 'homosexual' or 'lesbian' imply. Nonetheless, homoerotic desire is evinced in Shakespeare's plays, as intimate friendships slip into expressions of eroticism, and gender-segregated environments offer enticing alternatives to the conjugal bond. Polixenes' nostalgic reminiscence of his boyhood friendship with Leontes registers his longing for the experience of similarity untouched by gender difference:

> We were as twinned lambs that did frisk i'th' sun,
> And bleat the one at th' other. What we changed [exchanged]
> Was innocence for innocence. We knew not
> The doctrine of ill-doing, nor dreamed
> That any did. (*Winter's Tale* 1.2.69–73)

The affections of boyhood are given mature expression in the description of the battlefield deaths of the Duke of York and the Earl of Suffolk at Agincourt:

> Suffolk first died, and York, all haggled over,
> Comes to him, where in gore he lay insteeped,
> And takes him by the beard, kisses the gashes
> That bloodily did yawn upon his face,
> And cries aloud, 'Tarry, dear cousin Suffolk.
> My soul shall thine keep company to heaven.
> Tarry, sweet soul, for mine, then fly abreast,
> As in this glorious and well-foughten field
> We kept together in our chivalry.' . . .
> So did he turn, and over Suffolk's neck
> He threw his wounded arm, and kissed his lips,
> And so espoused to death, with blood he sealed
> A testament of noble-ending love. (*Henry V* 4.6.11–27)

Martial valour and honour are relayed in simultaneously religious and erotic terms: 'espoused to death', their union sealed with a kiss, they seek to fly together to heaven. Such language to describe bonds among noblemen suggests that certain forms of homoeroticism were not only tolerated, but sanctioned, especially within a military culture. When Coriolanus forsakes his *patria*, Rome, in order to fight alongside its arch-enemy, the general Aufidius embraces him with these words:

> Know thou first,
> I loved the maid I married; never man
> Sighed truer breath. But that I see thee here,
> Thou noble thing, more dances my rapt heart
> Than when I first my wedded mistress saw
> Bestride my threshold. (4.5.112–17)

Male homoerotic bonds are not always supported, however. In *Twelfth Night* and *The Merchant of Venice*, the characters named Antonio are associated with homoerotic desire, and it is they who are marginalized at the conclusion, left out of the inevitable heterosexual closure of Shakespearian comedy. Because of the importance of marriage, most intimate male friends, whether homoerotic or not, find a way to accommodate new alliances with women. Both *The Two Noble Kinsmen* and *The Two Gentlemen of Verona* focus on the threat women represent to male intimacy, and heighten the issue by positioning men as romantic rivals. The stakes in the transfer of male allegiance are powerfully articulated in Beatrice's response to Benedick's passionate avowal of love. Her demand upon hearing him say, in typical romantic hyperbole, that he will do anything for her, is 'Kill Claudio' (*Much Ado* 4.1.287).

Female homoeroticism likewise is present in Shakespearian drama, albeit in such a way that always suggests it is a thing of the past. In *A Midsummer Night's Dream*, as Helena perceives her childhood friend, Hermia, to have turned against her, she voices a pained admonition:

> Is all the counsel that we two have shared –
> The sisters' vows, the hours that we have spent,
> When we have chid the hasty-footed time
> For parting us – O, is all quite forgot?
> All schooldays' friendship, childhood innocence?
> We, Hermia, like two artificial gods,
> Have with our needles created both one flower,
> Both on one sampler, sitting on one cushion,
> Both warbling of one song, both in one key,
> As if our hands, our sides, voices, and minds
> Had been incorporate. So we grew together,
> Like to a double cherry: seeming parted,
> But yet an union in partition,
> Two lovely berries moulded on one stem.
> So, with two seeming bodies but one heart . . . (3.2.199–213)

Helena concludes this passionate appeal with the question, 'And will you rend our ancient love asunder. . . ?' (216).

So too, in *As You Like It* eroticism suffuses the speeches of Celia, who urges her cousin Rosalind to 'love no man in good earnest' (1.2.22–3) and who later asserts, 'We still have slept together, / Rose at an instant, learned, played, eat together, / And wheresoe'er we went, like Juno's swans / Still we went coupled and inseparable' (1.3.67–70). Celia reiterates Helena's sense of betrayal when she queries, 'Rosalind, lack'st thou then the love / Which teacheth thee that thou and I am one? / Shall we be sundered? Shall we part, sweet girl?' (1.3.90–2). Helena and Celia's poignant questions, which echo the rhetoric of the Anglican marriage ceremony, 'Those whom God hath joined together, let no man put asunder', posit female amity as parallel in emotional intensity and physical closeness to heterosexual marriage. Nonetheless, Shakespeare did not imagine the continuation of female–female desire into adulthood, instead rendering it in an elegiac mode, limiting it to a mournful expression of what *was* instead of what *is* or *might be*.

Before the advent of feminist and queer criticism, critical and editorial practices tended to erase such intimations of homoeroticism, assuming, for instance, that any reference to the genitals must allude to a male phallus and a female vagina, thus yielding a heterosexual coupling. Even when modern editors have inserted an explicitly sexual meaning into a text – as in a notorious textual crux in *Romeo and Juliet* (2.1.38), in which Mercutio refers to an 'open, or' (second quarto) or an 'open *Et caetera*' (first quarto), and which is emended in most modern editions to 'open-arse' – the result typically has been to foster an image of male–female intercourse.[12] As they have become more cognizant of the enormous flexibility of sexual positions and the variety of erotic desires circulating in early modern culture, editors have begun to revise their introductions and glosses accordingly; nonetheless, much remains to be done to establish the full range of erotic meanings to Shakespeare's language and characters.

Within the tradition of performance, similar elisions have occurred, although, perhaps in response to audience taste, such practices are no longer *de rigueur*. For directors looking for ways to cut the length of a production, homoerotic passages were often considered minor or expendable. Thus, Antonio's passionate speeches to Sebastian in *Twelfth Night* and the recollections of Hermia and Helena's shared childhood were typically excised, the homoerotic nature of their love silenced.[13] If directors once felt authorized to manipulate Shakespeare's plays to foster conservative interpretations of social roles, today's stage and film productions do so at their peril – for audiences increasingly recognize that Shakespeare's representations of gender and sexuality are as complex, various, and fascinating as our own bodies and selves.

Notes

1. Eric Partridge, *Shakespeare's Bawdy: A Literary and Psychological Essay, and a Comprehensive Glossary* (London: Routledge, 1947).
2. Kathleen McLuskie, 'The Patriarchal Bard: Feminist Criticism and Shakespeare: *King Lear* and *Measure for Measure*', in *Political Shakespeare: Essays in Cultural Materialism*, ed. Jonathan Dollimore and Alan Sinfield (Ithaca, N.Y.: Cornell University Press, 1985), pp. 88–108.
3. David Underdown, 'The Taming of the Scold: the Enforcement of Patriarchal Authority in Early Modern England', in *Order and Disorder in Early Modern England*, ed. Anthony Fletcher and John Stevenson (Cambridge University Press, 1985), pp. 116–36.
4. Susan Amussen, *An Ordered Society: Gender and Class in Early Modern England* (Oxford: Blackwell, 1988) and Merry E. Weisner, *Women and Gender in Early Modern Europe* (Cambridge University Press, 1993).
5. Peter Stallybrass, 'Patriarchal Territories: the Body Enclosed', in *Rewriting the*

Renaissance: The Discourses of Sexual Difference in Early Modern Europe ed. Margaret W. Ferguson, Maureen Quilligan, and Nancy Vickers (Chicago and London: University of Chicago Press, 1986), pp. 123–42.

6. Louis Adrian Montrose, *The Purpose of Playing: Shakespeare and the Cultural Politics of the Elizabethan Theatre* (Chicago and London: University of Chicago Press, 1996), p. 33.

7. Russ McDonald, *The Bedford Companion to Shakespeare: An Introduction with Documents* (Boston and New York: St Martin's Press, 1996), p. 153.

8. Eve Kosofsky Sedgwick, *Between Men: English Literature and Male Homosexual Desire* (New York: Columbia University Press, 1985).

9. The Norton edition includes three different texts of *King Lear*; I have used the conflated text.

10. Judith Bennett and Amy Froide, eds., *Singlewomen in the European Past* (Philadelphia: University of Pennsylvania Press, 1998).

11. C. L. Barber, *Shakespeare's Festive Comedy: A Study of Dramatic Form and its Relation to Social Custom* (New York: Princeton University Press, 1963).

12. Jonathan Goldberg, 'Romeo and Juliet's Open Rs', in *Queering the Renaissance* (Durham, N.C., and London: Duke University Press, 1994), pp. 218–36.

13. Laurie E. Osborne, *The Trick of Singularity: Twelfth Night and the Performance Texts* (University of Iowa Press, 1996); Trevor R. Griffiths, *Shakespeare in Production: A Midsummer Night's Dream* (Cambridge University Press, 1996), p. 161.

Reading list

Adelman, Janet, *Suffocating Mothers: Fantasies of Maternal Origin in Shakespeare's Plays, 'Hamlet' to 'The Tempest'* (London and New York: Routledge, 1992).

Barker, Deborah and Ivo Kamps, eds., *Shakespeare and Gender: A History* (London and New York: Verso, 1995).

DiGangi, Mario, *The Homoerotics of Early Modern Drama* (Cambridge University Press, 1997).

Dusinberre, Juliet, *Shakespeare and the Nature of Women* (New York: Barnes and Noble, 1975).

Erickson, Peter, *Patriarchal Structures in Shakespeare's Drama* (Berkeley and Los Angeles: University of California Press, 1985).

Garner, Shirley Nelson and Madelon Sprengnether, eds., *Shakespearean Tragedy and Gender* (Bloomington and Indianapolis: Indiana University Press, 1996).

Goldberg, Jonathan, ed., *Queering the Renaissance* (Durham, N.C., and London: Duke University Press, 1994).

Greene, Gayle, Carol Thomas Neely, and Carolyn Ruth Swift Lenz, eds., *The Woman's Part: Feminist Criticism of Shakespeare* (Urbana and Chicago: University of Illinois Press, 1980).

Hall, Kim, *Things of Darkness: Economies of Race and Gender in Early Modern England* (Ithaca, N.Y., and London: Cornell University Press, 1995).

Hendricks, Margo and Patricia Parker, eds., *Women, 'Race', and Writing in the Early Modern Period* (New York and London: Routledge, 1994).

Howard, Jean, *The Stage and Social Struggle in Early Modern England* (London and New York: Routledge, 1994).

Howard, Jean and Phyllis Rackin, *Engendering a Nation: A Feminist Account of Shakespeare's English Histories* (London: Routledge, 1997).

Jardine, Lisa, *Reading Shakespeare Historically* (London and New York: Routledge, 1996).

Kahn, Coppélia, *Roman Shakespeare: Warriors, Wounds, and Women* (London and New York: Routledge, 1997).

Man's Estate: Masculine Identity in Shakespeare (Berkeley: University of California Press, 1981).

Masten, Jeffrey, *Textual Intercourse: Collaboration, Authorship, and Sexualities in Renaissance Drama* (Cambridge University Press, 1997).

Montrose, Louis Adrian, "'The Place of a Brother", in *As You Like It*: Social Process and Comic Form', *Shakespeare Quarterly* 32:1 (1981) 28–54.

Newman, Karen, *Fashioning Femininity and English Renaissance Drama* (University of Chicago Press, 1991).

Orgel, Stephen, *Impersonations: The Performance of Gender in Shakespeare's England* (Cambridge University Press, 1996).

Rose, Mary Beth, *The Expense of Spirit: Love and Sexuality in English Renaissance Drama* (Ithaca, N.Y.: Cornell University Press, 1988).

Schwartz, Murray and Coppélia Kahn, *Representing Shakespeare: New Psychoanalytic Essays* (Baltimore, and London: Johns Hopkins University Press, 1980).

Smith, Bruce, *Homosexual Desire in Shakespeare's England: A Cultural Poetics* (University of Chicago Press, 1991).

Traub, Valerie, *Desire and Anxiety: Circulations of Sexuality in Shakespearean Drama* (London and New York: Routledge, 1992).

Wayne, Valerie, ed., *The Matter of Difference: Materialist Feminist Criticism of Shakespeare* (Ithaca, N.Y.: Cornell University Press, 1991).

Zimmerman, Susan, ed., *Erotic Politics: Desire on the Renaissance Stage* (London and New York: Routledge, 1992).

10

ANIA LOOMBA

Outsiders in Shakespeare's England

IMAGES of racial, national, religious, and cultural difference haunt Renaissance theatricals. Indians and Moors, gypsies and Jews, Ethiopians and Moroccans, Turks, Moors, Jews, 'savages', the 'wild Irish', the 'uncivil Tartars', and other 'outsiders' were repeatedly conjured up on early modern English stages, both public and private. Sometimes such outsiders occupied the centre-stage, in plays such as Shakespeare's *Othello*, or Christopher Marlowe's *The Jew of Malta*, or in court masques such as Ben Jonson's *The Masque of Blackness*, or in the pageants such as Thomas Middleton's *Triumphs of Truth* which were enacted before the citizens of London when a new Lord Mayor was appointed. At other times they played smaller roles, like the black Moor Aaron in Shakespeare's *Titus Andronicus* (whose picture, drawn by Henry Peacham, is the only surviving image from this time of a black character on the stage) or Portia's suitor, the Prince of Morocco, in *The Merchant of Venice*, whose blackness the upright lady fears and loathes: 'If he have the condition of a saint and the complexion of a devil, I had rather he should shrive me than wive me' (1.2.109–10). Some were just shadowy presences that were evoked but never appeared on stage such as the 'lovely boy stol'n from an Indian king' over whom Titania and Oberon fight in *A Midsummer Night's Dream* (2.1.22) or the Moorish woman who, we are told, has been made pregnant by Lancelot in *The Merchant of Venice*. Sometimes outsiders are only figures of speech, conjured up to establish a point of view: in Shakespeare's *Much Ado About Nothing*, for example, Claudio affirms his decision to marry Leonato's niece whom he has not seen by declaring, 'I'll hold my mind, were she an Ethiope' (5.4.38) and in *A Midsummer Night's Dream*, Lysander spurns Hermia by calling her an 'Ethiope' and a 'tawny Tartar' (3.2.258, 264).[1]

Shakespeare criticism has long commented on such images and figures but, until fairly recently, many influential critics insisted that racial outsiders are incidental to the themes usually regarded as central to the study of Shakespeare: 'Europe is Shakespeare's centre, and although things outside intrude now and then, like spectres from another world, his plots, themes, and scenes are almost exclusively European.'[2] Only in the last two decades or so has Shakespeare criticism (perhaps as a result of a wider scholarly as well as political focus on the genesis as well as effects of empire) come to pay more systematic attention to the ways in which representation of outsiders shapes the meaning and form of Shakespearian drama, both in its own context and subsequently.[3]

Such a critical history derives from the fact that since the early eighteenth century, Shakespeare has been widely regarded as the 'national poet' of England, which means that the connection between his writings and something called 'Englishness' has been posited as organic. Both Shakespeare and Englishness had to be moulded in particular ways in order for this alignment to appear natural and inevitable.[4] Shakespeare's centrality to 'English culture' was established in part by purging the plays, early modern England, and even Shakespeare's own life of anything that might be considered 'foreign' or un-English. For example, Sir Walter Raleigh, the first professor of English literature at Oxford, suggested that Shakespeare's bloodline could 'be traced straight back to Guy of Warwick and the good King Alfred'. During the First World War, Raleigh also interpreted Caliban, the 'deformed and savage slave' of *The Tempest*, not as a native of the New World but as a German.[5] Such an interpretation presumes that *The Tempest* portrays Caliban unambiguously as a brute and endorses his enslavement by Prospero, but it also demonstrates how outsider-figures become flexible templates of 'otherness' which can be made to fit the changing requirements of Englishness or Western civilization.

Not so long ago, students reading *Othello* were informed that Shakespeare had never seen a black man, and therefore could not have intended to portray Othello as a 'veritable Negro'. Such an assertion was provoked by the presumed contradiction between a high moral stature and blackness: if Othello is meant to be a noble and tragic hero then it follows that he cannot be black. The suggestion that early modern England had no black presence works to the same effect as readings which flatten Shakespeare's outsiders into simply evil or inferior beings: both create a 'merry England' which was either literally or ideologically homogeneous, where foreigners didn't exist or were hated or, at the very least, were completely unimportant to the lives and ideas of Shakespeare and his contemporaries. In numerical terms, there were indeed very few Africans or Turks or Jews in England during Shakespeare's time. However, the significance of blackness or Jewishness in English culture cannot be reckoned by numbers alone. Outsiders provoked more debates, anxieties, and representations than the population statistics might warrant. In this essay, rather than discuss particular outsider-figures in Shakespeare's plays, I want to indicate the contemporary resonance of issues of racial, religious, national, or cultural difference and outline the cultural vocabulary from which Shakespeare fashioned his own language of difference. We can then decide for ourselves to what extent he used the cultural language available to him and to what extent, in creating characters such as Othello, Caliban, Cleopatra, or Aaron, he departed from it.

It is not possible, in the space of a short essay, to convey the density or the details of the multiple histories and ideologies that contributed to such a language. However, I will indicate how attitudes to particular groups of outsiders, as well as the meaning of outside-ness in general, were fashioned from several intersecting histories – those of English nationalism, religious strife, overseas trade and empire, intra-European rivalry, and gender as well as class. I will suggest that if we examine attitudes to racial and religious outsiders in Shakespeare's England and their representations in drama, travelogues, and other literature, we can see how ideologies of 'race' and 'nationhood' changed during this period into something approaching their modern meanings; these changes were ushered in, in part, by the advent of colonial trade and settlement, which reworked older histories of contact between Europeans and those they considered foreign.

Questions of identity and difference became especially urgent in sixteenth- and seventeenth-century English culture because at this time the idea of an English nation developed and was articulated through a variety of media such as literature, law, cartography, or travel writing.[6] Liah Greenfeld suggests that 'A whole class of people emerged whose main preoccupation was to do research and write – chronicles, treatises, poems, novels and plays – in English about England . . . Everything English became an object of attention and nourished a new feeling of national pride.'[7] But 'everything English' was not a stable given: as in the nineteenth and twentieth centuries, so in the early modern period, Englishness was defined, in part, in opposition to everything *not* English. I want to suggest that the idea of difference is important in complicating our under- standing of the emergence of an English nation and in showing to what extent this was the result of an ongoing struggle to colonize, marginalize, or incorpo- rate different groups of people who lived both within and outside the geographic boundaries of England.

The idea of an English nation as such was itself relatively new in Shakespeare's time. Until 1534, when King Henry VIII broke with the Catholic Church, the religious head of England (the Pope) was not English at all. Monarchies in feudal Europe constantly warred and married with one another, and their wrangling and alliances remoulded the shapes of their nations. Thus, the monarch of one country could also become the sovereign of another, as happened in 1580 when Philip II of Spain also became King of Portugal, or indeed in 1603 when Elizabeth I died, and James VI of Scotland became James I, monarch of England. Benedict Anderson has suggested that the nation is an 'imagined community', born precisely by breaking from such a pan-European religious and feudal order in which the ruling elite bonded across national or linguistic boundaries, and by the forging of a different notion of community, in which people of different classes are supposedly united within a more bounded geography.[8] Although Anderson discusses a much later period, it is possible to view Elizabethan and Jacobean England as the crucible within which the English nation was beginning to be forged.

As Anderson reminds us, nations are *imaginatively* projected before they are realized. In Shakespeare's plays one of the most passionate evocations of

'England' is put into the mouth of a dying John of Gaunt, Duke of Lancaster in *Richard II*. Lamenting its imminent dissolution, Gaunt celebrates England:

> This royal throne of kings, this sceptred isle,
> This earth of majesty, this seat of Mars,
> This other Eden, demi-paradise . . .
> This blessèd plot, this earth, this realm, this England. (2.1.40–50)

Ironically, Shakespeare's play appropriates as a spokesman for England a fourteenth-century figure who had, in real life, pan-European rather than 'English' affiliations – the historical John of Gaunt's second wife was from Castille, and one of his daughters married the King of Portugal, the other a Spanish nobleman.

Nation-making was neither smooth nor free of contradictions. James I, a self-proclaimed father to a Protestant English nation, was Scottish and seen as pro-Catholic, and his attempt to effect a union between England and Scotland met with resistance from the House of Commons. James also tried to ensure that Scottish subjects born after his accession to the English throne in 1603 would be considered English subjects. The jurist Edward Coke suggested that one of the defining features of a subject was allegiance to the king, which could be either natural (that is stemming from birth) or acquired (when newly conquered or immigrated subjects transferred allegiance to the new ruler).[9] Such discussions generated as many contradictions as they attempted to negotiate – by paving the way for the Scots to be incorporated within the English (later British) nation, Coke's formulations also muddied the notion of a clear-cut, God-given natural Englishness. They could also potentially be used to argue for the admittance of Jews or Moors or Americans into the nation.

Nationalism attempts to create a community among people who have never met and who do not necessarily have interests or outlooks or even a language in common; historically, newspapers, novels, and other new forms of communication which Anderson calls 'print capitalism' were the channels for creating such shared culture, interests, and vocabularies. However, Anderson, as his critics have remarked, does not pay sufficient attention to the manner in which attempts to forge national identities also enact exclusions and create internal hierarchies within the newly formed community. Specifying who is part of the nation also entails identifying who may *not* be part of it, or who may be its 'lesser' member. In early modern England, the representation of outsiders, especially in travelogues and in the theatre, contributed to the creation of 'English' identity precisely by exploring, locating, indeed constructing notions of 'difference' and of a hierarchy of peoples, religions, and cultures.

Like the earlier epic and later the novel and newspapers, early modern travelogues take their readers through diverse landscapes, inviting them to view the unknown through the reassuring perspective of a familiar protagonist or narrator, making sense of the bewildering variety of the world by describing it in familiar terms. In Shakespeare's lifetime, travel narratives began to circulate on an unprecedented scale: Richard Hakluyt's monumental collection of voyages, *Principal Navigations* (1589; second edition 1599) made available the writings of both older travellers and newer voyagers, fables and maps, outlandish stories about 'men whose heads / Do grow beneath their shoulders' (*Othello* 1.3.143–44) as well as precise lists of foreign commodities and currencies. Hakluyt reminded his countrymen that they had lagged behind other European nations in gathering the riches of the two Indies, and he ardently advocated English participation in both 'Eastern trade' and 'Western planting'. Earlier, Richard Eden's notable collection *The History of Travayle in the West and East Indies* (1577) had also pleaded for English expansion overseas. But Hakluyt not only invited English people to contemplate their relationship to, and participate in, the European scramble for a fast-changing 'rest of the world' but he also (to use Richard Helgerson's evocative phrase) cast 'the nation as universal voyager' (p. 153). English readers were invited, in Hakluyt's pages (and later in the collections edited by Samuel Purchas) to view the rest of the world from the shared perspective of their common investments in overseas enterprises and to enjoy the prospect of future global success.

Overseas ventures, both colonial and mercantile, had intensified English contact and conflict with other European peoples, like the Spanish or the Dutch, and with a wide range of non-European and non-Christian peoples of far-away lands – Africans, Turks, native Americans, Indians, Moluccans, and others. Contact with the latter helped create the sense of a shared European or Christian culture; yet, somewhat contradictorily, it also heightened the rivalry between different European nations and Christian sects. Thus, for example, the differences between the Iberians and the English (and Roman Catholics and Protestants) are played up in travelogues or plays dealing with the Moluccas or North Africa, and yet they are also blurred as a wider gap is suggested between dark- and light-skinned peoples, Moors or heathens and Christians, non-Europeans and Europeans. At the same time, England's always volatile relationships with the peoples nearer or within home – the Welsh, the Scots, and especially the Irish – became even more fraught as English authorities grappled with the problem of how these people could be contained within the nation.

The development of 'Englishness' depended on the negation of 'Irishness', argue Andrew Hadfield and Willey Maley.[10] A wide spectrum of work has identified similar processes of English identity formation through the negation of other 'outsiders', whether they belonged to far-away lands, such as various 'Indians' and 'Moors', or lived in closer proximity, such as the Irish; whether they wandered like the Gypsies, or were hard to define, like the Jews. Such scholarship has been undertaken in the wake of Michel Foucault's work on a range of 'dividing practices' which define an inner normative territory by indicating what lies outside, or is deviant.[11] Edward Said extended Foucault's insights to suggest that colonial Europe's self-definition was crucially dependent upon its construction and 'othering' of the Orient.[12] Shakespeare scholarship has productively amplified such perspectives on 'otherness' to review the question of ethnic, religious, and national difference in the early modern period. Stephen Greenblatt's view that the Renaissance aristocratic and upper-class self was fashioned at least partly against the image of the newly discovered 'natives' of the New World has been extremely influential.[13] More recently, Kim Hall has shown that poetry (including Shakespeare's sonnets to the dark lady), plays, masques, paintings, jewellery, and travel writings reveal the growing obsession to define and grasp an elusive white English self that can only be represented or defined by being juxtaposed and contrasted with images of blackness.[14]

Normative or deviant sexual behaviour was also shaped, in part, by being compared with real or imagined foreign sexual practices. New World, African, or Eastern peoples were widely believed not only to be more libidinous than Europeans but also to indulge in same-sex erotic practices and to live in strange familial arrangements involving harems, polygamy, wife-sharing, and occasionally polyandry. These practices were demonized (and more rarely idealized) to construct pictures of normative families, women, and sexualities at home. Descriptions of African or Turkish 'tribades' were evoked to police same-sex eroticism in England, and fed into the construction of the 'lesbian' in Europe.[15] Accounts of Turkish repression of women served simultaneously to demonize the brutal Turks, to congratulate the English for their kindness to women, and to suggest that Englishwomen were given too much freedom and needed to be policed more strictly.

By this time, English voyagers such as John and Sebastian Cabot, Martin Frobisher, Sir Francis Drake, and Sir Walter Ralegh had literally charted new worlds for English consumption. Accounts of the New World, such as Walter Ralegh's 'Discovery of the large, rich and beautiful Empire of Guiana', painted elaborate pictures of the fabled Inca wealth and assured English authorities that, whoever conquered this new land, 'that Prince shall be Lord of more gold, and of a more beautiful Empire, and of more cities and people, than either the King of Spain, or the great Turk', reminding us that Spain and Turkey were the models for, as well as the greatest threats to, English imperial ambition.[16] Edmund Spenser described Ireland in almost identical terms as 'a most beautiful and sweet country as any is under heaven'; so full of nature's bounties that 'if some princes in the world had them, they would soon hope to be lords of all the seas, and ere long of all the world'.[17] The spectacular profits made by the first voyages to the East confirmed the promises of older travel stories – in March 1588, *The Hercules* returned from Tripoli in Syria, 'the richest ship of English merchant goods that ever was known to come into this realm'.[18] On 31 December 1600 the East India Company was set up with a capital of £50,000, four years after its Dutch counterpart. Queen Elizabeth granted monopoly of trade with the East to the company 'for the honour of our nation, the welfare of the people, the increase of our navigation, and the advancement of lawful traffic to the benefit of the commonwealth'.[19] By 1620, the company had trading stations in Sumatra, India, Japan, Java, Borneo, Malacca, Siam, and Malabar, among other places.

In Shakespeare's *The Merry Wives of Windsor*, Falstaff announces his intention to make simultaneous love to two women by declaring: 'They shall be my East and West Indies, and I will trade to them both' (1.3.63–5). Like Falstaff, England also seized the opportunity to traffic in both regions, although its *modus operandi* in each differed significantly. In the East, the English struggled to set up trading stations whereas in the Americas, by the middle of the seventeenth century, the imperial hallmarks of settlement and dispossession, violence, and plunder were already evident. The English presence in America was, several critics suggest, patterned on their adventures in Ireland – often the same individual colonists went out to both places. English administrators such as Edmund Spenser, Sir John Davies, or Fynes Moryson variously describe the Irish as wild, thieving, lawless, blood-drinking, savage, barbarous, naked – these are also the terms routinely used to describe New World Indians. However, whereas Indians residing far beyond English borders could at least occasionally be regarded as noble savages, and some colonists could advocate treating them gently, the Irish were subjects of the English crown and had to be dealt with far more harshly. Elizabethan writers on Ireland adopted the medieval distinction between civility and savagery.[20] Thus, ideologies of difference were both geographically and temporally mobile – not only did notions of outsiders honed in one part of the world shape attitudes in another, but older habits of thought were reinforced and reshaped by newer developments.

I have been suggesting that the formation of English nationhood is intricately interwoven with that of overseas trade and empire. By the early seventeenth century 'both the Indias, of Spice and Myne' (to use John Donne's words) had made their way to England with new commodities – spices such as pepper and cloves, cloths such as certain kinds of silk, artifacts, plants such as tobacco, potatoes, tomatoes and chilies, and even animals such as elephants. In 1599, the Swiss traveller Thomas Platter described the house of one Mr Cope, 'a citizen of London who has spent much time in the Indies' which was 'stuffed with queer foreign objects'. Platter's long list included 'An African charm made of teeth', 'Beautiful Indian plumes', 'Ornaments and clothes from China', 'A curious Javanese costume', 'A felt cloak from Arabia', 'Shoes from many strange lands', 'The Turkish Emperor's golden seal', 'A Madonna made of Indian feathers', and 'A long narrow Indian canoe'. The fact that it also included a 'Flying rhinoceros' or 'A round horn which had grown on an English woman's forehead' and other fantastic objects should not detract from its testimony that England was witnessing an unprecedented exposure to foreign ideas and images as well as material objects.[21] Even the queen received Platter 'with a whole bird of paradise for panache, set forward on her head studded with costly jewels'. European languages swelled with new vocabularies gleaned from languages the world over –

the word 'magazine', just to take one example, which is repeatedly used in plays and travelogues of the period to denote a repository of riches, was a recent import into English via the spice trade and derived from the Arabic *makkhasin*, meaning 'treasury'. Platter also mentions that at Hampton Court hung 'a lively life-like portrait of the wild man and woman captured by Martin Frobisher, the English captain, on his voyage to the New World, brought back to England alive' (p. 201). *The Tempest* possibly refers to the exhibition of this Eskimo couple in London: Trinculo remarks that even though the English 'will not give a doit to relieve a lame beggar, they will lay out ten to see a dead Indian' (2.2.30–1). Not all foreigners were helpless captives: London welcomed an embassy from the court of the Moroccan emperor Abd-el-Malek in August 1600, and many 'turbaned Turks' stayed in the city for nearly six months. While this embassy, according to some commentators, was not well treated, others argue that the English lavished their attention on the visitors, arousing the wrath of the resident Portuguese ambassador. Outsiders could thus be both objectified and glamorized, depending on where they came from, the colour of their skins, or their economic status in their homelands, as we shall soon see.

Of course, England had not been entirely homogeneous before this spate of mercantile and colonial travels – over the previous century, African servants had become increasingly popular in aristocratic households. Royalty had an even longer tradition of employing black entertainers: a black trumpet-player was employed by Henry VII and Henry VIII, and there was a group of Africans at the court of King James IV of Scotland. One was a drummer favoured by the king, who put together a dance for Shrove Tuesday festivities in 1505. That year, and then again in 1507, James installed a black woman as the Queen of Beauty and himself appeared as a 'wild knycht' who defended her. The lady's full lips, shining skin, and rich dress were described by the poet William Dunbar: the winner of the tournament was to be rewarded by the black lady's kiss while losers 'sall cum behind and kiss her hippis'.[22] Four black men are said to have danced naked in the snow (and later perished) at the wedding celebrations of James I and Anne of Denmark and in 1594, at their son's baptism celebrations, a 'Black-Moor' was made to pull a chariot originally meant to be harnessed by a lion.

It is not easy to chart the black and other 'foreign' presence among the larger population. According to one historian, one third of London's population in 1550 was foreign.[23] This number seems excessive, but James Shapiro reminds us that the word 'foreigner' was used by Londoners to describe those who had entered the city from the countryside (as indeed Shakespeare himself had). The terms 'stranger' or 'alien' were employed for non-English Europeans, as well as Africans and Jews.[24] In addition there were people from Scotland, Ireland, and Wales, who were neither fully outsiders nor insiders. Considering that London's population tripled in the years between 1520 and 1600, and that during every year in the first half of the seventeenth century, ten thousand people migrated to London from other parts of the country, it is hardly surprising that questions of difference should have been volatile and alive in the city (see chapter 8, The London Scene: City and Court, by Anne Barton). Throughout the sixteenth and seventeenth centuries both nationalist feelings and hostility to outsiders in England increased. Visitors to England were often amazed by English antipathy to outsiders. In 1517, there was a violent riot against foreign artisans resident in London which was suppressed by Cardinal Wolsey; in the same year, a preacher had moved his audience to violence by proclaiming that the increase in English poverty was due to the influx of aliens, and that God had earmarked that land exclusively for Englishmen. This riot was later represented in a play called *Sir Thomas More*, to which Shakespeare is thought to have contributed, and which was censored by the Master of Revels for its graphic depiction of the violence. In 1551, five or six hundred citizens had demonstrated before the Lord Mayor of London, threatening to kill foreigners. Anxieties about the foreign presence gave rise to rumours that there were as many as fifty thousand strangers in the city.

Thus, like imperial Portugal and Spain in the previous century, England displayed an increasing hostility to, and anxiety about, the presence of outsiders within its borders, even as it sought to expand its own frontiers. Various laws were proposed circumscribing the legal and economic rights of outsiders. Both Queen Mary and Queen Elizabeth issued proclamations against foreigners. The best known are Elizabeth's edicts of 1596 and 1601 seeking to expel some 'blackamoors' from the land. In 1596 Elizabeth sent an open letter to mayors of London and other towns, asking that ten black people be deported. A week later a warrant was sent to the Lord Mayor of London and other officers, informing them that Casper van Senden, a merchant from Lübeck, had offered to arrange the release of 89 English prisoners in Spain and Portugal in exchange for 89 'blackamoors' to be handed over to be traded as slaves. The queen thought this 'a very good exchange and that those kind of people may be well spared in this realm'. Clearly the land remained unpurged of blacks, for in 1601 Elizabeth proclaimed that she was

> highly discontented to understand the great numbers of Negroes and blackamoors which (as she is informed) are carried into this realm since the troubles between her highness and the King of Spain; who are fostered and powered here, to the great annoyance of her own liege people that which co[vet?] the relief which these people consume, as also for that the most of them are infidels having no understanding of Christ or his Gospel: hath given a special commandment that the said kind of people should be with all speed avoided and discharged out of this her majesty's realms . . .[25]

Elizabeth's argument that 'blackamoors' were depriving Christians of opportunities for food and employment demonstrates that the anxiety they generated was wholly disproportionate to the actual numbers of black people in the country. Her proclamation also implies a connection that is never specified –

between the 'fostering' of black people in England, and her tensions with Catholic Spain.

Such expulsions were of course not new: in 1290, King Edward I had expelled Jews from England and they were not officially allowed back until the middle of the seventeenth century, although as converts to Christianity, they had started returning soon after the expulsion. An obsession with racial and religious purity coincided, all over Europe, with both national consolidation and imperial expansion – in 1492, the same year in which Columbus sailed to the Americas, Jews were also expelled from Spain, and in 1497, they were forcibly converted to Christianity in Portugal. Spain complained that English monarchs were harbouring Jews; conversely, English authorities accused descendants of converted Iberian Jews (derogatorily called 'Marranos') of maintaining Spanish or Portuguese loyalties – thus the 1598 edition of John Florio's Italian–English dictionary, *A Worlde of Words*, defined 'Marrano' as 'a Jew, an infidel, a renegado, a nickname for Spaniard'.[26] Elizabeth's Portuguese–Jewish physician Roderigo Lopez was tried and later executed for high treason in 1594 for plotting against the queen under orders from Spain. The Lopez affair was followed by a revival of Marlowe's *The Jew of Malta* at the Rose theatre, and Shakespeare's *The Merchant of Venice* was written a few years later.

Precisely because there were no Jews who could openly live as Jews in England, Jewishness was 'a covert state, a state that entailed multiple creeds, nationalities, even names'.[27] Jews, who as one contemporary writer put it, 'have not for their Mansion, any peculiar country, but are dispersed abroad among foreign nations', were located by Mandeville's enormously popular *Travels* (first published in English in 1496 and reprinted seven times in the next century) in the hills beyond Cathay.[28] The 'dispersions of the Jewish nation' meant that Jews could be Spanish, Portuguese, Russian, or Turkish, and also English. The attempts to attribute hooked noses or a particular smell or a darker skin to Jews tell us that, as with the Irish, the lack of obvious physical distinctions between Jews and Christians was worrying to many English people. Given the Hebraic origins of Christianity, conversions between the two faiths were especially unsettling to those who looked for rigid demarcations between the two. Converts were suspected of secretly adhering to their former faith; at the same time, religious affiliation was not regarded as entirely a matter of choice: the idea that faith signified an inner essence was codified in Spain where the 'pure blood' laws were invoked to sift converts from Old Christians, and spread to the rest of Europe. Jews, it was suggested, *could* never fully convert to Christianity but intrinsically carried what one contemporary writer called 'the evil inclination of their ancient ingratitude and lack of understanding'.[29] In Shakespeare's England there were descendants of converted Iberian Jews who had been born and brought up in England, and debates about them or indeed latter-day English Jews were, as James Shapiro remarks, 'substitutes for what is really being fought over: the nature of Englishness itself and who has the right to stake a claim in it' (p. 4).

Englishness is similarly at stake in the critical debates on race, blackness, and difference. The question of conversion also surfaced in relation to the Moors, who had been allowed to live in Spain after 1499 only as *Moriscoes* or converts to Christianity. In 1501, over a million such converts were expelled from Europe, bringing to an end a long Muslim presence in Europe that had begun in the eighth century when Spain was conquered by people of mixed Arab and Berber blood and Islamic faith, called 'Moro' by the Spanish.[30] Like the Jews, these people were usually not dark-skinned, but over time Moorishness and blackness gradually began to be seen to overlap. Caesar Fredericke and other travellers to the East Indies tended to view Moors as Muslims, or of 'Mahomets sect'. But John Lok, who brought five black men from Barbary to England in 1554, calls people of Ethiopia 'Moores, Morens, or Negroes, a people of beastly living, *without a God, lawe, religion, or common wealth* . . .'[31] Here Moorishness is not a religion but equated with colour and a debased way of life. According to Leo Africanus' influential account of Africa, Moors come in various colours, and 'white, or tawny Moors' are the 'most steadfast in friendship', the most learned, and the 'most devout in their religion'.[32] It has been suggested that it was Africanus' translator, John Pory, who inaugurated the fusion of blackness and Islam in the English usage of the term Moor.[33] In Shakespeare's plays, the term 'Moor' primarily evoked blackness, while the religious connotation usually faded into apparent insignificance. *The Merchant of Venice* refers to the woman made pregnant by Lancelot as both a 'Moor' and a 'Negro' (3.5.32–3). Here, Moorishness is something that cannot be either acquired or shed. And in *Titus Andronicus* it is Aaron's colour rather than religion that audiences are invited to consider, although in the case of Othello, the Moor of Venice, a history of religious difference with the Turks or North Africans inscribes itself underneath the more overt references to colour.

Both blackness and Islam had been the target of hatred as well as fascination in medieval Europe, although the sources of this antipathy were not necessarily identical. By the time Shakespeare was writing, black skin became widely understood as the result of Noah's curse upon his son Ham's descendants. The English writer George Best was representative in rejecting the theory that blackness was a result of a hot climate and arguing instead that God had decreed that Ham's children be punished with skin 'so black and loathsome that it might remain a spectacle of disobedience to all the world'.[34] Understood in this way, the story of Ham anticipates certain key elements of later racism by reading skin colour as index of an inner quality, and also as something that is genetically transmitted from parent to child. Recent scholarship has indicated a historical irony, suggesting that a devaluation of dark skin might have been something that Iberian Christians learnt from Muslims, who had been making distinctions between their black and white slaves as early as the ninth century, assigning the more backbreaking work to the former and treating them as inferior. Persian and Arab scholars may have been responsible for introducing blackness into the Old

Testament story of Noah's curse: 'In Muslim cosmology, the sub-Saharan African emerged as the sons of Ham, destined to perpetual servitude. The Hamitic curse provided a justification for the increasing debasement of sub-Saharan Africans. Muslim vilification of blacks was constantly being refined as blackness and slavery came to be regarded as synonymous.'[35]

We must be cautious as we trace the multiple and intersecting intellectual histories of colour prejudice. Previously, some scholars had argued that Jewish commentaries on Noah's curse had provided the first association between blackness and Ham, and such arguments had worked to suggest that Jews are responsible for colour prejudice and the enslavement of Africans. The complex genealogies of Ham indicate not only the long intersection of Jewish, Islamic, and Christian thought, but also that 'otherness' is moulded by questions of gender and class: for example, Paul Freedman has demonstrated that Ham was seen too as the progenitor of serfs and peasants, and began to represent servitude.[36] Thus those who were later to be enslaved by Europeans and those Europeans whose labour was already being appropriated could be represented in overlapping ways. Peasants were 'others' too, regarded as inferior, darker, and almost a race apart from their masters. As Freedman cautions us, it would be a mistake simply to collapse all these 'others' into one, but by tracing the connections between them we can also avoid making the opposite mistake of isolating the history of racialized thought from that of class consciousness or gender ideologies.

In the West today, 'race' is most commonly understood in terms of skin colour. It has been argued that colour prejudice was not widely prevalent in early modern England at the time Shakespeare was writing *Othello* because it was primarily the European enslavement of black Africans that introduced both such prejudice and a negative view of Africans. It is true that colonial traffic in dark-skinned peoples was to institutionalize and deepen colour prejudice on an unprecedented scale. But, as we have seen, negative stereotyping of black people (and especially black Africans) pre-dates systemic European slavery and exploitation, and in fact such stereotyping often fed into justifications of slavery and colonial plunder. Certainly the stage was rife with such stereotypes: black people were routinely portrayed as lewd, unprincipled, and evil, and their appearance commented on as ugly and repulsive. Shakespeare repeatedly evokes the horror of blackness: in *Titus Andronicus*, Aaron himself says that black people's inability to blush invites popular comparison between them and black dogs (5.1.122), and the nurse calls his son (borne by Tamora the Queen of Goths)

> A joyless, dismal, black, and sorrowful issue.
> . . . as loathsome as a toad
> Amongst the fair-faced breeders of our clime. (4.2.66–8)

Aaron questions this, asking, 'Is black so base a hue?" (4.2.71), and displays a tenderness for his child that contests the stereotypical views of black inhumanity.

Shakespeare repeatedly stages such contests of perspective: in *Othello*, the hero's gentleness and nobility and Desdemona's passion for him are set against

Iago's use of bestial imagery to describe their alliance; the Venetian Senate's mild response to the inter-racial marriage (because Othello is so important to Venice in meeting the Turkish threat) is contrasted to Brabanzio's horror at his daughter's behaviour. *The Merchant of Venice* vividly evokes the difference perceived by both Jews and Christians between their two communities: Shylock says he bears 'an ancient grudge' against Antonio because the latter is a Christian who 'hates our sacred nation' (1.3.43), and the Christians refer to Shylock as a 'devil' (1.3.94; 3.1.19), 'old carrion' (3.1.31). At the same time, the play unsettles any assumptions of absolute difference by highlighting their shared mercantile culture: Portia, disguised as the learned legal man, asks 'Which is the merchant here, and which the Jew?' (4.1.169). Shylock stakes a passionate claim to a shared humanity (and right to revenge): 'Hath not a Jew eyes? Hath not a Jew hands, organs, dimensions, senses, affections, passions . . . If you prick us do we not bleed? If you tickle us do we not laugh? If you poison us do we not die? . . . And if you wrong us shall we not revenge?' (3.1.49–56).

The English attitude to outsiders was not uniformly one of smug superiority. Europeans viewed Turks (to take but one example) with a great deal of anxiety as well as a grudging admiration of their military strength and organization. As in the case of Judaism, Islam was especially threatening because it too was a religion of the Book (and offered an alternative interpretation of it) and because it had coexisted with Christianity in the very heart of Europe. By the sixteenth century, Islam was viewed as an 'unclean bird' that had been bred in Arabia, a 'poison' and a 'pestilence' that had 'infected' a large part of Asia, as well as Africa, and would overrun Europe if not checked.[37] As successful imperialists, the Turks were regarded as cruel and bloodthirsty, 'the scourge of Europe', but they were also covertly admired. As England tried to establish trading connections with Morocco and other Islamic territories, Elizabethan and Jacobean writers would occasionally suggest an affinity between Protestantism and Islam. In 1578 Morocco had, with English military aid, defeated the Portuguese at the famous battle of Alcazar. Edmund Morgan, a prominent merchant and later ambassador to Abd-el-Malek's court, and several others suggested that Muslims and Protestants had much in common as opposed to the idolatrous Catholics. Elizabeth herself claimed that both she and the Great Turk were enemies to idolaters. In my view, any implied affinity between Moors and English people was tenuous and expedient at best; anti-Islamic discourses never abated during the period, and contemporary writers regularly suggested an overlap between Muslims and Roman Catholics:

> If Mahomet, that prophet false,
> Eternity do gain
> Then shall the Pope, and you his saints,
> In heaven be sure to reign.[38]

Thus, schisms within Christianity complicated attitudes to religious and ethnic 'outsiders', as well as to national identifications.

Can we call early modern stereotyping of black people, Jews, Muslims, the Irish, and others racism? Would it be accurate to characterize antipathy to outsiders in Shakespeare's England as xenophobia? Various critics have rightly cautioned against interpreting early modern attitudes and institutions simply from our own perspectives. It would be equally wrong not to see how early modern attitudes were also different from still older histories of contact. However, as I have tried to show, during the modern period, the growth of European nationalisms and colonialisms generated crucial new ways of seeing racial and cultural others, and these ways establish intellectual, literary, and political genealogies for colonial views of race and nation. Of course, racism is more than simply colour prejudice; some critics define it as the translation of prejudice into unfair social advantage. Early modern England did not yet possess such advantage with regard to every kind of outsider, but it had already begun to invoke difference to justify its brutal practices in Ireland and the Americas, to outlaw Jews, expel Moors, and create internal hierarchies within its own population. Over the next century, attitudes outlined here would certainly feed into justifications of the slave trade, plantations, and unfair trading practices. It is useful to remember that 'the absence of an articulated doctrine of racial superiority does not necessarily imply behavioral tolerance in the relations between people of somatically different groups'.[39] Finally, in my view, a crucial feature of racism is the belief that there is a biologically or divinely ordained correspondence between the 'outside' and 'inside' of human beings, and that both external appearances and internal qualities are transmitted through bloodlines. In this sense, early modern notions of 'difference' had certainly begun to become racist. This is not to suggest that they were not also contested or contradictory or fraught with anxiety about the European 'self': for example, the invocation of the proverbial Ethiope who could not be 'washed white' clearly addressed the anxiety that colour lines were not inviolate.

Stage representations of outsiders were instrumental in influencing public opinion about outsiders (as about many other matters). By 1600, eighteen to twenty-four thousand Londoners were going to the theatre each week, so we can imagine how important a medium it was at a time when very few people were able to read or had access to books. According to Thomas Platter, 'the English pass their time, learning at the play what is happening abroad . . . since for the most part the English do not much use to travel, but prefer to learn of foreign matters and take their pleasures at home'.[40] Indeed, stage images influenced 'historical' accounts of the rest of the world: in the 1610 edition of Richard Knolles's influential book, *General History of the Turks*, the picture of Emperor Timur (or Tamburlaine) is possibly a drawing of the actor Edward Alley in the role of Tamburlaine in Marlowe's play of the same name (see plate 5). Outsiders or foreigners were always embodied on the stage by white male actors. Such impersonations had also had a long tradition in England. Since the medieval period, blacking up was a central part of representations of the grotesque, the evil, or the exotic. Mummers' plays,

5   Edward Alleyn (?) as Tamburlaine. From Richard Knolles's *General History of the Turks* (1610).

miracle plays, and Morris dancing all involved blackening the faces of performers. In more sophisticated circles too there was a sustained interest in the enactment of difference. In 1510, King Henry VIII and the Earl of Essex dressed themselves 'after Turkey fashion', their torchbearers and six ladies blackening themselves with cloth to appear 'like Moreskoes' or 'blacke Mores'.[41] Between 1510 and 1605, there are at least six documented instances of courtiers appearing as blacks: most famously, Queen Anne herself appeared as one of the black daughters of the River Niger in Ben Jonson's *Masque of Blackness* (1605). James I was especially fond of Jonson's *The Gypsies Metamorphosed* (1621) in which noblemen took the part of gypsies. These images of difference did not always hinge on the question of colour: court entertainments regularly included Irish characters who were white but whose alienness was enacted through their costumes (notably the Irish mantle) and through accented speech.

While the entertainments involved the impersonation of outsiders by insiders, they often depicted a movement in the opposite direction. Outsiders became insiders either by literally changing colour (as in *The Masque of Blackness*) or by changing their political allegiance or faith as in Jonson's *Irish Masque* (1617), wherein Irish gentlemen shed their mantles to indicate their submission of the Irish to the English monarch. On Shakespearian and other early modern stages, the outsider is not safely 'outside' at all – like the older figure of the wild man, he or she threatens to cross over the boundaries of racial or ethnic or religious difference. Othello is not simply an alien who crosses over by marrying Desdemona, he is also the exotic outsider who alone is capable of defending Venice against other outsiders such as the Turks. Shylock as well as Portia draw attention to the unstable divide between 'the merchant' and 'the Jew' in Venice, and Jessica's conversion to Christianity reminds the audience just how fragile the boundaries between communities really are. But these plays simultaneously reassert the difficulty of such crossovers: both Othello and Jessica in some senses remain outside the Christian fold. Thus, these plays explore the fragility as well as the tenacity of difference.

It has been suggested that the cultural anxiety represented by the converted Jew 'isn't about Marranism, or Jewishness, or even . . . about emerging ideas of race and nation, but about cultural change and a fluid sense of self that one could call "modern"'.[42] In my view, however, outsiders who mould themselves in the image of the dominant culture are not just a shorthand for an emerging 'modern' preoccupation with self-fashioning and mobility; rather, self-fashioning and mobility, indeed 'modernity' itself are, in part, the result of the religious, cultural, and racial changes that this chapter has been charting. The enactment of cultural and religious interchange and contact rehearsed fantasies of, as well as anxieties about, the incorporation of 'others' into the 'self' but also the potential crossing of racial, cultural, religious, and national boundaries by the European, Christian, white self. Shakespeare as well as other playwrights also depicted Europeans who (to use the vocabulary of a later day) 'went native'. In *Antony and Cleopatra*, for example, Antony is seduced by Cleopatra into abandoning Roman masculinity and becoming an 'effeminized' Egyptian.

The fear of Englishmen turning Turk was widely expressed in relation to English travellers and seamen in travelogues, sermons, and other writings of the period. Sexuality was of course the conduit for racial and cultural crossovers; hence women occupy a central place in the dramas of difference. Tamora, Desdemona, and Miranda are the means for the attempted cultural crossings of Aaron, Othello, or Caliban. When women themselves are the converts, like Jessica, or Hippolyta the Amazon queen in *A Midsummer Night's Dream*, they usually represent a more reassuring scenario of a safe assimilation of outsiders into the dominant culture. In each case, however, Shakespeare evokes the possibility that both difference and assimilation can be eroded.

The hardening of racial categories during this period was accompanied by proliferating images of hybridity and crossover. In a remarkable passage, a character called Irenius in Spenser's *A View of the Present State of Ireland* evokes the long history of multiple migrations of the Huns and the Vandals, and later the Moors, into Spain. Irenius laments that although the Moors were

> beaten out by Ferdinand of Aragon and Isabella his wife, yet they were not so cleansed but that, through the marriages which they had made and mixture with the people of the land during their long continuance there, they had left no pure drop of Spanish blood . . . So that, of all the nations under heaven, I suppose the Spaniard is the most mingled and most uncertain . . .

Irenius claims that he does not regard such mingling as negative,

> for I think there is *no nation now in Christendom nor much further but is mingled and compounded with others.* For it was a singular providence of God . . . to mingle nations so remote, miraculously to make, as it were, one blood and kindred of all people, and each to have knowledge of him. (p. 82; emphasis added)

Coming as it does after Spenser's horrified evocations of the English who have 'degenerated' into the 'wild Irish', this celebration of global hybridity, we can see, is a rather anxious attempt to place racial intermingling into a more reassuring framework. It also reminds us of the contradictions that beset contemporary discourses on 'difference' – according to the Bible (to take just one example) all human beings were children of the same God, and yet according to the same Bible, they were sorted out into servants and masters, the accursed and the blessed, the black and the white. English encounters with outsiders, at home and abroad, opened up possibilities of a material exchange of goods, which most English people were to regard as beneficial, and also of spreading the word of God among unbelievers. But such possibilities were also fraught with danger – encounters with outsiders could always blur precisely those lines of demarcation which guaranteed both material and ideological benefit, and conjured up the possibility of a reverse traffic, whereby the English turned into Turks, became Irish, or in other ways crossed the bounds of civility.

Shakespeare's depictions of outsiders draw upon and amplify such contradictions, exploring the romance as well as the tragedy of attempted crossovers. Whether we think that they worked to consolidate the nascent discourse of race, or to alert English audiences to its unfairness and instability, Shakespeare's 'others' remind us that we need expanded conceptual frameworks to analyse Renaissance culture, Shakespearian drama, and their modern-day legacies.

Notes

1. This chapter will focus, with a few exceptions, on religious or racial outsiders – there were also many French, German, Italian, Spanish, and Dutch people in England who are not discussed here. I should like to thank Lisa Lampert, Carol Neely, Michael Shapiro, and Richard Wheeler who helped me reshape and think through the concerns of this chapter.

2. G. D. Rogers's 1916 essay, 'Voyages and Explorations: Geography: Maps' is quoted and discussed by John Gillies, *Shakespeare and the Geography of Difference* (Cambridge University Press, 1994), p. 1.

3. Early exceptions to this critical pattern include Samuel Chew, *The Crescent and the Rose: Islam and England During the Renaissance* (New York: Oxford University Press, 1937); Eldred Jones, *Othello's Countrymen: The African in English Renaissance Drama* (London: Oxford University Press, 1965); Leslie Fiedler, *The Stranger in Shakespeare* (New York: Stein and Day, 1972); G. K. Hunter, *Dramatic Identities and Cultural Tradition: Studies in Shakespeare and his Contemporaries* (Liverpool University Press, 1978).

4. Michael Dobson, *The Making of the National Poet: Shakespeare, Adaptation and Authorship, 1660–1769* (Oxford: Clarendon Press, 1992); James Shapiro, *Shakespeare and the Jews* (New York: Columbia University Press, 1996).

5. Both instances are discussed by Terence Hawkes, 'Swisser-Swatter: Making a Man of English Letters', in John Drakakis, ed., *Alternative Shakespeares* (London: Methuen, 1985) p. 33.

6. Richard Helgerson, *Forms of Nationhood: The Elizabethan Writing of England* (Chicago and London: University of Chicago Press, 1992).

7. Liah Greenfeld, *Nationalism: Five Roads to Modernity* (Cambridge, Mass.: Harvard University Press, 1992), p. 67.

8. Benedict Anderson, *Imagined Communities: Reflections on the Origin and Spread of Nationalism* (London and New York: Verso, 1991).

9. Richard Marienstras, *New Perspectives on the Shakespearian World*, trans. Janet Lloyd (Cambridge University Press, 1985), pp. 99–125. I am indebted to Marienstras for his discussion of the status of foreigners.

10. Andrew Hadfield and Willey Maley, 'Introduction' in Brendan Bradshaw, Andrew Hadfield, and Willy Maley, eds., *Representing Ireland: Literature and the Origins of Conflict* (Cambridge University Press, 1993), p. 7.

11. See Paul Rabinow, ed., *The Foucault Reader* (New York: Pantheon Books, 1984), p. 8.

12. Edward W. Said, *Orientalism* (London and Henley: Routledge and Kegan Paul, 1978).

13. Stephen Greenblatt, *Renaissance Self-Fashioning: From More to Shakespeare* (University of Chicago Press, 1980); *Marvelous Possessions: The Wonder of the New World* (University of Chicago Press, 1991).

14. Kim Hall, *Things of Darkness: Economies of Race and Gender in Early Modern England* (Ithaca, N.Y.: Cornell University Press, 1995).

15. Valerie Traub, 'The Psychomorphology of the Clitoris', *Gay and Lesbian Quarterly* 2 (1995), 81–113. See also Katherine Park, 'The Rediscovery of the Clitoris, French Medicine and the Tribade, 1570–1620', in *The Body in Parts: Fantasies of Corporeality in Early Modern Europe*, ed. David Hillman and Carla Mazzio (New York and London: Routledge, 1997), pp. 171–94.

16. Sir Walter Ralegh, 'The discoverie of the large, rich, and beautiful Empire of Guiana . . .' in *The Principal Navigations Voyages Traffiques and Discoveries of the English Nation*, ed. Richard Hakluyt (Glasgow: James MacLehose and Sons, 1904–5), X, p. 355.

17. Edmund Spenser, *A View of the Present State of Ireland* in *Ireland under Elizabeth and James the First*, ed. Henry Morley (London: George Routledge and Sons, 1890), p. 54.

18. Hakluyt, *Principal Navigations*, III, 328.

19. Tripta Desai, *The East India Company: A Brief Survey from 1599 to 1857* (New Delhi: Kanak Publications, 1984), p. 3.

20. Andrew Hadfield, '"The Naked and the Dead": Elizabethan Perceptions of Ireland', in *Travel and Drama in Shakespeare's Time*, ed. Jean-Pierre Maquerlot and Michèle Willems (Cambridge University Press, 1996), pp. 32–54; p. 41.

21. *Thomas Platter's Travels in England*, trans. and introduced by Clare Williams (London: Jonathan Cape, 1937), pp. 171–2.

22. See Kim Hall, *Things of Darkness*, p. 271. For this and other histories of black people in England see Peter Fryer, *Staying Power: The History of Black People in Britain* (London: Pluto Press, 1984) and James Walvin, *The Black Presence: A Documented History of the Negro in England, 1555–1860* (London: Orbach and Chambers, 1971).

23. Hans Kohn, 'The Genesis and Character of English Nationalism', *Journal of the History of Ideas* 1 (January 1940), 69–94; p. 73. I am indebted to Kohn, Shapiro, *Shakespeare and the Jews*, Richard Marienstras, and Andrew Pettegree, *Foreign Protestant Communities in Sixteenth-century London* (Oxford: Clarendon Press, 1986) for my discussion in this paragraph.

24. See *Shakespeare and the Jews*, pp. 180–93.

25. 43 Elizabeth I (1601), in *Tudor Royal Proclamations*, ed. P. L. Hughes and J. F. Larkin, vol. III (New Haven and London: Yale University Press, 1969), p. 221.

26. Quoted by Shapiro, *Shakespeare and the Jews*, p. 18.

27. Peter Berek, 'The Jew as Renaissance Man', *Renaissance Quarterly* 51: 1 (Spring 1998), 128–62; p. 132.

28. 'Master Brerewood's Enquiries of the Religions Professed in the World' in *Hakluytus Posthumus*, ed. Samuel Purchas, vol. I (Glasgow: James Maclehose and Sons, 1905), pp. 324; Shapiro, *Shakespeare and the Jews*, p. 95.

29. Fray Prudencio de Sandoval, *Historia de la vida y hechos del emperador Carlos V* (1604), quoted in Jerome Friedman, 'Jewish Conversion, the Spanish Pure Blood Laws and Reformation: a Revisionist View of Racial and Religious Anti-Semitism', *Sixteenth Century Journal* 18 (1987), 3–29; pp. 16–17.

30. Ivan Hannaford, *Race: The History of an Idea in the West* (Baltimore and London: Johns Hopkins University Press, 1996), p. 124.

31. Hakluyt, *Principal Navigations*, VI, 167, emphasis added.

32. 'Observations of Africa, taken out of John Leo', in *Hakluytus Posthumus*, V, 357.

33. Anthony Gerard Barthelemy, who also provides a useful discussion of the term's lineage and history. *Black Face, Maligned Race* (Baton Rouge and London: Louisiana State University Press, 1987), pp. 6–17.

34. George Best's *A True Discourse of the last Voyages of Discoverie . . .* (London, 1578) quoted and discussed by Alden T. Vaughan and Virginia Mason Vaughan, 'Before *Othello*: Elizabethan Representations of Sub-Saharan Africans', *The William and Mary Quarterly*, 3rd series, 54: 1 (January 1997), 19–44; p. 27.

35. James H. Sweet, 'The Iberian Roots of American Racist Thought', *The William and Mary Quarterly*, 3rd series, 54: 1 (January 1997), 143–66; p. 149.

36. *Images of the Medieval Peasant* (Stanford University Press, 1999).

37. 'Master Brerewood's Enquiries', in *Hakluytus Posthumus*, I, 314–19.

38. John Phillips, *A Friendly Larum, Select Poetry Chiefly Devotional of the Reign of Queen Elizabeth*, ed. Edward Farr (Cambridge: Parker Society, 1845), part II, p. 528.

39. Orlando Patterson, *Slavery and Social Death*, quoted by Sweet, 'Iberian Roots', p. 165. I am indebted to Sweet's discussion of racism, as well as to Robert Miles, *Racism* (London: Routledge, 1989).

40. *Platter's Travels*, p. 170.

41. Jones, *Othello's Countrymen*, p. 28.

42. Berek, 'The Jew as Renaissance Man', pp. 130, 158.

Reading list

Anderson, Benedict, *Imagined Communities, Reflections on the Origin and Spread of Nationalism* (London and New York: Verso, 1991).

Barthelemy, Anthony Gerard, *Black Face, Maligned Race* (Baton Rouge and London: Louisiana State University Press, 1987).

Berek, Peter, 'The Jew as Renaissance Man', *Renaissance Quarterly* 51: 1 (Spring 1998).

Bradshaw, Brendan, Andrew Hadfield, and Willy Maley, ed. *Representing Ireland: Literature and the Origins of Conflict* (Cambridge University Press 1993).

Chew, Samuel, *The Crescent and the Rose: Islam and England During the Renaissance* (New York: Oxford University Press, 1937).

Dobson, Michael, *The Making of the National Poet: Shakespeare, Adaptation and Authorship 1660–1769* (Oxford: Clarendon Press, 1992).

Fryer, Peter, *Staying Power: The History of Black People in Britain* (London: Pluto Press, 1984).

Gillies, John, *Shakespeare and the Geography of Difference* (Cambridge University Press, 1994).

Greenblatt, Stephen, *Marvelous Possessions: The Wonder of the New World* (University of Chicago Press, 1991).

   Renaissance Self-Fashioning: From More to Shakespeare (University of Chicago Press, 1980).

Hakluyt, Richard, *The Principal Navigations Voyages Traffiques and Discoveries of the English Nation* (Glasgow: James MacLehose and Sons, 1904–5).

Hall, Kim, *Things of Darkness: Economies of Race and Gender in Early Modern England* (Ithaca, N.Y.: Cornell University Press, 1995).

Hannaford, Ivan, *Race, The History of an Idea in the West* (Baltimore and London: Johns Hopkins University Press, 1996).

Helgerson, Richard, *Forms of Nationhood: The Elizabethan Writing of England* (University of Chicago Press, 1992).

Jones, Eldred D., *Othello's Countrymen: The African in English Renaissance Drama* (London: Oxford University Press, 1965).

Maquerlot, Jean-Pierre and Michèle Willems, ed., *Travel and Drama in Shakespeare's Time* (Cambridge University Press, 1996).

Miles, Robert, *Racism* (London: Routledge, 1989).

Purchas, Samuel, ed., *Hakluytus Posthumus* (Glasgow: James Maclehose and Sons, 1905).

Said, Edward W., *Orientalism* (London: Routledge and Kegan Paul, 1978).

Shapiro, James, *Shakespeare and the Jews* (New York: Columbia University Press, 1996).

Tokson, Elliot H., *The Popular Image of the Black Man in English Drama 1550–1688* (Boston: G. K. Hall, 1982).

Vaughan, Alden T. and Virginia Mason Vaughan, 'Before *Othello*: Elizabethan Representations of Sub–Saharan Africans', *The William and Mary Quarterly*, 3rd series, 54: 1 (January 1997), 19–44.

11

DAVID SCOTT KASTAN

Shakespeare and English history

History in Shakespeare's England: from Caxton to Camden

SHAKESPEARE'S artistry uncannily animates the past. As one near contemporary insists, in a commendatory poem in the second edition of Shakespeare's collected plays (1632), the plays energetically present 'what story [i.e., history] coldly tells', and they even more literally enliven history in their ability 'to raise our ancient sovereigns from their hearse'. The stage makes the past present and allows its audiences vicarious emotional participation. When historical characters are represented in the theatre, 'the present age / Joys in their joy and trembles at their rage'. For the commendatory poet, this is value enough; we are 'by elaborate play / Tortured and tickled'.

Yet the representation of the past was of more serious concern to many in Shakespeare's England. History was unquestionably among the most influential forms of writing circulating among the ranks of an increasingly literate populace, and history plays were written not least to exploit in the theatre the enthusiasm for history that was evident in the bookstalls. But to understand what these history plays were (and were not) for the audiences that saw them, it is necessary to think about how the more traditional forms of history writing were understood and valued.

There was a general consensus that the past had meaning for the present, but less agreement about what this meaning was. History was sometimes recognized as a branch of theology, the record of God's providence, and sometimes it was seen as an exclusively secular concern, the record solely of human motives and actions. History was sometimes valued because it is truthful, that is, for its accurate recording of events; and sometimes it was valued because it is useful, that is, for its ability to provide compelling examples of behaviour to be emulated or shunned. History was sometimes understood as the record of noble deeds and matters of state, and sometimes its focus self-consciously widened to include the experiences of a greater slice of the population, implicitly insisting that the nation was more than just its aristocracy.

Although many in Shakespeare's England were well aware of the ambiguities and contradictions surrounding the practice of history writing, history unquestionably existed for them as a significant cultural enterprise, and indeed it is in this period that 'history' begins to form as an academic discipline.[1] History served the nation in various ways, and the multiple benefits of history writing were part of the familiar catalogues of praise that usually introduced it. Richard Stanyhurst, for example, in but one of the many sixteenth-century encomia of history, claimed that it serves as the 'marrow of reason, the cream of experience, the sap of wisdom, the pith of judgement, the library of knowledge, the kernel of policy, the unfoldress of treachery, the calendar of time, the lantern of truth, the life of memory, the doctress of behaviour, the register of antiquity, the trumpet of chivalry'.[2] And if no single example of history writing was likely to be all of these things, the variety of available historiographic practices indeed meant that history could function to recover and preserve the past, to instruct and inspire the present, to witness to God's providence, and to celebrate, perhaps even to define, the nation. Antiquarian, moral, theological, and political interests motivated both the writing and the reading of history, and could be discovered to various degrees in the wide range of historical texts that circulated.

Though history writing in Shakespeare's England would become most spectacularly available in the massive folio volumes of Foxe's *Acts and Monuments* (first published in 1563) or the collaborative project familiarly known as Holinshed's *Chronicles* (first published in 1577), already by the end of the fifteenth century history had emerged significantly both as a topic of serious thought and as a commodity. Indeed, the printing of history in England is virtually coextensive with the history of printing in England. Among the books printed by William Caxton in the years immediately after he founded the first English press in 1476, on Tothill Street in the shadow of Westminster Abbey, were two books of history writing: *The Chronicles of England* (1480), a translation of the *Brut*, an Anglo–French chronicle history of Britain beginning, as its name suggests, with its mythical founding by Brutus, a descendant of Aeneas, and continuing to the battle of Halidon Hill in 1333; and a translation of Ranulph Higden's *Polychronicon* (1482), a universal history in seven books, that began with Adam and Eve and continued to 1358, with Caxton himself adding an eighth book in his printed edition extending the narrative to 1460.

History was, of course, not all that Caxton printed (though interestingly the very first book that he did print, while still working in Bruges in 1474, was *The Recuyell of the History of Troy*, an English translation of Raôul Lefèvre's French version of two alleged eyewitness accounts of the Trojan War).[3] Nonetheless, the fact that Caxton so eagerly took on the printing and publishing (and even the writing) of history suggests how important the genre was – both to him and to the emerging reading public that enthusiastically greeted the supply of affordable copies allowed by the new technology. Caxton's versions of both the *Brut* and the *Polychronicon* went through multiple printed editions. By 1530, the *Brut*, which in its enlarged form had become known as 'Caxton's Chronicles', had been published thirteen times; the *Polychronicon* six.

Caxton's *Brut* and *Polychronicon* were the first two printed histories that a reader could consult in English, and they set the pattern for much of what was to come. The *Polychronicon* arranges human time according to the seven ages of the world, a structure of history derived ultimately from Augustine, in which worldly events find meaning in relation to the defining rhythms of salvation history; it is, however, no less than the more obviously nationalistic *Brut*, a work of secular and patriotic history designed for lay reading, in which the past takes its ordering principle from political institutions – regnal or mayoral years marking time – rather than from God's providential scheme.

Not least because of its independence from the structure of salvation history, the chronicle form evident in Caxton's two histories became a significant and successful genre, responding to the demands not only of an aristocratic readership but also of an increasingly literate middle 'sort' for histories that would help explain and secure their growing prestige. Numerous other chronicles were written, perhaps most significantly that by Robert Fabyan, a London draper, which would serve as both source and pattern for the chronicles of Hall and Holinshed that would later influence Shakespeare.

Fabyan's *New Chronycles of Englande and Fraunce* appeared posthumously in 1516. In the next half-century, Fabyan's work was printed six more times. Divided into seven parts, Fabyan's history begins with the Romans' appearance in ancient Britain and carries the history forward until 1485. The bulk of the book, however, covers the period 1066 to 1485, that is, from the Norman Conquest to the end of the Wars of the Roses. Additions first present in the 1533 edition extended the history to 1509, bringing it up through the reign of Henry VII.

Fabyan did little if any original scholarship, depending for most of his history on the accounts that were readily available to him in the augmented editions of the *Polychronicon* and the *Brut*, and in Geoffrey of Monmouth's *Historia Regum Britanniae*. But if Fabyan was not noticeably ambitious as a scholar – he describes his book merely as 'The Concordance of Histories' – he did compare his sources and often recognized contradictions between them. Indeed he saw as a major part of his task 'the stories and years to make accordant',[4] though his principle of adjudication was usually merely quantitative. Where one source varied 'from other writers of authority', he would rely on that which 'accordeth best with other stories and chronicles' (p. 35), with no apparent recognition that agreement might prove only common dependency rather than greater reliability. Nonetheless, in places he does show some sophistication about source material, insisting, for example, that the bias of the historian must be factored into one's reading, as with Geoffrey of Monmouth, who Fabyan realized omitted material that might taint the British past with 'dishonour': 'for he was a Briton, he showed the best for Britons' (p. 36).

Fabyan's chronicle, however, itself 'showed the best for Britons'. Although his occasionally voiced scepticism about received traditions would become the very mark of modern historiography, he wrote a history primarily designed to preserve and celebrate the English past, to 'spread / The famous honour of this fertile Isle' (p. 3). If he was suspicious of some of the Arthurian material that derived from Geoffrey, he, nonetheless, usually included it, because it provided a useful genealogy for sixteenth-century England's own energies and ambitions.

A more scholarly tradition of historiography was almost simultaneously established in England. The Italian cleric, Polydore Vergil, who had been educated at Padua and Bologna, had come to England in 1502, officially as the deputy collector of Peter's pence. He was encouraged by Henry VII to rewrite England's history, and he was hard at work on it by 1506. He had probably completed a version by 1513, though a printed edition of the *Anglica historia* was not available until 1534.

Vergil's history, written in Latin (and not published in English until the middle of the nineteenth century), demonstrated the scholarly rigour of continental humanism, even as it produced a history that would bolster the legitimacy of the Tudor reign. Vergil examined primary materials, such as statutes and other governmental documents, interviewed people who had first-hand knowledge of events, and, for the earlier history for which such direct evidence could not be assembled, energetically sought historical accounts that might be more accurate or more extensive than the *Brut* or the *Polychronicon*. He brought to the practice of history writing a methodological self-consciousness previously absent from the writing of English history,[5] a self-consciousness that led him to reject the historicity of the Arthurian material that made up much of the early chronicle material and accounted in large degree for its great popularity.

If Fabyan and Vergil superficially produce similar kinds of history, each organizing the swirl of event in terms of successive monarchical reigns, they differ in crucial ways that would shape the future directions of history writing. What counts as history for Fabyan could be seen as more capacious than what counts for Vergil. Fabyan focuses his narrative on the 'acts and deeds' of noble men, but fills his chronicle also with information irrelevant to the high politics of the nation. He writes as well of drought and dearth, of urban affairs and local customs. Clearly he is content to be one of those '*Chroniclers*' who do, as a seventeenth-century satirist put it, 'confound grave matters of estate / With plays of *Poppets*, and I wot not what'.[6] For Fabyan, history is the history of the nation's people, a history of the world that they experience.

For Vergil, history is the history of the nation's rulers and its governmental institutions. His is a history from above, almost exclusively a history of great men and the 'grave matters of estate' that Fabyan's capaciousness confounded. But it is also a history that is more plot than story, perhaps suggesting how powerful patronage might make for powerfully narrativized history. Fabyan's popular history is largely paratactic, that is, a history in which many things happen but not necessarily in any relation to one another nor moving towards any particular end. Indeed Edward Hall, while praising the 'diligence' of Fabyan's research, criticized the capacious chronicle itself as 'far shooting wide from the butt of a history'.[7] Hall complains that Fabyan's history lacks a 'butt', or target; it lacks, that is, teleological design. Vergil's history, however, unmistakably has such a 'butt': the coming of the Tudors to power. Unlike Fabyan's, his narrative is hypotactic: events are seen in causal relation as they unfold towards a known and desired end.

Fabyan and Vergil represent two separate impulses of English history writing. Fabyan's inclusive, popular history would give rise to the great chronicle tradition of Grafton, Holinshed, and Speed, while Vergil's more learned and critical practice would find its fulfilment in the seventeenth century in the work of Francis Bacon and John Selden. But the two historiographic traditions were never completely distinct.

Their interrelations can perhaps be seen most clearly in the work of Edward Hall. Hall, a London lawyer educated at Eton and Cambridge and a member of Parliament, made explicit Vergil's effort to use history for present purposes. His *Union of the Two Noble and Illustre Famelies of Lancastre & Yorke* (first published in 1548) recounts the emergence of the Tudor dynasty from the chaos of the Wars of the Roses. History, as for Vergil, is organized by individual monarchical reigns, stretching from 'The unquiet time of King Henry the Fourth' to 'the triumphant reign of King Henry the VIII'. But Hall has, like Fabyan, a more robust sense of what counts as history, filling his pages also with trial records and legislative debates, natural occurrences and local events, texturing the historical romance that was his chief interest: 'as King Henry the fourth was the beginning and root of the great discord and division: so was that godly matrimony [i.e., the marriage of Henry Richmond to Elizabeth of York], the final end of all dissensions, titles and debates' (sig. A2[r]).

But in spite of the conspicuous achievements of both the popular chronicle and the more learned historical writing, achievements that would in time prove decisive for the practices and protocols of English historical scholarship, most English readers would have encountered their history elsewhere. Almost everyone would have somewhere seen (if not necessarily read) the great volumes of John Foxe's *Acts and Monuments*, often known as *The Book of Martyrs*, that were chained, along with the Bible, to lecterns in cathedrals and in many parish churches. The two volumes of the 1570 edition run to approximately two-and-a-half million words printed on somewhat more than 2,300 large folio pages (14½ inches (36.8 cm) by 9½ inches (24 cm)). Foxe's history stands in two senses as a monumental witness to what Foxe calls 'the secret multitude of true believers'. It is monumental both in size and in intent, an imposing memorial to the martyrs whom Foxe sees as witnessing to and suffering for the Protestant faith. Foxe's history is a genealogy of and a justification for the Reformation itself, and, if not a claim that England is *the* elect nation, a recognition that England is *an* elect nation, whose position as bulwark against the forces of the Antichrist the book would both celebrate and reinforce.

If the various editions of Foxe's *Acts and Monuments* (eight between 1563 and

1641) offer massive evidence of the importance of history writing in the sixteenth century, equally telling evidence can be found in miniature, in the reduced form in which most readers would in fact have read historical texts. The big folios of Foxe, and other historians, were both unwieldy and expensive, and soon a supply of cheap and small-format histories, summaries or abridgements of larger works, began to fill the bookstalls. Even Foxe was abridged, first by Timothy Bright in 1589 in a quarto edition selling for five shillings, and subsequently in ever smaller redactions, eventually appearing in a version by John Taylor in 1616, which improbably reduced Foxe's book to two hundred and thirty eight couplets published in 64mo, its pages measuring a mere 1⅝ inches (4 cm) by 1¼ (3 cm).

Less spectacular reductions in size were of course the norm. Recognizing that few readers had either the money or the time to spend on the large chronicles, historians produced summaries or abridgements of the chronicles in inexpensive octavo and duodecimo formats, designed, as Alexander Ross said in his preface to *The Marrow of History* (1650), to be 'more portable, more legible, and more vendible, than the great Book'. The first of these abridgements was Thomas Cooper's *Epitome of Cronicles* (1549), a work begun by Thomas Languet, who had died having brought the history only up to the birth of Christ. Others soon followed Cooper's example, most notably Richard Grafton and John Stow. Though both published large folio editions of their histories, their abridgements were the great commercial successes – and generated an often bitter rivalry.[8] Grafton's *Abridgement of the Chronicles* was issued six times between 1563 and 1572, the year of his death; and Stow's *Summary of the English Chronicles* five times in that period, with an additional fourteen editions appearing between 1573 and 1618 (the last three of which were edited by Edmund Howes after Stow died in 1605).

Some forms of history writing, however, did not readily lend themselves to abridgement, most obviously the form that was generally known as chorography, combining historical data and geographic detail. Place and family names, local customs, topographic features, coins, inscriptions, ruins, monuments, and buildings are all described and analysed, enabling the history of a particular locale to come into view. But chorography resists abridgement because its logic is not narrative but accretive; more is always better. Details do not obscure the main point; they are the main point.[9]

William Camden, an undermaster at Westminster School, wrote the most influential version of this kind of history. His *Britannia*, published first in 1587 in Latin, was enlarged and reprinted five times before 1607; it was translated into English in 1610 by Philemon Holland, and an enlarged version of the English translation was published in 1637. *Britannia* was conceived as a guidebook to Roman Britain. Camden traced the Roman occupation of Britain, often following the path of the Roman roads as he searched for archaeological evidence of Britain's Roman past. Camden's interest was in part to connect the nation to

Imperial Rome, giving it a genealogy that would establish its links to the rest of Europe; but in part it was also a more general interest in the way the land absorbs and speaks its history.

Camden's geographic focus offers a fourth understanding of the nation, not as its people or as its rulers, as in Fabyan or Vergil, nor as the battlefield on which the forces of Christ and Antichrist waged war, as in Foxe, but the nation as the land itself – country, that is, as countryside. Though *Britannia* sought to describe the entire nation, after Camden the chorographic impulse tended to produce local histories of counties and towns. Local chorography could be seen as mere antiquarianism and evidence of regional pride; but its effects, if not its explicit motives, were less anodyne. It fractured the imagined wholeness of the nation, as it celebrated parochial interests over the centralizing impulses of the monarchy and reminded its readers how multiple and unstable the meanings of 'country' could be.

History, then, wrote the nation in various registers. It became progressively obvious that there wasn't a single past; rather, there were different pasts in which different conceptions of the nation became visible and were buttressed. If this made history a matter of considerable governmental concern (in 1599, for example, leading to an order insisting that all works of history be authorized by the Privy Council), it also made history a matter of significant public interest. Throughout the sixteenth century, history was read ever more widely, initially mainly among aristocratic and wealthy merchant readers but in the last quarter of the sixteenth century finding an increasingly broad audience for whom the complexly interrelated histories of the English nation were legible in the multiple forms and formats in which they could be read.

'*Time past made pastime*': Shakespeare's plays as history

In Ben Jonson's *The Devil is an Ass*, squire Fitzdottrel proclaims:

> Thomas of Woodstock
> I'm sure was Duke, and he was made away
> At Calais, as Duke Humphrey was at Bury;
> And Richard the third, you know what end he came to.

With sarcasm, Meercraft grants that this gull is 'cunning i' the chronicle', but the dense Fitzdottrel proudly admits to a different source of knowledge: 'No, I confess I ha't from the play-books / And think they're more authentic' (2.4.8–14).[10]

Whether Jonson's fun is here aimed more at the unreliability of the chronicles than at the unreliability of the history play isn't quite clear, but rates of literacy alone assure that many in Shakespeare's England would, like Fitzdottrel, have encountered their history in the drama rather than on the pages of works by professional historians. Indeed even in the nineteenth century, the Duke of Marlborough, as Coleridge relates, 'was not ashamed to confess that his principal acquaintance with English history' was derived from Shakespeare's plays.[11]

Although Marlborough is hardly alone in this regard, the fact that Shakespeare has served many as a source of historical knowledge does not make him a historian. In 1612, Thomas Heywood enthusiastically claimed that history plays have 'instructed such as cannot read in the discovery of all our *English Chronicles*',[12] but, if indeed the plays present lively images of historical events and personages, it is not obvious that they are to be primarily thought of as forms of historical writing.

Undeniably English history was an important subject for playwrights of Shakespeare's time. By the time of the publication of the First Folio (1623) each of the twenty-four monarchs from William the Conqueror to Elizabeth had been represented in a play, and at least one play on an English historical subject had been published in twenty-five of the previous thirty years. But however eagerly dramatists embraced this English history, it served them mainly as a repository of plots for the many new plays that the successful professional theatres demanded rather than as an identifiable dramatic genre.

It isn't clear that Shakespeare thought of his plays on English history in any precise sense as history plays. The designation comes from the organization of the First Folio, the collected volume of Shakespeare's plays put together by John Heminges and Henry Condell in 1623, seven years after the playwright's death. The ten plays that are grouped there as 'Histories' and differentiated from the more familiar genres of comedy and tragedy are obviously linked by their common subject-matter, an origin specifically in post-conquest English history; but it is not clear that the grouping defines a common generic commitment. The early printings of *3 Henry VI*, *Richard II*, and *Richard III* refer to each of those plays as tragedies; and Francis Meres, in *Palladis Tamia* (1598) praising Shakespeare 'for Tragedy', indiscriminately includes as examples 'his *Richard the 2*, *Richard the 3*, *Henry the 4*, *King John*, *Titus Andronicus*, and his *Romeo and Juliet*' (sig. OO2r). Shakespeare's histories may be, then, more a result of Heminges and Condell's generic imagination than of Shakespeare's own.

But whether or not Shakespeare had a specific idea of what a history play should be, clearly his dramatic imagination was sharply drawn to English historical subjects. The ten history plays are a number greater than any other playwright of the period wrote on English history, and they cover a large swath of that past, *King John* and *Henry VIII* defining the chronological limits of Shakespeare's wide focus. *King John* opens soon after the king has been crowned, an event that took place in 1199, and *Henry VIII* (probably co-written with John Fletcher) ends with the birth of Elizabeth, which occurred in 1533, and looks forward to the reign of James I, during which it was written and acted. The eight other historical plays, usually considered as two discrete 'tetralogies', cover the tumultuous period between 1397 and 1485 that ended with the Tudors coming to power. *Richard II*, the two *Henry IV* plays, and *Henry V*, plus the three *Henry VI* plays and *Richard III*, traverse England's medieval history from the deposition of Richard II to the end of the Wars of the Roses and Henry Richmond's crowning as the first of the Tudor monarchs.

It is no doubt tempting to see these eight plays *in toto*, as many have, as a dramatic version of Hall's *Union of the Noble and Illustre Famelies*, that is, as Shakespeare's account of the political effects of the deposition of Richard II playing themselves out in history until England's tribulations end in Tudor glory. Nonetheless, a major difficulty of maintaining such a view is that the two tetralogies were not written in the order in which the history unfolded. The culminating historical events were dramatized first by Shakespeare in the three *Henry VI* plays and *Richard III*; and only after did he take up the story that was the supposed point of origin. At the very least one must then say that Shakespeare did not begin writing these eight histories with the intention of dramatizing Hall's moralized history. Second, the plays themselves are so very different, even in their use and understanding of history, that it is hard to see them as the tesserae of a single grand mosaic.

No single model of history emerges from the plays. They do not uniformly enact God's providential design, nor do they inevitably assert the truth of a machiavellian *Realpolitik*; the pious Henry VI is destroyed by a machiavellian monster, but that monster is in turn undone by the actions of providence. The plays experiment with different formal strategies as they seek a form for history: homiletic tragedy, saturnalian comedy, the prodigal son play, epic history, and these often in improbable mixtures that bring incompatible visions of history into contact and conflict.

Yet whatever their complex generic impulses, the individual plays themselves can hardly serve as reliable history. They do not attempt in any exacting way to recollect and rehearse the past. Obviously there are the purely fictional characters and events: 'the humorous conceits of Sir John Falstaff', for example, that compete with the historical plot on the title page of the quarto of *1 Henry IV* as well as on the stage. But historical material is itself often reordered or even ignored. Queen Margaret's bitter choric presence in *Richard III* is Shakespeare's creation, as she had returned to France in 1476 and indeed had died by the time of Richard's accession. Arguably, her role as a fury promising revenge for past wrongs is somehow appropriate for one returned from the dead, but her forbidding presence on stage has no historical warrant. Examples could be endlessly multiplied. In every one of the historical plays, events are selected, sometimes invented, and always shaped so that what Sidney calls the 'bare was' of history is dressed with dramatic purpose and power or simply cast aside.

This does not mean that Shakespeare had free rein to rewrite history. The pressure of historical fact is heavy upon him in these plays, if only because the broad outlines of the history would be generally known. He could not, for example, have the English lose the battle at Agincourt in his *Henry V*, but he can

– and does – structure the encounter there so that dramatic relationships are clarified in the absence of historical evidence or even in the face of it.

At Agincourt, an outnumbered and exhausted English army defeats a much larger force of French troops. On this, the play is in complete agreement with the chronicles. The historical sources, however, report that the improbable victory was gained in large part by superior military strategy: the 'politic invention', as Holinshed says, of placing 'stakes bound with iron sharp at both ends to the length of five or six foot to be pitched before the archers, and of each side the footmen like a hedge, to the intent that if the barded [i.e., armoured] horses ran rashly upon them, they might shortly be gored and destroyed' (Bullough, IV, 393). Even *The Famous Victories of Henry V*, a Queen's Men play of the 1580s that significantly influenced Shakespeare's conception of the reign, notes the 'brave policy' of the 'stakes of the trees' (lines 1168–73).

Shakespeare, on the other hand, makes no mention of the device; indeed his Henry proudly claims that victory came 'without stratagem, / But in plain shock and even play of battle' (4.8.107–8). The defeat of the French against the 'fearful odds' (4.3.5) that the English faced on the battlefield would no doubt be more explicable if mention were made of the sharpened stakes that Henry had ordered to be placed before his archers to prevent the French horsemen from overrunning his troops; but Shakespeare goes out of his way to emphasize the almost miraculous nature of the victory.

The casualty report delivered after the battle reinforces this intent. The French, as in the chronicles, are said to have lost ten thousand men, while the English lose only

> Edward the Duke of York, the Earl of Suffolk,
> Sir Richard Keighley, Davy Gam Esquire;
> None else of name, and of all other men
> But five-and-twenty. (4.8.97–100)

This is almost an exact transcription of the account in Holinshed, but it omits the rest of the sentence, where Holinshed says that it is only 'as some do report' (Bullough, IV, 400). Edward Hall adds even more sceptically: 'if you will give credit to such as write miracles' (*The Union of the Two Noble . . . Famelies*, 1548, sig. d2ʳ). Both historians are well aware that 'other writers of greater credit affirm', that there were slain above five or six hundred persons' (Bullough, IV, 400; Hall, *Union*, sig. d2r).

Even at the larger number, the victory is of astonishing proportions, and Shakespeare's acceptance of the report of least credit (along with his omission of the emphasis in the historical accounts upon the strategy of the sharpened pikes) suggests that probability is not here Shakespeare's goal. The credible is rejected in favour of the miraculous; the historical logic of probable cause abandoned in favour of the poetic logic of giantkilling.

The play as a whole reveals the same transformative process. Shakespeare has inherited a well-known history, most immediately from the account in Holinshed's *Chronicles*. Scenes and even speeches can be traced directly to the pages of the historical work. Nonetheless, Shakespeare does not merely dramatize what he finds on the pages of the chronicle. He structures his history to give it a shape that the historical records deny.

The nine-and-a-half years of Henry's rule was the shortest of the Lancastrian reigns but also the most successful. But in his handling of the historical material, Shakespeare turns the received story of the 'famous victories' of Henry V into an even more remarkable history, giving the reign almost mythic shape and significance. Shakespeare structures his history in part by omission. First, the anti-Lancastrian rebellions and the Lollard activity that dominated the first eighteen months of Henry's rule are completely ignored by Shakespeare, replacing the reality of a tense and divided country with the dramatic illusion of a unified England enthusiastically committed to the will of its king. Second, the events of the French war are themselves selected and compressed so that the great victory at Agincourt leads directly to the peace at Troyes, omitting the chronicles' account of the intervening four years of intensive fighting before the peace was achieved in 1420, with Henry's marriage to Catherine celebrated twelve days after the treaty was signed. Finally, the peace treaty in Shakespeare's play concludes the hostility, promising a time of 'Christian-like accord' (5.2.325). In the chronicles, however, the Dauphin refused to accept the terms of the treaty, forcing Henry to return to France. This subsequent invasion met with greater resistance than the first, and Henry died in 1422 of an illness contracted during the long siege of Meaux in the winter of 1421–2, having failed to subdue the Dauphin's forces, and indeed having failed even to outlive the French King Charles and so never in truth becoming King of France.

Thus Shakespeare's dramatic version of the history, through omission and compression, gives the achievement of the reign a clarity and coherence it lacked in fact. Shakespeare's Harry leads a small band of valiant soldiers against a much larger force of arrogant Frenchmen. The astounding victory at Agincourt ends the French resistance, confirming England's moral and military superiority. The shape of this restructured history is a cliché of propagandistic plotting, evidence of Shakespeare's deliberate transformation of history into patriotic myth.

In *Henry V*, Shakespeare clearly wants Henry V to appear even more irresistibly heroic than he does in the chronicles. But if Shakespeare makes Henry's heroic energies unmistakable, he does not allow us to take them as the whole truth about the English King. His political and military successes are given great emphasis, but Shakespeare embeds their telling in a complex set of non-historical qualifying frames – the idealizing choruses and the comic plot – that make the restructured historical material seem manifestly partial, and that leave Henry's glory vulnerable to the contrasts and contradictions that are produced.

Certainly the truth of the reign is in part the heroic conception of the king that Shakespeare inherits and intensifies, but Shakespeare uses the other aspects of his plot to expose and explore the costs, both ethical and psychological, of Henry's triumphs. We do see Henry V as hero, but the play as a whole makes us see more clearly than ever Henry does exactly what this means. Much has been won, but some things have been lost. Shakespeare's story, of course, is the story of Henry's 'famous victories', but Shakespeare, unlike his sources, insists that those victories were achieved by the exercise of an imagination too ready to sacrifice moral excellence for effective political leadership, too willing to subordinate humane values to imperial ambitions. In the multiple angles of vision that Shakespeare's play provides, as history's authority is subordinated to Shakespeare's dramatic design, we discover the fallible humanity of even this 'mirror of all Christian kings' (2.0.6).

'To take advantage of the absent time': Shakespeare's plays as historiography

In whatever sense, then, that Shakespeare's plays can be seen as forms of history writing, they cannot be valued primarily as reliable accounts of the historical events on which they are based. They are not living chronicles, or 'quick books', as the Corpus Christi plays were termed. But if Shakespeare's history plays will not serve as accurate representations of the English past, they do serve as provocative explorations of the nature of history and of history writing.

In *Richard III*, one of the young princes presciently inquires about the Tower. 'Did Julius Caesar build that place, my lord?', Edward asks Buckingham; and the duke replies that Caesar did begin its building, 'which since succeeding ages have re-edified'. The prince then asks the source of the duke's knowledge: 'Is it upon record, or else reported / Successively from age to age, he built it?' Buckingham assures him that it is 'upon record', but the prince's historiographic anxiety has been piqued:

> But say, my lord, it were not registered,
> Methinks the truth should live from age to age,
> As 'twere retailed to all posterity
> Even to the general all-ending day. (3.1.69–78)

It is a rich and complicated exchange. The prince's curiosity about architectural history is motivated less by antiquarian interest than by his obvious anxiety at Richard's suggestion that he await his coronation in the Tower. But the exchange itself raises important issues central to the play – and to the histories at large. It provides various criteria by which historical evidence can be evaluated.

The prince's hope that the truth of the past could be preserved 'even if it were not registered' is an innocent desire for memory to function to save everything from oblivion, with nothing either disregarded or distorted. Perhaps the truth 'should' so 'live from age to age', but it does not. Both individual and cultural memories inevitably shape the past, forgetting and inventing, to make it accord better with present desire.

Buckingham's assurance, however, offers an apparently more secure ground of historiographic confidence: Julius Caesar's responsibility for the building of the Tower rests firmly 'upon record' rather than upon the shifting sands of mere report. But, in spite of Buckingham's claim, there is no 'record' of Caesar's building of the Tower. John Stow records that 'it hath been the common opinion, and some have written (but of none assured ground) that Julius Caesar . . . was the original author and founder', but Stow can find no confirming evidence and indeed finds 'in a fair-register-book, containing the acts of the Bishop of Rochester, set down by Edmond de Hadenham, that William I, surnamed Conqueror, built the Tower of London'.[13]

Buckingham's appeal to 'record' is thus either disingenuous or merely mistaken, but even if it were accurate, the play makes us see that it would not really offer more certainty. Records are not neutral, objective facts, but are themselves texts, written for purposes that must be evaluated when considering their evidentiary value. Soon after the scene with the prince, a scrivener enters with 'the indictment of the good Lord Hastings' (3.6.1) that he has copied fair. Here is a 'record', documentary evidence of the state's intention to bring charges against Hastings. Except Hastings has already been killed. In the previous scene, Lovell and Ratcliffe have entered with his bloody head. The scrivener's eleven hours of laborious copying is to produce an *a posteriori* justification for the illegal act. A 'palpable device' (11), says the scrivener, but not so palpable for later historians who will discover only the 'record' with its timing and motives probably lost in the unrecorded past.

Why should the play, in these two almost incidental scenes in its middle, make the uncertain ground of historical reconstruction visible? It is perhaps not an accident that they appear in *Richard III*. Tudor historians were in general agreement about the truth of the reign, not least because in spite of the multiple tellings, almost all are derived immediately from Thomas More's *History of King Richard III* (c. 1518), which was incorporated, often unacknowledged, into later works, including Grafton's, Hall's and Holinshed's chronicles, before it made its way to Shakespeare. More's Richard is the deformed monster, unnatural both in body and behaviour, that haunts the Tudor imagination.

Shakespeare would have found little to contravene this view, and his play, of course, provides its most memorable telling. Nonetheless, Shakespeare seems aware of how much his 'misshapen' Richard (1.2.237) has been shaped by desire. 'The historical figure of Richard' can mean only the figure of Richard that history gives us – and history, Shakespeare knows, is never identical with the past it narrates, but is constructed from the often inarticulate or misleading 'record' left by the past and written by the interests of the present.

In the case of Richard III, it is at least questionable whether his well-known deformity was an anatomical fact. 'No contemporary document or portrait attests to it', observes Peter Saccio; 'and the fact that he permitted himself to be stripped to the waist for anointing at his own coronation suggests that his torso could bear public inspection'.[14] Even this evidence, however, is inconclusive. Perhaps it does suggest that Richard's notorious deformities were 'quite unlikely', as Saccio supposes. But it might suggest, alternatively, that Richard's power made comment on any defect unwise, and 'the fact' that he allowed his body to be displayed might be a brazen assertion of that power, or even a manipulative technique by which it might be gained. Nonetheless, Tudor interests were well served by the 'fact' of Richard's misshapen body, and indeed it may be that it is their invention to help legitimate the Tudor succession.

Richard's deformity can be taken, then, as the sign of history itself, the distortion that history works upon the past.[15] Richard luxuriates in his own claim that he has been

> Cheated of feature by dissembling nature,
> Deformed, unfinished, sent before my time
> Into this breathing world scarce half made up. (1.1.19–21)

But the Richard who has been sent into the world of the theatre has certainly been at least 'half made up', in the idiom of a later age; he is as much a creature of fiction as of fact. He is not so much cheated of feature by dissembling nature as he is the recipient of feature from an assembling history, which, out of the facts it finds in the past, makes the history it needs in the present.

Not just *Richard III*, but all the histories are self-conscious about their making. King John in his death throes sees himself as 'a scribbled form, drawn with a pen / Upon a parchment' (5.7.32–3). But what is any historical figure but such a scribbled form? This is not to see the plays, as some have done, as meta-drama,[16] but to see them as meta-history. The plays are fundamentally about the difficulty of preserving the past. In *2 Henry VI* (*First Part of the Contention*), Gloucester sees that the marriage of Henry and Margaret will negate the achievements of recent history,

> Blotting your names from books of memory,
> Razing the characters of your renown,
> Defacing monuments of conquered France,
> Undoing all, as all had never been! (1.1.96–9)

The heroic past is annulled by the 'shameful' actions of the present, deconstructing history itself, 'undoing all as all had never been'.

In the so-called first tetralogy, history is always at risk of being undone by present desire, as the glorious achievements of Henry V are quickly forgotten. The later histories, however, reverse the focus but not the motive: history there is self-consciously *achieved* by present desire, as the second tetralogy drives towards Henry's acceptance of his heroic destiny. Henry IV's 'unthrifty son' (*Richard II* 5.3.1) manipulates his own history throughout the second tetralogy to emerge as England's hero–king; but that history is in turn discovered to have been manipulated by the plays' 'bending author' (epilogue, line 2), bent over his desk, bowed by his task, and contorting history itself as he locates Henry's 'small time' (line 5) within the 'little room' (line 3) of the stage and the printed page.

Shakespeare finds in the act of writing histories the deepest truth of history writing: that it is not the representation of the *past*, but is the *representation* of the past. The past cannot be fully recovered from 'the swallowing gulf / Of dark forgetfulness and deep oblivion' (*Richard III* 3.7.128–9), and its representation is therefore inevitably partial, in both senses of the word, a product both of the incomplete traces that have survived and the shaping concerns of those who seek and study them. Shakespeare knows that history is always as much invented as found, speaking the interests of the present as much as those of the past that it would bring into view. His histories may be undependable registers of historical fact, but they are brilliant meditations on the nature of history itself.

Notes

1. In October 1622, Degory Wheare was appointed to the first chair in history at Oxford, a professorship established by a bequest from William Camden. Five years later, Fulke Greville endowed a lectureship in history at Cambridge, which was filled by Isaac Dorislaus, though Greville had been trying to establish the position as early as 1615.
2. Raphael Holinshed, *The Chronicles of England, Ireland, and Scotland* (London, 1587 edn), v. 2, sig. A4ᵛ. The spelling and punctuation here, as in all quotations in the essay, have been modernized. Where possible, quotations from Holinshed will be cited from Geoffrey Bullough, *Narrative and Dramatic Sources of Shakespeare*, 8 vols. (London: Routledge and Kegan Paul, 1957–75).
3. The two accounts, by Dictys and Dares, in fact were not contemporaneous with the events they putatively witnessed, but date from the fourth and fifth centuries AD respectively. They were first combined by Benôit in 1160, translated into Latin in 1287 by Guido della Colonna, and back into French by Lefèvre in 1464. On Caxton, see N. F. Blake, *William Caxton and English Literary Culture* (London: Hambledon Press, 1991).
4. Fabyan, *The New Chronicles of England and France*, ed. Sir Henry Ellis (London, 1811), p. 239.
5. Arguably that self-consciousness was anticipated in some of the historical work of twelfth-century monastic scholars, most obviously William of Malmesbury. See R. W. Southern, 'Presidential Address: Aspects of the European Tradition of Historical Writing: 4. The Sense of the Past', *Transactions of the Royal Historical Society*, 5th series, 23 (1973), 243–64.
6. 'Papers Complaint, compild in ruthfull Rimes', in *The Complete Works of John Davies of Hereford*, ed. A. B. Grosart (rpt; New York: AMS, 1967), II, 77.
7. *Union of the Two Noble and Illustre Fameles of Lancastre & Yorke*, facs. rpt 2nd edn, 1550 (Menston: Scolar Press, 1970), sig. Aiiᵛ.
8. See my 'Opening Gates and Stopping Hedges: Grafton, Stow, and the Politics of Elizabethan History Writing', in *The Project of Prose in Early Modern Europe and the New World*, ed. Elizabeth Fowler and Roland Greene (Cambridge University Press, 1997), pp. 66–79.
9. A very few were attempted (unlike the numerous chronicle abridgements). *The*

Abridgement of Camden's Britannia was published in 1626 by John Bill, nominally so its 'small chorographical descriptions' would not be 'troublesome or tedious' to the king (sig. a2ʳ); but the abridgement emphasizes its maps over its descriptions, making it more an atlas than a chorography.

10. Some of the material in this and the next few paragraphs has been adapted from my *Shakespeare and the Shapes of Time* (London: Macmillan, 1982), esp. pp. 56–76; and '"To Set a Form Upon that Indigest": Shakespeare's Fictions of History', *Comparative Drama* 17 (1983), 1–16.

11. *Coleridge's Writings on Shakespeare*, ed. Terence Hawkes (New York: G. P. Putnam, 1959), p. 223.

12. *An Apology for Actors* (London, 1613), sig. F3ʳ

13. Stow, *The Survey of London*, ed. H. B. Wheatley (London: Dent, 1987), p. 42.

14. Peter Saccio, *Shakespeare's English Kings: History, Chronicle, and Drama* (Oxford University Press, 1977), p. 159.

15. See Marjorie Garber's 'Descanting on Deformity: Richard III and the Shape of History', in *Shakespeare's Ghost Writers: Literature as Uncanny Causality* (New York: Methuen, 1987), pp. 28–51.

16. See James L. Calderwood, *Metadrama in Shakespeare's Henriad: 'Richard II' to 'Henry V'* (Berkeley: University of California Press, 1979).

Reading list

Fergusson, Arthur B., *Clio Unbound: Perception of the Social and Cultural Past in Renaissance England* (Durham, N.C.: Duke University Press, 1979).

Hampton, Timothy, *Writing From History: The Rhetoric of Exemplarity in Renaissance Literature* (Ithaca, N.Y.: Cornell University Press, 1990).

Helgerson, Richard, *Forms of Nationhood: The Elizabethan Writing of England* (University of Chicago Press, 1992).

Howard, Jean and Phyllis Rackin, *Engendering a Nation: A Feminist Account of Shakespeare's Histories* (London: Routledge, 1997).

Kamps, Ivo, *History and Ideology in Early Stuart Drama* (Cambridge University Press, 1996).

Kastan, David Scott, *Shakespeare and the Shapes of Time* (London: Macmillan, 1982).

Kelley, Donald R., 'The Theory of History', in *The Cambridge History of Renaissance Philosophy*, ed. Charles B. Schmitt and Quentin Skinner (Cambridge University Press, 1988), pp. 746–61.

Kelley, Donald R. and David Harris Sacks, eds., *The Historical Imagination in Early Modern Britain: History, Rhetoric, and Fiction, 1500–1800* (Cambridge University Press, 1997).

Kingsford, Charles Lethbridge, *English Historical Literature in the Fifteenth Century* (Oxford: Clarendon Press, 1913).

Levy, F. J., *Tudor Historical Thought* (San Marino, Calif.: Huntington Library, 1967).

McKisack, May, *Medieval Historians and the Tudor Age* (Oxford: Clarendon Press, 1971).

Patterson, Annabel, *Reading Holinshed's Chronicles* (University of Chicago Press, 1994).

Rackin, Phyllis, *Stages of History: Shakespeare's English Chronicles* (Ithaca, N.Y.: Cornell University Press, 1990).

Saccio, Peter, *Shakespeare's English Kings: History, Chronicle, and Drama*, 2nd (Oxford University Press, 2000).

Woolf, D. R., *The Idea of History in Early Stuart England* (University of Toronto Press, 1990).

12

LOIS POTTER

Shakespeare in the theatre, 1660–1900

When the British monarchy was restored in 1660 and Charles II ended Parliament's eighteen-year ban on public playhouses, he entrusted the task of theatrical restoration to two playwrights who had been active at his father's court. They received patents giving them the exclusive right to perform plays in London and the existing dramatic repertory was divided between them, with the stipulation that it should be 'reformed' – that is, made fit for a stage different from the playhouse of the past. Boy actors were to be replaced by women; scenery and music would create the kind of theatre which, before the war, had been used only for court masques. The history of Shakespeare production for the next 150 years would continue to be one of reform and restoration, though the meanings of these words would be constantly changing.

Theatrical reform was accomplished quickly. The first play to feature a woman actor (as opposed to a singer) was probably *Othello*; the date may have been 8 December 1660. For those who remembered productions with all-male casts, the mere presence of women, even when they were not much more than animated scenery, must have been as revelatory as all-male productions are today. The scenery itself, like that of the French theatre which was its model, was primarily decorative: one prison scene, one garden scene, and so on, served for the entire repertory. After the scene had been opened by sliding shutters in grooves, the actors normally came forward to play on a projecting apron stage. Because their background could be changed behind them while they remained on stage, the plays of Shakespeare and his contemporaries could still be played with something of the fluidity of the unlocalized stage for which they were written.[1]

The first Restoration adaptors approached Shakespeare much as Shakespeare had approached his predecessors, modernizing his language and complicating his plots. In *The Law Against Lovers* (1662), William Davenant, one of the new patentees, combined the plots of *Measure for Measure* and *Much Ado About Nothing* (Angelo is Benedick's brother). His motives were both political and theatrical: Angelo's draconian moral legislation clearly satirizes the recent Commonwealth government, but other inventions – like Beatrice's younger sister, who sings and dances with castanets – simply respond to the desire for women and music on the stage. Similarly, his *Macbeth* (1663) contrasts the idealized royalist Macduffs with a demonized tyrant intended to recall Cromwell, but also expands the witches' songs and dances to almost operatic length. In 1667 he collaborated with the young John Dryden in revising *The Tempest*. The adaptors provided Miranda with a sister, and provided the sister with a second young man, played by a woman, who has never seen a woman. They also turned Caliban's conspiracy into a comic parody of the Commonwealth. Dryden's prologue opens with a striking comparison between the dead Shakespeare and a tree that has been cut down, with the adaptation as a new branch springing up from its 'secret root'. Since the felled oak tree had been used by many writers as an image for the regicide, audiences could have been forgiven for thinking that Shakespeare had been beheaded like Charles I.

It is, however, misleading to see Restoration adaptations as merely political. Significantly, Samuel Pepys, who loved the new *Tempest* and called its romantic plot 'innocent', nevertheless thought on a second viewing that the political characters were 'a little too tedious'.[2] What he really liked best was the music, and others must have felt the same, since in 1674 Thomas Shadwell made the adaptation into an opera. A long-standing tradition of Shakespearian burlesque was inaugurated when Thomas Duffet parodied the opera in *The Mock-Tempest*, where Prospero pimps for his daughters.

As Charles II had no legitimate children, his presumed successor was his Roman Catholic brother James. The tense political situation after 1678 had a direct impact on the theatres, since fear of violence decreased attendance to such an extent that the two companies finally merged between 1682 and 1695. As fears and rumours of a 'Popish plot' produced mob violence and the threat of a new civil war, Shakespeare's classical plays and English histories, largely neglected (except when they dealt with Falstaff), acquired a new relevance. Dryden's *All for Love* (1678), a new play rather than an adaptation, replaced *Antony and Cleopatra* so completely that it was often played under that name. His *Troilus and Cressida, or Truth Found Too Late* (1679) is an interesting attempt to salvage a play not seen in its original form until the twentieth century. Although Dryden whitewashes Cressida (as the title indicates, she is misunderstood), he keeps much of Thersites' strong language and even makes Ulysses defend the therapeutic effect of his 'satire'. Both plays reserve their harshest treatment for priests and for characters who put public affairs ahead of private relationships. The titles of two other adaptations speak for themselves: John Crowne's *The Miseries of Civil War* (1681), based on the Cade and York rebellions of the Henry VI plays, and Nahum Tate's rewriting of *Coriolanus* as *The Ingratitude of a Commonwealth* (1682). But the censorship seems to have been opposed to any depiction of a successful uprising or regicide, however much it was condemned. Tate's version of *Richard II* (*The Sicilian Usurper*, 1681) was banned after a few performances, though it altered history to make Richard an innocent victim.

It is surprising that Tate's famous adaptation of *King Lear* (1681), which omits the Fool, marries Edgar to Cordelia, and ends with the king's restoration, is usually explained as a concession to neoclassicism. Tate's political intention is obvious from his reversal of the opening scenes so that the first character to appear is the bastard Edmund, arguing his right to replace a legitimate heir – this, when Charles II was under pressure to declare the legitimacy of his bastard son, the popular and Protestant Duke of Monmouth. The Fool's omission would later be approved as the removal of an archaic irrelevance, but his real offence was probably that he speaks disrespectfully to a king. In theory, Restoration critics believed in poetic justice (the artist's duty to correct the injustices of real life), but in practice playwrights and their audiences enjoyed the pathetic deaths of the innocent as much as the sensational deaths of the wicked; both Edward Ravenscroft's *Titus Andronicus* and Tate's Coriolanus play add considerably to the original death toll, with the young sons of Aaron and Martius among the victims. The final scene of the revised *Lear* shows Lear saving Cordelia from death by fighting off the murderers until help arrives. Though Samuel Johnson later defended Tate's ending because the death of Cordelia so obviously contravened poetic justice, it was probably the heroic fight that made actors and audiences reluctant to give it up.

After 1688, when James II had been replaced by William and Mary (his own daughter), Tate's ending, with Lear abdicating in favour of Edgar and Cordelia, was too close to reality; a satirist in 1689 called Mary 'worse than cruel, lustful Goneril' and the play disappeared from the stage for the rest of the century.[3] When it returned, it was in harmony with the new trend to sentimental drama. Audiences wept for pity at the sufferings of Lear and Cordelia (now a much more important character), then wept for joy when their virtue was rewarded. For a hundred and fifty years, the greatest British actors, including David Garrick and Susanna Cibber (see plate 6), would play Lear and Cordelia in this version. Even after the Shakespeare text had been restored, actors throughout the nineteenth century still kept many of Tate's changes, such as his placing of the curse on Goneril at the end of Act 1, where it ensured that the curtain would fall to thunderous applause.

The longest-lasting of all Shakespeare adaptations was Colley Cibber's *Richard III* (1700), which was still being played in the twentieth century and can be heard at two points in the Laurence Olivier film of 1956. It initially got into trouble because the licenser feared that Henry VI in the Tower (Cibber began with *3 Henry VI* 5.6) might remind audiences of the exiled James II. If Cibber had a conscious political intention, it was quite different. Whereas Crowne's *Miseries of Civil War* made Edward IV a generous, open-hearted womanizer and Richard Gloucester a puritan who hypocritically condemns vices that he commits himself, Cibber's Richard is successful enough with women to resemble a Restoration – or Stuart – rake. In the final scenes he is also heroic, thanks to Cibber's borrowing of the eve-of-battle Chorus from *Henry V,* some battle rhetoric from the *Henry VI* plays, and a death speech (since Shakespeare had neglected to write one) based on Northumberland's desperate curse in *2 Henry IV* 1.1. The success of Cibber's *Richard* meant that Northumberland disappeared

6   *Mrs Cibber in the Character of Cordelia*, after Peter van Bleeck. She is seen in the
storm scene of Tate's *King Lear*, accompanied by her maid Arante. In the background
are two ruffians sent by Edmund to abduct her and the disguised Edgar, about to inter-
vene.

from the acting version of *2 Henry IV* (published in 1720), which was now little
more than the story of Falstaff. The practice of transferring lines from play to
play has persevered: in a nineteenth-century *Richard II*, 'the queen mourns over
Richard's body in words adapted from those of the dying Lear' – who, as Stanley
Wells points out, had not died on stage for 150 years.[4] Many twentieth-century
versions of the early histories, such as John Barton's *Wars of the Roses* (1962),
employ a similar collage technique.

Cibber's *Apology* (1740), the first great theatre autobiography, is also a reminder that actors were as important to Shakespeare's afterlife as authors. Indeed,
many of them were authors. Thomas Betterton was not only the most famous
actor of the age, acclaimed as Hamlet and Falstaff and everything in between, but
also a playwright himself and the probable author of several adaptations. Because

of his long career (1660–1710), he is virtually the only Restoration actor to be described in detail by eyewitnesses. Cibber provided a touchstone for all subsequent Hamlets in his description of Betterton's reaction to the first sight of his father's ghost. It is significant that it began with a 'pause of mute amazement' – in other words, Betterton held what would later be called an 'attitude', or pose. It is generally believed that Elizabethan acting style was rapid and continuous, forcing concentration on the words. Betterton's pause was a kind of visual coding, a product of the view that the actor's job was to indicate the various passions that Shakespeare had delineated. His importance was recognized by scholars and playwrights of the day. When Nicholas Rowe, who was both, published the first edited text of Shakespeare's plays in 1709, he broke off his preliminary biography of Shakespeare to pay tribute to Betterton's acting.

Rowe also reflects stage practice in such matters as the vagueness of his scene headings. In *Coriolanus*, for instance, he distinguishes only between Rome and Corioles, and it was not until Theobald's edition of 1733 that *As You Like It*, which Rowe placed simply in 'the Forest', acquired its notorious scene heading, 'Another Part of the Forest'. Partly because of the flurry of affordable editions that followed Theobald's, this period began to raise Shakespeare to almost superhuman status. Far from encouraging a return to unadapted texts, however, the increasing reverence for his reputation often seemed to mean cutting and altering whatever might prevent him from being properly appreciated. But the sometimes bitter battles fought in the footnotes of eminent editors over the proper way to stress a line also aroused curiosity to see more of the plays staged. The battle between the two licensed theatres, Drury Lane and Covent Garden, encouraged the search for novelty or, in a few cases, the mounting of competing productions of the same play. At the end of 1740 Drury Lane announced three Shakespeare comedies in rapid succession. The playbills associate all three revivals with 'the particular desire of some Ladies of Quality' – members of the newly founded Shakespeare Ladies' Club, who had previously encouraged revivals of other rarely performed plays.[5] *Twelfth Night* (15 January 1741), although timed to fall near the holiday after which it was named, had only a short run. However, *As You Like It* (20 December 1740) was a revelation both of the play and of the unsuspected potential in the role of Rosalind. Contemporary comments suggest that Hannah Pritchard, whose talent had gone unrecognized until now, was helped by her unusually clear diction, which conveyed both the meaning and the breathless excitement of Rosalind's longer speeches. The other actors also played as they liked it: the brilliant Kitty Clive making the most of Celia's comic opportunities, James Quin giving Jaques the benefit of his clear but monotonous delivery, and old Adam becoming so tearful as he offered to accompany Orlando into exile that much of the audience (believing that this role had once been played by Shakespeare) wept as well.[6] A month later, *The Merchant of Venice* (14 February 1741) was an equal surprise for the audience, and perhaps for the actors as well. Since rehearsal time was brief and devoted mainly to repeating lines and movements, it is possible that no one realized that Kitty Clive, a celebrated mimic, had decided that in the courtroom scene Portia should give an imitation of a well-known judge. As for Charles Macklin, he had been doing research on the costume of Jews in Venice (hence the red hat that he wore) and on the behaviour of merchants in the London Exchange. His Shylock, a fine example of realistic acting, hardly seems to belong in the same play, but he, and the role, became famous at once.

Later in 1741, David Garrick made a sensationally successful acting debut, and his exceptional qualities led him rapidly to the top of his profession. As manager of Drury Lane from 1747 to 1776, he must have been capable of controlling the aggressive individualism of his fellow-actors, since he revived not only Shakespeare but Jonson, who demands well-timed ensemble playing. His productions moved, as he did, rapidly. It was his own acting of many roles, both tragic and comic, that created their success. Eyewitnesses consistently praise his energy, his lightness of touch, and the expressiveness of his face. Some of his choices were considered definitive – for instance, the famous 'start' in *Hamlet*, which aspiring actors tried to imitate. In Hannah Pritchard he found his best partner, with *Macbeth* (1747) as their greatest success. *Much Ado About Nothing* had been briefly revived a few times since 1721; in 1748 the combination of Garrick and Pritchard made it a regular part of the repertory. While many other actresses also played opposite him (Peg Woffington, Clive, Susanna Cibber, Frances Abingdon), he paid tribute to Pritchard's Lady Macbeth by dropping the play once she had retired from the stage.[7] The actor-centred nature of the theatre affected the choice of revivals. Before 1750, *Othello* and *Julius Caesar* were the third and ninth of Shakespeare's plays in popularity; they were ninth and twenty-sixth between 1750 and 1800.[8] One reason must be that neither Othello nor Brutus suited the short, mercurial Garrick, though both plays were performed at the rival Covent Garden.

Garrick was the last actor considered by his contemporaries to have done as much for Shakespeare as Shakespeare had done for him. Betterton had been commemorated, in a theatre opened after his death, by a painting above the auditorium showing him in conversation with Shakespeare and Jonson. Even in Garrick's lifetime, tributes to Shakespeare, like the famous Jubilee in his honour in 1769, had a way of becoming tributes to Garrick. Patriotic enthusiasm for the symbiotic relationship of actor and author – both of them, in an era of wars with France, somehow associated with British freedom – constituted the 'politics' of Garrick's audience. Ironically, Garrick himself was a francophile, and also, despite his reputation as a worshipper of Shakespeare, one of his main adaptors. His *Catherine and Petruchio* (1754) displaced *The Taming of the Shrew* until 1886. He shortened *The Winter's Tale* as an afterpiece called *Florizel and Perdita* (1762). His *Macbeth* was mainly Shakespeare's rather than Davenant's, but much of the spectacle still remained and a death speech by Garrick replaced the one by Davenant. His *Romeo and Juliet* revised an otherwise defunct Restoration adaptation, Otway's *Caius Marius*, in which Juliet awakens for a brief, pathetic scene with Romeo before the poison takes effect. She continued to do so well into the nineteenth century, and in the final scene of Charles Gounod's opera (1867). Garrick's last adaptation, of which he seems to have been genuinely proud, although audiences disliked it, was a *Hamlet* (1771) that omitted the grave-diggers and the final fencing match, probably because French critics regarded them as a symbol of all that was ridiculous in English tragedy. Garrick may even have been influenced by Jean-François Ducis, whose adaptations of *Hamlet* and other Shakespeare plays would be the basis of many 'translations' into other languages.[9]

A crucial development in the years following Garrick's retirement was the constant enlargement of the theatres. The Licensing Act of 1737 had reinforced the monopoly initially created by Charles II. Outside the two licensed theatres, Shakespeare could be performed only as puppet show, pantomime, equestrian drama, or melodrama – a new and popular form, involving brief dialogue spoken over music, which would come to influence Shakespearian acting style. With only two locations for serious drama, in a city with a growing population at all income levels, the managers were encouraged to expand. By 1815 both theatres held nearly four thousand spectators, prepared to start a riot whether over politics or the price of seats. Every famous actor from Garrick to Macready had at some time to face a large and hostile audience. Its presence had to be acknowledged: actors were taught the importance of responding to applause with a graceful bow and to boos by miming apology for the fault that had caused them. Lines with a general or topical meaning were often spoken out front rather than to their supposed addressee. The theatre was never again so close to royalty as when Charles II lent it his coronation suit to use as a costume, but royal visits to the theatre, particularly after major public events, gave new meaning to any performance. The absence of *King Lear* from the stage from 1811 to 1820, the period of George III's final illness, which was thought to be insanity, shows how relevant the play was still felt to be – as does the fact that both theatres put it on within three months of his death.

Against this background, John Philip Kemble – who assumed control of Drury Lane in 1788 – moved to Covent Garden in 1802, and retired in 1817, was ideally cast as a reactionary, classicizing actor-manager, especially since his best role was generally thought to be Coriolanus. No Kemble production consisted, like the 1740–1 comedy revivals, of shooting stars going off in all directions. As his biographer puts it, he wanted to 'produce a tragedy on the stage, through the whole of whose characters, illustrious, or mean, one correct, presiding mind should be clearly discerned'.[10] He was helped by the presence in his company of several members of his family. In particular, his sister, Sarah Siddons, became a legend as soon as the public had seen her 'towering' and 'majestic' Lady Macbeth, though she also astonished her admirers by her delicacy as Ophelia and Desdemona. She was never very successful as Shakespeare's comic heroines; she may simply have inspired too much awe, but one factor must have been her refusal to wear anything remotely like a convincing male disguise, although she later gave public readings in which she played male roles superbly. Like her brother, she made a special study of statuary, which inspired her carefully draped costumes and striking attitudes. Reform of costume was in fact one virtue with which his successors credited Kemble. His scenes were more definitely localized than his predecessors', his crowds larger, his expenses – and prices – higher. He took great care over his acting editions (the names he gave Shakespeare's anonymous minor characters appear in theatre programmes throughout the nineteenth century) but not over textual authenticity. His *Coriolanus* was partly by James Thompson and partly by Shakespeare. Like Garrick, he replaced some of Tate's *Lear* with the original text, but retained its three main features: the love interest, the omission of the Fool, and the happy ending.

When Kean came out of nowhere in 1814 and took the theatre by storm as Shylock at Drury Lane, he was immediately seen as a new and exciting alternative to Kemble. Before his career ended in 1833, wrecked by drink and scandal, he inspired some of the most exciting theatre reviews ever written. They praise his rapid transitions of mood and tone, which appealed to audiences familiar with melodrama; his fine singing and verse-speaking, particularly in poetic passages like Othello's 'farewell forever'; and his agility (he was a trained Harlequin). But his visual effects – sometimes copied from statues or pictures – captured the imagination still more. Above all, he could convey a sense of the intellectual and the diabolical. Only 5 foot 4 inches (1.6m) tall, he reminded the Romantics of their flawed hero Napoleon, and Byron acknowledged that some lines in his 'Ode to Napoleon' had been inspired by the sight of Kean's brooding Richard III silently tracing his plan of battle on the ground.[11] By contrast with the famous 'start' of Betterton and Garrick, Kean was not so much interpreting a passion as providing a subtextual glimpse of Richard's unspoken thoughts. In a large theatre, where his voice was often ragged by the end of the evening, such silent moments were probably the most accessible parts of his performance.

Kean's reputation as a romantic rebel derived more from his private life than from his attitude to the Shakespeare text. He attempted some unusual revivals – even a *King Lear* with a tragic ending and a conflation of the Henry VI plays – but quickly fell back on the versions the audience preferred. Meanwhile, European anglophiles who had been struggling to read Shakespeare in the original were arriving in England to experience the great symbol of freedom at first hand, only to find themselves watching Tate's *Lear*, Cibber's *Richard*, and a host of Garrick adaptations. Much of this was soon to change, beginning with William Macready's brief periods as actor-manager (1837–9 at Covent Garden, 1841–3 at Drury Lane). Like Kemble, he wished to see 'one great presiding mind' in his productions, but he hoped that the mind would be Shakespeare's. He read the Choruses of *Henry V* as an opportunity to 'illustrate' Shakespeare: in his production, the opening Chorus was spoken by Father Time, while Henry

7   Covent Garden Theatre with the stage set for *As You Like It* in Macready's 1842
production, showing the vastness of the auditorium.

stood with three Furies 'leashed in like hounds'. The battle of Agincourt, initially a painting seen through the smoke of battle, gave way to the sight of real
actors in motion.[12] The gauze and lighting did what Macready himself thought
he was doing: bringing Shakespeare back through the mists of the past, as
Shakespeare had brought Henry and his followers (see also chapter 15,
Shakespeare on the Page and the Stage, by Michael Dobson). His most famous
accomplishment was to bring back the original *King Lear* in 1838, not only delet-
ing all Tate's lines but reintroducing the Fool, who was played, by a woman, as
'a fragile, hectic, beautiful-faced, half-idiot-looking boy' (Downer, p. 170; see
plate 8). His concern with the text became so well known that on a royal visit to
Drury Lane Prince Albert inquired whether the *As You Like It* he had just seen
was 'the original play' (it was).[13]

Macready retired just before the Act for Regulating the Theatres (1843) finally
ended the long theatrical monopoly. In the second half of the century the two
large theatres were finally found more suitable for opera, while the most innovative productions took place in other venues under Samuel Phelps (Sadler's Wells
Theatre, 1844–62), Edmund Kean's son Charles (Princess Theatre, 1850–9) and
Henry Irving (Lyceum, 1878–1902), all of whom gradually won back the
middle-class audiences lost in earlier years. As an actor, Phelps had a range that
extended from Christopher Sly to King Lear and Falstaff. He transformed the

8   William Macready as King Lear at Covent Garden, 1838, by George Scharf.
Macready is acting in the 'restored' text, with Priscilla Horton as the Fool.

rowdy Sadler's Wells public into a genuinely attentive one, partly through a slow
and emphatic delivery intended to make Shakespeare intelligible to an unsophis-
ticated audience. With simple (and now old-fashioned) wings and backdrops
instead of the new and more elaborate 'box sets', he revived many Shakespeare
plays for the first time in years, in texts still closer to the original than
Macready's. One of his finest achievements was *A Midsummer Night's Dream*
(1853), in which sets, costumes, and the new gas lighting combined in a triumph
of illusionistic theatre. Phelps's playing of Bottom was part of this conception;
reviewers called him 'a man seen in a dream'.[14] Like Macready's fragile boy fool
in *Lear*, the comic character was integrated into a theatrical whole.

   Both Macready and Phelps were part of a new kind of Shakespeare criticism
insisting on the organic unity of his works and on the significance of every line,
however apparently irrelevant. Charles Kean, equally characteristically, gave a
sense of unity to the same play in 1856 by setting it in Periclean Athens, with
the Acropolis in the background and a carefully researched Athenian carpenter's shop for the mechanicals. Still more than Macready, this manager created
a world rich in detail. His gigantic crowd scenes – made possible by the cheap
labour gathered about the stage door, to be drilled by the prompter – located the
protagonists in a wider social context. Several hundred of these extras crowded
the stage in *Richard II* (1857) as Richard and Bolingbroke rode into medieval
London. Kean deliberately echoed this famous scene in *Henry V* (1859 (see

9   Henry V's return to London after the victory at Agincourt, from Charles Kean's production, Princess Theatre, 1859. The scene was meant to parallel the entry of Richard II and Henry Bolingbroke in Kean's earlier production of *Richard II*.

plate 9)), suggesting that the crowd welcoming the victorious Henry contained some who remembered Richard – a rare example of a director creating links between the history plays. Part of the pleasure of theatregoing now was learning about another age. Producing Shakespeare meant studying books on the history of costume, architecture, and furniture; characters were surrounded by their environment instead of playing in front of it. When Irving at the Lyceum followed Wagner's Bayreuth in darkening the auditorium so that the audience no longer saw each other, the illusion was complete. But it came at a price. The cathedral setting of the wedding in Irving's *Much Ado About Nothing* (1882) required fifteen minutes to build.[15] Not surprisingly, Irving sometimes rearranged episodes and cut lines in order to reduce the number of scene changes. His *King Lear* (1892) lost 46 per cent of the text, including much of the subplot and the blinding of Gloucester. What it offered instead were stunning images, like the death of Lear beneath Dover Cliff, his face lit by the red glow of a setting sun (see plate 10).[16]

Most actor-managers of the nineteenth century had little faith in the drama of their own time. Kemble was frankly uninterested in new plays, asking, 'what could be expected now in the way of the regular drama, that previously had not been better done?' (Boaden, II, 100). Dramatists hoping to be performed wrote blank-verse plays on historical subjects, and Shakespearian language soon became almost second nature to them. Because Irving dominated the London

10   Hawes Craven, *The Death of King Lear*, as depicted in Henry Irving's production at the Lyceum Theatre, 1892.

theatre scene, his continued encouragement of this kind of drama, rather than the 'new' Ibsenite prose plays, began to make Shakespeare, once embraced by the radicals, seem a figure of repression. Irving's leading lady, Ellen Terry, incarnated one Shakespeare heroine after another, always radiant, loving, and beautifully costumed, while Bernard Shaw, who longed to see her in one of his own plays, kept pointing out that a drama which was still trying to sound Elizabethan could not express issues of interest to the late nineteenth century.

In fact, as that century drew to an end, a variety of new influences had begun to modify attitudes to Shakespeare production. Once, it had been only the British who took the national dramatist abroad; now, with the aid of improved public transport, individual actors – and, later, whole productions – crossed the seas. The black American Ira Aldridge, whose Covent Garden debut in 1832 had been blighted by racial prejudice, played in the provinces and finally ventured abroad in 1852, playing in English opposite German, Russian, and Polish actors using their own language. His Othello and (in whiteface) his Macbeth and Lear had a powerful effect on audiences still acquainted with Shakespeare only in heavily adapted translations. Some of them felt that they would never again be satisfied with Othello in blackface, but it was only in the last years of his career, that he was invited to act at a major London theatre. By then, foreign actors of Shakespeare were a more familiar sight. The American Charlotte Cushman – the most famous of a surprisingly large number of what are now called cross-dressed performers – played Romeo in 1855 at the Haymarket, and Queen Victoria praised her in her journal because 'no one would ever have imagined she was a woman' (Rowell, p. 74). Charles Fechter's Hamlet (1861), was seen as 'modern' because he was constantly touching and shaking hands with people. Physical contact between actors on the English stage was still minimal: in 1875, when Ellen Terry had her first big success as Portia in *The Merchant of Venice*, at the moment when Bassanio has chosen the correct casket and she is able to express her suppressed excitement, Henry James recorded that the woman next to him gasped, 'Good heavens, she's touching him!'[17] 1875 was also the year when Tommaso Salvini's powerful and passionately sensual Othello came to Drury Lane, both shocking and inspiring a whole generation of theatregoers.

The history of Shakespeare in the theatre tends to be told in terms of figures like Betterton and the other actor-managers mentioned here, because they influenced everything from the choice of repertory to the way a text was cut and acted. Though many of these men sound very much like directors in the modern sense, the fact that they often played the leading roles in their own productions naturally focused theatrical and critical attention on the plays' heroes at the expense of many other things. The visit to England by the Saxe-Meiningen company in 1881 is often seen as a forerunner of what would now be called 'directors'' theatre. The Duke of Saxe-Meiningen did not act in his own productions and his company had no stars. He compensated for the lack of strong leading actors by careful disciplining of the crowd scenes, often achieving excellent performances in the minor roles and scenes that had so often been cut or rushed through in English productions.

Thus, it is probably fair to say that there was more Shakespeare, in every sense, at the end of the century than during the previous two hundred years. Even the long works, usually thought unplayable in their entirety, were coming into their own again. William Poel gave an experimental matinée of the first quarto *Hamlet* at St George's Hall in 1881. Forbes-Robertson's *Hamlet* (Lyceum, 1897), partly through Bernard Shaw's influence, gave the audience more of the text than ever before; Frank Benson's touring company played an uncut *Hamlet* at the Stratford-upon-Avon Memorial Theatre in 1899, and again at the Lyceum in 1900. The first director to treat the history plays as a cycle was Franz Dingelstedt, who, inspired by Wagner's *Ring* cycle, produced the two tetralogies in sequence at Weimar in 1864. Benson would also perform a history sequence at Stratford in 1901, though neither tetralogy was complete. In 1908 he would do the entire sequence apart from *Richard III*.

Were the new productions as exciting as the old ones? There is no way to test the accuracy of the glowing descriptions of the great eighteenth- and nineteenth-century actors. Perhaps the authors were simply gloating over experiences their readers had not been able to share. But there are several reasons why audiences of the period might have found Shakespeare's plays particularly meaningful and immediate. For much of the period, the actors' extensive repertory of roles, their reuse of the same scenes and costumes for several plays, and their audience's tolerance for under-rehearsed productions, allowed a dialogue between the theatre and public events – as when, to take a trivial example, the violent storms of 1703 were followed by revivals of *The Tempest*. When, in 1820, George IV was trying to divorce his estranged wife on the grounds of adultery, speeches in *Othello* and *Cymbeline* about falsely accused wives provoked near-riots on her behalf.[18] This kind of topicality became rarer as Macready and his successors increasingly felt the need to provide each play with new scenery and costumes corresponding to its peculiar atmosphere. Macklin probably rehearsed his famous Shylock in two to three weeks; Macready seems to have had under a month to mount *King Lear*; Irving usually spent eight to ten weeks on a new production. If the theatre obviously gained in polish and the total artistic effect, it also lost something in immediacy. But, while actors and audiences liked to believe in the universality of Shakespeare, they were probably glad when he was no longer inflammatory. Macready claims that he spoke Lear's 'poor naked wretches' speech directly at Queen Victoria (Rowell, p. 25), but he also told an audience that 'art and literature have no politics' (Downer, p. 173). Performances in Irving's theatre were still (though less frequently) interrupted by applause, but now it was for the sets, costumes, and performances rather than the perceived relevance of the plays.

In another respect, too, the Shakespeare of 1900 was more firmly embedded in the past. German scholars, beginning with Ludwig Tieck's fanciful model of the Fortune Theatre in 1836, had been calling for a return to Elizabethan staging as the only way to recover the true meaning of plays written in that period.[19] Though an experimental 'Elizabethan' *Taming of the Shrew* was put on by Ben Webster in 1844, it seems to have been only a curiosity and had no immediate successors. By the end of the century, however, the movement towards a restored Elizabethan stage was under way. William Poel's Elizabethan Stage Society, founded in 1895, was created to produce plays without scenery, using a stage and costumes as close as possible to those that Shakespeare would have known. If this looks like the appropriation of the theatre by scholarship, it is worth noting that the decisive factor in Poel's choice of a theatrical career was the experience of watching Salvini's Othello – the same experience that also inspired a still more important twentieth-century figure, Konstantin Stanislavsky. By 1900, the imitation of Shakespeare's language, except for the purpose of parody, was virtually over. Shakespeare's main influence, for much of the new century, would be on dramaturgy and theatrical space. The dramatist who had once been championed as a force for both poetic language and realistic psychology would now be invoked instead to justify non-mimetic theatre, Brechtian political drama, fluid staging, and a post-modern treatment of character.

Notes

1. George C. D. Odell, *Shakespeare from Betterton to Irving*, 2 vols. (New York: C. Scribner, 1920), I, 18–23.
2. *The Diary of Samuel Pepys*, ed. Robert Latham and William Matthews, 11 vols. (Berkeley, Calif.: University of California Press, 1970–83), 7 Nov. and 13 Nov. 1667.

3. 'The Female Parricide', in *Poems on Affairs of State*, vol. v: 1688–97, ed. William J. Cameron (New Haven: Yale University Press, 1971), p. 157.

4. Stanley Wells, 'Shakespeare on the English Stage', in *William Shakespeare: His World, His Work, His Influence*, ed. John F. Andrews, 3 vols. (New York: Charles Scribner's Sons, 1985) III, 603–28; p. 617.

5. Michael Dobson, *The Making of the National Poet: Shakespeare, Adaptation, and Authorship, 1660–1769* (Oxford: Clarendon Press, 1992), pp. 146–62.

6. [John Hill], *The Actor: A Treatise on the Art of Playing* (London, 1750), pp. 44–5.

7. Philip Highfill *et al.*, *A Biographical Dictionary of Actors, Actresses, Musicians, Dancers, Managers and Other Stage Personnel in London, 1660–1800* (Carbondale: Southern Illinois University Press, 1973–93), 'Pritchard', p. 187.

8. Charles Beecher Hogan, *Shakespeare in the Theatre, 1701–1800*, 2 vols. (Oxford: Clarendon Press, 1952 and 1957), I: Appendix B, pp. 460–1; II: Appendix C, pp. 716–19.

9. Frank Hedgcock, *David Garrick and His French Friends* (London: Stanley Paul, n.d.), pp. 194–9, p. 77n., pp. 292–3.

10. James Boaden, *Memoirs of the Life of John Philip Kemble*, 2 vols. (London, 1825, rpt New York and London: B. Blom, 1969), I, 326.

11. F. W. Hawkins, *The Life of Edmund Kean*, 2 vols. (London, 1869), I, 213–14.

12. Alan S. Downer, *The Eminent Tragedian: William Charles Macready* (Cambridge, Mass.: Harvard University Press; London: Oxford University Press, 1966), pp. 248–9.

13. George Rowell, *Queen Victoria Goes to the Theatre* (London: Paul Elek, 1978), p. 41.

14. Gary Jay Williams, '*Our Midnight Revels': A Midsummer Night's Dream in the Theatre* (University of Iowa Press, 1997), pp. 110–14.

15. Michael Booth, *Victorian Spectacular Theatre* (London: Routledge and Kegan Paul, 1981), p. 55.

16. Alan Hughes, *Henry Irving, Shakespearean* (Cambridge University Press, 1981), p. 118, pp. 135–7.

17. Quoted in Nina Auerbach, *Ellen Terry: Player in Her Time* (New York and London: W. W. Norton, 1987), p. 173.

18. E. A. Smith, *A Queen on Trial: The Affair of Queen Caroline* (Dover, N. H.: A. Sutton, 1993), pp. 138–9.

19. See Simon Williams, *Shakespeare on the German Stage*, vol. I (1586–1914) (Cambridge University Press, 1990), pp. 153–61, and ch. 9.

Reading list

Bate, Jonathan, and Russell Jackson, eds., *Shakespeare: An Illustrated Stage History* (Oxford University Press, 1996).

Boaden, James, *Memoirs of the Life of John Philip Kemble*, 2 vols. (London, 1825, rpt New York and London: B. Blom, 1969).

Burnim, Kalman A., *David Garrick, Director* (University of Pittsburgh Press, 1961).

Cibber, Colley, *An Apology for the Life of Colley Cibber*, ed. B. R. S. Fone (Ann Arbor: University of Michigan Press, 1968).

Dobson, Michael, *The Making of the National Poet: Shakespeare, Adaptation, and Authorship, 1660–1769* (Oxford: Clarendon Press, 1992).

Donohue, Joseph, *Theatre in the Age of Kean* (Oxford: Basil Blackwell, 1975).

Downer, Alan S., *The Eminent Tragedian: William Charles Macready* (Cambridge, Mass.: Harvard University Press; London: Oxford University Press, 1966).

Foulkes, Richard, ed., *Shakespeare on the Victorian Stage* (Cambridge University Press, 1986).

Hawkins, F. W., *The Life of Edmund Kean*, 2 vols. (London, 1869).

Highfill, Philip, Kalman A. Burnim and Edward A. Langhans, *A Biographical Dictionary of Actors, Actresses, Musicians, Dancers, Managers and Other Stage Personnel in London, 1660–1800*, 18 vols. (Carbondale: Southern Illinois University Press, 1973–93).

Hogan, Charles Beecher, *Shakespeare in the Theatre, 1701–1800*, 2 vols. (Oxford: Clarendon Press, 1952 and 1957).

Hudson, Lynton, *The English Stage, 1850–1950* (London: Harrap, 1951).

Hughes, Alan, *Henry Irving, Shakespearean* (Cambridge University Press, 1981).

Marshall, Herbert, and Mildred Stock, *Ira Aldridge, the Negro Tragedian* (London: Rockliff, 1958, and Washington, D.C.: Howard University Press, 1993).

Odell, George C. D., *Shakespeare from Betterton to Irving*, 2 vols. (New York: C. Scribner, 1920).

Price, Cecil, *Theatre in the Age of Garrick* (Oxford: Basil Blackwell, 1973).

Rowell, George, *Queen Victoria Goes to the Theatre* (London: Paul Elek, 1978).

Theatre in the Age of Irving (Oxford: Basil Blackwell, 1981).

Speaight, Robert, *Shakespeare on the Stage: An Illustrated History of Shakespearian Performance* (London: Collins, 1973).

Sprague, Arthur Colby, *Shakespeare and the Actors: The Stage Business in His Plays, 1660–1905* (Cambridge, Mass.: Harvard University Press, 1944).

Terry, Ellen, *The Story of My Life* (London: Hutchinson, 1908).

Van Lennep, William, Emmett L. Avery, Arthur H. Scouten, George Winchester Stone, Jr, Charles Beecher Hogan, *The London Stage, 1660–1800*, 5 Parts, 11 vols. (Carbondale: Southern Illinois University Press, 1965–78).

13

PETER HOLLAND

Shakespeare in the twentieth-century theatre

In April 1987 the Royal Shakespeare Company opened a production of *Titus Andronicus* at the Swan Theatre in Stratford-upon-Avon, a theatre with a thrust stage and an audience capacity of 430. The play was the first to be directed for the RSC by Deborah Warner who had come to the company on the success of her Shakespeare productions with her own small touring company, Kick Theatre. There was no set other than the architectural form of the stage itself, no music other than that performed by the actors themselves (including a song from Walt Disney's *Snow White* whistled by Titus as he prepared to cook his monstrous pie). The costumes mixed styles from many periods and many contexts: the victorious Titus on his first entry wore Roman breastplate and modern trousers; for the final scene, he appeared 'like the *chef de cuisine* at a smart restaurant . . . in tall white chef's hat and starched white overalls'.[1] Warner did not cut a single line of the text and allowed the audience all the laughter that the play might provoke while also ensuring that it revealed all the horror that its violence demanded.

Warner's *Titus*, as it became known, was a theatrical triumph, for many critics the finest Shakespeare production of the decade, but it also exemplifies many of the questions that need to be asked of any twentieth-century performance. The size of theatre, the shape of the stage, the experience of the director, the nature of the company, the choice of play, the decisions about set, music, and costumes, the range of emotional responses encouraged from the audience, the cutting of the text and the critical reception – not to mention the work of the actors themselves – are all crucial elements in our understanding of any Shakespeare production. This chapter does not offer a chronological account of Shakespeare performances this century; such accounts are available in some of the books listed at the end. Instead, it explores some of the problems and solutions, drawing heavily, though not exclusively, on examples from England.

Productions of any Shakespeare play, even one as rarely performed as *Titus Andronicus*, invite comparison with other explorations of the same text. Peter Brook, the most radical and inventive English director of Shakespeare since Harley Granville-Barker in his revolutionary seasons at the Savoy Theatre in London from 1912 to 1914, had directed *Titus Andronicus* in 1955 at the Shakespeare Memorial Theatre, then the only theatre in Stratford. Where

11 *Titus Andronicus*, Act 3, scene 2: Titus (Brian Cox) feeds Lavinia (Sonia Ritter), directed by Deborah Warner at the Swan Theatre, Stratford-upon-Avon, 1987.

Warner would seem innovative simply by using no set and no conventional theatre music, Brook had worked within the scenic practices of mid-century productions: he designed a simple set of three massive but mobile pillars that suggested Rome and created powerful stage spaces without making the production's world too overtly realistic. But he also wrote emotive *musique concrète* (an early form of electronic music) to accompany the action at crucial moments.

Though the set dwarfed the actors, the performances of the cast, especially Laurence Olivier as Titus, were on a heroic scale, making *Titus Andronicus* into a powerfully solemn precursor of the later tragedies. But Brook accomplished this act of rescuing the play from the obscurity into which assumptions about its stage-worthiness had consigned it by cutting nearly 700 lines, trimming the text until it would conform both to his own conception of its value and to audience assumptions of what kind of play a tragedy should be. Critics hardly noticed the cutting: Evelyn Waugh thought that 'Mr Brook had to make few adjustments of

12   *Titus Andronicus*, Act 2, scene 4: Chiron (Kevin Miles, left) and Demetrius (Lee Montague) watch Lavinia (Vivien Leigh), directed by Peter Brook at the Shakespeare Memorial Theatre, Stratford-upon-Avon, 1955.

the text.'[2] There was no space in such a production for audience laughter; instead the production became famous for the frequency with which paramedics had to give aid to spectators overcome with shock at the play's violence. The violence itself was, however, represented in a stylized fashion: people fainted at the sight of Lavinia, played by Vivien Leigh, with her hands and tongue cut off, but the horrifying mutilations were signalled by ribbons of red velvet at her mouth and wrists, not by the use of stage-blood. Such restraint, as with Brook's choosing to move off stage some of the violence that the play puts on stage, brought the play's barbarity closer to the high classical forms of Greek tragedy. The contrast with the blood that welled from Lavinia's mouth in Warner's production could not be starker but it also demonstrates a crucial tension in twentieth-century explorations of the translation of Shakespeare to the stage, the tension between realism and stylization, between an emphatic immediacy and an equally emphatic distance in style and conventions. Warner's immediacy was aided by the smaller size of the Swan Theatre, Brook's grandeur by the vastness of the Shakespeare Memorial Theatre. Brook's *Titus Andronicus* justified the play as a work of the man who would later write *King Lear* but only by resolutely toning down the kind of action that prefigured the blinding of Gloucester.

There are many kinds of histories of twentieth-century Shakespeare production that could be written. By choosing two examples of performances of *Titus Andronicus* I have hinted at one: the rediscovery, at regular intervals across the period, of plays that seemed to have slipped from the canon of Shakespeare in the theatre. *Troilus and Cressida*, a play whose cynical examination of the supposed heroism of war and of the corruption and confusions of sexual desire has made it so often performed in the last twenty-five years in England and Germany, has, in effect, no stage history in England from its putative first performances until 1907, other than a few of Dryden's adaptation between 1679 and 1734. But it was William Poel's production in 1912, in Elizabethan costume on a bare stage for the Elizabethan Stage Society, that showed the play's potential as an anti-war statement. Poel's work, a conscious attempt imaginatively to recreate his version of an Elizabethan theatre, complete with costumed onstage spectators, was not only a matter of archaeological accuracy. The play's impact had less to do with its being another of Poel's string of such historicized performances than with its timeliness as a warning against war as the self-defined Great Powers armed across Europe. Where Poel's productions are most often viewed as part of a different history, the history of explorations of early modern staging to which I will return, his expansion of the range of plays staged belongs, in this case, firmly to the history of the curious way in which a play will find its right time, re-emerging from the scholar's study to claim its necessary place on stage as the theatre seeks to comment on contemporary concerns.

It is no surprise then that *Troilus and Cressida* should have been produced in September 1938, directed by Michael Macowan at the Westminster Theatre in London, presenting the characters as 'the *bon vivants* of a 1930s clubbish set' and the play as 'vividly topical' in the very month that 'Neville Chamberlain was caving in to the Nazis at Munich'[3]. If it is now little more than a cliché to costume a Shakespeare production in modern dress, for Macowan's audience it was still comparatively innovatory. Such innovative experiments can be difficult to date but it seems that modern-dress productions were invented by Barry Jackson while he ran the Birmingham Repertory Theatre, starting with his *Cymbeline* in 1923. Being radical in the provinces had little impact, however, and it was Jackson's *Hamlet* at the Kingsway Theatre in 1925, with Colin Keith-Johnston as Hamlet in a dinner-jacket, that established the curiosity, as a reviewer put it, 'to be able to judge *Hamlet* as though . . . a modern playwright, say Tchekhov [*sic*], had written it'.[4] Jackson's updating, carefully advertised as '*Hamlet* in Modern Dress' as if to warn audiences of the visual shock to their expectations, proclaimed the play's modernity, denying convention to enable the play to become immediate, demanding, and necessary. Shakespeare's actors wore contemporary dress and Garrick too wore costumes that befitted an eighteenth-century gentleman but each period was working within the conventional practices of their contemporary theatre. Jackson's device forced audiences to treat the familiar classical text as unfamiliarly new, just as Macowan's *Troilus* asked audiences to reflect just as forcibly on the disconcerting parallels with contemporary politics. Yet Macowan was seeking an effect not dissimilar from Poel's, for all that the latter eschewed any gesture towards the time of his own production. Macowan's means of seeking immediacy might be compared with Orson Welles's production of *Julius Caesar* in 1937 for the Mercury Theatre in New York, where the play acquired a subtitle, 'The Death of a Dictator', and the costume designs made explicit its reading of contemporary history with Caesar as a Mussolini figure, greeted with fascist salutes.

Troilus and Cressida had, by this time, become an appropriate play to use to reflect on war. Subsequent productions, for example by Robert Atkins at the Regent's Park Open Air Theatre in 1946 or by John Barton and Peter Hall at Stratford-upon-Avon in 1960, similarly chose the play to represent the disillusion or tension of a society facing the aftermath of one war or the tensions of a cold-war anticipation of another. In 1985 Howard Davies directed *Troilus and Cressida* for the RSC, setting the play roughly at the time of the Crimean War and thereby exemplifying the tendency of post-war directors and designers to seek a style that dated the set and costumes to a period of history serving as some kind of analogy that would, in their view, speak more immediately to the audience than the styles of either the play's original date of production or the historical moment that the play described. The Crimean War was therefore chosen to suggest an international conflict fought by countries whose imperial power was waning.

But *Troilus and Cressida* had, by 1985, become open to another kind of pressure and another form of rereading. Cressida had been viewed consistently unsympathetically in British productions, unlike the far more imaginative response to her as the victim of male behaviour in Joseph Papp's New York production in 1965 – a sign of Papp's different kind of responsiveness to contemporary issues in a very different cultural context. Juliet Stevenson in Davies's production refused to play Cressida as a faithless woman. Stevenson was well aware of the risks in her approach:

> If you are interested in how women are portrayed on stage and in re-investigating Shakespeare's women from scratch, you feel a responsibility to the women that does not necessarily go hand in hand with creativity, because you go into the rehearsal room feeling slightly defensive of them. You react against the way tradition and prejudice have stigmatised them – Cressida the whore, Kate the shrew, and every time they're judged you feel protective. Perhaps too protective.[5]

Significantly, Stevenson is marking a performer's decisive intervention into the production's sexual politics while indicating her anxiety about how the actor's response that creates the rereading may work too strongly. If the history of twentieth-century production is most often described, usually lamentingly, as the rise of directors' theatre so that productions have often become known by the identity of the director rather than the star – or indeed the playwright – Stevenson demonstrates a way in which the processes of rehearsal may involve a different kind of accommodation, not of actors to the will of the director but of the production to the demands made by an actor. The result was a revaluation of

Cressida, now seen as a woman nearly raped by the Greek generals and turning to Diomede not out of natural female inconstancy and faithlessness but as a desperate response to a dangerous situation.

Such a response, reconsidering Shakespeare's constructions of gender and the ways in which traditional modes of performance have taken a consistently unquestioning view of them, had already necessitated the transformation of expected ways of ending performances of certain texts. Where Katherine, in *The Taming of the Shrew*, had always been seen as being brought properly into conformity with the male view of wifely behaviour, it was now possible for a production to question the value and meaning of what had happened to her. Michael Bogdanov's production for the RSC in 1978 showed Katherine (Paola Dionisotti) delivering her final long speech on the value of a wife's obedience with absolute sincerity but to a Petruccio horrified by what he now realized he had made of her. As Dionisotti described it,

> My Kate was kneeling and I reached over to kiss his foot and he gasped, recoiled, jumped back, because somehow he's completely blown it. He's as trapped now by society as she was in the beginning . . . The lights went down as we left – I following him, the others hardly noticing we'd gone. They'd got down to some hard gambling. They just closed ranks around the green baize table. (Rutter, p. 23)

Where the play in production had previously spoken of the change in Katherine as a positive socializing of the unsocial woman, it could now be seen as a condemnation of the forms of socialization to which women are forced to assent. But, in addition, this broadly feminist argument was also seen, by Dionisotti herself, to be a dissection of the construction of masculinity, as Petruccio too is trapped by social expectations. Other women, for example Sinead Cusack for Barry Kyle (RSC, 1982) or Fiona Shaw for Jonathan Miller (RSC, 1987), would find different solutions to the problem of the play's ending, but what was irrevocably in place was an acceptance that the final speech had now become problematic, that the end of the play could not be left as an unquestioned celebration of the taming of a shrew into the delights of normative matrimony, unless the production was to shirk its responsibilities both to the play and to its modern audience.

Measure for Measure, another play whose previously skeletal stage-history has filled out at a remarkable rate in the period since 1945, posed a similar problem of ending. John Barton's production (RSC, 1970) ended with Isabella (Estelle Kohler) alone on stage, shocked by the Duke's proposal. Peter Brook had in 1950 placed the emphasis on Isabella's learning the necessity of pleading for mercy for Angelo, an event pinpointed in performance by the immense pause that preceded Isabella's kneeling in intercession for Angelo's life. Barton found that the text suggested a different gap that needed to be demonstrated in performance, a gap embodied in Isabella's silence in response to the Duke's two proposals of marriage. Though often described as a production in which Isabella refused the Duke, it offered instead a woman shocked by the proposal itself and hence unsure

13   *The Merchant of Venice*, Act 3, scene 1. Shylock (Antony Sher, right) and Tubal (Bill McGuirk), directed by Bill Alexander at the Royal Shakespeare Theatre, Stratford-upon-Avon (1987).

what kind of response she could make. Again, the assumption that marriage could be confidently seen as the inevitably desirable ending of a comedy was being called into question. It is no accident that *Love's Labour's Lost* also began to be produced more often, a play whose celebration of language and courtship is circumscribed by the women's rejection of the move towards marriage and the extension of the demands beyond the play's own temporal limits:

King. Come, sir, it wants a twelvemonth an' a day,
   And then 'twill end.
Biron. That's too long for a play. (5.2.863–4)

Starting with Peter Brook's production at Stratford in 1946, *Love's Labour's Lost* changed from an infrequently performed example of a frothy comedy of arcane language-games to a frequently troubling, melancholy, and dark drama that audiences accepted and understood.

   Such reconsiderations of the performance of gender relations across the range of Shakespearian comedies can be seen as a parallel to the reconsiderations of the performance of race. *The Merchant of Venice*, widely performed in Germany under the Nazis to demonstrate the evil of Jews, became a very different play after the end of the Second World War, with the awareness of the Holocaust making it almost impossible to see Shylock as a representative of his race and difficult even to see him as unmitigatedly evil; instead it necessitated a view of the play as an exploration of Venetian anti-semitism and Shylock as a man separated by his thirst for revenge from the other Jews in Venice. But Belmont also needed revaluing and Portia's line after the failure of the Prince of Morocco to choose the right casket, 'Let all of his complexion choose me so' (2.7.79), could no longer be excused as a comment on his temperament rather than his colour.

Shakespeare's black characters (Aaron in *Titus Andronicus*, Morocco, and Othello but, noticeably, not Cleopatra) were not only beginning to be cast more consistently with black actors but race became a newly important problem. When Paul Robeson played Othello in London in 1930, the first major production with a black actor in the role since Ira Aldridge in the nineteenth century, race was certainly a concern but it was far more emphatically so in Robeson's performances in 1943 which toured across America – or at least those parts of the country which would not have required Robeson to perform in front of racially segregated audiences. The production attracted a new audience, particularly among servicemen on leave, an audience often unused to the theatre as well as to Shakespeare but one immediately caught up in the contemporaneity of the drama where Othello's kissing Desdemona on arrival in Cyprus caused a gasp from the audience every night. Laurence Olivier's Othello at the National Theatre in 1964 seems, in retrospect, a reactionary performance, with his careful mimicking of a racially different stance, walk, and voice rhythms now only able to be read as teetering on the edge of being offensive. By 1997 when Patrick Stewart played Othello for the American Shakespeare Theatre in Washington it seemed that the only way in which a white actor could play the role was in a photo-negative production with Othello and Bianca the only white actors in an otherwise black company. Peter Sellars's production of *The Merchant of Venice* in 1994 for the Goodman Theatre, Chicago, showed that a contemporary view of race could be used to overlay an early modern one with the Jews played by black actors and with film of racial attacks in Los Angeles shown on television monitors on stage. But the effect of race is more widespread across Shakespeare production than ethnicity: Michael Langham's production of *Henry V* at Stratford, Ontario in 1956 altered the audience's responses to the French by casting French-Canadians in the roles in a country where, unlike England, the French have not been seen as the natural enemy of the state; and the same play's exposition of the disunited kingdom of English, Welsh, Scots, and Irish is heard differently in different parts of Great Britain.

In the USA in particular, Caliban in *The Tempest* was, from the 1970s onwards, frequently played by an African-American actor so that the play's view of colonialism could be related directly to American anxieties about slavery and racial oppression. While there were few black actors in the classical theatre in England through much of the century, by the 1970s black actors began to be cast in Shakespearian roles other than those explicitly defined by race. 'Colour-blind' or 'non-traditional' casting allowed black actors to play a far wider range of roles with Josette Simon, for instance, cast as Rosaline in *Love's Labour's Lost* (1985) and Isabella in *Measure for Measure* (1987) for the RSC.

Though some theatre critics continued to argue that such racially transgressive casting was unacceptable, it could be seen as a parallel to other kinds of explorations, such as cross-gendering or the age of a character, that casting was designed to reveal. There is a long history of women playing Hamlet, but Fiona Shaw played Richard II at the Royal National Theatre in 1995, Kathryn Hunter King Lear at the Young Vic in 1997, and Mark Rylance Cleopatra at the Shakespeare's Globe theatre in 1999, the last an effect which was no more connected to the Globe's investigations of historically authentic modes of performance than the all-male casts for *As You Like It* at the National Theatre in 1967 and for Cheek by Jowl in 1991. Such unusual casting decisions increased the range of roles available for men and women, and supported strong interpretative approaches to the plays. Cross-gender casting makes gender into a performative process, rethinking for twentieth-century audiences the ways in which gender had, after all, been explored in early modern theatre when all women were played by boys.

There was one further significant change in casting across the century: a rethinking of the relationship of the actor's age and the age of the character. In part this was a theatrical response to audiences' expectations derived from their experience of film. Where it had been possible for actors to continue to play, say, Romeo and Juliet well into their forties, directors now looked to find young actors, especially after Franco Zeffirelli's production with John Stride and Judi Dench (Old Vic Theatre, London, 1961). Though an actor in his forties could play King Lear (for example Paul Scofield at age forty in Peter Brook's production for the RSC in 1962), youth seemed no longer able to be achieved solely by make-up. The texts' statements about the age of a character began to be responded to in more noticeably realist terms, exactly the reverse of the thinking that allowed cross-racial or cross-gender casting. Characters whose age had been left unstated by Shakespeare had often come to be assumed to have a particular age but the traditions were also rethought: the Duke in *Measure for Measure* was no longer an elderly figure but, as in Roger Allam's performance (RSC 1988), a man in his thirties, throwing his proposal of marriage to Isabella into a wholly new light. But, especially in productions of cycles of Shakespeare's English histories, where a character ages in the course of the plays, actors could still be seen to perform the right age rather than being the right age, for example Peggy Ashcroft as Margaret in *The Wars of the Roses*, the condensing of Shakespeare's three parts of *Henry VI* and *Richard III* into three plays (RSC, 1963).

The kinds of concerns I have been exploring over gender, race, and age are primarily concerned with the actor's body. If there has been one central opposition in critics' comments on Shakespearian performance across the century it has been between body and voice. It is usually phrased as an assumption that the voice beautiful is to be preferred to the body heroic. It is the classic opposition of Gielgud, the epitome of voice, and Olivier, an actor who always sought to disguise his body in some way so that, for example, his performance as Shylock emerged from his demand to wear false teeth and his interpretation of Othello was created through the definition of skin colour in the painstaking application of layers of make-up rubbed to a sheen with a length of silk. But there is also a common assumption that the great age of verse-speaking belongs irretrievably in the past. More generally it displays a fundamental anxiety about how Shakespeare's plays are heard rather than watched, about the extent to which the playgoers are audience (hearers) rather than spectators (watchers). Theatre history too, not least by virtue of the nature of its evidence, can more easily write of what a production looked like than what it sounded like.

Nonetheless, if there has been one crucial transformation across the century in the staging of Shakespeare it can be located in the changing responses to the demands of set design. Reviewing a 1981 Stratford production of a double bill of *Titus Andronicus* and *The Two Gentlemen of Verona*, Michael Coveney complained 'Christopher Morley's messy design of trunks, clothes racks and artificial trees is topped off with a large gauze canopy. It amounts to as uncommitted a visual statement as could be imagined.'[6] For Coveney, set design ought not to be neutral but a palpable definition of the director's and designer's intentions. Set design had changed since the start of the century: from being a group of well-painted conventional representations of the fictive world of the play, identified with varying degrees of archaeological accuracy and theatrical tradition, sets had become capable of independent meaning, a meaning that could control the audience's response and the actor's rehearsals. No longer likely to have been taken from a theatre company's substantial stock of scenery, the design, often now presented to the actors on the first day of rehearsal, was redefined for each production. There are no longer assumptions about what a Shakespeare production should or indeed might look like.

The theatre's revolution in stage design, inaugurated by Adolphe Appia and Edward Gordon Craig, did not immediately have an impact on Shakespeare production in England. Craig himself only once directed and designed a Shakespeare play in England, a production of *Much Ado About Nothing* in London in 1903, notable for the scene of Hero's rejection (4.3) for which Craig created a perspective corridor through curtains, candles, and coloured lights suggesting stained-glass windows. His mother, Ellen Terry, played Beatrice but the setting was far from the kind she had been used to when playing opposite Irving at the Lyceum. In Moscow in 1912 Craig designed *Hamlet* for Stanislavsky's Moscow Art Theatre, using for the first time on stage monochrome flats as mobile screens to create metamorphic stage spaces. He also created a startling image for Claudius' court (1.2) as a gigantic gold cloak cascaded downstage to a trap-door from the shoulders of Claudius and Gertrude standing far upstage; courtiers poked their heads through holes in this golden sea while Hamlet sat, a lone figure downstage apparently in a totally different world from the others. The first English responses could be seen in Harley Granville-Barker's productions in 1912 to 1914 which tentatively explored the possibilities of abstraction so that Norman Wilkinson's designs for *A Midsummer Night's Dream* (Savoy Theatre, London, 1914) represented the wood by a mound on the stage floor, heavy curtains painted with abstract images of trees and a wreath in mid-air of leaves and fairy-lights rather than with the tradition of canvas flats or even real trees. But the designs left little progeny and English theatre continued to work with its nineteenth-century conventions for much of the early part of the century.

Elsewhere in Europe, however, the effects of the kinds of new staging Craig had advocated were even bolder and the implications more complex. Leopold Jessner's *Richard III* (Berlin Staatstheater, 1920), designed by Emil Pirchan, for instance, explored expressionist staging, modulating between a simple wall with an archway in its centre and a walkway on its top (a style that could easily be used for the kinds of staging Shakespeare's text requires) and the use of lighting, for instance to project a gigantic shadow of Richard against the back wall, a device that seems familiar enough now but which was shockingly new in 1920. In the second half of the production Jessner used what had become his design 'trademark . . . a gigantic flight of steps rising from the proscenium line to the lower wall in narrowing sections, effectively occupying the playing space'.[7] Jessner, like many other directors before and after, interpolated a scene to show a part of the action that Shakespeare had chosen not to dramatize: staging the coronation in brilliant red, Jessner made the costumes of the attendants, Richard's robe, and the steps themselves merge into a crimson sky 'as though an electric charge of evil had leapt the gap between heaven and earth' (Michael Patterson, quoted by Kennedy, p. 87). Such a strong line on the play's meaning and one which was so emphatically staged through design had consequential losses. Jessner's abstractions denied the actors any opportunity to explore their characters' psychological complexity. Instead an intellectual concept was made visible and Jessner was content to sacrifice more conventional aspects of performance to that end.

Such continental styles as Jessner's were slow in reaching England. In 1932, for the first season of the newly built Stratford Memorial Theatre, Theodore Komisarjevsky directed *The Merchant of Venice* on a set of comically leaning bridges and odd perspectives; he used Jessner's famous steps for the opening scene of *King Lear* there in 1936 as Bridges-Adams had for Coriolanus' triumphal entrance in his production at Stratford in 1933. But English theatre sought a less extreme solution to design and found it in the work of Motley, a design-team of three women (Elizabeth Montgomery, Audrey and Margaret Harris) whose work with Gielgud in the 1930s began a new form of flexible staging which did not dominate the actors in the way other experiments in design seemed to. Motley's work still provided directors with locales for each scene, precise visual definitions of where exactly each scene was conventionally imagined (by directors and audiences) as being located but, by adroit use of curtains across the stage, their designs also made for fluid and rapid staging with none of the lengthy

14   Theodore Komisarjevsky's 1936 production of *King Lear* (Act 1, scene 1) at the Shakespeare Memorial Theatre, Stratford-upon-Avon.

pauses, clumsy spectacle or need for enormous stage-crews for scene-changes with traditional designs. A typically English compromise, midway between abstraction and realistic representation, Motley's staging proved a powerful influence, particularly after their designs for Gielgud's *Romeo and Juliet* in 1935 (New Theatre, London). Productions on the largest stages in Stratford or at the Royal National Theatre in London are still strikingly derived from their kinds of solutions to the problems of accommodating the traditions of English Shakespeare to the demands of the modern stage. The theatre has found it difficult to reconcile the tension between, on the one hand, the possibilities and conventions of the modern stage and, on the other, the nature of the plays themselves with their limited concerns with realistic place and their greater interest in a mobile, imaginary space which is often no more or less than a bare stage platform.

When Brook directed *Titus Andronicus* in Stratford only one theatre was available; when Warner directed the same play she had a choice of three theatres. The Shakespeare Memorial Theatre was a grand conventional building designed with a vast gulf between stage and audience: as the actor Baliol Holloway commented in 1934, 'On a clear day . . . you can just about see the boiled shirts in the first row. It is like acting to Calais from the cliffs of Dover.'[8] Subsequent redesigns of the theatre auditorium tried to diminish this space that distanced actor (and action) from audience while increasing its capacity from an initial 1,000 to, currently, 1,500.

But the development of an alternative mode of fringe theatre through the 1960s suggested the need for a different kind of space in which to perform Shakespeare. In 1974 Buzz Goodbody directed a version of *King Lear* (retitled *Lear*) as the first production in The Other Place, a chamber theatre for an audience of 140. A corrugated-iron shack converted from a stage store, The Other Place denied the plush experience of the Royal Shakespeare Theatre (as the Stratford Memorial Theatre has been renamed). Goodbody's *Lear* and, in 1975, *Hamlet* rethought the plays as chamber-pieces, with the audience closer to the action than would ever have been possible in a larger house. Simple sets and modern dress were visible signs of Goodbody's style but it encouraged detailed psychological acting and a kind of relevance that chimed with her left politics, something that was also apparent in the low admission price (70p). Such an exploration of Shakespeare in a small space seems to be unprecedented. Shakespeare had, of course, been performed in theatres as small as The Other Place for centuries but the idea of a company choosing a small space when a large one was also available is distinctively different. It made it possible to explore Shakespeare in close-up, to import into the theatre the kinds of attention that film and television had made available. The plays – and it was particularly the tragedies that immediately benefited from this new style – lost their national and international politics but gained, through the domesticity of the space, a riveting concern with the politics of family.

When in 1976 Trevor Nunn completely reworked for The Other Place the overblown production of *Macbeth* that he had staged at the Royal Shakespeare Theatre in 1974, the result terrified audiences in its exploration of evil in an extraordinary way. Played on a bare wood floor outlined with a circle of paint with those actors not in a scene often seated on boxes watching the action in close proximity to the 'real' audience, *Macbeth* became a study in good and evil in which Ian McKellen's Macbeth could do more with a small gesture or a coldly murderous stare than could be achieved with far larger effects on a larger stage. Lighting, too, could be extreme, with Macbeth's melancholic despair in Act 5 lit by a single light bulb suspended over Macbeth's head and which he set swinging to and fro, making his face alternate from darkness to harsh light.

Some of the RSC's finest work in the ensuing years was a response to the opportunity for new discoveries that The Other Place offered: John Barton's *The Merchant of Venice* (1978), Adrian Noble's extension in 1982 of the domestic view of *Antony and Cleopatra* that Peter Brook had attempted in the Royal Shakespeare Theatre in 1978, Trevor Nunn's detailed realism for *Othello* in 1989. Such productions were the work of directors with strong interpretative 'readings' of the plays. But The Other Place and its style of chamber Shakespeare, later extended by, for instance, the Royal National Theatre's productions in its smallest theatre, the Cottesloe, also seemed to give the plays back to the actors: the very closeness of actor to audience made for a new authority of actor over design, responding in part to the call by John Russell Brown in his book *Free Shakespeare* (1974) to return Shakespeare to the actor and to deny the overweening power of the director. If the work in The Other Place grew in part out of the RSC's experience of small-scale touring, particularly their productions as Theatregoround from 1965, it also grew out of the close connection with the new plays which the company worked on in the same space, giving Shakespeare a kind of modernity and relevance that was rarely available elsewhere.

But production of Shakespeare also needed a different context, the context provided by placing his work alongside that of his contemporaries. The Swan Theatre opened in 1986 in the rebuilt shell of the first Stratford Memorial Theatre. Its horseshoe seating around a thrust stage and the light colour of the wood that formed its galleries were derived from an imaginative reworking of some of the forms of early modern theatres. In no sense a slavish reconstruction of an indoor theatre like the Blackfriars for which Shakespeare had written, the Swan was a venue designed specifically for the revival of other plays from 1570 to 1700, the kinds of plays which the RSC had occasionally mounted in the main theatre. Productions of Shakespeare at the Swan – and the first play performed there was *The Two Noble Kinsmen* – invited comparison of Shakespeare's dramaturgy with that of his contemporaries, not in terms of authenticity but in a mode of modern rediscovery.

The search for authentic Shakespeare had, however, been a recurrent concern throughout the century, from the work of William Poel and the Elizabethan Stage Society onwards, spurred by the discovery in 1888 of the 1596 'de Witt' drawing of the Swan. In 1921 Nugent Monck, a disciple of Poel's, opened a tiny version of an Elizabethan theatre like the Fortune as the Maddermarket Theatre in Norwich and used it throughout the decade to explore how Shakespeare might have been staged. There were further experiments, but the culmination of the process was the opening in 1997 of a reconstruction of the Globe on Bankside, as close as was practicable to the original site. A result of extensive collaborations between scholars and architects – and driven by the concern of the American actor Sam Wanamaker for a living memorial to Shakespeare on the site where his plays had first been produced – the Globe is a reasonable approximation to authenticity, within the limits prescribed by commercial demands and fire regulations. If the productions to date have not been of outstanding worth, with poor companies and poorer directors, the physical structure of the theatre, especially the sight-lines and relationship from stage to audience, have allowed a new view of how the texts work in performance to begin to emerge.

But what, after all, is the nature of the text itself? Recent textual scholarship has made scholars realize that the text is provisional and unstable but the traditions of the theatre have always been prepared to rework the plays. Apart from the long history of adaptation, theatre remakes each text in the act of producing it. Warner's *Titus Andronicus* was remarkable for its refusal to cut; much more often, the texts are substantially reduced since the rhythms of contemporary staging, and assumptions about the audience's ability to comprehend Shakespeare's language when spoken at speed, necessitate cutting if the plays are not to run unsociably long. But the plays are also rewritten: the RSC's staging of the first tetralogy of history plays as a trilogy renamed *The Wars of the Roses* (directed by Peter Hall and John Barton, 1963) meant not only extensive cutting but also the inclusion of hundreds of lines written by John Barton to provide bridges and explanations. Rearrangements of the text are equally common with lines transferred between characters, not only because of directorial rethinking of the nature of character but also as a result of the smaller cast sizes of late-twentieth-century theatre; for example, *Timon of Athens* in the Royal Shakespeare Theatre in 1965 had a cast of forty-six, whereas the 1999 production had only twenty.

In non-anglophone production, of course, the text is automatically and necessarily rewritten through translation, and the remaking of the text into subsequent cultural contexts by retranslation is a continual process. Shakespeare on stage in France is not the same as Shakespeare on stage in England or Japan or Germany, not only because of the differing cultural meanings action has but also because the text changes its meanings in translation. Every culture creates the Shakespeare it needs so that, for instance, *King Lear* in two separate productions in Moscow in 1994 became a play about the break-up of the Soviet state and the consequential chaos; widely different though Sergei Zhenovach's version at Malaya Bronnaya Theatre and Alexei Borodin's at the Detsky Theatre were in theatrical style and interpretative meanings, both were recognizably theatrical responses through *King Lear* to the same social context.

But Shakespeare has also been the location for intercultural experiment: Ariane Mnouchkine's production of *Richard II* for her company, the Théâtre du Soleil, at the Cartoucherie (Paris, 1981) made extensive use of Asian techniques of mask and formalized movement derived from Noh, Kabuki, Kathakali, and Peking Opera, an eclectic orientalism to remake the rituals of a medieval court. Peter Brook's production of *The Tempest* (as *La Tempête*, Paris, 1990) turned to African rituals of shamanism to provide the forms for Prospero's magic. In what is possibly the most extreme such experiment yet, Karin Beier's version of *A Midsummer Night's Dream* (Düsseldorfer Schauspielhaus, 1995) used actors from many different European countries, each speaking his or her own language, a Euro-babel of conflicting tongues through which the politics of relationships in the play took on a wholly new urgency of meaning. Against such radical rethinking of the nature of the Shakespearian text for performance and of the cultural contexts within which it has meaning, main-stream English productions can make central institutions like the RSC or the Royal National Theatre appear staunch bastions of conservatism. But they are also the inheritors of a tradition of exploring the text, finding, often with enormous subtlety and great theatrical distinction, new ways in which to reveal potential meanings in the plays.

Notes

1. Robert Smallwood, 'Directors' Shakespeare', in *Shakespeare: An Illustrated Stage History*, ed. Jonathan Bate and Russell Jackson (Oxford University Press, 1996), pp. 176–96; p. 182.
2. Stanley Wells, ed., *Shakespeare in the Theatre: An Anthology of Criticism* (Oxford: Clarendon Press, 1997), p. 254.
3. William Shakespeare, *Troilus and Cressida*, ed. David Bevington, The Arden Shakespeare (Walton-on-Thames: Thomas Nelson, 1998), p. 96.
4. Wells, *Shakespeare in the Theatre*, p. 204.
5. Carol Rutter, *Clamorous Voices: Shakespeare's Women Today*, ed. Faith Evans (London: The Women's Press, 1988), p. xviii.
6. Michael Coveney, *The Financial Times*, 7 September 1981.
7. Dennis Kennedy, *Looking at Shakespeare: A Visual History of Twentieth-Century Performance* (Cambridge University Press, 1993), p. 87.
8. Sally Beauman, *The Royal Shakespeare Company: A History of Ten Decades* (Oxford University Press, 1982), p. 113.

Reading list

Bate, Jonathan, and Russell Jackson, eds., *Shakespeare: An Illustrated Stage History* (Oxford University Press, 1996).

Beauman, Sally, *The Royal Shakespeare Company: A History of Ten Decades* (Oxford University Press, 1982).

Berry, Ralph, *On Directing Shakespeare: Interviews with Contemporary Directors* (London: Hamish Hamilton, 1989).

Brockbank, Philip, Russell Jackson, and Robert Smallwood, 4 vols. to date, *Players of Shakespeare* (Cambridge University Press, 1980–).

Brown, John Russell, *Free Shakespeare* (London: Heinemann Educational, 1974).

David, Richard, *Shakespeare in the Theatre* (Cambridge University Press, 1978).

Hill, Errol, *Shakespeare in Sable: A History of Black Shakespearian Actors* (London: University of Massachusetts Press, 1987).

Hodgdon, Barbara, *The Shakespeare Trade: Performances and Appropriations* (Philadelphia: University of Pennsylania Press, 1998).

Holland, Peter, *English Shakespeares: Shakespeare on the English Stage in the 1990s* (Cambridge University Press, 1997).

Hortmann, Wilhelm, *Shakespeare on the German Stage: The Twentieth Century* (Cambridge University Press, 1998).

Kennedy, Dennis, *Looking at Shakespeare: A Visual History of Twentieth-Century Performance* (Cambridge University Press, 1993).

Kennedy, Dennis, ed., *Foreign Shakespeare: Contemporary Performance* (Cambridge University Press, 1993).

Mullin, Michael, *Design by Motley* (Newark: University of Delaware Press, 1996).

Mulryne, J. R., and Margaret Shewring, *Shakespeare's Globe Rebuilt* (Cambridge University Press, 1998).

Rutter, Carol, *Clamorous Voices: Shakespeare's Women Today*, ed. Faith Evans (London: The Women's Press, 1988).

Styan, John L., *The Shakespeare Revolution* (Cambridge University Press, 1977).

Trewin, J. C., *Shakespeare on the English Stage 1900–1964* (London: Barrie and Rockliff, 1964).

Wells, Stanley, ed., *Shakespeare in the Theatre: An Anthology of Criticism* (Oxford: Clarendon Press, 1997).

Worthen, William B., *Shakespeare and the Authority of Performance* (Cambridge University Press, 1997).

14

RUSSELL JACKSON

Shakespeare and the cinema

Films based on Shakespeare's plays are best considered in terms of their vision – that is, the imaginary world they create, and the way of seeing it that they offer the viewer rather than the degree of their faithfulness to a Shakespearian original. However, Shakespearian films often arise from the director's desire to do justice to what are perceived as the original's salient qualities – attempting to encompass each 'necessary question of the play' (to borrow Hamlet's term.) To an extent, the history of Shakespearian film-making is one of variations on this theme: shifting attitudes to the Shakespearian source material, varied objectives, and changing techniques.[1]

Probably the first – and certainly the earliest surviving – 'Shakespeare film' is the brief glimpse of Sir Herbert Beerbohm Tree as the dying King John exhibited in 1899. Within a decade, the narrative cinema rapidly grew in technical resource and cultural diversity. Shakespearian subjects served as a source of familiar scenes and characters and a well-accredited bank of cultural respectability on which the new medium might draw. Before the advent of fully synchronized sound, in the relatively 'silent' but in fact only speechless cinema, Shakespeare's plays provided the basis for more than 400 films. The more modest of these included the terse one-reelers (10–15 minutes in duration) made in New York between 1908 and 1912 by the Vitagraph company, or the short films made on stage at Stratford-upon-Avon, featuring Frank Benson's company in scenes from a number of plays – of which only *Richard III* (1911) survives. More ambitious projects included the 59-minute British *Hamlet* (1913) featuring Sir Johnston Forbes-Robertson in the title role; Sven Gade's striking *Hamlet, A Drama of Revenge* (Germany, 1920) in which Asta Neilsen plays a prince who is *in fact* a woman; and the grandly designed *Othello* (Germany, 1922) directed by Dmitri Buchowetski with Emil Jannings (Iago) and Werner Krauss (Othello).[2]

The more expansive among these films, which attempt to convey the play's narrative without reliance on the audience's prior knowledge of the text, often illustrate divergences of technique between the theatrical original and the increasingly sophisticated devices of the new medium. Hamlet, in the British film of 1913, cannot meaningfully soliloquize, but he can (by the use of outdoor locations) be seen in the context of a natural world unavailable even in the pictorial theatre of the 1900s. By the 1920s, the cinema's ability to suggest psychological states by lighting, *mise-en-scène* and the juxtaposition of images had expanded enormously. In Buchowetski's film Krauss as Othello twists and gnaws at the handkerchief which becomes not merely evidence of Desdemona's perfidy but an icon of the Moor's jealous agony and the physical cruelty he will visit on her. Sven Gade's *Hamlet* begins from an extraordinary premise: Hamlet was a female child, born when her father was presumed dead in battle. Her true gender was concealed by her mother to preserve the dynasty, and the pretence maintained after the revelation that Hamlet senior was alive. Gade exploits in intimate close-up the heavy-lidded, pallid expressiveness of Neilsen's face, contrasting the elegance of her slim, androgynous, black-clad figure with the grossness of her villainous uncle and the commonplace womanliness of Gertrude. Often in the film, the gestural language of German expressionism is combined with stark clarity in lighting and sets. For all its quirkiness, the film's engagement with issues central to the play itself makes Gade's work a powerful vision of *Hamlet* and of Hamlet himself. As an intervention in the critical and artistic dialogue with Shakespearian originals, it is more telling than many more 'faithful' cinematic renderings of the plays' plots and characters.

The advent of fully synchronized sound complicated the cinema's relationship with Shakespeare. Verbal description, the Elizabethan theatre's principal means of establishing a sense of location, could now exist alongside the images that had hitherto replaced but now rivalled it. Dialogue and soliloquy were now available to the film-maker, but archaic language and rhetorical patterning were likely to be as much of an embarrassment as an advantage. How would the 'talkies' and the popular audience take to Shakespearian speech?

The first full-length Shakespeare sound film was *The Taming of the Shrew* (USA, 1929), directed by Sam Taylor with and for Douglas Fairbanks and Mary Pickford. Taylor was an experienced director of silent comedies, and the movie is remarkable for its vitality and broad (and physical) comedy, and for Pickford's ability to suggest that even in capitulation Katherine has the whip hand. It also gained from press interest in the turbulent off-screen relationship of the two stars.

If the film can be said to propose a 'vision', it is that of a lavishly picturesque Italian Renaissance society that incorporates the happy-go-lucky world of slapstick humour. The sets alone must have accounted for a good deal of the half a million dollars allegedly spent on production. Inevitably, the wedding is shown rather than described and, just as inevitably, its physical comedy is developed beyond Gremio's description in the play. Fairbanks is recklessly but amiably boisterous, Pickford (playing more adventurously against her usual saccharine type) a whip-wielding termagant who is tricked into marriage but manages to subvert the taming campaign. Overhearing his plans to make the wedding-night a nightmare, she takes each of Petruccio's tricks (pulling off bedclothes, and so forth) in her stride, adopting, as Kate does not in the text, the very strategy Petruccio announced when he undertook to woo her. She manages to land him a resounding blow on the head with a stool, but then comforts him in her arms, and burns her whip in the bedroom grate. This is only a show of acquiescence: in the concluding scene her bandaged and punch-drunk husband lolls at the head of the table, but with a wink at the 'headstrong women' whom she lectures Katherine makes it clear that she has won her way, whatever her recommendation of 'submission' may seem to be saying.

The next Shakespeare sound film from Hollywood, *A Midsummer Night's Dream* (1935), was altogether more ambitious, both in production values and as an importation of 'high' culture into the movies. One of the greatest European theatre directors of his time, Max Reinhardt had staged at least eighteen productions of the play before the screen version he and William Dieterle co-directed for Warner Brothers. Over the years Reinhardt had developed a vision of the play that encompassed lyricism, pageantry, and natural magic.[3] On the Warner Brothers' sound stages, built to accommodate the grandest screen musicals, he had constructed an elaborately naturalistic forest and a baroque 'Athenian' palace. Casting largely from the studio's contract players, he acquired a musical-comedy Lysander in Dick Powell, Mickey Rooney as Puck, and a superb, nervously overweening Bottom in James Cagney. Dances were arranged by Bronsislava Nijinska, and music rearranged from Mendelssohn by Erich Wolfgang Korngold. The film was handsomely photographed in black-and-white, with many effective optical tricks (including a shimmer of stars across the whole screen for some of the fairy sequences), and an erotically charged choreographic sequence in which Oberon's dark-skinned, bat-winged male fairies engulf the crouching, tinsel-haired (and exclusively female) entourage of the Fairy Queen.

A Midsummer Night's Dream was an expensive film ($1.5m) and its commercial failure seems to have convinced the producers that such bids for prestige were too highly priced: earlier announcements that Reinhardt would go on to direct a series of Shakespeare films were forgotten. By the end of the decade, when he was an exile rather than a distinguished visitor in Hollywood, there were no film projects for him. In Britain in 1936 another refugee from the German-speaking theatre, Paul Czinner, directed an ornate and studio-bound *As You Like It* with his wife, the waifish, winsome, and charmingly accented Elisabeth Bergner as Rosalind (she had played the part to great acclaim in Berlin) and Laurence Olivier as Orlando. Neither this, nor the sumptuous *Romeo and Juliet* directed by George Cukor for Irving Thalberg at MGM provided any reassurance that Shakespeare might lead to either box-office success or adventurous film-making. Cukor's extensive back-lot Verona (a skilful anthology of the city's architecture) provided the setting for processions and crowd scenes; the Capulet garden was worthy of a Hollywood mansion. Unfortunately the film's one dynamic presence was John Barrymore as Mercutio. Fatally restrained and dignified performances by an excessively mature pair of lovers (Leslie Howard and Thalberg's wife, Norma Shearer) drained the plot of its excitement and urgency. The well-bred mellifluousness of their speaking and the sumptuousness of the 'accurate' period setting were indicative of a deadly reverence for the cultural property appropriated on behalf of the studio. Expenditure again set a record – this time $2m. If the film possessed any vision it was of high culture, achieved by conspicuous consumption in the service of the supposedly irreproachable (but in the event not irresistible) combination of Shakespeare and the Italian Renaissance.

Laurence Olivier's first attempt at directing a Shakespeare play on screen, *Henry V*, was filmed in Technicolor in Great Britain in 1943 and released (after the Normandy landings) in the autumn of the following year. After the claustrophobia of Czinner's *As You Like It* and the pieties of Cukor's *Romeo and Juliet*, it seemed revolutionary: a vision of the past that was colourful but stylized rather than leadenly naturalistic, and also an assertion of what film-making might be after cross-fertilization with Elizabethan theatre. The quasi-documentary tone of its spirited opening sequences in Shakespeare's London (clean, idealized) and his own theatre (democratic, good-humoured, speaking to the people) are used to validate for the cinema an archaic and rhetorically ordered mode of speech. This is capped by the subsequent move, not into 'reality' but into a picture-book version of medieval France. The genuine open air is reached only with the climactic battle of Agincourt and its thrilling cavalry charge (shot on location in neutral Eire, where the skies were clear of air-traffic). By omitting such episodes as the traitors' plot and its discovery, Olivier suggests a nation unanimous in support of its leadership, and finesses Henry's aggressive territorial campaign into a foreshadowing of the Allied liberation of Europe. He even circumvents the problems of having France as the enemy by indicating that the country is merely ill-led, its half-crazed king bullied by a cadre of militarists resembling milder versions of the Nazis. Henry has the virtues that contemporary fiction, film, and theatre celebrated in the British officer: modesty, enough of the common touch to reassure his men without seeming to patronize, and the ability to keep his anxieties out of sight. Olivier's film does not emphasize the horrors of warfare, perhaps sufficiently vivid in everyday life at the time: he does include (somewhat awkwardly) a tableau-like illustration of Burgundy's speech about the ravaged land of France. The film is of course patriotic, both in its typical British wartime plot (a disparate band of amateur 'warriors for the working day' rather than militaristic professionals are united as an effective fighting force) and the very scale of its artistic achievement at such a time.

    In its creation of a picturesque, imaginative, and at the same time plausible style for screen Shakespeare, hospitable to the play's own artificiality, *Henry V* seemed to point a way forward. Olivier's own next step in Shakespearian film-making was *Hamlet* (1948), a neo-gothic psychological study which strips away the political material from the play and announces itself in the opening moments as 'the story of a man who could not make up his mind'. In fact, as has been pointed out, that is not the principal problem facing Olivier's Hamlet, who is energetic and athletic enough (especially in his death-dealing leap onto Claudius in the final scene) for his bouts of melancholy to seem passing moods. Violent with Jean Simmons's fragile Ophelia, and hyperactive both during the 'Mousetrap' and in his mother's bedroom, Hamlet seems to be working out his psychological conflicts in action. Roger Furse's designs for this almost entirely studio-bound film create a castle of dark recesses and archways and vertiginous staircases, where the great hall (its ceiling high above the camera's view), is the only lofty space, and Ophelia's chamber the only one to command a view of the outside world. The shadowy black-and-white photography and empty, mostly stone-walled chambers and passages (there is hardly any furniture) have been said to evoke both the psychological intensity of *film noir* and the mannerisms of German 1920s expressionist film.

As if in contrast to this sombre psychological thriller, Olivier's next Shakespeare film, released in 1955, was colourful and pageant-like, presenting the events of *Richard III* (with acknowledged additions from old stage versions by Colley Cibber and David Garrick) as one of the 'legends' attached to the crown of England. The film's first section, a *tour de force* of acting and camera-work, has Richard of Gloucester guiding the spectator through the personalities and intrigues of Edward IV's court, played out in a brilliantly designed single set of adjoining rooms, lobbies, and streets. In *Henry V* Olivier had tackled the problem of energetic 'public' theatrical speech by having the camera pull back and up from the king during his exhortation outside the walls of Harfleur. In the first section of *Richard III* Olivier makes the most of direct address to the camera, allowing Gloucester the benefit of looming close-ups to offer his own point of view, beckoning the camera into his confidence and offering sardonic comment: only as Richard achieves power, and his gradual decline begins, does the camera cease to accept his invitations. By the battle at the end of the film (shot with rather sparse numbers in Spain) Richard is left to his own devices, a con-vulsed, grotesque animal, looked down on now from a detached distance.

Olivier's two films based on history plays had shown how the fluid stagecraft and rhetorical address of the originals could find a cinematic equivalent, and all three of his films offered a coherent and pictorially sophisticated interpretation of the world of each play in relation to (or in *Hamlet* as a projection of) the char-acters' thoughts, words, and actions. Combined with the presence of British and therefore seemingly 'authentic' acting talent, this seemed to offer a way of com-mending Shakespeare to a sizeable cross-section of the larger cinema-going public as well as to art-film enthusiasts and the growing educational market. The *Julius Caesar* of Joseph L. Mankiewicz, produced in Hollywood and released in 1951, deploys a fine international cast (including Marlon Brando, John Gielgud, and James Mason) in a very full version of the play's script. The sets, the costuming, and the staging of such mass scenes as that of the funeral speeches, are handsome and convincing without dominating the film. Like many other productions of the play, this one is let down by the final scenes of battle and self-immolation, but it succeeds in accommodating Shakespeare to an established realist mode of film-making. At the same time, however, other ways of making Shakespeare films were being explored by an altogether more wayward actor and director than either Olivier or Mankiewicz.

The film career of Orson Welles, launched spectacularly in 1941 with *Citizen Kane*, was in many respects a continuation by other means of his innovative theatrical and radio work. The Shakespeare films Welles completed in the following decades – *Macbeth* (1948), *Othello* (1952), and *Chimes at Midnight* (1965) – share the adventurousness and technical innovation of his other movies, and of such enterprises as his 'Voodoo' stage production of *Macbeth* (1936) and modern-dress *Julius Caesar* (1937) or the startling radio adaptation of *The War of the Worlds* (1938). Himself an actor, a devotee both of Shakespeare and *legerdemain*, Welles did not hesitate to cut and rearrange the texts he used: although sometimes the chaotic circumstances of production and post-production can be held responsible, the startling incongruities and expressive dislocations in Welles's Shakespeare films are largely the result of artistic strategy.[4] In *Macbeth* and *Othello* Shakespeare is made a collaborator in Welles's explorations of extreme psychological states, and in *Chimes at Midnight* the figure of Falstaff (like Macbeth and Othello, played by Welles himself) represents an eloquent defence and embodiment of hedonistic, humane values in a colder world of political expediency. To banish this plump Jack is indeed to banish a good deal of the world.

Macbeth (1948), filmed within a tight budget (less than $1m) on a studio set of moderate size, probably benefits from the atmospheric murkiness of its black-and-white photography (if not from the muddied soundtrack) in presenting a world prey to night's black forces. The witches, first seen kneading a clay 'voodoo' doll of the hero, are pitted against the poor defence offered by a 'holy man' (in any case an equivocal figure) and aided by the uncompromisingly evil feminine power of Lady Macbeth. Welles himself delivers a powerful, haunted Macbeth, his considerable bulk swathed in furs, and crowned with a generically 'primitive' head-dress. The oppressive atmosphere (fog and filthy air), the vampish Lady Macbeth, and the hero's tortured state of mind are suggestive of *film noir*, and the additional element of the supernatural makes a metaphysical rather than psychological thriller. One senses that Welles's Macbeth would benefit little from the attentions of a Freudian analyst, while Olivier's Hamlet might well be cured of a good deal of mental strife (and Denmark spared a few murders) by a course of treatment. However, the notable difference between all Welles's Shakespeare films and those of Olivier and most other directors working in the plays' original language is the degree to which Welles is content to allow speech to be overheard, slurred, and generally subordinated to other priorities of staging and filming.[5] By comparison, the verbal clarity of Olivier's films seems theatrical. Welles's camera seems to have stumbled on a passionate and often incoherent world, and to be caught up in its emotions.

Othello (1952) was filmed on a much bigger scale than *Macbeth*, far better (if fitfully) funded and immeasurably better acted. The element of pyschological expressionism persists, indeed dominates: once the action has left Venice Welles effectively transfers the signifiers of the hero's mental state onto the bright skies and white walls of the North African locations that serve for Cyprus. The film begins with the funeral of Othello and Desdemona, during which Iago is dragged to an iron cage in which he is hoisted up to begin his punishment. This antici-pation of the conclusion frames the subsequent events, and the film announces its dominant visual language of tilted camera-angles, and the repeated use of bars and shadows across faces or intervening between the viewers (within the film and outside it) and events. Much of the editing is frenetic, and the camera-angles are frequently vertiginous. Dapper, earnest, and incisive (even though deprived of his soliloquies) Michéal MacLiammóir's Iago presses against the physically for-midable but inwardly vulnerable Othello, while Suzanne Cloutier's Desdemona is all but eclipsed by the deadly game being played among the men.

Chimes at Midnight (1965) – also known as *Falstaff* – derives from the direc-tor's lifelong obsession with the history plays, and specifically with the title role he assumes. The film draws mainly on the two parts of *King Henry IV*, with some material from *Richard II*, *Henry V*, and a few lines from *The Merry Wives of Windsor*. Shooting again in black-and-white, Welles creates in his Spanish loca-tions a medieval world that is far from a conventionally warm and homely 'merrie England'. The film opens with Falstaff and Shallow, with Silence in tow, trudg-ing across a snowy field that would not seem out of place in a production of *King Lear*. The forest in which the Gadshill robbery takes place and the windy plain on which the unremittingly brutal battle of Shrewsbury is fought could scarcely be less like their authentic locations. Henry Bolingbroke (John Gielgud) inhab-its a high-vaulted and bleak palace that is indeed a disused monastery church, and only the low-ceilinged, half-timbered interiors of the Boar's Head offer any real warmth and – implicitly – human comfort. Although it is relieved by the comedy of Norman Rodway's Hotspur, Jeanne Moreau's genially sensuous Mistress Quickly and the resilient good humour of Falstaff himself, the tone of the film is effectively set by Keith Baxter as Hal, whose level delivery and cold-eyed gaze make him a worthy heir to Gielgud's remote and querulous king. The battle is one of the grimmest montages of combat ever filmed, during which Falstaff is occasionally glimpsed running round in his complete armour like a pot-bellied stove on legs. At its conclusion, after Hal has endorsed his old friend's claim to have killed Hotspur, the king looks at his son contemptuously and turns away: the transaction seems to take place in another world from that natural to Falstaff.

At times it must have seemed as though the uncompromising world of film finance had as little time for Welles as Bolingbroke (and ultimately Hal) had for Falstaff. None of his projects was easily financed or accomplished, and among the unfinished work he left behind him were plans for a *King Lear* and an editing print of an almost-complete *Merchant of Venice*, set in the eighteenth century: surviving footage includes a striking scene of Shylock confronted in a low-ceilinged chamber by a suavely grinning Antonio (Charles Gray) and a crowd of masked and cloaked associates. Like the completed Shakespeare films, this again shows the hero/victim (played by Welles) in oppressive architectural spaces, captured by expressive camera angles and at the mercy of forces, societal and personal, beyond his control.

Welles's work extended the perceived cinematic possibilities for the expression of psychological complexity and the manipulation of the spectator's point of view in Shakespeare films. Other points of departure were indicated by two film-makers working in languages and film traditions outside Europe and America: Akira Kurosawa in Japan and Grigori Kozintsev in the Soviet Union.

Throne of Blood – the title by which *Kumonosu-djo* (*Cobweb Castle*, 1957) is best known in English – transposes *Macbeth* to Japan during a period of civil wars some four centuries ago.[6] The hero Washizu (Toshiro Mifune) exists in a world of contending warlords and is prompted to overreach himself by the prophecies of a ghostly seer he and Miki (the Banquo figure) encounter in the haunted 'Spider's Web Forest', and by the solicitings of his power-obsessed wife. As in Kurosawa's later *Lear*-derived epic *Ran* (*Chaos*, 1985) legitimacy of rule is a matter of military power supported by a code of honour: the ruler to be deposed is simply another warlord, rather than a divinely appointed monarch. Announced in its opening moments by an off-screen chorus as a fable of evil and retribution, and of the transience of worldly power, *Throne of Blood* combines epic breadth of canvas – notably in its scenes of combat – with scenes of intense emotional and political confrontation, particularly those between Washizu and his wife Asaji. At the film's climax, Washizu in his castle keep is surrounded on the outside of the wall by the avenging forces, and within the wall is confronted by a host of his own retainers. At first they simply remain silent as he urges them to repulse the enemy, then they begin to fire arrows at him. The hail of arrows from both directions grows in intensity until Washizu, covered like a porcupine in arrow shafts, is transfixed through the throat and topples from the tower. In the concluding sequence the chorus is heard again and the camera reads the inscription on the memorial pillar marking the site of the now-vanished 'Cobweb Castle'.

Kurosawa finds in Shakespeare's play a fable that fits into the historical period that preoccupies him: the social world around the warring factions is less acutely defined than in his *Seven Samurai* or *Yojimbo*, and the tragic fable has some of the archetypal quality of the *Noh* drama and is performed with some borrowing from its technique. At the same time, the finale evokes the epic cinema of DeMille and D. W. Griffith, and the westerns of John Ford. The later *Ran* repeats some of the same elements, this time concentrating on the Lear-like figure of Hidetora. Having delegated authority to two of his sons this cruel and ruthless warrior (he has made war on the families of two of his future daughters-in-law, and blinded the brother of one of them) suffers what seem like the inevitable and predictable consequences. Kaede, the second wife of one of Hidetora's disloyal sons, emerges as a Lady Macbeth-like character, and like Washizu's wife in *Throne of Blood* is more closely identified than any of the male characters with a Noh figure – her grim mask-like face is combined with elaborately folded robes and minimal, stylized movement. The ultimate message of *Ran* seems even bleaker than that of *Throne of Blood*: in the final moments the blind Tsurumaru taps his way towards the edge of an abyss, and the parchment he is carrying falls from his hands – taking with it any sense of redemptive knowledge or insight, beyond recognition that Buddha (and any other supernatural power) is indifferent.

The two Shakespeare films of Grigori Kozintsev, *Hamlet* (1964) and *King Lear* (1969), are in another 'epic' cinematic mode, associated with the great Russian film-maker Sergei Eisenstein. Kozintsev places an emphasis on the social framework of the stories, establishing an Elsinore that is at once rugged on the outside, in touch with the elements of air, earth, water, and fire (sky, stone, seascape, and torchlight are present in the very first moments, and recur throughout) and sophisticated and suavely administered within. Claudius runs his kingdom by proclamations to the peasants, communiqués to ambassadors, and persuasive exposition for the benefit of his privy council. Hamlet (Innokenti Smoktunovski) moves through the crowd of witnesses, the observed of all observers, an intellectual surviving in an oppressive regime by diving deeper into his own thoughts. At the same time, the film achieves a gothic romanticism even grander than Olivier's. The Ghost, his cloak billowing behind him, strides across a high terrace; the 'Mousetrap' is performed in torchlight with the sea behind the players' platform; Hamlet and Horatio seem to have stepped from a painting of the Romantic period. As well as its native filmic heritage, Kozintsev's *Hamlet* draws on a century and a half of Russian obsession with this hero's significance – 'Hamletism' as a means of resistance as well as escape.

In *King Lear* (1970) the monarch himself is strikingly untrue to type: a slight, unimposing figure with a face set in what already seems a childish wilfulness combined with the assumption of absolute authority. The common people are present throughout: in the opening moments, a long sustained shot following a crowd of peasants (perhaps pilgrims?) to their vantage point overlooking Lear's stockaded castle. In the storm sequence the 'hovel' is shared by Lear, Kent, Edgar, and the Fool with a host of the wretched of the earth among whom Edgar as Tom has taken his place. The final battle has clearly ravaged the kingdom rather than merely taken place in it. Taking advantage of the cinema's ability to stage scenes on a grand scale, Kozintsev has Edgar fight Edmund on a muddy battlefield surrounded by a crowd of armed men, and shows Cordelia's hanged body swinging out from the castle towers in full view of the assembled soldiery. The devastation is general and vividly presented, a tragic and final answer to the questioning gaze of the peasants with whom the film began.

The second wave of major English-language Shakespeare films was effectively inaugurated by the work of an Italian director, Franco Zeffirelli. By the mid-sixties he had made a reputation in opera and theatre with productions rich in atmospheric visual effects, recreating (and enhancing) the past in abundant picturesque detail. His 1960 production of *Romeo and Juliet* on the stage of the Old Vic was admired for its authentically 'Italianate' heat, urgency, and passion – qualities he was able to reproduce in his film (1968) with the far fuller resources of an Italian studio and locations. Choosing a Romeo (Leonard Whiting) and Juliet (Olivia Hussey) who would convince as teenagers, trimming the play effectively and choreographing its action to a sumptuous sentimental score (by Nino Rota), Zeffirelli created the first film version of the play to appeal to a large – and apparently young – international audience. Romeo and Juliet themselves speak the verse acceptably, but with no great show of skill, which may be appropriate for the tentativeness and simplicity of the relationship the film suggests. John McEnery's Mercutio (aggressive, cynical, and eloquent) and Susan Henshall's nurse (warm, sympathetic, but ultimately unavailing) more than make up for the blandness of the lovers and the over-frenetic mugging of some other characters. The fights, the dance, and the funeral are effectively staged, and the film is full of striking visual effects. Unlike the painstaking outdoor location work and historical authenticity of Renato Castellani's earlier English-language production (1954) – sunk by dull performances and a leaden screenplay – or the sterile opulence of the 1936 Cukor film, Zeffirelli's version creates a vigorous and stylish emotional and physical environment that is matched by the performances and camera work.

Although superficially similar, his earlier venture, *The Taming of the Shrew* (1966), is self-consciously artificial, beginning not with a view over the rooftops of a 'real' Italian city in the morning mist, but with a painting that comes to life – or rather to a stylized sort of life. The play is set in a kind of 'merrie Italy', where comic excess reigns, and in which Katherine and Petruccio, for all their extremity, stand out as the most authentic or 'normal' human beings. Because the roles were played by Richard Burton and Elizabeth Taylor, notorious for the vagaries of their off-screen relationship, the film had a curiosity value not unlike that of the 1929 Fairbanks–Pickford version. The skilfully trimmed and rearranged script delivers more of the play than the earlier production, but follows its lead in showing the wedding scene that Gremio describes. Katherine's growing but hidden admiration for Petruccio is intimated by glimpses of her watching him, supported by a 'love' theme in the soundtrack, and the 'submission' speech is delivered as a straightforward gesture of love, without any of the irony expressed in Mary Pickford's wink. Zeffirelli's *Shrew* is effective as a colourful, sentimental love story accompanied by boisterous physical humour, but it hardly reflects any of the misgivings that the play has aroused ever since its reappearance in the theatre (replacing shortened acting texts) at the end of the nineteenth century. Nor does it address any of the sterner questionings of the feminist movement that was already gaining momentum when it was made.

Roman Polanski's *Macbeth* (1970) did address contemporary critical issues. The Polish director's combination of macabre evocations of the supernatural with surface realism, and his use of violence were thought shocking at the time of its release and still retain their power. The film also achieved notoriety for the depiction (in fact relatively mild) of sexuality and the unavoidable connection with not only the director's earlier story of demonic possession, *Rosemary's Baby* (1968), but the savage murder of his wife, Sharon Tate, and a group of friends by the 'family' of Charles Manson's followers. Beyond this, the film was also informed by notions of authority and kingship derived from *Shakespeare our Contemporary* (1964), the widely influential collection of essays by Polanski's countryman, Jan Kott. Polanski makes Macbeth and his wife young, sexually attractive (and implicitly, active), and upwardly mobile figures of the 1960s. He intimates a general cynicism about political power through the sinister figure of Ross, here both king-maker and turncoat, and with the indication in the final scene that Donalbain, brother of the newly crowned Malcolm, is himself going to consult the witches. The gruesome sights begin in the opening moments with the three witches burying a severed arm on a seashore and culminate in Macbeth's on-screen decapitation. In this world of explicit and vivid visions, it might be expected that the air-drawn dagger would be shown to the audience, but more surprising – and effective – is the moment when we share Lady Macbeth's view of the stigmata-like blood on her hands. Polanski's well-calculated and vivid sensationalism brings the play firmly into line with the popular cinema as a violent thriller with sexual and supernatural overtones.

To a considerable extent their directors' readiness to emulate Polanski in embracing popular genres explains the commercial success of some Shakespeare films made in the subsequent decades of the twentieth century. The refusal to follow that path also explains the relative commercial failure of others. Among the latter, *Othello* with Laurence Olivier in the title role (1966) suffers the consequences of its stubborn recreation of the National Theatre stage production on which it is based and the lack of adjustment in scale of the leading actor's performance to the pitiless intimacy of the cinema medium. Peter Hall's *A Midsummer Night's Dream* (1968) makes more of an attempt to translate the qualities of a successful stage production (by the Royal Shakespeare Company), in this case by adopting the jump-cuts, dislocations and eccentric colouring and lighting of 'alternative' film, but falls down on the poor technical quality of the end-product and the stilted, over-theatrical performances of its distinguished RSC cast. Peter Brook's austere *King Lear* (1971), with Paul Scofield in the title role, follows a successful stage production by the same company (1962) and owes more to the new cinema of France, Italy, and Scandinavia than to Hollywood. Austere black-and-white cinematography, a steadfast refusal to make concessions to 'classic' conventions of story-telling, and arresting visual effects for the storm are allied to an unremittingly bleak landscape. Brook will not allow any sense of redemption of perception in the process of Lear's degradation and destruction.

More winning in its refusal to play the game of commercial cinema is Derek Jarman's *The Tempest* (1979), which achieves a real sense of mystery and disturbing eroticism in the dilapidated mansion that serves as Prospero's island. Heathcote Williams is a romantically dishevelled Prospero, Toyah Wilcox a punkish, provocative but innocent Miranda, and Jack Birkett a leering, grotesque but un-monstrous Caliban. Ariel (Karl Johnson) wears white overalls, which make him look like a supernatural garage hand. A sense of extravagant pleasure is secured in the masque by replacing Shakespeare's script with Elizabeth Welch's rendition of 'Stormy weather' amid a troupe of cheerful *mâtelots*. As an exploration of the 'otherness' in magic and sexuality, the film has a direct relation to Jarman's more professedly 'queer' work: as an accessible and often lyrical adaptation that could only be made in its chosen medium, it shows a commendable fearlessness in using Shakespeare for cinema. (A less easy-going, determinedly intellectualized, presentation of the play followed in 1991: Peter Greenaway's *Prospero's Books*.)

Screen Shakespeare in the mid-1980s was dominated by another medium, through the widespread marketing of the BBC/Time–Life television series, at first dutifully wedded by contract to 'traditional' costuming and uninventive naturalism. Many of the acting performances were impressive, and some of the later productions were more imaginatively directed and designed: the work of Jonathan Miller and Jane Howell was outstanding.[7] Meanwhile in the cinema there was little apparent sign of interest in Shakespeare.

In 1989 the success of a new film of *Henry V*, directed by the young actor Kenneth Branagh, seemed to suggest that Shakespeare might after all have box-office potential. Branagh employed relatively modest resources, and many of the film's scenes are intimate, in medium shots or close-ups (wider shots which show more are more expensive), but it remains insistently cinematic rather than televisual. The film begins in darkness, with the chorus (Derek Jacobi) lighting a match to illuminate his face before he throws a master-switch to illuminate the clutter of a sound-stage. It is to this darkness that the film finally returns, with the rueful reference to the mishandling of Henry's legacy by his successor, and a good deal of the interim is filled with the imagery of conspiratorial politics and muddy and bloody warfare. The story of a king obliged against his better nature to undertake an unpleasant task, and the heroism of those who support him, is punctuated with reminders of the life he has put aside. In this his tavern companions are handled less jovially and innocently than in Olivier's film, and Henry has to watch while Bardolph is hanged, and Pistol (Robert Stephens) is seen scavenging on the battlefield. There is much painful marching in the rainy fields. Where Olivier's grandest, most expansive scene was the charge of the doomed French cavalry, Branagh follows a graphic battle (owing much to Welles's battle of Shrewsbury and such post-Vietnam films as *Platoon*) with a long travelling shot in which Henry carries the dead boy across a field littered with corpses. In wooing Katherine (Emma Thompson) Branagh encounters a firmer opposition than that mounted against Olivier's Henry by Renée Asherson, and the final 'treaty' scene is less picturesque and more sombre than its 1944 equivalent. In Branagh's hands *Henry V* is the story of a young man's maturation, with the heartening support of his immediate peer group (in both senses, as they are all peers of the realm) and one avuncular figure, Exeter (Brian Blessed). Although its representation of combat is unflinching, it hardly throws a searching light on the motivations of the military campaign.

Branagh's next Shakespeare film, *Much Ado About Nothing* (1993), depicts a sunny Tuscan version of Messina – rural rather than urban – in which a priggish but not unlikable Claudio (Robert Sean Leonard) is shown what seems to be 'his' Hero in an explicitly sexual encounter with Borachio. Because the audience is also shown the sight (as in the cinema they probably must be) the young man's error seems all the more pardonable. A pleasing romantic story, told with no little wit and a strong sense of festivity, and with central performances by Branagh himself and Emma Thompson, *Much Ado* proved popular at the box-office (and on video) but failed to charm critics who looked for a darker, less comfortable reading of the play. Like *Henry V*, it drew on a strong cast of British Shakespearian actors, many of them associated with the Renaissance Theatre Company founded in the mid-1980s by Branagh and his fellow-producer David Parfitt. This time North American favour (and finance) was courted with some familiar Hollywood talent: as well as Robert Sean Leonard, there were Denzel Washington (Don Pedro), Keanu Reeves (Don John) and Michael Keaton as an alarmingly deranged Dogberry.

Even more than *Henry V*, *Much Ado About Nothing* reflects Branagh's love of cinema. This is nowhere more apparent than in the lyrical and energetic opening, when an idyllic picnic (Beatrice reads 'Sigh no more' as she sits picturesquely in a tree, book in one hand and a bunch of grapes in the other) is succeeded by the mock-heroic arrival of Don Pedro's party on horseback *à la Magnificent Seven*. This is intercut with frantic domestic preparations, including shower-baths for the women and a splashy communal soaking for the men, and climaxes in a final swing into the formal choreography of the two groups' first encounter in the villa courtyard.

The full-length, four-hour, *Hamlet* (1996) filmed by Branagh in the 'epic' 70 mm format, shares *Much Ado*'s adoption of international casting and offers further evidence of the director's penchant for cinematic brio, although critical opinion has been divided as to the wisdom of using for a film the 'full' conflated text of *Hamlet*, Q2 and Folio – or indeed the full text of any play. The greater scope and range of the story, as represented in Branagh's version, has been compared with that of a nineteenth-century novel, and many of the performances have been admired (notably Derek Jacobi and Julie Christie as Claudius and Gertrude, and Richard Briers as Polonius.) Branagh's own performance, his fourth in the role, is a *tour de force*, and although some aspects of his adaptation and direction (particularly the flashback showing Hamlet and Ophelia in bed together) have been severely criticized, his insistence that the play should be given the greatest possible scale and impact has won respect.

Although the world of film finance is in most respects as difficult to fathom and as unpredictable as any branch of commerce, it appears to be true that at least moderate success on the part of one film – say, *Henry V* – can engender temporary enthusiasm on the part of 'the money' for other mixtures with some or all of the same ingredients. Multinational finance brings with it responsibility to multinational market pressures, in which the demands of the cinema-going and video-viewing public of the USA carry the greatest weight. Smaller-scale projects, with finance gathered mainly from local or (in Europe) even governmental sources, are freer to innovate and more likely to retain a strong sense of their national origin than those dependent to a greater extent on Hollywood money. At the same time, the appeal of the unusual, or even 'foreign' film can sometimes effect a 'crossover' from one market (that is, 'art-house') to another. At the time of writing (January 2000) at least the first two of Branagh's first three Shakespeare films seem to have made this transition, as have the inventive, spectacular, and stylish *Richard III* of Richard Loncraine and Ian McKellen (1995) and the wholly 'youth'-oriented *Romeo + Juliet* of Baz Luhrmann (1996). Both of these effect a more radical shift of period and milieu than Branagh's *Much Ado About Nothing* and *Hamlet* (1930s fascism for *Richard III* and Latin-American gang warfare for *Romeo + Juliet*). In the first, the cast is dominated by prominent British actors with substantial experience of Shakespeare; in the second the emphasis is on the casting of a cult film star (Leonardo di Caprio) as Romeo and the pervasive visual techniques of music videos – the play reworked for MTV. Like Branagh's films (and indeed Olivier's) *Richard III* has a strong stage production in its background, so that at least one performance (specifically, that of McKellen as Richard) and the *mise-en-scène* are a cinematic adaptation of ideas previously worked through in the theatre. *Richard III* is not, however, a documentary about 1930s politics, or indeed fascism in general. Richard is not clearly either a racist or an imperialist, and has no discernible policies beyond the achievement of power. Like Luhrmann's film, which hardly amounts to a sociological study of youth and its problems, *Richard III* constructs a framework for the play's events and characters that will be believable and in some important respects familiar to its target audience.

In Shakespeare films, as in productions in any medium, a distinction should be made between the *resonance* of a given production – in its own time and after – and the conscious pursuit of *relevance*. Although Loncraine and McKellen's *Richard III* alludes explicitly to 1930s politics there is little real engagement with the politics of the film's own century, either in the 1930s or the 1990s. By contrast, Mankiewicz's 1951 conventionally toga-swathed *Julius Caesar*, even though it lacks the episode in which the mob kills Cinna the poet, had an unmistakable relevance to the political situation in post-war (and McCarthyite) America, with a fear both of demagogues and of totalitarianism. We should remember that – like play scripts but unlike the stage productions of them – films exist both in their own time and for years afterwards, and that like dramatic scripts, their effect on viewers and readers changes with their age. There is an unavoidable complexity of allusion in the film-making process, with its references to contemporary views, events, and fashions, both within the realm of film-making and more generally. Some films have also engaged in a more-or-less direct and playful way with earlier work. Michael Hoffmann's handsome *A Midsummer Night's Dream* (USA, 1999) draws on a host of references in symbolist art of the late nineteenth century but creates a haunted wood that also seems to glance at the sound-stage claustrophobia of Reinhardt and Dieterle. At the same time, Hoffman's Tuscan location for 'Athens' and his extensive cultivation of 'local colour' suggest at least a reliance on the proved formulas of Zeffirelli and Branagh, if not a conscious *hommage*. Branagh's own *Love's Labour's Lost* (Great Britain, 2000) transposes its original to the mannered sound-stage world of the 1930s Hollywood musical, and its script accords with the director's penchant for stories of disparate characters coming together to form a positive, creative community.[8]

This post-modern sense of films speaking to and about one another, as well as to (and through) Shakespeare's text, has been intensified by the advent of video-tape and (recently) DVD, which have made the greater part of the surviving library of film material accessible in the home. At the same time this revolution has divorced the movies from the conditions of their original commercial, theatrical exhibition. Shakespeare films, like other motion pictures, have moved in the course of their first century from more or less inadequate imitation of what could be offered on stage, initially to an exploitation of what only the cinema screen could offer, and then to a situation where cinema showings may seem to suffer from their lack of the participation and manipulation available to consumers of videos, CD-ROMs and DVDs. But the images and sounds – the visions – that Shakespeare has provoked in film-makers will remain potent in the context of any medium. Olivier's French cavalry charge, Welles's Falstaff in the snow and Kurosawa's arrow-pierced Washizu could not have existed without Shakespeare, could only have been achieved for the cinema, and will continue to imprint themselves on the way viewers perceive not only other Shakespeare films, but also their play-script originals.

Postscript

Since this *Companion* went to press, two notable Shakespeare films have been released. Julie Taymor's sumptuous *Titus* situates *Titus Andronicus* in a post-modern mixture of ancient Rome and contemporary Italy, with Anthony Hopkins in the title role. Michael Almereyda's low-budget *Hamlet* takes place in twenty-first century Manhattan, where Claudius (Bill Murray) is C.E.O. of the Denmark Corporation and Hamlet (Ethan Hawke) his bitterly disenchanted nephew. In their different ways, both directors refuse to abide by the conventions of 'classic' film realism.

Notes

1. In addition to the feature-length films considered in this chapter, there have been many Shakespeare-influenced films, with greater or lesser pretensions to conveying salient features of the plays.
2. On Shakespeare in the silent cinema see the book by Robert Hamilton Ball and the filmography by Rothwell and Melzer listed below in the Reading list.
3. For an account in English of Reinhardt's theatrical productions of the play, see J. L. Styan, *Max Reinhardt* (Cambridge University Press, 1982), ch. 5.
4. On the circumstances of Welles's films, see Michael Anderegg, *Orson Welles, Shakespeare and Popular Culture* (New York, Columbia University Press, 1999).
5. See Dudley Andrew, *Film in the Aura of Art* (Princeton University Press, 1984), p. 167: '. . . we might think of [Olivier's] *Henry V* or *Hamlet* as films based on Shakespeare's *writing* whereas *Chimes at Midnight* is tied to the actor's *voice*'.
6. The most authoritative and informative source on Kurosawa's work is Donald Richie, *The Films of Akira Kurosawa*, 3rd edn, expanded and updated (Berkeley, Los Angeles, and London: University of California Press, 1996).
7. On the BBC/Time–Life Shakespeare series see Susan Willis, *The BBC Shakespeare Plays: Making the Televised Canon* (Chapel Hill, N.C., and London: University of North Carolina Press, 1991).
8. I am thinking here not only of Branagh's *Henry V* and *Much Ado* but also of the gentle, Ealing-style comedy *In the Bleak Midwinter*, in which a ramshackle acting company manages to stage *Hamlet* in the forlorn village of Hope at the behest of an ardent idealist.

Reading list

Reference
Luke McKernan and Olwen Terris, eds., *Walking Shadows: Shakespeare in the National Film and Television Archive* (London: British Film Institute, 1994. (With informative introduction, historical essays and bibliography: lists only material held in the NFTA)).
Kenneth S. Rothwell and Annabelle Henkin Melzer, eds., *Shakespeare on Screen: An International Filmography and Videography* (New York and London: Neal Schumann, 1990). (Comprehensive and detailed, with a valuable introduction and notes on each film).

General
(A full and detailed bibliography will be found in Kenneth S. Rothwell, *A History of Shakespeare on Screen*, listed below).

Ball, Robert Hamilton, *Shakespeare on Silent Film: A Strange Eventful History* (London: George Allen and Unwin, 1968).

Boose, Lynda E., and Richard Burt, eds., *Shakespeare the Movie: Popularising the Plays on Film, TV and Video* (London: Routledge, 1997).

Buchman, Lorne M., *Still in Movement: Shakespeare on Screen* (New York: Oxford University Press, 1991).

Burnett, Mark Thornton and Ramona Wray, eds., *Shakespeare, Film, Fin de Siècle* (Basingstoke and London: Macmillan, 2000).

Burt, Richard, *Unspeakable Shaxxxspeares: Queer Theory and American Kiddie Culture* (New York: St Martin's Press, 1998).

Collick, John, *Shakespeare, Cinema and Society* (Manchester University Press, 1989).

Crowl, Samuel, *Shakespeare Observed: Studies in Performance on Stage and Screen* (Athens: University of Ohio Press, 1992).

Coursen, H. A., *Shakespearian Performance as Interpretation* (Wilmington: University of Delaware Press, 1990).

Shakespearian Production: Whose History? (Athens: University of Ohio Press 1996).

Davies, Anthony, *Filming Shakespeare's Plays* (Cambridge University Press, 1988).

Davies, Anthony, and Stanley Wells, eds., *Shakespeare and the Moving Image: The Plays on Film and Television* (Cambridge University Press 1994).

Donaldson, Peter S., *Shakespearian Films/Shakespearian Directors* (Boston, Mass.: Unwin Hyman, 1990).

Eckert, Charles W., ed., *Focus on Shakespearian Films* (Englewood Cliffs, N. J.: Prentice Hall, 1972).

Jackson, Russell, ed., *The Cambridge Companion to Shakespeare on Film* (Cambridge University Press, 2000).

Jorgens, Jack J., *Shakespeare on Film* (Bloomington: Indiana University Press, 1977).

Klein, Holger and Dimiter Dapkinoff, eds., *'Hamlet' on Screen, Shakespeare Yearbook*, 8 (Lampeter: Edwin Mellen, 1997)

Kliman, Bernice W., *'Hamlet': Film, Television and Audio Performance* (London and Toronto: Associated University Presses, 1988).

Manvell, Roger, *Shakespeare and the Film* (London, 1971; rpt, Cranbury, N.J.: A. and S. Barnes, 1979).

Pilkington, Ace G., *Screening Shakespeare: From Richard II to Henry V* (Newark: University of Delaware Press, 1991).

Rosenthal, Daniel, *Shakespeare on Screen* (London: Hamlyn, 2000).

Rothwell, Kenneth S., *A History of Shakespeare on Screen: A Century of Film and Television* (Cambridge University Press, 1999).

Shaughnessy, Robert, ed., *Shakespeare on Film*, New Casebooks (Basingstoke and London: Macmillan, 1998).

15

MICHAEL DOBSON

Shakespeare on the page and the stage

WHICH conventional phrase best describes the author of *Hamlet*, 'the world's greatest poet' or 'the world's greatest playwright'? The two are often used interchangeably, but their different emphases, defining Shakespeare as first and foremost a literary artist or as primarily a man of the live theatre, adumbrate a genuine and enduring demarcation dispute between the library and the playhouse which has conditioned the reproduction of Shakespeare's works from his own lifetime to the present. At its heart is the question of how we are to understand the relation between the publication and the performance of Shakespeare's works. Is a play's printed text to be seen as prior and superior to its theatrical embodiments, which if so are only belated, partial, and imperfect glosses upon an essentially literary artifact? Or is that text itself to be seen as only a belated, partial, and imperfect souvenir of a theatrical event, the incomplete written trace of a dramatic work which can only fully be realized in performance? The ways in which this issue has been approached over the centuries since the writer's death, and the changing boundaries between its possible resolutions, have done much to shape both conceptions of Shakespeare and the nature of Shakespeare studies, and it is a problem which remains close to the centre of current debates in editing, in performance studies, and in biography. Some understanding of its origins and progress is therefore essential to any account of their development.

The disagreement as to whether Shakespeare wrote incidentally actable poems or incidentally poetic scripts has endured firstly because we know so little about the working practices of Shakespeare and his company (we do not really know, for example, if they had what we would recognize as rehearsals, let alone how far these might have modified scripts between first draft and first performance), and, secondly, because the early editions of his works are often ambiguous, if not downright contradictory, about how even Elizabethan publishers (let alone writers, readers, and theatregoers) understood the relations between texts and performances. This is famously exemplified by the case of *Troilus and Cressida*. In February 1603 the Stationers' Register records the intention of one Mr Roberts to publish 'the book of Troilus and Cressida as it is acted by my lord Chamberlain's Men': significantly, this entry makes no mention of Shakespeare, apparently envisaging a printed text whose claim to authority would be not its fidelity to a single author's intentions but the accuracy with which it remembered a company's stage performances. When the play finally did appear in quarto in 1609, its title page, although adding the name of the playwright, at first made much the same claim, offering 'The History of Troilus and Cressida. As it was acted by the King's Majesty's servants at the Globe. Written by William Shakespeare'. Although it assumes that there are at least some potential book-buyers who will be attracted by Shakespeare's literary reputation, this title page's first appeal is to discriminating theatregoers, people who, even if they missed the production this text here purports to record, will recognize that a play which has been acted by the King's Men at the Globe is likely to be preferable to one which has not. While the edition was being printed, however, this title page was withdrawn and replaced by another, which rechristens the play 'The Famous History of Troilus and Cressid. Excellently expressing the beginning of their loves, with the conceited wooing of Pandarus Prince of Lycia. Written by William Shakespeare'. Gone is the boast about the play's stage history, replaced by a titbit of its literary content, so that Shakespeare now features not as a company's scriptwriter but as an author in his own right, capable of excellently expressing the love and wooing of these famous characters from legend and poetry. The change is heavily underlined by an added epistle to the reader, which proclaims that so far from being an established hit from the boards of the Globe this is in fact 'a new play, never staled with the stage, never clapper-clawed with the palms of the vulgar'.[1] The advertising pitch has been inverted: rather than being sold as a script seasoned and approved in performance, *Troilus and Cressida* is now being offered as a work of literary art which has mercifully escaped being corrupted by the exigencies of the public stage. Even during Shakespeare's lifetime, there coexisted diametrically opposed accounts of what a play's text actually represented – even of what the same edition of the same play's text represented.

This uncertainty as to the status of Shakespeare's texts in relation to their performance, moreover, is not clarified even in the case of the posthumous 1623 Folio, which – as a monument to Shakespeare the poet assembled by two colleagues of Shakespeare the actor, John Heminges and Henry Condell – sends distinctly mixed signals as to the relative priority of page and stage (see also chapter 2, The Reproduction of Shakespeare's Texts, by Barbara A. Mowat). In some respects it is very much a theatre-oriented edition, belatedly bringing print up to date with what has already happened in the playhouse. The texts it supplies, as one would expect given its compilers' position as fellow members of Shakespeare's acting troupe, usually have a theatrical provenance: as is the case with *Troilus and Cressida* (where the 1609 quarto text, apparently derived from an authorial draft, appears to have been updated by reference to a manuscript which has been used in the theatre),[2] the Folio seems generally to reproduce Shakespeare's plays as they were last performed by the King's Men. This feature of the book is glanced at in its prefatory materials: 'so much were your Lordships' likings of the several parts, when they were acted, as before they were published, the volume asked to be yours',[3] remarks Heminges and Condell's dedicatory letter to the Earls of Pembroke and Montgomery, promising that they are simply providing the book of the shows. Their subsequent address 'To the great Variety of Readers' assures potential buyers that the book has in effect received rave reviews in advance in the form of the applause the plays have enjoyed in the play-houses, treating the critical assessment of printed drama as simply theatre criticism after the fact: '. . . though you be a magistrate of wit, and sit on the stage at Blackfriars, or the Cockpit, to arraign plays daily, know, these plays have had their trial already, and stood out all appeals . . .'[4] It is very much in keeping with this remark that the last piece of information the Folio supplies before the reader settles down to enjoying (or revisiting?) the first play is a list of 'The Names of the Principal Actors in all these Plays'. Even more appropriate is the accidental reappearance of two names from this list in a few speech-prefixes in *Much Ado About Nothing*, when the actors William Kemp and Richard Cowley temporarily take precedence over the fictitious Dogberry and Verges: here the volume registers the actors as co-creators of the roles it officially credits to Shakespeare.

This example, however (which the Folio simply takes over from the 1600 quarto), is a brief and isolated one, and otherwise the volume nowhere records which actors from the list took which parts, laying its chief stress on the individual authorship of Shakespeare. Treated solely as a record of specific performances, the Folio is remarkably frustrating, sometimes appearing more interested in suppressing the theatrical nature of the scripts it reproduces than in celebrating it. It provides no clues as to where or when the different plays were first performed, nor in which order (arranging them within the volume in a strictly literary manner, by genre), and such stage directions as their texts supply vary enormously in the level of information they provide as to how they have hitherto been realized, tending towards the barest minimum. Despite the instances quoted above, the volume's prefatory pages overall are less interested in presenting the plays as collaborative products of a theatre company than in proclaiming the Folio itself as the life achievement of an author: the first words it contains, for example, are Ben Jonson's lines on Droeshout's portrait engraving, directing our attention from Shakespeare's picture not to his enacted plays but to his 'book'. Taken together with the quartos, the Folio, thus divided between privileging Shakespeare the author or Shakespeare the member of the King's Men, can provide the materials for radically different kinds of subsequent editions (and stage productions) of Shakespeare, and over the course of the century which followed its publication two very different traditions would emerge – each of them, however, oddly and persistently haunted by the other. One of them insists on the direct connection between Shakespeare and performance, albeit strictly contemporary performance rather than the plays' original productions: the other seeks ultimately to remove Shakespeare from the theatre altogether. Our own time's chief efforts in the staging and the publication of Shakespeare alike can perhaps best be understood as attempts to reconcile the two.

Stage over page

Apart from reprints of the Folio and the quartos themselves, the first new editions of Shakespeare plays to be printed after 1623 would belong emphatically to the theatre: so emphatically, indeed, that many of them do not even confess to belonging to Shakespeare. The first, published in 1661, makes its view of publication as only secondary to present-day performance resoundingly clear both on its title page and in an introductory epistle from 'The Stationers to the Reader'. This is *The Merry Conceited Humours of Bottom the Weaver* ('As it hath been often publically acted by some of His Majesty's comedians, and lately privately presented by several apprentices for their harmless recreation, with great applause'), an abbreviation of *A Midsummer Night's Dream* originally prepared for clandestine performance during the Puritan interregnum. It is now being printed, according to Francis Kirkman and Henry Marsh, solely in order to remember successful past performances and enable future ones:

> Gentlemen, the entreaty of several persons, our friends, hath induced us to the publishing of this piece, which (when the life of action was added to it) pleased generally well. It hath been the desire of several (who know we have many pieces of this nature in our hands) that we should publish them, and we considering the general mirth that is likely very suddenly to happen about the King's coronation, and supposing that things of this nature will be acceptable, have therefore begun with this, which we know may easily be acted . . .[5]

A play, by this account, scarcely exists when unperformed, and publishing anything as incomplete as a mere script seems almost to call for an apology, or at very least the assurance that the play it remembers pleased generally well 'when the life of action was added to it', and could easily do so again. Nothing could have less to do with literary reputation, or literary property: Kirkman and Marsh mention neither Shakespeare, nor the person who has adapted his old play (the actor Robert Cox, who had died in 1655), neither of whom, after all, have played any active part in either the recent stage performances which have prompted this publication or in the printing of the edition itself. Appropriately, the only person this edition does mention, apart from the 'Stationers', is the king, Charles II, whose return to the throne in 1660 and coronation the following year have restored professional theatre and provided the occasion for amateur performances. An important part of the publishing history of Shakespeare's plays, no less than their stage history, thus begins all over again at the Restoration, as a pattern establishes itself by which editions of single plays, their *dramatis personae* supplied with actors' names so as to double as souvenir cast lists, are produced primarily to record (and supplement) performances. For the remainder of the seventeenth century and most of the eighteenth, individual Shakespeare plays would often reappear strictly under the aegis of the two royal theatre companies who now enjoyed a monopoly on performing them, each title page purporting to offer the play 'As it was Acted'.

Since these companies staged many of Shakespeare's plays only in versions heavily revised to suit Restoration playhouses and Restoration tastes, this produced major discrepancies between the expensive Shakespeare of the Folio (a comparatively slow seller, reprinted in 1663–4 for the first time since 1632, then reappearing only in 1685)[6] and the acted Shakespeare of new quartos like *The Merry Conceited Humours*. During the early Restoration, such differences were apparently barely noticed, but the revised theatrical Shakespeare would gradually develop an explicit consciousness of the older authorial Shakespeare as the decades passed. In the 1660s and 1670s, stage adaptations were as often as not printed without any reference to their original author at all: among Sir William Davenant's pioneering efforts in this mode, for example, his versions of *The Two Noble Kinsmen* and *Macbeth* are attributed only to the playhouse which was performing them, while *The Law Against Lovers* (a conflation of *Measure for Measure* and *Much Ado About Nothing*) is printed in Davenant's own posthumous folio without any acknowledgement of Shakespeare. Of his other two adaptations, *The Tempest, or the Enchanted Island* mentions no authors on the title page of its 1670 quarto (professing only to be 'A Comedy. As it is now acted at his Highness the Duke of York's theatre'), and is only admitted to be an alteration of a Shakespeare play in the preface and prologue supplied by Davenant's co-adaptor John Dryden.[7] In the 1660s and 1670s, clearly, Shakespeare's plays belonged more securely to the playhouses, and to anyone prepared to carry out the work of making them actable there, than they did to the author of the Folio.

The last of Sir William's stage versions to reach print, however, does give Shakespeare precedence over Davenant on its title page, albeit giving the theatre precedence over both. One of Shakespeare's plays, at least, was already too famous as such for its text to be wholly subordinated to the needs and fancies of its current stage performers, even in an edition in part selling itself as a memento of their work. In 1676 appeared *The Tragedy of Hamlet Prince of Denmark. As it is now Acted at his Highness the Duke of York's Theatre. By William Shakespeare*, a quarto which supplies a conservatively adapted acting text probably evolved during the 1660s by Davenant in conjunction with the actor who would still be playing the title role nearly fifty years later, Thomas Betterton. More interesting than the minor clarifications and modernizations of Shakespeare's diction, however, is the typographical feature advertised in a preliminary address 'To the Reader': 'This Play being too long to be conveniently Acted, such places as might be least prejudicial to the Plot or Sense, are left out upon the Stage: but that we may no way wrong the incomparable Author, are here inserted according to the Original Copy with this Mark.'[8] This is the first instance of an acting edition paying such elaborate homage to the Shakespearian source-text it might otherwise appear to be trying to supplant, and the result is a printed text which seems even more conflicted than did the Folio itself about the relative claims of the literary and the theatrical. Any reader of this 1676 *Hamlet* is made painfully aware of the incompleteness either of reading *Hamlet* or of seeing it performed. The marginal inverted commas continually remind contemporary playgoers that they have not seen all of *Hamlet* acted, highlighting those ghostly passages of Shakespearian poetry cut off from the theatre's current prompt-book but now returning to haunt it in print; at the same time they insistently remind readers of Shakespeare's *Hamlet* that it is full of material which can easily be left out without prejudicing either plot or sense.

As the device of marginal inverted commas develops it is revealed even more fully as a symptom of the stage's incipient bad conscience about Shakespeare as literature. When they next appear in an acting edition, in the printed text of Colley Cibber's adaptation of *Richard III* (1700), they are there not to draw attention to Shakespearian passages which have been left out in performance, but to confess which sections of the script are composed of Shakespearian poetry as rewritten by Cibber:

> Though there was no great danger of the readers mistaking any of my lines for Shakespeare's; yet, to satisfy the curious, and unwilling to assume more praise than is really my due, I have caused those that are entirely Shakespeare's to be printed in this *Italic Character*; and those lines with this mark (') before 'em, are generally his thoughts, in the best dress I could afford 'em: What is not so marked, or in a different character is entirely my own. I have done my best to imitate his style, and manner of thinking . . .

While Cibber's business as an adaptor for the stage is to produce a consistently 'Shakespearian' play, he feels obliged as the author of a printed text to make the distinction scrupulously visible. Reading here seems to trump playgoing. The Restoration theatre's desire to keep sole possession of Shakespeare's plays, updating their scripts to suit its changing needs and printing the resulting adaptations simply as commemorative side-effects of successful productions, could apparently no longer be realized. The scripts were now too old for contemporary playwrights to add new material without adopting a pseudo-archaic style as they did so, and such dramatists were increasingly aware that in doing so they would face the scrutiny not only of theatregoers but of judicious readers more and more inclined to treat Shakespeare's unaltered texts as classics, albeit not invariably actable ones.

Page over stage

This increasing consciousness of the distinction between Shakespeare as acted and Shakespeare as read would become still more inescapable when affordable copies of a strictly Folio-based Shakespeare became widely available, with the publication of Nicholas Rowe's six-volume quarto edition of the plays in 1709.

It is an irony of Shakespeare's reception that this publication, which would play a decisive role in the claiming of Shakespeare for a strictly study-oriented notion of literary value, should have been prepared by a working playwright, and one whose work on Shakespeare's text consisted very largely in making it more, rather than less, theatrically practicable – apart from making verbal emendations to the 1685 Fourth Folio (without consulting the quartos), Rowe mainly confined himself to supplying stage directions (especially entrances and exits) implied by Shakespeare's dialogue but not hitherto marked. His edition, furthermore, inadvertently preserves a good deal of visual information about the rewritten Shakespeare of the Restoration stage in the form of three frontispieces to individual plays (*A Midsummer Night's Dream*, *The Taming of the Shrew*, and *The Tempest*), where the nameless artist has been influenced less by Rowe's texts than by the adaptations he has seen in the contemporary theatre. Nonetheless, one of the immediate consequences of the wide dissemination of this edition was a dawning sense that the theatres were not doing full justice to the venerable English poet celebrated in Rowe's biographical preface. In 1710 Charles Gildon appended an unauthorized seventh volume, adding the poems and his own commentaries on the plays, and it appropriately contains the first attack in print on Davenant and Dryden's stage version of *The Tempest*, now minutely compared to the original: according to Gildon, the added material is 'scarce guilty of a thought which we could justly attribute to Shakespeare . . . the alteration has been no benefit to the original'.[9]

This realization that the playhouses were in many instances performing only corrupted texts of Shakespeare is drastically and influentially back-dated by Rowe's editorial successor, Alexander Pope, whose own edition of the plays (1723–5) sets out to argue that the theatre always has been the source of whatever is corrupt about Shakespeare's texts, responsible not only for spurious interpolations but for the errors of taste committed by Shakespeare himself. Pope's edition is determined above all to rescue Shakespeare the gentleman-poet from Shakespeare the crowd-pleasing scriptwriter: all that he finds vulgar in the plays he attributes to Shakespeare's willingness to make a living by pleasing 'the meaner sort of people' who then frequented the theatres, and his concomitant association with those mercenary dregs of society, professional actors. 'And in this view it will be but fair to allow', he explains,

> that most of our author's faults are less to be ascribed to his wrong judgement as a poet, than to his right judgement as a player . . . I think the two disadvantages which I have mentioned (to be obliged to please the lowest of people, and to keep the worst of company) . . . will appear sufficient to mislead and depress the greatest genius on earth.[10]

If the theatre is thus blamed for the literary failings of the Shakespeare corpus, it is held no less responsible for its textual shortcomings: professing the utmost contempt for Heminges and Condell, Pope assures his readers that the 'innumerable errors' in all previous texts of Shakespeare 'have risen from one source, the ignorance of the players, both as his actors, and as his editors' (p. xiv). His edition accordingly relegates what he regards as 'trifling and bombast passages' (p. xvi) found only in the Folio to the foot of the page, blaming them on the players, and, lamenting that the actors responsible for transcribing the copy did not know prose from verse, Pope silently 'corrects' Shakespeare's metre throughout the edition, emending the plays to suit his own views of poetic style, scansion, and decorum. Where Davenant and his peers had rewritten Shakespeare to keep him alive in the theatre as a contemporary playwright, Pope did so more discreetly to transform him into a polite Augustan poet, redeemed as far as could be managed from his degrading associations with the stage.

Pope thus corrected Rowe's Folio-based edition by appealing to the quartos (and to his own instincts as a poet); Pope would in his turn be corrected by Shakespeare's next editor, Lewis Theobald; and a seemingly endless argument between rival editors and their critical readers about the rights and wrongs of particular emendations and interpretations had begun, an argument which would ultimately find its home in the cumulatively expanding footnotes of the Variorum editions. It was an argument, significantly, which largely ignored the contemporary theatre, a discussion carried out in print (in pamphlets, in the pages of journals such as *The Critical Review* and *The Gentleman's Magazine*, in critical monographs, and in the editions themselves) about how Shakespeare's texts should themselves appear in print. Although the mid-eighteenth century saw Shakespeare's plays achieving unprecedented popularity in the theatres, it also saw Shakespeare increasingly treated as a strictly literary author, a subject for library busts and ever larger and more lavishly bound library editions; an annotated native classic to be appreciated by gentlemen in their studies. The irony here is that much of this intensely literary activity would necessarily be preoccupied, as was Pope's preface, with the Renaissance theatre, archaeologically exhumed – with whatever levels of distaste – in order more fully to bring to light the lost meanings of Shakespeare's texts. The 1821 Malone–Boswell edition, for example, than which few artifacts could seem more remote from the world of Elizabethan popular entertainment, devotes a whole 550-page volume to Edmond Malone's exhaustive 'Historical Account of the Rise and Progress of the English Stage' before reprinting a single Shakespeare text: the intensely scholarly, genteel and literary enterprise of editing Shakespeare is thus perennially haunted by the oral, promiscuous institution from which it attempts to rescue him.

On the rare occasions when eighteenth-century editors and critics take notice of contemporary staged Shakespeare, their highest praise for actors is usually that they are 'judicious commentators',[11] their performances perceived merely as animated footnotes to plays which have their definitive existence only on paper. This ascendancy of reading over playgoing is visible even in a publication which might otherwise appear to mark the finest hour of the older, 'As it is Acted' school of Shakespearian publishing, *Bell's Edition of Shakespeare's Plays, as they are now performed at the Theatres Royal in London; Regulated from the Prompt Books of each House by Permission* (1774). This first complete acting edition of Shakespeare's plays entirely shares Pope's view of Shakespeare as a literary genius unfortunately compromised by the theatre in which he worked: 'all our author's faults may justly be attributed to the loose, quibbling licentious taste of the time'; explains Francis Gentleman's prefatory 'Advertisement',

> he, no doubt, upon many occasions, wrote wildly, merely to gratify the public . . . why then should not the noble monuments he has left us, of unrivalled ability, be restored to due proportion and natural lustre, by sweeping off those cobwebs, and that dust of depraved opinion, which Shakespeare was unfortunately forced to throw on them? . . . can any degree of critical taste wish the preservation of dark spots, because they have grown upon dramatic sunshine? is not the corrective hand frequently proved to be the kindest?[12]

Fortunately, Gentleman goes on to observe, 'the Theatres, especially of late, have been generally right in their omissions', so that Bell can now print their prompt-books in the confidence that his edition will thereby show more consistent aesthetic and moral judgement than those produced by undiscriminating scholars and antiquarians, with their lingering attachment to Shakespeare's archaisms and obscenities. Gentleman hastens to add, however, that any gems of poetry cut by performers solely on grounds of length will be scrupulously retained, suggesting in the process that when Shakespeare was at his most inspired he appropriately forgot the hampering practicalities of the stage altogether: 'As an author, replete with spirited ideas, and a full flow of language, especially one possessing *a muse of fire*, cannot stop exactly where stage utterance and public attention require; some passages, of great merit for the closet, are never spoken; such, though omitted in the text, we have carefully preserved in the notes' (1, 7–8). The most remarkable claim of the Advertisement, though, concerns one of the practical purposes this compact publication is designed to serve. As early as 1660 Samuel Pepys had tried the experiment of taking a Shakespearian text (*1 Henry IV*) with him to the theatre, regretting that he had diminished the pleasure of the performance as a result ('it did not please me, as otherwise I believe it would . . . my having a book, I believe did spoil it a little', 31 December 1660). Gentleman, however, approves wholeheartedly of this practice, imagining the public playhouses transformed into communal reading rooms in which the actors can at last be judged as fairly by the audience as by the prompter as to the accuracy with which they are incidentally supplementing the written text: 'from this part of our design, an evident use will arise; that those who take books to the theatre will not be so puzzled themselves to accompany the speaker; nor so apt to condemn performers of being imperfect, when they pass over what is designedly omitted' (p. 6). Bell's edition may appear to surrender Shakespeare's text once more to the actors, but its underlying model of how performance works subordinates the actors entirely to the printed word. This Advertisement, in its support for the censorship of Shakespeare's 'indelicacies' and its sense of Shakespeare as a transcendent genius beyond the merely mechanical requirements of the playhouse, clearly anticipates two profoundly anti-theatrical publications of the following generation, the Bowdlers' *Family Shakespeare* (1807), intended solely to be read in the home, and Charles Lamb's essay 'On the Tragedies of Shakespeare' (1811), with its Romantic commitment to a Bard whose masterpieces can only be travestied by performance: 'It may seem a paradox, but I cannot help being of the opinion that the plays of Shakespeare are less calculated for performance on a stage than those of almost any other dramatist whatever.' Bell's edition is on its way to transferring Shakespeare from the public playhouse to the Romantic theatre of the mind.

Bell's edition, however, had its more pragmatic successors too: as both provincial and amateur theatre expanded around the start of the nineteenth century, still smaller and cheaper editions of individual Shakespeare plays were produced to enable the current working scripts in use at London theatres to generate further productions, in such series as *Inchbald's British Theatre* (1800–17, and much reissued) and *Cumberland's British Drama* (which took over from *Dolby's British Theatre* in 1817, and was similarly much reissued, 'As performed at the Theatres Royal, Drury Lane and Covent Garden: printed under the authority of the managers, from the prompt book').[13] Such series often supply meticulous instructions for costume and blocking (marking at the end of each act, for example, the 'Disposition of Characters at the Fall of the Curtain'), reducing the provincial casts who used them to more or less faithful puppets. In the London theatres too, actors were now being judged according to their adherence to a strictly page-bound conception of Shakespeare: John Philip Kemble, for example, brought vociferous scholarly controversy into the stalls in 1789 by pronouncing 'aches' with two syllables in *The Tempest* out of a concern for historical accuracy, earning a supportive footnote from Edmond Malone by so doing.[14]

Page and stage reconciled?

Apparently displaced from the centre of things Shakespearian by literary and textual criticism, nineteenth-century actors and producers could nonetheless achieve notice through the sheer zeal of their new-found fidelity to Shakespeare's text (see also chapter 12, Shakespeare in the Theatre, by Lois Potter). One actor hereby achieved the accolade of having an entire edition dedicated to him on his retirement, *The Illustrated Tallis's Shakspere* (1850), offered 'To William Charles Macready, Esq., the regenerator of the stage, who restored to it the pure and unsullied text of the immortal Shakspere' in celebration of Macready's determination that 'the corrupt editions and unseemly presentations of past days will never be restored, but . . . the purity of our great Poet's text will henceforth be held on our English stage in the reverence it should ever command'.[15] Performers had at last, apparently, accepted the textual critics' perspective on Shakespeare, but in doing so had entitled themselves to venture into those critics' own purlieus: in this publication Macready is so thoroughly acclaimed for his loyalty to Shakespeare the poet as substantially to displace him. The edition begins with an extensive memoir of Macready, together with a full transcript of the speeches made at his farewell performance and subsequent farewell banquet, and tucks away its cursory biography of Shakespeare in the sixth of its seven volumes. Throughout each volume, meanwhile, the plays' texts are explained less by their light annotations than by engravings of Macready and his company acting them, their performances so thoroughly legitimated by their use of Shakespeare's unaltered texts as to claim equally definitive status.[16]

This apparent truce between text and performance in nineteenth-century theatre and publishing might even, in a critical climate preoccupied with Shakespeare's private imagination, allow the stage to reclaim at least a local ascendancy, purporting to transcend the Shakespearian text by fully embodying the airy nothings the author had thereby succeeded only partially in giving a local habitation and a name. Kemble himself had set a precedent here by imposing lavishly researched costumes and sets on Shakespeare's history plays, retrospectively supplying the Bard with the spectacular concern for antiquarian and heraldic accuracy he had himself never expressed, so that his production of *King John*, designed by J. R. Planché in 1823, could claim more fully to show 'The life and death of King John' than the text printed in the Folio.[17] This approach reached its apogee at the Princess's Theatre in the 1850s in the work of Charles Kean, whose lavishly pictorial productions were so committed to minute historical verisimilitude as occasionally to warrant what is in this context less adaptation than emendation. Staging *The Winter's Tale* in 1856, for example, Kean explicitly favoured the spirit of the play over the letter, adopting Sir Thomas Hanmer's long-discredited alteration of 'Bohemia' to 'Bithynia' in the interests of making his production consistently and educationally classical:

> Chronological contradictions abound throughout the five acts . . . It is evident that when an attempt is made to combine truth with history, conflicting epochs cannot all be illustrated; and I have therefore thought it permissible to select a period which, while it accords with the spirit of the play, may be considered the most interesting, as well as the most instructive.[18]

This explanation for Kean's choice of decor occurs in the course of the dense eleven-page introduction to a souvenir edition more scholarly than most library editions, its dialogue annotated by copious reference to the best authorities, and its scenery described in extensive archaeological detail (after each act, five pages of notes cite sources in classical authors and in the British Museum for every prop and costume used in its staging). So far from being a production which merely glosses the text of Shakespeare's *The Winter's Tale*, this is one which mandates the publication of an entire new (and improved) edition of the play as its complement and gloss. If the eighteenth-century rivalry between page and stage had begun in 1709 with the playwright Rowe inadvertently betraying the primacy of the stage's Shakespeare by turning textual critic, its nineteenth-century continuation here finds the actor-manager Kean reasserting that primacy by invading the territory of the editors. In this second career he would be followed on an even larger scale by his most famous successor, Henry Irving, who would supplement his own box-office receipts by the publication not only of individual souvenir editions ('as arranged for the stage by Henry Irving') but of a complete *Henry Irving Shakespeare* (8 volumes, London, 1888–90).

What is more ominously prophetic about Kean's souvenir editions, though, from the point of view of the live theatre, is their stress on the educational value of the Shakespearian productions they gloss. The most rapidly expanding market for Shakespeare in the later nineteenth century was provided not by playgoers or actors or gentlemen with literary pretensions, but, with the expansion of compulsory vernacular education and the emergence of English as an academic discipline, by schoolchildren and students. This was a market (despite the traditions of school and university drama) with much less interest in contemporary live performance than in minute textual exegesis. The editions which proliferated to meet this demand took little cognizance, if any, of the work of actors since Burbage (who feature, if at all, only as villainous adulterers of the true text), often treating stage directions less as records of either past or possible stage action than as aids to reading the play without reference to either.[19] The Shakespeare of early twentieth-century academic criticism was more often seen as a dramatic poet than as a poetic dramatist, a tendency which found one extreme in the desire of conspiracy theorists to believe that the author of the Complete Plays was a courtier, aristocrat, or even monarch. (This tendency finds more moderate expression in the view that Shakespeare's plays are 'too long to be conveniently acted' because Shakespeare was in part writing them for genteel circulation in manuscript – a practice of which, in Shakespeare's case, there are unfortunately no records.)[20] In part as a result, the theatrical souvenir edition had largely died out by the 1940s, and it survives now only in the diminished form of the elaborate programmes published by subsidized theatre companies such as the Royal Shakespeare Company and the National Theatre. These, however, are designed less to commemorate and celebrate Shakespearian stage productions in print than to legitimate what happens on stage by appeal to written academic authorities, guaranteeing (for an audience often dominated by schoolchildren only present because they are about to sit a compulsory examination about the play) the classical theatre's compliance with strictly literary standards. Today's descendants of the Victorian theatrical souvenir edition are instead book-of-the-film publications such as *Much Ado About Nothing by*

William Shakespeare: Screenplay, Introduction and Notes on the Making of the Movie by Kenneth Branagh (New York: Norton, 1993), reminders that at the end of the twentieth century more people are encountering Shakespeare on film – as neither quite performance nor quite text – than either in the theatre or in print.

In more recent scholarship, however, the stage has at last regained ground against the dominance of the exclusively literary treatment of Shakespeare's plays. In Shakespearian publishing, for example, a wholly new kind of edition has emerged, what might be described as the dramatic variorum, designed to record not the conjectures of successive textual scholars but the cuts, transpositions, and stage business of successive performers. The most elaborate example to date has been William P. Halstead's unwieldy *Shakespeare as Spoken: A Collation of 5,000 Acting Editions and Promptbooks of Shakespeare* (12 volumes, Ann Arbor: American Theatre Association, 1977–9), but a similar interest in tracing the different staged lives of Shakespeare's plays informs series such as *Plays in Performance* (founded in 1981, now *Shakespeare in Production*)[21] and *Shakespeare in Performance* (established by Manchester University Press at much the same time). This has coincided with an increased willingness among textual scholars explicitly to treat Shakespeare as a writer whose plays found their fullest expression in performance: it is this commitment which animates the one-volume Oxford edition (1986), determined 'to formulate a text presenting the play when performed by the company of which Shakespeare was a principal shareholder in the theatres that he helped to control and on whose success his livelihood depended',[22] and thus presenting itself as a sort of four-centuries-belated souvenir edition of the stage productions remembered in the Folio and quartos. Biographers, too, have long abandoned the Romantic view of Shakespeare as a poet too good for either his own theatre or any other, and in criticism the recognition of the pragmatic and performative dimensions of Shakespeare's plays (already crucial to the work of William Empson in the 1930s and 1940s) has been a notable feature of some of the most influential work of the last two decades.[23] Whether all this constitutes the page praising the stage or burying it remains to be seen: but what is certain is that the 'living monument' constituted by Shakespeare studies today is more visibly than ever before a monument to an actor and theatrical shareholder as well as to a poet.

Notes

1. William Shakespeare, *Troilus and Cressida*, ed. Kenneth Muir (Oxford University Press, 1984), p. 193. See also pp. 1–4.
2. *Ibid.*, pp. 1–5.
3. Stanley Wells and Gary Taylor, eds., *The Complete Oxford Shakespeare* (Oxford: Clarendon Press, 1986), p. xlii.
4. *Ibid.*, p. xliii.

5. *The Merry Conceited Humours of Bottom the Weaver* (London, 1661), 'The Stationers to the Reader'.

6. There is some evidence that a fifth Folio was begun at some time early in the 1700s but abandoned – perhaps when Rowe's edition (1709) came onto the market. See Eric Rasmussen, 'Anonymity and the Erasure of Shakespeare's First Eighteenth-century Editor', in *Reading Readings: Essays on Shakespeare Editing in the Eighteenth Century*, ed. Joanna Gondris (Cranbury, N.J.: Associated University Presses, 1998), pp. 318–22.

7. On contemporary understandings of the relation of this text to Shakespeare's authorship, see Michael Dobson, *The Making of the National Poet: Shakespeare, Adaptation and Authorship, 1660–1769* (Oxford: Clarendon Press, 1992), pp. 38–41, 59–61.

8. *The Tragedy of Hamlet Prince of Denmark. As it is now Acted at his Highness the Duke of York's Theatre. By William Shakespeare* (London, 1676), 'To the Reader'. This quarto was reprinted in 1683.

9. *The Works of Mr. William Shakespeare*, ed. Nicholas Rowe [and Charles Gildon], 7 vols. (London, '1709' [1710]), VII, 272.

10. *The Works of Shakespeare, Collated and Corrected*, ed. Alexander Pope, 6 vols. (London, 1723–5), I, vii–ix.

11. Cf. Francis Gentleman on David Garrick, 'the best illustrator of, and best *living comment* on, Shakespeare, that ever has appeared, or possibly ever will grace the British stage', *Bell's Edition of Shakespeare's Plays, as they are now performed at the Theatres Royal in London; Regulated from the Prompt Books of each House by Permission*, 8 vols. (London, 1774), I, 4.

12. *Ibid.*, p. 5.

13. These would themselves be succeeded by long-lived Victorian acting editions such as Phelps's and Lacy's.

14. See *The plays and poems of William Shakspeare, with the corrections and illustrations of various commentators . . .* ed. Edmond Malone and James Boswell, 21 vols. (London, 1821), XV, 57 (*The Tempest*, 1.2.423).

15. *The Illustrated Tallis's Shakspere*, 7 vols. (London, 1850), I, 9.

16. It became quite widespread in the nineteenth century even for purely reading editions of Shakespeare, though devoid of reference to the theatre since Shakespeare's time in their introductory materials or notes, to be illustrated with engravings (and, increasingly, photographs) of contemporary actors performing the plays – an instance, perhaps, of the printing press's bad conscience about the theatre it has displaced.

17. On this production, see Nicola J. Watson, 'Kemble, Scott, and the Mantle of the Bard', in *The Appropriation of Shakespeare*, ed. Jean Marsden (Hemel Hempstead: Harvester-Wheatsheaf, 1991), pp. 73–92; James Boaden, *Memoirs of the Life of John Philip Kemble, Esq . . .*, 4 vols. in 2 (London, 1825), II, 279.

18. *Shakespeare's Play of the Winter's Tale, arranged for representation at the Princess's Theatre, with historical and explanatory notes by Charles Kean. As first performed on Monday, April 28th, 1856* (London, 1856), p. v.

19. The most famous example here would be John Dover Wilson's Cambridge edition of *Hamlet* (1930), which interpolates stage directions to enable readers to watch, strictly in the theatre of the mind, his particular interpretation of the play, further developed in *What Happens in Hamlet* (Cambridge University Press, 1935).

20. See Richard Dutton, 'The Birth of the Author', in *Elizabethan Theatre: Essays in Honor of S. Schoenbaum*, ed. R. B. Parker and S. P. Zitner (Newark: University of Delaware Press, 1996), pp. 71–92.

21. See, for example, *Plays in Performance: Richard III*, ed. Julie Hankey (London: Junction Books, 1981. From 1996 the series was published by Cambridge University Press under the new title *Shakespeare In Production*.)

22. Stanley Wells, 'General Introduction', in *The Complete Oxford Shakespeare*, p. xxxiii.
23. See, for example, Harry Berger, *Imaginary Audition: Shakespeare on Stage and Page* (Berkeley: University of California Press, 1989).

Reading list

Berger, Harry, *Imaginary Audition: Shakespeare on Stage and Page* (Berkeley: University of California Press, 1989).

Billington, Michael, ed., *Directors' Shakespeare: Approaches to Twelfth Night by Bill Alexander, John Barton, John Caird, Terry Hands* (London: Nick Hern, 1990).

Brooks, Douglas A., *From Playhouse to Printing House: Drama and Authorship in Early Modern England* (Cambridge University Press, 2000).

de Grazia, Margreta, *Shakespeare Verbatim: The Reproduction of Authenticity and the Apparatus of 1790* (Oxford: Clarendon Press, 1991).

Dessen, Alan C., *Shakespeare in Performance: Titus Andronicus* (Manchester University Press, 1989).

Hankey, Julie, ed., *Plays in Performance: Othello* (Bristol Classical Press, 1987).

Knapp, Robert S., *Shakespeare – The Theater and the Book* (Princeton University Press, 1989).

Osborne, Laurie, *The Trick of Singularity: Twelfth Night and the Performance Editions* (University of Iowa Press, 1996).

States, Bert O., *Great Reckonings in Little Rooms: On the Phenomenology of Theater* (Berkeley: University of California Press, 1985).

Taylor, Gary, *Moment by Moment by Shakespeare* (London: Macmillan, 1989).

Warren, Roger, *Text and Performance: A Midsummer Night's Dream* (London: Macmillan, 1983).

Wells, Stanley, *Literature and Drama* (London: Routledge, 1970).
  Re-editing Shakespeare for the Modern Reader (Oxford: Clarendon Press, 1984).

16

DENNIS KENNEDY

Shakespeare worldwide

'It is normally supposed that something always gets lost in translation. I cling obstinately to the notion that something can be gained'
(Salman Rushdie, *Imaginary Homelands*)

SHAKESPEARE is so deeply ingrained in English-speaking culture, and the appreciation of his work so thoroughly intertwined with the study of the English language, that it seems almost incidental that he is also the world's best-known playwright. Regularly at or near the top of lists of the most performed and most studied dramatists in diverse countries and languages, Shakespeare has been disseminated broadly and incorporated into the lives of people far removed from his homeland and his native tongue. The globalized nature of contemporary culture has expanded the reception of Shakespeare further through material means: widespread sales of the texts for schools by British publishers, world tours by the Royal Shakespeare Company (the first ones occurring in the early 1960s, soon after its founding), and international distribution of films of the plays. Is this a logical result of Shakespeare's overriding genius, another example of English cultural imperialism, or just clever marketing in the post-modern manner?

The idea that Shakespeare belongs to the world is certainly not new. Elizabeth's reign witnessed the first major period of England's expansion, initiating and encouraging an overseas empire that continued until the late twentieth century, and many plays of the period carry indicators of the early modern fascination with foreign shores, exotic peoples, global wealth. From *Titus Andronicus* to *The Tempest* Shakespeare's work repeatedly turns to themes touching on the stranger, the alien, the other, and often deals openly with questions of empire and colony. In an environment so absorbed with the great world, it is not surprising that Shakespeare's company, the Lord Chamberlain's Men, in 1599 named their new theatre the Globe. The name suggests that like Atlas their work carried the world, just as the 'wooden O' of their playhouse symbolically contained it.

From the start of Shakespeare's afterlife as a dramatist two issues have been consistently present: claims for his universality and his appropriation into foreign environments. The earliest declaration of Shakespeare's universality came in the first substantial piece of Shakespeare criticism, the dedicatory poem by Ben Jonson in the Folio edition of 1623. Jonson memorialized his friend and rival as one who shone brighter than all other dramatists and poets:

> Triumph, my Britain, thou hast one to show
> To whom all scenes of Europe homage owe.
> He was not of an age, but for all time . . . (41–3)

But universality is a tricky concept: often what we believe to have comprehensive attraction turns out to be more local or more time-bound than we think. Because Shakespeare's texts appear open – intellectually and theatrically unstable and subject to divergent understanding and assessment – vastly different audiences have been able to read themselves into them or see them as reflections of their own condition. The wide appeal Shakespeare has enjoyed over time and space may be the result of the indeterminacy of his work rather than its universality. Or perhaps that is what universality in art ultimately means: resilience to change based on an artifact's elasticity.

Turning to the extension of the plays into other lands and languages, the argument for universality gives way to a more complex observation: when Shakespeare proved functional in disparate cultural circumstances, it was usually because the plays were adapted, often drastically, to fit distinct needs. We do not have to leave native shores to witness this, of course, since the texts as performed in Britain and Ireland were rewritten with heavy hands throughout the seventeenth and eighteenth centuries and well into the reign of Victoria. (Though not usually discussed in the same context, they continue to be heavily rewritten today when they are filmed.) But the expatriation of the plays is a different case. Intriguingly, the first example of Shakespeare abroad occurred while the poet was still alive and serves to demonstrate the phenomenon.

In 1592 the London actor Robert Browne led a band of his underemployed associates on a journey to the court of the Duke of Brunswick (Braunschweig) in what is now the middle of Germany. Thereafter Browne and a number of others, generically called 'English Comedians', travelled central and eastern Europe as itinerant players, the need for their journeys influenced by the changing fortunes of the London theatres (and after 1618 often disrupted by the Thirty Years' War).[1] The playing conditions of the English Comedians were severely restricted: the early troupes did not speak German, were performing for audiences without a contemporary theatrical tradition and often in outdoor, makeshift locales that permitted little or no spectacle and only limited spectator attention. While we cannot be positive, it is most likely that their repertory included versions of some of Shakespeare's plays, versions that must have reduced the work of a great poet to little more than dumb show. In this first exporting of Shakespeare, it is already clear that there would be great differences between the fashioning of his work in foreign climes and in the land of his birth.

To say that in another way: for some time Shakespeare has been taken for granted in England and the English-speaking world but other nations had to find reasons to read and perform him. In this chapter I will look at three major manifestations of that desire, each representing a different observance. The first is the example of Germany, which drew upon Shakespeare for nationalist reasons in the eighteenth century, urged by powerful literary voices from within who appropriated him for a distinctive cause. The German model led the way for much of the rest of Europe. The second is the nineteenth-century example of colonial India, where Shakespeare's work was imported as part of the cultural baggage of Empire but later took a series of distinctive turns unanticipated by British promoters. The last is the twentieth-century example of Japan, which serves to illustrate a third way: neither nationalist nor colonial, Japanese Shakespearians have dodged the political implications of adopting so foreign a writer in favour of an ideal of intercultural understanding.

Germany

Despite its political and cultural antagonism to Britain, France actually led the way in the awareness of Shakespeare outside the Anglophone nations, initiated by Voltaire's praise of the dramatist in 1734, though the dry translations that followed were more Louis XV than Elizabeth I. A twenty-volume prose edition by Pierre Letourneur was published between 1776 and 1783, the first foreign-language complete edition, even though France remained hostile to Shakespeare in the theatre until well into the nineteenth century. The model of foreign desire for Shakespeare was established in neighbouring Germany, in direct opposition to French hegemony, a century and a half after the English Comedians. We can say 'Germany' only in a qualified sense; in the eighteenth century the German-speaking lands of the Holy Roman Empire were not a nation but a disunited group of petty principalities. Each had its own court and attendant cultural institutions in the aristocratic mode – chapel singers, concert musicians, poets, opera, and theatre – which generally followed the royal tastes of the Austrian or French Empires.

Under Enlightenment influence, and eventually taking heart from the American and French Revolutions, the German romantic movement began to question both aristocratic governance and neoclassic art. One supported the other, of course: neoclassicism, especially in the theatre, was obsessed with order, regularity, and class distinction. Shakespeare had almost no place in that world as his plays were seen as sprawling, untutored, and far too often concerned with rebellion. It was precisely those qualities, however, that the romantics admired, attracted as they were to the individual over the group, emotion over rationality, freedom over order. The writers of the *Sturm und Drang* ('storm and stress') school of the 1770s, which included the early Goethe, took Shakespeare as a dramaturgical epitome in their longing to throw off the French monarchist example.

Yet for all his value as prototype, Shakespeare was to have a much greater importance. Since the small German states did not constitute a modern country, they did not have a shared literature. At the same time that Shakespeare was being enshrined as the English national poet, German nationalists saw an opportunity to make him theirs as well. For Goethe, and particularly for Friedrich Schiller (1759–1805), Shakespeare was to become the basis for the development of a theatre that would engage German-speakers in the project of creating a nation. Paradoxically, it was Shakespeare's foreignness that made him useful: the lack of a Shakespearian history in Germany was the main attraction, allowing the romantic movement to recreate him as a visionary of freedom.

Shakespeare's effect in this environment was dependent upon translation. Though some important literary figures read English, the national theatre Schiller dreamed of would have to find its form in German. A translation of *Titus Andronicus* was published as early as 1620, though that was anomalous. After a few half-hearted versions in the 1740s and 1750s, the first concerted efforts were the prose versions made by Christoph Martin Wieland, who published twenty-two plays between 1762 and 1766. It was Wieland's work that made possible the *Sturm und Drang* reliance on Shakespeare and that brought the plays to a wide reading public and occasional productions. G. E. Lessing praised Shakespeare in *Hamburg Dramaturgy* (1767–9), though Hamburg audiences had small opportunity to see the plays until F. L. Schröder acted in an adaptation of *Hamlet* in 1776. In the next three years Schröder staged eight more plays, but it was *Hamlet* – with its protagonist who faces an internal struggle against external forces, a struggle entirely compatible with the romantic notion of individual heroism – that drew most attention, and productions multiplied. 'Where in Germany is a troupe of actors', a critic asked in 1781, 'that has not performed *Hamlet*?'

Theatrical activity prompted new translations, which in turn created more productions and much wider awareness of Shakespeare's utility in the German cause. The most important were the highly romantic versions of J. J. Eschenburg called the Mannheim Shakespeare, published between 1775 and 1782, and those begun by August Wilhelm von Schlegel in 1797. Schlegel, both critic and dramatist, translated seventeen of the plays in accessible versions; his work was continued by Ludwig Tieck, Tieck's daughter Dorothea, and Wolf von Baudissin. Individual plays appeared as their translations were completed and the full result, *Shakespeare's Dramatic Works*, was published in twelve volumes in Berlin in 1839–40.

The Schlegel–Tieck versions rapidly became the standard German translation. Simon Williams notes that despite the variety of translators the edition has stylistic unity, is reasonably faithful to the original and yet catches, in Schlegel's words, 'part of the innumerable, indescribable beauties which do not lie in the letters but hang about it like a ghostly bloom'.[2] The text became highly popular with readers and gave Shakespeare a literary status greater in Germany than in his native land. When a single-volume edition was published in 1891, 25,000 copies were bought in the next two years, and the translation is still frequently used in schools and in the theatre. *Unser* Shakespeare – 'our Shakespeare' – was an unfeigned appropriation, dissociated entirely from the original condition of the work and from Shakespeare's position in Britain in the eighteenth century. England's national poet had become a German writer.

And has remained so: in the twentieth century Shakespeare held an unparalleled position in German thought and performance. During the First World War, when Shakespeare was almost absent from the London stage, Berlin saw the number of productions increase. In 1915 Gerhart Hauptmann said in an address to the Deutsche Shakespeare-Gesellschaft (the world's oldest Shakespeare society, founded in 1864), 'There is no nation, not even the British, which is more entitled to call Shakespeare its own than Germany . . . Though he was born and buried in England it is in Germany that he is truly alive.' At the Deutsches Theater Max Reinhardt mounted a major celebration of Shakespeare in honour of the tercentenary of his death, allowing Germany to claim that it valued England's national dramatist more than the enemy did. The extreme expression of *unser* Shakespeare was given by the playwright Ludwig Fulda in the same year when he noted that there were more performances of Shakespeare in Germany annually than in an entire decade in England, and they were better performed and better understood as well:

> Our Shakespeare! Thus we may call him, even if he happened to be born in England by mistake. Thus we may call him by right of spiritual conquest. And should we succeed in vanquishing England in the field, we should, I think, insert a clause into the peace treaty stipulating the formal surrender of William Shakespeare to Germany.[3]

One of the underlying reasons for the continuing German ease with Shakespeare is the modernity of translations. In most foreign-language performance the text has been translated into a contemporary vernacular, so losses to poetic subtlety are offset by ease of understanding. English-speakers, especially those professionally involved in the teaching and reproduction of Shakespeare, quite understandably think that any translation of the plays is a reduction, lacking both the authenticity of the original and the essential relationship of style to meaning (*traduttore, traditore*, the punning Italian proverb goes: a translator is a traitor). There is no doubt that this is true. Nonetheless, while Shakespeare's poetry is a marvel of human accomplishment, its archaism and obscurity place substantial barriers between it and contemporary audiences in theatre and film. For English-speakers who have not been trained to understand or value it, Shakespeare's language can be a major reason for avoiding him. Paradoxically a translation, which by definition misses much of the original's qualities, nonetheless has advantages in performance. Even the Schlegel–Tieck version, the oldest of the translations still in regular use, is two centuries closer to us than the original and is much closer to the German of today's Berlin or Vienna than Shakespeare's language is to the English of London, not to mention Los Angeles. Imagine if Shakespeare had been rewritten by Coleridge and you have some idea of the Schlegel–Tieck use of idiom. Further, it is common practice to make new translations every generation, or even for each new production, so that *Hamlet* in foreign environments can sound like a new play, whereas in English it often sounds like a series of obsolete and self-conscious quotations.

Of course the modernity of translation can apply to any non-English language. While chronicling Shakespeare's general position in Europe is beyond the scope of this chapter, I can note in passing that other European countries soon followed the German lead in requisitioning Shakespeare for their national stages, publishers, and schools. Russia and a number of eastern European lands began translation projects in the first third of the nineteenth century, often with a political impetus similar to that of German romanticism and usually based on the German or French versions rather than the original. In the twentieth century the political use of Shakespeare actually increased, especially during the Cold War period. Frequently prohibited from staging new plays with even implicit criticism of their Stalinist regimes, theatres in the Soviet Union and eastern Europe, including East Germany, often used productions of Shakespeare as coded messages about current circumstances, as if the original text had been a message sent across time in a bottle. Today the theatres of all European countries are easily familiar with Shakespeare.

But Germany has remained Shakespeare's second home and has treated him with the familiarity of a family member, and with the gentle abuse that sometimes goes with kinship. While there have been many productions that have been 'respectful' of the text, in general terms German-speaking directors have used Shakespeare as a vehicle for personal or social commentary more openly than English-speaking ones, in part because of the more volatile and deadly politics surrounding them, in part because the translated text cannot have the same almost sacred resonance as the original has in Anglophone environments. As examples, I will look briefly at three productions of *Hamlet* spanning the twentieth century. 'Germany is Hamlet', Ferdinand Freiligrath famously wrote in 1844, and the complex affair between the country and the play has heavily marked German theatre history.

First, Leopold Jessner, the director of the Berlin State Theatre during the Weimar Republic, who made a number of productions that quite consciously commented on the regressive policies of the deposed Kaiser's government, starting with an extraordinary expressionist mounting of *Richard III* in 1920 (see also chapter 13, Shakespeare in the Twentieth-century Theatre, by Peter Holland). His modern-dress *Hamlet* of 1926 was even more direct in its condemnation of the previous regime. Claudius and his court appeared as Prussian military officers with shoulder brushes and breastplates, Gertrude carried an ostrich fan, but

Fritz Kortner as Hamlet wore informal contemporary clothes; when he returned from England he had on foul-weather gear with sailor's watch cap, and smoked a pipe. The message was clear: the Kaiser and his cronies had been corrupt murderers, not far removed from Richard III, and Hamlet's more democratic modern manner was to be preferred – yet clearly was endangered by rising fascism. Jessner, a communist and Jew, seriously angered conservative political forces with his criticism. As if to confirm his worries about regressive politics, after the 1930 elections he was removed from his position and in 1933 left Germany for permanent exile.

I jump forward a half-century to a transformed world where *Hamlet* could become a site for general cultural commentary. Hansgünter Heyme's production of 1979 in Cologne was one of the first that radically commented on the position of the play in a post-modern manner. Rather than Jessner's political allusions, this 'electronic' *Hamlet* was interested in how the personal and cultural schizophrenia of the time is created by and reflected in high technology. Here nothing, especially the most famous play in the world, could be experienced directly, but only through heavy mediation. Instead of conversing in dialogue form, actors turned a video camera upon each other, its images multiplied by eighteen monitors lined up on the stage. Hamlet was split in two, the onstage one unable to talk and lost in video replications of himself, while a disconnected amplified voice recited his lines in the Schlegel translation – the civilized and traditional language in direct contrast to the fractured television images. A tragedy of the individual, Heyme implied, is no longer possible in a world where electronic apparitions are more alluring than contact with the person. His production also suggested that Germans now know *Hamlet* so well that the play can be read through their obsessions and become whatever they wish it to be.

Finally, Heiner Müller's version in East Berlin in 1990 was mounted as a seven-and-a-half-hour performance of his translation interrupted by amplified passages from his own by-product play *Hamletmachine*, which he calls 'the shrunken head of the Hamlet tragedy'.[4] Here the theme had changed from unsettled post-modernity to loss, plain and simple. An autistic Hamlet, powerless to effect change, was again surrounded by television monitors, isolated and alienated from the political chaos in a corrupt Denmark, itself standing for the rickety government of the German Democratic Republic. Events caught up with the production and seemed to confirm it: during the lengthy rehearsal period the Berlin Wall came down and, having just celebrated its fortieth anniversary, the state collapsed and reunited with its western double. 'I was Hamlet', Müller writes in the opening lines of *Hamletmachine*, 'I stood at the shore and talked with the surf BLABLA, the ruins of Europe in back of me. The bell tolled the state-funeral.' At the end of the communist experiment – and in Müller's view at the end of the European world – our Shakespeare remains: cracked, damaged, shrunken, outworn, but still alive and still important.

India

Shakespearian interpretation in eurocentric countries, even when wildly outlandish in English eyes, has occurred in systems of culture of the same Western tradition. Greco-Roman civilization, Judeo-Christian observance, the Renaissance, the Enlightenment, the scientific and industrial revolutions – these are references Europeans and their transplanted descendants obviously share. Shifting Shakespeare from one such country to another involves cultural displacement but not cultural trauma. When we move outside the range of the West, however, we are likely to encounter traditions and mores that are vastly different from those of the humanist tradition of early modern Europe, and Shakespeare must be transmuted into a different creature if he is to make sense and flourish.

In 1607, about the time he was writing *Antony and Cleopatra*, and while the English Comedians were probably performing his earlier plays on the European continent, another intriguing exportation of Shakespeare occurred much further afield. Captain William Keeling, commander of the third voyage of the East India Company en route to the court of the 'Great Mogol', was becalmed off the coast of Sierra Leone for six weeks. To keep the sailors 'from idleness and unlawful games or sleep', Keeling arranged for them to give amateur performances of *Hamlet* and *Richard II* on board his vessel. Within sight of Africa, Shakespeare already appeared as a useful pastime for the early English imperial project. In the land of the Great Mogol, India itself, Shakespeare was made into an ally of political dominance in the nineteenth century, demonstrating once again that the inherent ideology of the texts is much less significant than the cultural meanings that can be assigned to them. Attempting to create a subcontinental copy of English society, the Empire inducted Shakespeare as an edifying agent in its educational and cultural systems. But colonial authority is always ambiguous or doubled-edged. Shakespeare in India could be taken as the champion example of English superiority or, parallel to the example of German romanticism, as an inciter of nationalism – as if the people of India had said, 'We will learn your game of cricket and then beat you at it.'

This ambiguity is apparent from the rise of modern Indian theatre when, starting in the 1770s in Bombay and Calcutta, independent stages in Western likeness were established for the Raj. Shakespeare was a crucial writer for them, and has remained so for their successors. But what kind of Shakespeare? To make a complex issue simple, there have been three types. First, the imperial model, in which British actors, often amateur, performed for the ruling class, their subordinates and educated Indians. This type of theatre expected – whether consciously or unconsciously – to demonstrate the righteous inevitability of European dominance. When Indian actors were co-opted for such performances, they established all the more the virtue of authoritarian rule and were often given a stature borrowed from English celebrities: the actor Ganpatrao Joshi was called the Garrick of Maharashtra, the manager K. P. Khatau was called the Irving of

India, and the translator Agha Hashr Kashmiri was known as the Shakespeare of India. This type of Shakespeare was imperialist because it kept itself culturally separate from the population at large and from native languages, marking difference clearly and loudly.

But it rapidly widened to the Indian bourgeoisie and in so doing transformed into the second type of Shakespeare, which we can call the colonial model because of its integration into the lives of the subordinate people. As with most successful colonial practice, the burden of enrichment and the promise of advancement were subtle. No one was forcing Indians to attend the theatre; they wished to do so in emulation of their foreign leaders and to 'better' themselves through Western high culture. A glimpse of the growing hybridity of the colony can be seen in the example of the Hindu Theatre of Calcutta, the first Bengali playhouse, which opened in December 1831 with a double bill of scenes from *Julius Caesar* and an English translation of a classic Sanskrit play. Thereafter the Western notion of theatre spread widely into the regions, providing the main source of urban drama. The language of performance could vary enormously, from Urdu or Hindi in the north to Bengali or even Tamil in the south. As Ania Loomba notes, the fact that these theatres often performed Shakespeare 'is merely another of colonial India's many ironies'.[5]

Colonial Shakespeare assumed a humanist approach: because he wrote about a human condition believed to be unchanging, Shakespeare could be valued by all peoples regardless of their nationality or gender or race. Since the ideology behind the promotion of a universalist Shakespeare was hidden, the texts were easily subsumed into the political and cultural hegemony as components of the general project of edification. Shakespeare's work appeared unproblematic; it could be read and studied in schools for its transcendent appeal to the spirit without having to question the process of dominance which had brought an English dramatist to the subcontinent in the first place. As Macaulay's foundational 1835 Minute put it, a small number of British masters could govern the teeming millions in India only if sufficient numbers of 'interpreters' or mediators stood between them, a 'class of persons Indian in blood and colour but English in tastes, in opinion, in morals and intellect'. The power of this idea has remained strong, despite the enormous political changes in India in the second half of the twentieth century. Loomba notes that in the University of Delhi alone some 20,000 students study Shakespeare each year and *The Tempest* is still taught in some Indian classrooms 'completely divorced from its colonial theme'.[6]

But the best example of colonial Shakespeare operated, ironically, in the post-colonial period. I refer to the case of Geoffrey Kendal, made famous by the Merchant–Ivory film *Shakespeare Wallah* (1965), with Kendal playing a fictionalized version of himself. Together with his wife Laura Liddell, Kendal formed a troupe of chiefly British actors called Shakespeariana that criss-crossed India from 1946 to the early 1960s, playing in theatres, grand houses, and makeshift huts, before audiences as diverse as school-children, merchants, and maharajas, the last imperial viceroy and the first Indian prime minister. Kendal's was a British export product; since there was little of India in his Shakespeare, it could survive in its colonial clothes after independence in 1947. He thought Indian audiences were the best in the world but he constructed them a bit like children, willing receptors of a culture inherently worth knowing and a dramatist unquestioned in his instructive authority.[7] Kendal tilled a fruitful ground and Indian theatre companies have planted in his furrows, performing Shakespeare in English in a neocolonial mould. India is a land of many languages, none of them universally spoken. English has been a medium of communication among the regions for well over a century. Where English abides, it seems, so Shakespeare is – a cultural lingua franca.

The third type of Shakespeare in India follows the appropriative model, naturalizing the plays into indigenous theatre or dance forms. For simplicity's sake I wish I could call it post-colonial, but I cannot; just as Kendal's colonial Shakespeare operated after independence, so appropriative Shakespeare began much earlier. Though the first moves were colonialist, desiring to imitate English culture like the Hindu Theatre mentioned above, they were already hybrid in nature. In 1893, for example, a version of *Macbeth* in Calcutta was designed by 'European artists' but performed by Bengali actors; *The Englishman* newspaper reported that 'A Bengali Thane of Cawdor is a living incongruity, but the reality is an astonishing reproduction.'[8] From the middle of the nineteenth century a number of Indian theatre companies progressively used Shakespeare as raw material, adapting and revising the plays for local tastes and dramatic forms, interested more in their extravagant plots than in imitating Western theatre methods. The crucial issue for Shakespeare in the subcontinent has always been whether English or a domestic language will be spoken on stage. Once translated into Gujarati, for example, nothing stood in the way of transforming Shakespeare into a naturalized dramatist.

One of the best illustrations of appropriative Shakespeare is found in the career of Utpal Dutt, a Bengali actor and director who began his work with Kendal in 1947. Dutt soon rejected his Western education and made a radical turn to traditional culture. 'The fact that he could recite Virgil and Shakespeare dismayed him',[9] so starting in 1951 he set about using his elite background to create a revolutionary popular theatre for working-class and rural audiences. His *Macbeth*, for example, toured in remote areas of the state, performing in Bengali, drawing upon the lively traditions of Jatra, a ritualized folk theatre that normally plays outdoors to huge crowds. Jatra had been the basis of new plays produced by the Communist Party in Bengal in the 1940s and 1950s to convey social messages, so Dutt's company was following both ancient and modern traditions. Relying upon declamatory speech and song, melodramatic exaggerated gestures and a background of music, Dutt made Shakespeare part of the mythic life of villagers who had never seen themselves as part of the colonial world.

A further example shows a Shakespeare even more remote from Western models. It is the strange case of Mizoram, a remote tribal area in north-eastern India whose people have become obsessed with *Hamlet*. Translated into Mizo a half-century ago, the play is now variously performed in amateur venues and in the open air, usually in condensed forms or in selected segments. 'When Hamlet came to Mizoram', the protagonist says at the start, 'he became a Mizo' – a fully naturalized member of the local race – despite the fact that performances are in European costumes, apparently because the Mizos have no theatrical tradition of their own. Tape recordings of *Hamlet-drama*, as the Mizos call it, 'blare out at little market kiosks' and are copied for personal use. The text is drawn upon for instruction for young children and they in turn recite its lines in their games.[10] This is an instance of Shakespearian reproduction barely recognizable to a Western literary critic, though perhaps more familiar in the complex anthropology of colonialism. Taking *Hamlet* fully into their community, yet aware of its utter foreignness, the Mizos have created a Shakespeare that is neither British nor Indian, though it is possible only as a distant result of imperial conquest. Most Indians, in fact, already view the Mizo as alien, a people literally on the margins of the subcontinent. But like the novels of Salman Rushdie, the Mizoram *Hamlet-drama* exists not so much on the margin of a culture as caught in mid-scene, a place neither here nor there but only in between.

Japan

After a short period of international trade in the seventeenth century, Japan remained closed to the West until the Meiji era in 1868. Though some early partial versions of Shakespeare plays appeared in the late nineteenth century, and a complete translation of *Julius Caesar* was published in 1883, no notable activity took place until the first decade of the twentieth century. Shôyô Tsubouchi's standard translation of the complete works began with *Hamlet* in 1909. Published by Waseda University Press in Tokyo, the project was completed in thirty-nine volumes in 1928. Unlike the nationalist case of Germany or the colonial one of India, Japan from the start assumed a curiously discrete relationship to Shakespeare and other classic authors of Europe. In India, despite the immense differences in people and civilization, the reception of Shakespeare was preceded by English models of culture and behaviour. No such attenuation was present in Japan, where arrangements for daily life, morality, and aesthetics today still differ substantially from Western patterns. Indeed the entire fabulistic, mythical, and religious backdrop of Shakespeare is irrelevant in the Japanese case, or at least it was at the beginning of the twentieth century.

In the theatre the distance to Shakespeare was at least as great. Because Japan had a flourishing and more or less unbroken set of traditional forms – the oldest, noh, considerably more ancient than the theatre of Elizabeth – the appearance of European drama at the turn of the century created a constructive paradox: it appeared as an attack on indigenous theatre and thus on established culture, but it was also perceived as an extension of the official policy of modernization. Almost anywhere in the West, and by extension in India and other British colonies, Shakespeare has been seen as the classic *par excellence*. His work entered Japan, however, as *shingeki* or 'new drama'. Despite Shakespeare's antiquity and exemplary status, to the Japanese he belonged to the same reforming movement as Ibsen or Chekhov. What was most notable about Shakespeare, to put it another way, was his utter novelty.

Since the end of the Second World War Shakespeare has become a familiar sight and the number of productions has risen substantially. In 1964, when Europe and North America were heavily engaged in celebrating the quatercentenary of the dramatist's birth, there were only four Shakespeare productions or adaptations in Tokyo; in 1994 there were thirty-three, more than in London. But the plays still are seen as part of the *shingeki* enterprise, and thus they occupy a station very different from that in India, or almost anywhere else including other East Asian nations. In China, for instance, reception in the same period was almost entirely controlled by political exigency: Shakespeare was ignored when foreigners were distrusted in the early century, became consequential after the 1949 Communist Revolution because of his importance for Soviet critics, and was erased entirely during the Cultural Revolution. But in Japan, fed by a burgeoning scholarship and a general desire to emulate Western cultural models, Shakespeare gained high art prestige in the universalist mould.

While Japanese Shakespearian commentary remains deferential, some directors have taken innovative approaches. Before the war the most important of these was Koreya Senda, whose career was heavily influenced by his close contact with the political theatre of Berlin. After his return to Japan in the 1930s he directed leftist-inspired productions that put him into continual trouble with the authorities. His *Hamlet* of 1964 was an attempt to recapture some of the pre-war German political thinking he learned from epic theatre, though it was received with respectful nods rather than revolutionary fervour. The post-war generation of *shingeki* directors have had a larger effect. These include Tadashi Suzuki, whose strict system of physical training for actors governed his adaptations of *Macbeth* in 1975 and *King Lear* in 1988, and Hideki Noda, whose radical revisions in the 1990s placed *Much Ado About Nothing* in the world of Sumo wrestling and *A Midsummer Night's Dream* among a group of cooks at the base of Mount Fuji.[11]

The most notable of this generation is Yukio Ninagawa, schooled in the zealous Tokyo alternative theatres that replaced Senda's Marxist analysis. Fascinated by Western culture, he has made his mark as a director of Shakespeare, Greek tragedy, and twentieth-century American plays – but knows he stands far apart from the worlds they inhabit. He has called himself a 'listener' to foreign culture: visiting Italy, he said, he preferred to read about the Adriatic than swim in it. In an interview conducted while he was preparing *The Tempest*

(1987) he admitted that he had never seen a production of the play, could not remember reading it before he agreed to direct, and did not find the work particularly impressive when he did read it. Yet his work on the text was revelatory.

Inspired by the fact that Zeami, the founder of noh, was exiled like Prospero for political motives, Ninagawa staged the play as a rehearsal of a noh drama on Sado, the island of Zeami's exile. The fictional director of the noh play gradually took on the role of Prospero but recalled Zeami at the same time. Stylistically the production followed from this intercultural mixing. Visually it appeared to be from the samurai world of noh, but it also used Western mood music, psychological acting, and overtly emotional moments. Ninagawa says that 'he is trying to break down the artificial barriers between different forms of theatre by combining ritual, naturalism, kabuki, noh, Hollywood musicals, and film westerns'.[12] His other stagings have included a violently beautiful *Macbeth* (1980) that drew on Buddhist and kabuki traditions, *A Midsummer Night's Dream* (1994) incorporating a Kyoto stone garden and two actors playing Puck as Beijing Opera acrobats, and a *Hamlet* (1995) that combined ancient samurai life with modern Western clothing and manners. His fusion of East and West is distancing for the Japanese, who, he holds, like their Shakespeare treated conventionally. Because he is sponsored by a large Japanese entertainment company, Ninagawa takes most of his productions to Europe as well. Ironically, in British venues – *Macbeth* in Scotland, *Hamlet* in London – they are seen as intensely foreign and exotic, despite the many elements familiar to Western modes of theatre. It is fair to say that Ninagawa's Shakespeare, like so many contemporary cultural products, exists both in and out of the country of its origin.

This dislocating interculturalism returns us to the opening questions, whether Shakespeare's dominating position as the world's playwright is due to his innate greatness, English cultural imperialism, or a form of globalized marketing. The answer, as I hope this chapter shows, is all of the above. There has never been in history a single Shakespeare, particularly in lands foreign to his language: different ages and different peoples, starting most probably with the English Comedians four centuries ago, have forged him into the artist they wanted or needed. It is clear that something powerful in the plays continues to appeal widely, but it is not so clear what the something is, especially when the text is translated and adapted to fit circumstances utterly alien to those of Elizabethan or modern London. Because it is difficult to summarize Shakespeare's appeal it has been comparatively easy to transfer his work to myriad circumstances, from high art to popular culture, from ballet to advertising, from the established lustre of the Royal Shakespeare Company, which continues to mount some eight productions of Shakespeare annually, to the adolescent frivolity of the Reduced Shakespeare Company, which performs the 'complete works, abridged' in 97 minutes. In festivals and conferences, in classrooms and in films, in serious scholarship and in the cultural tourism of the new Shakespeare's Globe theatre in

London, for better or worse Shakespeare has a hold over the imagination of much of the world. How long that fascination will continue is anybody's guess, but it seems reasonable to conclude that we will go on raiding, for our own purposes and for some time to come, his eminently plunderable texts.

Notes

1. Simon Williams, *Shakespeare on the German Stage, 1586–1914* (Cambridge University Press, 1990), pp. 28–9. See also Jerzy Limon, *Gentlemen of a Company: English Players in Central and Eastern Europe, 1590–1660* (Cambridge University Press, 1985).
2. Williams, *Shakespeare on the German Stage*, pp. 151–2.
3. Both quotations are from Wilhelm Hortmann, *Shakespeare on the German Stage: The Twentieth Century* (Cambridge University Press, 1998), pp. 3–4.
4. Quoted by Carl Weber in the introduction to his translation, Heiner Müller, *Hamletmachine and Other Texts for the Stage* (New York: PAJ Publications, 1984), p. 50. The lines from the play quoted below are from p. 53.
5. Ania Loomba, 'Shakespearian Transformations', in *Shakespeare and National Culture*, ed. John J. Joughlin (Manchester University Press, 1997), p. 117.
6. Ania Loomba, '*Hamlet* in Mizoram', in *Cross-Cultural Performances: Differences in Women's Re-Visions of Shakespeare*, ed. Marianne Novy (Urbana: University of Illinois Press, 1993), p. 232.
7. See Geoffrey Kendal with Clare Colvin, *The Shakespeare Wallah: The Autobiography of Geoffrey Kendal* (London: Sidgwick and Jackson, 1986).
8. Quoted in Jyotsna Singh, 'Different Shakespeares: the Bard in Colonial/Postcolonial India', *Theatre Journal* 41:4 (1989), 453.
9. Rustom Bharucha, *Rehearsals of Revolution: The Political Theatre of Bengal* (Honolulu: University of Hawaii Press, 1983), pp. 55–6.
10. Loomba, '*Hamlet* in Mizoram', pp. 236–9.
11. See Akihiko Senda, 'The Rebirth of Shakespeare in Japan: from the 1960s to the 1990s', in *Shakespeare and the Japanese Stage*, eds. Takashi Sasayama *et al.* (Cambridge University Press, 1998), pp. 15–37.
12. See Dennis Kennedy, 'Shakespeare and the Global Spectator', *Shakespeare Jahrbuch* 131 (1995), 50–64.

Reading list

Hortmann, Wilhelm, *Shakespeare on the German Stage: The Twentieth Century* (Cambridge University Press, 1998).
Kennedy, Dennis, *Looking at Shakespeare: A Visual History of Twentieth-Century Performance* (Cambridge University Press, 1993).
Kennedy, Dennis, ed., *Foreign Shakespeare: Contemporary Performance* (Cambridge University Press, 1993).
Sasayama, Takashi *et al.*, eds., *Shakespeare and the Japanese Stage* (Cambridge University Press, 1998).
Stříbrný, Zdeněk, *Shakespeare in Eastern Europe* (Oxford University Press, 2000).
Williams, Simon, *Shakespeare on the German Stage, 1586–1914* (Cambridge University Press, 1990).

17

HUGH GRADY

Shakespeare criticism, 1600–1900

SHAKESPEARE, Ben Jonson assured us, was 'not of an age but for all time'. He might have added that the many eras and countries beyond his own which have appropriated Shakespeare have done so through their own terms and critical categories. The story of Shakespeare's reception by subsequent generations and societies thus involves complex processes of cultural transmission and recontextualization, a pouring, as it were, of Shakespeare's old wine into new cultural bottles that remarkably transforms the wine as it passes from one era or country to the next. It is a story in which we separate at our peril the dance from the dancer, the work from its interpretation. Until very recently, the story of Shakespeare's reception was almost always told as one in which the world gradually came to terms with Shakespeare's inherent and unchanging greatness, so that the post-Romantic apotheosis of Shakespeare as supreme artist was the fixed *telos* of the narrative of peoples, eras, and nations. Today, however, the separation between our own critical evaluations and the inherent worth of the works of art we are perceiving is less self-evident, and we are less confident that Shakespeare – or any other artist – is for all times and places.

During his lifetime Shakespeare was virtually unknown outside his island nation. If he was recognized by some in England as a pre-eminent poet and dramatist, he was also occasionally eclipsed by his rivals, and his reputation was always undercut by the controversial status of London's public theatres. The godlike esteem he has achieved today around the world would have been incomprehensible in his own time, both to him and to his peers.

This is especially true of Shakespeare's first recorded critic, the disgruntled playwright Robert Greene, who in 1592 described Shakespeare as 'an upstart Crow, beautified with our feathers'. By 1598, however, after publication of his Ovidian *Venus and Adonis* and *The Rape of Lucrece*, and after performances of plays like *Richard II*, *Romeo and Juliet*, *A Midsummer Night's Dream*, *The Merchant of Venice*, and *1 Henry IV*, he was accounted one of the leading contemporary poets of England. Francis Meres singles out Shakespeare in a treatise which attempts to establish a canon of English poets to compare with those of ancient Greece and Rome. His praise for Shakespeare is high; he calls him 'the most excellent in both kinds [tragedy and comedy] for the stage', matching the separate accomplishments of Plautus and Seneca in Latin literature, and he is paralleled to Plautus for his 'fine filed phrase' as well. There are numerous other short references in Shakespeare's lifetime both to his 'wit', manifest especially in the ingenuity of his poetic figures, and to his fluent, 'easy', or 'sweet' poetic style, especially in the non-dramatic poems *Venus and Adonis* and *The Rape of Lucrece*. The students at St John's College, Cambridge, who wrote and performed the so-called Parnassus plays between 1598 and 1601 referred to 'Sweet Mr. Shakespeare' and grouped him with Chaucer, Gower, and Spenser. This praise may be tinged with irony, for they also include Shakespeare among the commercial writers they contrast with the learned academic tragedians whom they may have admired more. The difference is enunciated by a character named 'Will Kemp', clearly meant to represent the famous comic actor prominent in Shakespeare's theatre troupe the Chamberlain's Men. Kemp is made to show his ignorance of Latin literature by taking *The Metamorphoses* to refer to the name of an author rather than to one of Ovid's most famous works, but the contrast he draws is significant: 'Few of the university men pen plays well, they smell too much of that writer Ovid, and that writer Metamorphoses, and talk too much of Prosperina and Juppiter. Why, here's our fellow Shakespeare puts them all down, ay, and Ben Jonson too.'

The allusion to Jonson (who had begun to write plays for the London stage in 1597) is equivocal, since it is unclear in this wording whether Jonson joins Shakespeare in putting down the academic writers or is one of those whom Shakespeare is putting down. But Jonson, evidently the better self-promoter of the two, soon helped promulgate a version of this opposition, in which he was seen as a learned student of the classics and Shakespeare an untutored child of nature. Jonson did not invent the terms of this contrast: they derive from famous lines in Horace's *Ars Poetica*, and their earliest recorded use in reference to Shakespeare is found in a poem to Ben Jonson by his fellow playwright Francis Beaumont, dated by E. K. Chambers to about 1615. Subsequently it would be repeated and elaborated in commendatory verses by Leonard Digges (published posthumously in 1640) and John Milton (1630). In fact, this association of Shakespeare's poetry with native talent rather than learning and acquired skill developed into the single most repeated and most variously interpreted critical commonplace on Shakespeare in critical history.

In the beginning, it had a decidedly double edge: on the one hand, the naturalness of Shakespeare's art bespoke its truth, beauty, and depth; on the other hand, it suggested unevenness, naïveté, and lack of learning. The popularity of Shakespeare's plays with contemporary audiences may have contributed to the idea of Shakespeare as a natural rather than a learned poet. Leonard Digges pointedly contrasted Jonson's small audiences with Shakespeare's larger ones in terms which must have irritated so competitive a spirit as Jonson. Digges wrote that the revenues earned by Jonson's best plays at times 'have scarce defrayed the seacoal fire / And door-keepers' – that is, the box-office receipts paid for little more than a warming fire and a ticket-taker – while Shakespeare's *Othello*, *1* and *2 Henry IV*, *Twelfth Night*, and *Much Ado About Nothing* brought in crowds.

Jonson himself saw both sides of the coin. In his most generous pronouncement, in the verses composed for the 1623 First Folio of Shakespeare's works, he praised Shakespeare as 'Soul of the age! / The applause, delight, the wonder of our stage'; went beyond Meres's previous poetic pantheon by ranking Shakespeare above Chaucer, Spenser, and Beaumont and found him the equal of the Greeks and Romans in tragedy and superior to them in comedy. Jonson goes further still. To the poet to whom he attributed in earlier lines of the same poem 'small Latin and less Greek', he adds to his gift of nature the accomplishments of art:

> Yet must I not give nature all: thy art,
> My gentle Shakespeare, must enjoy a part.

In Jonson's 1619 conversation with William Drummond of Hawthornden, he put his viewpoint much less ambivalently: 'Shakespeare wanted art.' For a gloss on this observation, we can turn to the lines on Shakespeare in Jonson's posthumously published *Timber: Or Discoveries Made Upon Men and Matter* (1641), where Jonson elaborates on the issue of Shakespeare's 'wanted art', with a rebuke to Shakespeare's fellow players and First Folio editors, John Heminges and Henry Condell. In their preface to the First Folio his two fellows had praised Shakespeare's fluency in writing, which was such, they wrote, 'that we have scarce received from him a blot in his papers'. Jonson replied, 'Would he had blotted a thousand', and went on to explain that Shakespeare's weakness was in yielding to his own talent for words and so falling into 'those things which could not escape laughter'. Here Caesar's supposed line, 'Caesar did never wrong but with just cause', is the example given, and Jonson later delighted to add the reference in *The Winter's Tale* to the non-existent coast of Bohemia. After Shakespeare's death, Jonson, as an esteemed classicist and Royalist favourite, would age well in the Cavalier culture of the mid-seventeenth century. In fact, along with Shakespeare's successor John Fletcher, Jonson would outshine Shakespeare in literary prestige both before and immediately after the Commonwealth interregnum.

The critical estimate of Shakespeare from his own contemporaries, then, emerges as generous but not overwhelming. His greatest praiser, Ben Jonson, is also his greatest detractor. And Jonson's view of Shakespeare as a great natural poet with certain faults would descend to Restoration critics and then dominate much of the Age of Reason's critical estimate of Shakespeare.

Milton, for example, not only praised Shakespeare in commendatory verses attached to the 1632 Second Folio, but also applied the contrast between art and nature to Jonson and Shakespeare in 'L'Allegro':

Then to the well-trod stage anon,
If Jonson's learned sock be on,
Or sweetest Shakespeare fancy's child,
Warble his native woodnotes wild . . .

But references to Shakespeare elsewhere in Puritan culture – and in the mid-seventeenth century more generally – are rare, not only because of the hostility between the Puritans and the theatre, but also because among Royalists Shakespeare was partially eclipsed by Jonson and Fletcher. However, King Charles I, it was said, in his last days before execution, was reading Jonson and Shakespeare, and as John Dryden reported after the Restoration, Shakespeare had been a favourite of the learned John Hale (1584–1656), Fellow of Eton, who boasted, in Dryden's words, that 'there was no subject of which any poet ever writ, but he would produce it much better treated of in Shakespeare'. This would appear to be the beginning of a practice, still represented in the books of familiar quotations of our own day, of treating Shakespeare as a kind of secular Bible, a source of saws and observations for public speaking and writing. Hale's claim is perhaps the earliest treatment of Shakespeare as a literary classic rather than a contemporary or near-contemporary playwright. Such high respect in the mid-seventeenth century, however, was exceptional. Between 1642 and 1660, a period which in the absence of dramatic performances saw many publications of play-scripts, including a Folio edition of the plays of Francis Beaumont and John Fletcher, only three of Shakespeare's plays were reprinted.[1]

In the Restoration, then, not only the monarchy, but Shakespeare had to be reinvented, and for an age and culture whose ideas of what constituted good drama had been radically altered. Neoclassical aesthetics, developed by the French from materials they had imported from Italian Renaissance critical theory, began to influence English taste and English writing. In its earliest stages neoclassicism was a paradoxical component of a developing European Enlightenment still of strong Royalist inclinations. It seemed a 'natural' approach to literary culture for the court of a restored monarchy which had been exiled in France. Nor were its tenets confined to the court. After the Restoration, spurred on by a developing economy, a new bourgeois class emerged. New media of communication and discussion – newspapers, magazines, cheaper books, coffee houses – facilitated the now much discussed emergence of a public sphere in which literary criticism played a major role. A new Shakespeare developed, characterized by a number of conflicts and contradictions. While the tenets of neoclassicism required stable aesthetic ideas on which could be based authoritative judgements concerning the value of art and culture, the clashing discourses of the new public sphere revealed the extent to which even neoclassical principles ('the rules') could not prevent disagreement about culture. The prevalence of the new ideas did lead, however, to much censuring of Shakespeare for his 'irregularity', but the trend throughout the century was one of increasing tolerance for such 'faults' and a growing appreciation for Shakespeare's 'genius'.

In the early Restoration, both the new neoclassical rigour and the tastes of the first and second Caroline courts had led, as previously mentioned, to a consensus ranking Shakespeare beneath Jonson and Fletcher. The most influential playwright, poet, and critic of his day, John Dryden, acknowledged this received reputation, even as he attempted to modify it in 'An Essay of Dramatic Poesy' (1668):

> . . . and however others are now generally preferred before him [Shakespeare], yet the age wherein he lived, which had contemporaries with him Fletcher and Jonson, never equalled them to him in their esteem; and in the last king's court, when Ben's reputation was highest, Sir John Suckling, and with him the greater part of the courtiers, set our Shakespeare far above him.

Dryden said he admired Jonson – for his versification, his diction, his classical correctness – but that he loved Shakespeare:

> He was the man who of all modern, and perhaps ancient poets, had the largest and most comprehensive soul. All the images of Nature were still present to him, and he drew them, not laboriously, but luckily . . . Those who accuse him to have wanted learning, give him the greater commendation: he was naturally learned; he needed not the spectacles of books to read Nature; he looked inwards, and found her there.

Thus Dryden continued and elaborated the commonplace of Shakespeare as child of nature, and in his positive moments he was if anything even more enthusiastic in his praise than was his neoclassical forebear Ben Jonson. However, both in this essay and elsewhere, Dryden could be exceedingly critical of what neoclassical theory regarded as Shakespeare's faults. Perhaps the best way to define Dryden's contradictory relation to Shakespeare would be to say that he began the trend which was gradually to transform Shakespeare's image and interpretation in the eighteenth century: Shakespeare moved from being the least of three classic English playwrights of the era Dryden referred to as 'the last Age' to pre-eminence among them.

Dryden's Preface to his adaptation of *Troilus and Cressida* (1679) might be taken as a typical example of his mixed attitude. There Dryden suggests that Shakespeare was England's Aeschylus – not necessarily its leading tragedian, but a great one who could be improved through adaptation. Aeschylus himself had been criticized by Quintilian for his obscurity of phrase, and Dryden believes Shakespeare has similar problems; the essay, of course, is a justification for his own adaptation of *Troilus and Cressida*, and he goes on to explain the deficiencies of language and dramatic construction that he has been forced to alter from the original to conform to his own age's sense of decorum and art.

In his explanation of the neoclassical concept of tragedy, Dryden had reason to refer to the earlier work on this subject by Thomas Rymer, who appears to be second only to Dryden in his influence on late seventeenth-century critical opinion. But where Dryden equivocated about Shakespeare, Rymer was consistently critical of Shakespeare for his failure to follow decorum and the three dramatic unities (time, place, action) of neoclassical critical theory. His 1693 critical essay *A Short View of Tragedy* illustrates the extent to which English culture had been transformed in less than a century. Rymer centres his remarks on *Othello*, a play which had survived changes in taste to remain a favourite of the first and second Caroline epochs. But for this much admired late seventeenth-century neoclassical critic the play had simply become aesthetically incomprehensible. Rymer found *Othello* wanting in just about every category of analysis of Aristotle's *Poetics*. Rymer's tone, as Brian Vickers remarked, is peculiar, almost as if Rymer were personally insulted,[2] and a reader of today can easily intuit the racism of Rymer's reactions to Othello's sexual relations with a white woman. Rymer embodied what many of today's cultural theorists see as the dark underside of the Enlightenment, illustrating the closed, dogmatic forms of thought that could be produced in the name of universal Reason, the unquestioned assumptions of cultural, racial, and male superiority which many believed were the unprejudiced outcome of the new rationality. Rymer was simply the most rigorous practitioner of the new critical paradigm which had been created in the Restoration and continued into the next century: a neoclassicism produced by the conjuncture of forces I have been sketching and which, taken in all, continued to assume and even depend on Shakespeare's high status in developing histories of English literature. However, particularly in the first third of the eighteenth century, Shakespeare's 'faults' received sustained attention from critics, so that it was Rymer's more critical estimate of Shakespeare rather than Dryden's mixed but often positive evaluation that dominated critical writing. But the severe tone of much of the censure was misleading. As the object of such attention in coffee-house conversations and new cultural organs like *The Spectator* and *The Tatler*, Shakespeare was constructed as a literary classic – and an English figure to set beside those of the French and of the Ancients themselves. He soon found defenders. According to Michael Dobson's study of the evolution of Shakespeare's reputation from 1660–1769, it was through a series of steps over several decades of the eighteenth century that Shakespeare began to be seen as England's greatest poet, and one to be compared with any the world had produced. All this took place through a complex, uneven cultural process, much of which continued to adhere to a framework of neoclassical critical assumptions. But beginning in the middle decades of the eighteenth century, neoclassical strictures loosened, and more importance was granted to the role of genius and nature, as Shakespeare's reputation began its ascent to apotheosis.

Shakespeare's status as a classical English writer in the eighteenth century was embodied in a series of critically annotated editions of his work, beginning with Nicolas Rowe's 1709 edition, the first which went beyond reprinting the Folio, using some quarto editions to supplement the text (see also chapter 2, The Reproduction of Shakespeare's Texts, by Barbara A. Mowat). These halting scholarly beginnings were greatly advanced by Lewis Theobald's edition (1733), the first systematic and 'modern' attempt at editing the plays, and one whose introductory essay is an encomium of Shakespeare as a wondrous poet of multiple dimensions and excellencies – a perfect example of the more approving attitudes towards Shakespeare which developed as the century progressed. The tradition culminates in the 1790 edition of Edmond Malone, which as Margreta de Grazia argued in *Shakespeare Verbatim*, establishes for Shakespeare the essential components of the post-Enlightenment 'author': stable texts, an established chronology of composition, a critical life of the author, transhistorical subjectivity and value, and transparent, single-levelled meaning.

Of the numerous editions of Shakespeare's works from 1709 to 1790, however, the most critically consequential was the 1765 edition of Samuel Johnson, with its Preface which synthesized and expressed in a celebrated Augustan prose style the new, moderate English neoclassicism that the evolution of taste and opinion over the course of several decades of the Age of Reason had produced. Following a developing trend, for example, Johnson abandons the earlier practice of criticizing Shakespeare for not adhering to the 'three unities' of neoclassical tragic theory, instead praising *Hamlet*, to take a crucial instance, as Shakespeare's greatest triumph in dramatic 'variety'. Instead of taking Shakespeare to task for mixing the comic and the tragic, as Rymer and others had done, Johnson praises Shakespeare's skill in composing scenes 'diversified with merriment and solemnity; with merriment that includes judicious and instructive observations, and solemnity not strained by poetical violence above the natural sentiments of man'.

Above all else, however, Johnson's criticism of Shakespeare is marked by the supreme self-confidence of one able to follow Shakespeare's artistry to regions unexplored in received neoclassical theory yet to judge it coolly when it fails to live up to the standards of Enlightenment taste. 'The poet is accused of having shewn little regard to poetical justice', he writes of *Hamlet*,

> and may be charged with equal neglect of poetical probability. The apparition left the regions of the dead to little purpose, the revenge which he demands is not obtained but by the death of him that was required to take it; and the gratification which would arise from the destruction of an usurper and a murderer is abated by the untimely death of Ophelia, the young, the beautiful, the harmless, and the pious.

This stance of disinterested rationality, with its judicial attitude towards the texts, was of course not only Johnson's – he is merely the most assured practitioner of the method and requisite tone – but that of the age as a whole in discussing the figure who had become by the end of the century the uncontested national poet. His new pre-eminence was underpinned by the notions of universal and unchanging rationality that our own age has subjected to intense critical scrutiny, but which for the Enlightenment entitled every gentleman to discuss literature. The list of Augustan essayists, novelists, playwrights, and men of letters who did so is impressive. A few women – Charlotte Lennox, Elizabeth Montague, and Elizabeth Griffith were the most prominent examples – were admitted into the discussion as well. If the criticism of this age must now seem anachronistic and even tedious in the assuredness with which it adopts what appear to be empty banalities as its bedrock principles, it remains impressive as a cultural practice which – its class, gender, and racial biases notwithstanding – was a crucial forerunner to all subsequent forms of democracy.

It was in the eighteenth century as well that Shakespeare's works first began to have a significant impact outside Britain. Shakespeare became not just an English author but a European one. The crucial first step of this development came through the flowering of German culture in the second half of the century.

Shakespeare had been introduced to an international audience earlier, by the great French *philosophe* Voltaire, in his 1733 *Philosophical Letters*, a report to a curious Continental readership on the startling civil society that had emerged in post-Restoration, parliamentarian, and capitalist England. Voltaire himself was a popular tragic playwright in France for whom the neoclassical rules and unities were the *sine qua non* of rational dramatic practice. Accordingly, he found Shakespeare 'a fecund genius, full of vigour, ranging from simple naturalness to the sublime, without the least glimmer of taste or the slightest knowledge of the rules'.[3]

Only a few years later in Germany, however, a new sensibility was arising that questioned Voltaire's assumptions and found in Shakespeare precisely the foil it needed to a French neoclassicism which it regarded as stifling and rigid. Shakespeare, wrote the German critic and playwright Gotthold Ephraim Lessing in 1767, is a less philosophical playwright than Voltaire, but he is a more poetical one whose ghost in *Hamlet* is not merely a dramatic device but a character who makes the audience believe in ghosts, even in an enlightened age.[4] This identification of Shakespeare with a restored sense of enchantment in a disenchanted, post-Enlightenment world is one of the clearest eighteenth-century examples of how Shakespeare was reinterpreted as an embodiment of a new aesthetic destined to restructure the perception and consumption of all subsequent forms of art. We associate these late Enlightenment ideas with the romantic movement which they led to, and literary history commonly identifies Germany as the cradle of European romanticism. However, it is Shakespeare who, even in Germany, is the key figure of the transnational movement. It is around discussion of his work that a new aesthetic emerges in marked opposition to neoclassicism. One of the key documents of this complex movement was from an author who styled himself a classicist but whom the non-German world has insisted on seeing as a consummate romantic pioneer, Johann Wolfgang von Goethe. In his 1795 autobiographical novel *Wilhelm Meister's Apprenticeship*, Goethe inserted a meditation on *Hamlet* which is still perhaps the most influential interpretation of the play ever penned, and while it has been (perhaps justly) pilloried throughout the twentieth century for its sentimentality and one-sidedness, it embodied new ways of reading Shakespearian texts which, in their essentials, are still in place. The (already) famous inconsistencies of *Hamlet*, Goethe's Wilhelm argues, are not to be used as evidence in a judicial inquiry in search of Shakespeare's 'faults', à la Johnson, Voltaire, and many other eighteenth-century critics; instead, Wilhelm assumes that if common-sense rationality finds *Hamlet* wanting, the fault is not in *Hamlet* but in common-sense rationality. A work of art like Shakespeare's great drama has its own rules and rationality, and the critic's job is not to measure the art-work on a Procrustean bed of supposed universal artistic norms, but to find instead the unique organic unity of true art. What many earlier critics saw as inconsistencies, Wilhelm took as clues to the play's portrait of 'a lovely, pure, noble and highly moral being, without the strength of mind which forms a hero, [who] sinks beneath a load which it cannot bear and must not renounce'. The key to the art-work that is *Hamlet*, in other words, is the would-be artist Hamlet, alienated and trapped in a cruel world. The romantic relationship between the aesthetic and the hostile world in which it is encased has been invented, along with a quasi-religious understanding of art as holding the deepest truths about the nature of reality itself. Shakespeare is both instance of and figure for this epochal development, the very epitome of the new conceptions of art, beauty, and the sublime which had been developing in the late Enlightenment and which crystallized in German and then European romanticism. It was a decisive turn against the aesthetics of French neoclassicism of which Voltaire was a late, relatively enlightened proponent.

Germany's celebrated translator of the Shakespeare who became a classic of German literature was August Wilhelm Schlegel, and he elaborated the new sensibility into a treatment of Shakespeare's works far more developed than any contemporaneous criticism of Shakespeare in England. His example clearly helped inspire Coleridge's highly influential commentaries on Shakespeare in England as well. Later nineteenth-century German criticism of Shakespeare, however, was decisively influenced by Hegelian philosophy, especially in Germany's nineteenth-century universities, pioneers of Western academic professionalism. Hegel was less important for anything he specifically said about the individual plays than for his systematizing synthesis of his day's commonplaces about tragedy, subjectivity, the Renaissance, and modernity. It was Hegel, for example, who wrote, 'to genuine *tragic* action it is essential that the principle of *individual* freedom and independence, or at least that of self-determination, the will to find in the self the free cause and source of the personal act and its consequences, should already have been aroused', and he believed that this was the explanation why tragedy had arisen only in the West.[5] These ideas and others like them entered the discussion of Shakespeare and the Renaissance more generally in several nations, whether in the influential generalizations on the Italian Renaissance by Jacob Burckhardt, the theories of Nietzsche on tragedy, Karl Marx's insights into Shakespearian themes, or A. C. Bradley's ideas of the tragic. Two Hegelian German professors of the mid-nineteenth century, Hermann

Ulrici and G. G. Gervinus, produced massive philosophizing surveys of Shakespeare's complete works that remain impressive monuments to nine-teenth-century ideas of Shakespeare as an inaugurator of modernity. Gervinus, the more secular, was especially influential in late nineteenth-century Britain and the USA, praised by the seminal twentieth-century modernist critic of Shakespeare, G. Wilson Knight as a formidable influence on his early enthusiasm for Shakespeare.[6]

The praise of Shakespeare came later to France than it did elsewhere in Europe, but in Stendhal and Victor Hugo Shakespeare found cogent and influen-tial champions who helped establish Shakespeare as a classic of world literature in France. Stendhal in his 1823–5 pamphlets *Racine et Shakespeare*, then Hugo in his manifesto, the preface to his drama *Cromwell* (1827), championed Shakespeare as a model for nineteenth-century French drama. Hugo returned to the subject at length in his 1864 *William Shakespeare*.

In the Britain of the Age of Romanticism, the praise of Shakespeare, reinvig-orated by the foreign appreciation, reached new levels of critical encomium. Samuel Taylor Coleridge's sojourn in Germany and reading in German litera-ture had a profound impact on his highly influential lectures and writings on Shakespeare, which helped raise Shakespeare's prestige even beyond its late eighteenth-century heights. Not only was Shakespeare the great national poet, but Shakespeare for Coleridge and the new romantic sensibility was 'himself a nature humanized, a genial understanding directing self-consciously a power and an implicit wisdom deeper than consciousness'.[7] Taking as his target a century or more of neoclassical censures and echoing the German romantics, Coleridge asserted that far from obscuring his beauties in formal mistakes and careless judgements, Shakespeare's judgement was equal to his genius, and the forms of his plays were unique, organic embodiments of the highest aesthetic and philosophical perceptions. With such views Coleridge helped fix the new understanding of Shakespeare that dominated the nineteenth and twentieth cen-turies: Shakespeare as a supreme artist of the imagination whose massive achievement challenges our comprehension rather than calls forth censure. Coleridge, Jonathan Bate has argued, was a synthesizer of theoretical German romanticism and a native English empiricism whose originality consists precisely in his application of German ideas to the details and minutiae of Shakespeare's plays.[8] However we decide the tangled issue of his indebtedness, there can be little doubt that Coleridge was the most pretigious and influential enunciator of the new Romantic paradigm in nineteenth-century Britain.

It was the romantic Shakespeare that was taken up across the Atlantic as a self-conscious American literature began to form in the New England transcenden-talist movement. Shakespeare became a major topic for such outstanding figures as Ralph Waldo Emerson, Herman Melville, Mark Twain, and many others. In addition, an American Shakespeare scholarship began to take part in a develop-ing international discussion. The later nineteenth century saw the development of scores of Shakespeare societies in both the United States and in Britain. These were private groups of amateur Shakespeare devotees who typically met once or more a month to read aloud, and sometimes to discuss, a series of Shakespeare plays. The more serious of these laid much of the foundation for a later academic Shakespeare scholarship, and their popularity testifies to the degree to which familiarity with Shakespeare had permeated the public sphere. Even more than in the eighteenth century, Shakespeare was a cultural icon to be contested from different political, national, and even gender perspectives.

While praise for Shakespeare's ability to create vivid dramatic characters can be traced back as far as the 1664 remarks of Margaret Cavendish, a new Enlightenment interest in psychology and aesthetics was evident in Samuel Johnson's attention to Shakespeare's characters and in such pioneering studies as the 1774 *A Philosophical Analysis and Illustration of Some of Shakespeare's Remarkable Characters* by William Richardson, *Remarks on Some of the Characters of Shakespeare* (1785) by Thomas Whateley, and the inimitable *An Essay on the Dramatic Character of Sir John Falstaff* (1777) by Maurice Morgann. Morgann's work is a Shandean disquisition with many links to Fielding's and Sterne's comic novels, but it is perhaps the first work of criticism to claim for a Shakespeare character the kind of life-like transcendence of its fictional context that is associated with the critics of the nineteenth century.

As the nineteenth century developed, the interest in Shakespeare's characters inherited from the previous century took a romantic turn to become a crucial part of the romantic emphasis on the personal, subjective, and individual, eventually even finding its way into later nineteenth-century discussions of realism. Character criticism is perhaps the best known of nineteenth-century approaches to Shakespeare, and while Coleridge's example is seminal and early, it comes down to us highly decontextualized in editions which extract from larger works and conceal much of Coleridge's conservative political agenda. In addition, Coleridge discussed in detail only eight plays, whereas William Hazlitt surveyed all Shakespeare's works in *Characters of Shakespeare's Plays* (1817), one of the most accomplished and ground-breaking works of nineteenth-century Shakespeare criticism. Hazlitt was explicit where Coleridge was coy in defining his general critical indebtedness to Schlegel, and he was judicious in identifying Samuel Johnson as the English interpreter of Shakespeare whom it was necessary to supersede. Hazlitt clearly was building on his predecessors Schlegel and Coleridge, but he was often strikingly original. Hazlitt, for example, was the first critic to say openly that between Prince Hal and Falstaff, Falstaff 'is the better man of the two'. And it was Hazlitt who wrote of *Hamlet*, 'It is *we* who are Hamlet.' But the romantic discourse on Shakespeare had many interpreters; Charles Lamb, famous for his argument that the richness of Shakespearian drama is inevitably impoverished by stage performance, and Thomas de Quincey, author of the 1823 essay, 'On the Knocking at the Gate in *Macbeth*', were influential voices from the romantic era.

The British Shakespeare criticism of the second half of the nineteenth century has often seemed a straightforward development of the romantic impulses of the early years of the century, but there were distinct new voices and methods as well. The Victorian era underwent a significant cultural divide as opinions varied over how to apply the era's notable scientific and technical advances within the literary sphere. For some a new cultural iconoclasm developed, while elsewhere the deification of Shakespeare continued unabated. A new attention to details, and a consequent lengthening of critical studies resulted.

The most irreverent voice in these debates was that of George Bernard Shaw, who tirelessly argued that after Ibsen, Shakespeare must henceforth be seen as antiquated, even aesthetically reactionary, part of the baggage of tradition-minded England that would need to be set aside as the new age of reform and rationality unfolded.[9]

From the other side of the developing Victorian divide between science and tradition, A. C. Swinburne took aim in the name of art and intuition against the scientistic versification analyses of Shakespeare promoted by Frederick James Furnivall and F. G. Fleay in a book-length study of Shakespeare's versification, *A Study of Shakespeare* (1880). Swinburne approached the Shakespeare texts with a reverence which testified to the effects of the romantic revolution in the understanding of Shakespeare in Britain – and increasingly the world. For Swinburne, not only had Shakespeare's works become classics beyond criticism, but they represented the very mystery of the universe destined never to be grasped by an imperializing science. Shakespeare, wrote Swinburne, borrowing his figure from Hugo, was an ocean, but one which would always elude attempts to systematize and measure it.[10]

Edward Dowden's *Shakspere: A Critical Study of His Mind and Art* (1875) represented another Victorian attempt systematically to define Shakespeare's greatness, but Dowden had recourse to a speculative spiritual biography, attempting to portray the great soul behind the great works of Shakespeare. Adopting and developing suggestions from Gervinus, he divided Shakespeare's life and works into four periods – apprenticeship ('in the workshop'), first worldly success ('in the world'), the tragic period ('in the depths'), and finally the serene late middle age of the late plays ('on the heights'). This synthesis of several trends of the nineteenth century produced a cultural monument which has been often ridiculed in the twentieth century but which remains an intensely imagined embodiment of late Victorian aestheticism and narrativization. The celebrated fictional discussion of *Hamlet* in Joyce's *Ulysses*, for example, would have been impossible without Dowden.

A. C. Bradley's 1904 *Shakespearean Tragedy* stands as another grand synthesis of several of these nineteenth-century currents and one which has proved even more durable than Dowden's. Bradley borrowed the character-analysis methods of Coleridge and Hazlitt and developed them in greater detail than ever before. Taking Coleridge one step further, his discussions of character were in turn intermingled with philosophical inquiries from Aristotle and Hegel on the nature of human meaning and tragedy. In comparison with the German Hegelians especially, however, Bradley's discussions of the plays reflected a *fin-de-siècle* aestheticism, a rejection of both neoclassical and Hegelian moralizing in favour of a view of the plays as idealizing explorations of human extremes not always subject to ordinary moral strictures. Yet this lack of moralizing is relative, not absolute, for Bradley tended to read the tragedies at another level as structured by a virtually metaphysical clash of good against evil, and he tended to understand tragic suffering as necessary to some greater good.

At yet another level of his complexly layered synthesis, Bradley was influenced by the aesthetic realism of the great novels and dramas of the late nineteenth century. It was primarily through him that the assumption passed into Shakespeare criticism that behind the imperfectly transparent media of language and dramatic action could be intuited a solid reality to be reconstructed by the astute critic. The result was the notorious series of speculations – for example, on where Hamlet was when his father died, or on where Lear had planned to live before Cordelia's silence – that L. C. Knights had such sport with in his 'How Many Children Had Lady Macbeth?' (1933). But Bradley has survived Knights' critique, and he appears likely to survive into a twenty-first century still in search of an elusive Shakespearian meaning always just ahead of us – because we ourselves create it in a complex cultural process as we move ahead into history, our eyes always fixed, as Walter Benjamin said, on what we have just passed.

Notes

1. Gary Taylor, *Reinventing Shakespeare: A Cultural History from the Restoration to the Present* (New York: Weidenfeld and Nicolson, 1989), p. 10.

2. Brian Vickers, Introduction, *Shakespeare: The Critical Heritage*, vol. II: 1693–1733 (London: Routledge and Kegan Paul, 1974), p. 2.

3. Voltaire, *Philosophical Letters*, trans. Ernest Dilworth (New York: Bobbs-Merrill, 1961), p. 85.

4. Gotthold Ephraim Lessing, *Hamburgische Dramaturgie*, Letters 11 (5 June 1767) and 12 (9 June 1767), (Stuttgart: Verlag, 1958), pp. 42–53.

5. G. F. W. Hegel, *The Philosophy of Fine Art*, trans. R. P. B. Osmaston (London, G. Bell, 1920), vol. IV, 248–348.

6. G. Wilson Knight, *Neglected Powers: Essays on Nineteenth- and Twentieth-Century Literature* (New York: Barnes and Noble, 1971), p. 9.

7. Samuel Taylor Coleridge, *Coleridge's Shakespearean Criticism*, 2 vols., ed. T. M. Raysor (Cambridge, Mass.: Harvard University Press, 1930), I, 198.

8. Jonathan Bate, *Shakespeare and the English Romantic Imagination* (Oxford: Clarendon Press, 1986), pp. 12–14.

9. G. Bernard Shaw, *Shaw on Shakespeare: An Anthology of Bernard Shaw's Writings on the Plays and Production of Shakespeare*, ed. Edwin Wilson (New York: Dutton, 1961). Most of the writings date from the 1890s.

10. Algernon Charles Swinburne, *A Study of Shakespeare* (1880; rpt New York: AMS Press, 1965), p. 2.

Reading list

Bate, Jonathan, *Shakespeare and the English Romantic Imagination* (Oxford: Clarendon Press, 1986).

Bate, Jonathan, ed., *The Romantics on Shakespeare* (Harmondsworth: Penguin, 1992).

Bristol, Michael D., *Shakespeare's America: America's Shakespeare* (London: Routledge, 1990).

de Grazia, Margreta, *Shakespeare Verbatim: The Reproduction of Authenticity and the Apparatus of 1790* (Oxford: Clarendon Press, 1991).

Dobson, Michael, *The Making of the National Poet: Shakespeare, Adaptation and Authorship, 1660–1769* (Oxford: Clarendon Press, 1992).

Dunn, Esther Cloudman, *Shakespeare in America* (New York: Macmillan, 1939).

Eastman, Arthur M., *A Short History of Shakespearian Criticism* (New York: Random House, 1968).

Grady, Hugh, *The Modernist Shakespeare: Critical Texts in a Material World* (Oxford: Clarendon Press, 1991).

Gundolf, Friedrich, *Shakespeare und der Deutsche Geist* (Berlin: Georg Bonde, 1914).

Haines, C. M., *Shakespeare in France: Criticism, Voltaire to Victor Hugo* (London: Oxford University Press, 1925).

Klein, Holger and Jean-Marie Maguin, eds., *Shakespeare in France. Shakespeare Yearbook* 5 (Lewiston, N.Y.: Mellen Press, 1995).

Munro, John, ed., *The Shakespeare Allusion Book: A Collection of Allusions to Shakespeare from 1591 to 1700*, 2 vols. (1909; rpt Freeport, N.Y.: Books for Libraries, 1970).

Pascal, R., ed., *Shakespeare in Germany, 1740–1815* (Cambridge University Press, 1937).

Taylor, Gary, *Reinventing Shakespeare: A Cultural History from the Restoration to the Present* (New York: Weidenfield and Nicolson, 1989).

Vickers, Brian, ed., *Shakespeare: The Critical Heritage*, 6 vols. (London: Routledge and Kegan Paul, 1974–81).

18

R. S. WHITE

Shakespeare criticism in the twentieth century

In 1961 a Polish critic, Jan Kott, published a book which, when translated into English under the title *Shakespeare Our Contemporary* (1964), seemed to herald a brave new world of Shakespearian study. With a preface by Peter Brook, the most daring theatre director of the time, it struck a note which led away from tradition into uncharted but exciting 'contemporary' waters. Now it seems dated and influenced by the theatre of Samuel Beckett, but it remains true that as an 'event', Kott's book was a symptom of change in the 1960s. Attempting to explain the changes, Hugh Grady wrote in 1991 of Shakespeare criticism, 'Around 1970 . . . doubtless under the impact of the Vietnam era and the student insurgency which marked the late Sixties and early Seventies in both American and British universities – a fundamental change begins to occur: a paradigm crisis, usually the preliminary stage of a paradigm shift, can be observed to begin.' However, there are as many continuities as discontinuities between 'modernism' and 'post-modernism', which call into question Grady's notion. We should avoid the all too seductive course of denying any significance to earlier critics and celebrating a new maturity in Shakespearian criticism, or alternatively of berating theory-driven criticism and returning nostalgically to an earlier, cosy consensus. This is not to deny the possibility of a paradigm crisis or shift having occurred as Grady suggests, but I leave the question open.

Certainly there have been waves of change in the way that Shakespeare is treated. If I had been writing this chapter in about 1970, I would have given a roll-call of individual critics, indicating 'who's in, who's out', implying a general progress in the field and predicting only incremental changes in the future. I would have been able to assume a general reverence for Shakespeare, and for the sanctity of his texts as stable and identifiable artifacts. There would have been little need to address theoretical or ideological groupings amongst critics or, with some exceptions, to talk about 'schools'. Most significantly of all, I would not have needed to justify the enterprise of writing a history of Shakespearian criticism, or to address theoretical challenges to the study of Shakespeare.

Things would have been very different if I had been writing in 1985. With the rise of literary theory and cultural studies, the very enterprise was 'problematized', requiring a defensive tone, an awareness of warring factions within Shakespeare studies, and an uneasy acknowledgement that the texts of

Shakespeare might not survive in importance into the twenty-first century. A flavour of this bristling period emerges from collections like *Alternative Shakespeares*, edited by John Drakakis (1985), *Political Shakespeare*, edited by Jonathan Dollimore and Alan Sinfield (1985), Peter Erikson's *Patriarchal Structures in Shakespeare's Drama* (1985), and *The Shakespeare Myth*, edited by Graham Holderness (1988). Even the notion of 'the text' of a play has been eroded by textual critics and theatrical practice. *The Division of the Kingdoms: Shakespeare's Two Versions of 'King Lear'*, edited by Gary Taylor and Michael Warren (1983), argued that Shakespeare, far from never blotting a line, painstakingly revised his plays for different occasions. Stephen Orgel in an article 'The Authentic Shakespeare' argues that there is no such thing as 'the authentic Shakespeare', either in word or spirit.[1] Moreover, sociological approaches were breaking down any binary distinction between 'high' and 'low' culture – everything is equally interesting as a social signifying system, and no place of privilege or 'canonical status' was allowed any individual writer. In fact, Roland Barthes had memorably pronounced 'the death of the author', and concepts like individual creativity, universality, and genius were derided. From another direction, the assault on Shakespeare seemed devastating. Cultural studies proclaimed that the centrality of Shakespeare in school syllabuses ('the canon') and theatrical repertoires was a ruling-class conspiracy intended to create populations in the British Commonwealth who would be docile to authority and accept the status quo by naturalizing a writer who represented tradition and orthodoxy. Some feminists mounted a similar argument on gender grounds. Shakespeare was a man who wrote for men, perpetuating a tenacious hold on a patriarchal system that subjugated women, inveterately heterosexual in inclination. Under these and other pressures, it seemed that 'Shakespeare' was in danger of becoming a spent force, and that his works would be unceremoniously jettisoned from schools and universities, as attention turned to more topical issues.

Now, writing in 2000, a different approach again is possible and necessary. Some of the internecine battles were settled or bypassed in a kind of *de facto* way. Cultural studies theorists found it impossible to counter the sheer weight of evidence that Shakespeare is still (or again) overwhelmingly popular, and they accordingly reclaimed him in new guises. In the relatively new and undoubtedly mass media of film and video, the plays were suddenly given wholly new and astonishingly large audiences of young people who, judging from their behaviour at box offices around the world, still find Shakespeare compelling. Baz Luhrmann's *Romeo + Juliet*, Kenneth Branagh's four-hour *Hamlet*, and the 'ficto-biography' *Shakespeare in Love* scripted by Tom Stoppard and Marc Norman have been only the most spectacular successes among many. A whole new field of criticism is opening up, Shakespeare on film.[2] Any question of the 'British conspiracy' was refuted by the continuing work of scholars and critics in nations which have no vested interest in the British Empire: Russia, Germany, Japan, and even in 'post-colonial' countries, like the USA, India, and Australia, expected to be antagonistic to their colonial oppressors. Shakespeare sites are all over the internet, the newest medium to date, some serious in intention, others frivolous, and Shakespeare was hailed on the front cover of *Newsweek* on 23 December 1996:

> Shakespeare Rocks. A Bard for the '90s: Why He's Hot Now. He's gone to Hollywood. He's on the Web. He's got theme parks and teenage fans. How can we miss Shakespeare if he won't go away?

Feminist criticism, by and large, has mellowed from a polemical mission of reading male writers resistantly, to the more descriptive 'gender studies', accepting writers like Shakespeare as open to feminist and gay readings. In this climate, then, it is not necessary to be over-defensive, or for that matter, to attack Shakespeare. Most important of all, if Shakespeare's status amongst critics can shift so rapidly and radically, then his works, although in one sense rooted in Elizabethan England, are in another sense transposable to ever-new cultural and historical contexts.

I should make apologies and admit limitations. Shakespeare has in the twentieth century been performed and studied in many countries and translated into many languages. Germany, India, Russia, and Japan have produced scholars and critics who provide original insight and powerful scholarship. With a few exceptions I have not incorporated their work, largely because of the nature of publishing which leads to the prominence in libraries and bookshops of works by those writing in the English language. I am also avoiding theatrical practitioners and critics such as Bernard Shaw, Bertolt Brecht,[3] and Harley Granville Barker. At the same time, there is a close connection between theatre, criticism, and scholarship as exemplified in the omnivorous interests of successive editors of the journal *Shakespeare Survey*: Allardyce Nicoll, Kenneth Muir, Stanley Wells, and Peter Holland.

What definitely grew after 1970 was a new professionalism in literary scholarship in general, which encouraged tolerance of many views rather than rancorous disagreement or elitism. With the proliferation of PhD theses and thousands of books and articles, there is no longer room for any 'party line', least of all one asserting universality and conservative values. Plurality and diversity have challenged and replaced 'ruling class' agreements. The broadening of the syllabus was both a part of this change and a facilitating agency for it. In this climate some older critics now seem more important and influential than others.

A. C. Bradley: moral philosophy and the dramatic poem

The roots of twentieth-century criticism lay in the nineteenth. S. T. Coleridge and A. W. Schlegel stressed the philosophical, metaphysical, and poetic qualities of Shakespeare, and the later critic who developed these aspects was A. C. Bradley[4] (see also chapter 17, Shakespeare Criticism, 1600–1900, by Hugh

Grady). The rise of Shakespeare criticism as the 'industry' we know today was linked to the accommodation of English literature as a university subject at the turn of the century, and the first bulky figure we encounter in this context is Bradley.[5] His *Shakespearian Tragedy* (1904) has long been acknowledged as the first serious and sustained work of academic literary criticism that matters. Bradley was a Scottish rationalist who was uncomfortable with the high anglicanism of Oxford and steadily moved up Britain, first to Liverpool and then to Glasgow, as if distancing himself from centres of conformity. His secularism, refusal to accept received dogma, and a capacity always to question and explore with an open mind are qualities that still emerge from his writing. He is fascinated by the 'mystery' of Shakespeare's plays, their apparent exfoliating from some inner principle of growth (Coleridge's 'organic unity' or Leavis's 'deep centre'). But being a philosopher and the brother of metaphysician F. H. Bradley, he probed to find some explanation for the mystery, something that links the surface factuality and realism of Shakespeare's plays with their inferred mythological meanings and conceptual significance.[6] It is a shame for Bradley that the most easily visible aspect of his contribution, respectively taken up and criticized by successors, was characterization, for it is only a part of his more general interest in the plays as unique structures with their own systems of implied thought, philosophical unity, and stylistic and linguistic expressiveness. In his general view of tragedy Bradley anticipates existentialism. He posits a metaphysical 'system or order', itself 'vast and complex', which is external to human action and which can loosely be called 'fate'. He sees this order as a 'blank necessity, totally regardless alike of human weal and of the difference between good and evil or right and wrong' (p. 30). Evil, such as Iago's, is of special fascination to Bradley, as it may have been to Shakespeare, for its very inexplicability. Humans act within this order, and in doing so create their own individual destinies, which makes the centre of human tragedy 'action issuing from character' (what some now call 'agency'). Assertion of individuality is usually ineffectual or catastrophic because each of Shakespeare's exemplary figures has a one-sidedness or individual predisposition which stems from good qualities but is, when tested, fatally incapacitating, for each a 'tragic trait which is also his greatness'. Bradley suggests that in witnessing the struggle between the flawed individual and larger circumstances, 'we do not judge', we 'watch what is' (p. 30). In their common debt to Hegel we find a surprising link between Bradley and his contemporary, Karl Marx, another great reader of Shakespeare.[7]

Bradley also writes on 'construction' of plays, the ways they are put together, as distinct from the 'substance of tragedy' which is his metaphysic. Bradley may well have agreed with Herbert Marcuse's epigram 'The medium is the message', for he sees Shakespeare as a 'conscious artist' (p. 70) who often in a calculated way sins against 'art' to achieve some effect. Under the head of construction, Bradley includes, 'for example, Shakespeare's methods of characterization, his language, his versification, the construction of his plots'. Where all the general structural considerations intersect with the philosophical is perhaps in

Shakespeare's creation of dramatic 'atmosphere', and it is here, arguably, that Bradley is at his strongest and most unique, showing that in a play by Shakespeare the parts are gathered into an atmospheric whole which is infinitely greater than its constituent parts. Language, poetry, and imagery are central to this phenomenon. His chapter on *Macbeth*, arguably the most powerful in *Shakespearian Tragedy*, is in itself a sustained prose poem which synthesizes the various strands of Bradley's approach into a rhythmic whole.

Bradley saw each play as a 'dramatic poem' (he calls *King Lear* Shakespeare's 'greatest poem' (p. 330)), subsuming characterization and imagery under a poetic whole that transcends its parts. So did T. S. Eliot (whose weighty influence and idiosyncratic vocabulary hung like a dark cloud over criticism for many decades), F. R. Leavis and the *Scrutiny* school (including its best Shakespearian, James Smith), although Bradley was never so judgemental and morally dismissive as Eliot or Leavis. Many American critics like Maynard Mack, Clifford Leech, Harold Bloom, and others have followed. Stanley Cavell is a self-consciously philosophical critic, although of a more sceptical school than Bradley. British critics who continue to share an affinity with Bradley's philosophical, formal, and poetic approach are G. K. Hunter and Barbara Everett (*Young Hamlet: Essays on Shakespeare's Tragedies* (1989)), while Emrys Jones in *Scenic Form in Shakespeare* (1971) has extended the study of structure into Shakespeare's mastery of the unit of the scene, and his use of 'two-part structure' in plays.

But Bradley's truest successor was G. Wilson Knight, whose output spans the whole of the mid-century. Knight's book on tragedy, *The Wheel of Fire* (1930), was a brilliant successor to Bradley's vivid impressionism, perhaps overemphasizing Christian readings in a way that the sceptical Bradley avoided. *The Crown of Life* (1947) gave critical respectability to Shakespeare's late plays, the romances. Knight was against judgemental 'criticism' in the spirit of Eliot and Leavis, and all for 'interpretation' which seeks to find meaning in every line and to 'recreate' Shakespeare. He wrote of each play as 'a visionary unit bound to obey none but its own self-imposed laws' which often lead us imaginatively into 'paradox and unreason'.[8] The play is an 'extended metaphor' which has a 'soul-life' and is made up of 'poetic symbolism'. With this rhetoric, it is not surprising that one of Knight's books on the 'Final Plays' is entitled *Myth and Miracle*. He accepts Bradley's assumptions about 'dramatic poems', but his approach is more intuitive where Bradley is rational, and he is influenced by the developing discipline of cultural anthropology. Northrop Frye, particularly in *Anatomy of Criticism: Four Essays* (1957), extended this mythopoeic and archetypal approach well beyond the texts of Shakespeare, and the approach had its heyday in the 1960s.

William Empson and radical ambivalence

A quite different, antithetical approach to Shakespeare developed alongside 'the line of Coleridge and Bradley'. William Hazlitt deserves credit as the Romantic precursor of resistant and radical readings of Shakespeare.[9] A nonconformist republican, he challenged contemporary high anglicans like Coleridge in his onslaughts on Shakespeare's kings as dissolute, power-hungry, and idle. Hazlitt also demonstrated ways of undermining notions of stable characterization in drama, even though his major work was entitled *Characters of Shakespear's Plays*. He talks of 'mixed motives' and shows in his theatre criticism that actors could interpret roles in politically charged ways. The actor he most admired, Edmund Kean, consistently radicalized plays, whereas others like John Philip Kemble, Hazlitt points out, could highlight conservative elements. Taken as a whole, his body of Shakespearian criticism constantly avoids universalism and metaphysical explanations, and instead stresses that plays can be read and performed in radically different ways.

Hazlitt's natural successor in the twentieth century is William Empson, who maintained a congenitally sceptical point of view encapsulated in the word 'ambiguity'. Writing at a time when literary study was seeking to give itself credentials as a science, and when the theory of relativity dominated physics, Empson used ambiguity as a quasi-scientific tool of analysis. His book, *Seven Types of Ambiguity* (1930), is one which now matters less for its local insights and perceptions than for its overall argument that the richness of Shakespeare's poetry and drama lies in multi-dimensionality and refusal to yield up single meanings. His 'first kind of ambiguity' is encapsulated in the statement that 'The fundamental situation, whether it deserves to be called ambiguous or not, is that a word or grammatical structure is effective in several ways at once' (p. 2), and he memorably analyses the line in Sonnet 73, 'Bare ruined choirs where late the sweet birds sang', to establish that 'the machinations of ambiguity are among the very roots of poetry' (p. 3). "'Ambiguity'", Empson argues, 'itself can mean an indecision as to what you mean, an intention to mean several things, a probability that one or other or both of two things has been meant, and the fact that a statement has several meanings' (p. 15). In arguing this, he undermined much of the criticism of his own day, which sought to establish unitary meanings, themes, and texts. He anticipated such 'recent' discoveries as 'indeterminacy', *lacunae*, deconstructive techniques, and the surprising phenomenon that through contextual irony the writer may be saying exactly the opposite from what he appears to be saying through his character. Poetry for Empson is interesting language *because* it revels in contradiction, paradox, and multiple ambiguities, embracing ambivalence and unresolvable contradictions.

Many of Empson's examples in *Seven Types* come from Shakespeare and secondarily from the poet who seems linguistically most Shakespearian, John Donne. Similarly, in *The Structure of Complex Words* (1951) we find detailed analysis of multiple ambiguous uses of the word 'honest' in *Othello*, 'dog' in *Timon of Athens*, 'sense' in *Measure for Measure*, and 'fool' in *King Lear*. What emerges as part of the methodology of ambiguity is an emphasis on contextualization: words mean different things in different contexts and from different ideological perspectives, ideas which have been tenets of virtually all criticism since about 1980. Anticipating reader response and reception theory, Empson also contemplates the idea that there will be as many readings as there are readers, whimsically hypothesizing, for example, '4,096 possible movements of thought, with other possibilities' derived from the simple line, 'They that have power to hurt and will do none'.[10] In his analysis of structure, he says, for example, of the *Henry IV* plays, 'I think indeed that the whole Falstaff series needs to be looked at in terms of Dramatic Ambiguity'[11] and those capital letters indicate that he is thinking in terms of general principle.

Empson is always informally happy to leave questions open. The contemporary critics whom he continually berates, John Dover Wilson, E. M. W. Tillyard, Derek Traversi, and, we might add, Lily B. Campbell, are constructed as the dogmatic voices. In Dover Wilson, Falstaff emerges as wholly bad, Henry V as wholly good, while Empson's own account is balanced and ultimately non-judgemental. In an anticipation of deconstruction and cultural materialism, he also suggests why the 'rather royalist critics' should be so sure of themselves:

> . . . Dover Wilson, as I understand, was working on his edition of the Falstaff plays during the Second World War, and felt a natural irritation at any intellectualist fuss against a broad issue of patriotism. He felt that *Henry V* is a very good patriotic play, and the man Henry V is the ideal king, and Falstaff is a ridiculously bad man, and if you can't face that you had better wince away from the whole subject.[12]

Empson's own experience led him to be less parochially patriotic. From 1931 he taught English at Tokyo University, then at the Peking National University in China. During the Second World War he was Chinese editor at the BBC, after which he returned to Peking and taught there from 1947 to 1952. He had no narrow vested interest in English patriotism, and was impatient with those who had and who assumed Shakespeare did. Habits of speculative provisionality and tolerance of ambiguity are evident also in Empson's essay on *Hamlet* in which he canvasses all the approaches up to his time of writing, finding fault with all, but also suggesting interesting half-truths in each:

> We need to step back here, and consider why it is possible for such radically opposed theories to be held by careful readers; it would be trivial merely to jeer at the long history of theories about *Hamlet*, because they bear witness to its peculiar appeal. The only simple view is that the play was constructed so as to leave them open.[13]

His viewpoint allows him to pick up whimsically such intriguing points as that, in allowing Puck to make a girdle round the earth in forty minutes, Shakespeare anticipated one of the twentieth century's technological feats in fuelling the Sputnik satellite to do precisely this. In general, recent literary theorists have found Empson more original than other twentieth-century critics.[14]

At least two books consciously kept ambiguity alive: A. P. Rossiter's *Angel with*

Horns (1961) maintained the existence of 'radical ambivalence' in the history plays, and Norman Rabkin's *Shakespeare and the Common Understanding* (1967) coined the term 'complementarity' to describe the phenomenon, most acutely observed in *A Midsummer Night's Dream*. J. L. Calderwood's methodology of 'metatheatrical criticism', building on Anne Righter's *Shakespeare and the Idea of the Play* (1962), foregrounds statements within the plays, drawing attention to the fact that we are watching a theatrical event. Such an approach implicitly recognizes ambiguity in the status of theatrical experience as both 'real' and unreal.

'New critics' in post-war America, who stress the ahistorical, internal complexity of individual works, employing techniques of close, analytical reading, may acknowledge their debt to I. A. Richards as their leader, but we must remember that its most potent tools of detailed explication were sharpened by his much more tentative and open-minded student, Empson, who so generously dedicated *Complex Words* to his more flat-footed Silenus. Nowadays linguistic and narrative ambiguity is taken for granted in Shakespeare criticism and the result is, at least to my optimistic mind, a state of healthy tolerance of pluralism and diversity in Shakespearian criticism.

L. C. Knights and historicism

While L. C. Knights also practised the kind of close stylistic analysis identified with new criticism, what emerges in retrospect as more significant in his work is the study of texts in their historical context with a decidedly Marxist and materialist orientation. Although he wrote directly on 'Shakespeare's politics' and on the history plays from a historical point of view, his most important book mentions Shakespeare only occasionally. *Drama and Society in the Age of Jonson* (1937) can in many if not most ways be seen as the precursor of new historicism. It is startling to find somebody in 1937 asserting 'the fact that "the materialist interpretation of history" has not yet been pushed far enough' (p. 15), and writing chapters entitled 'Shakespeare and Profit Inflations', 'The Development of Capitalist Enterprise', and 'Social Theory'. The book begins by detailing 'The Inherited Economic Order under Elizabeth' and then from a Marxist viewpoint outlining changes in the Elizabethan and Jacobean economic order: inflation, the growth of a new money market, monopolies in industry, enclosures and the agricultural economic basis, poverty, unemployment, and trade depressions. In this book Knights reveals his contextual approach to literature *via* politics, economics, and history, and he goes on to apply it mainly to Jonson but also to citizen comedy, Dekker, Heywood, and Middleton.

Knights never systematically applied historical foregrounding to Shakespeare but he gives enough hints to suggest that it was always a part of his thinking. His inaugural lecture at Bristol, *Poetry, Politics and the English Tradition* (1953–4) is not only an attack on critics of the 1950s who tried to implicate Shakespeare in order-based conservative political doctrine but a plea for literary critics to use the kind of local, 'history from below' approach being pioneered by Marxist historians like Christopher Hill and later E. P. Thompson. He argues strongly that Shakespeare reveals no political dogma or single doctrine, but that he was inveterately interested in politics as a reflection of the daily relations between men 'in the sphere of public life' (p. 8) – the personal is political, as many said in the sixties. Significantly, the examples he gives of '*concrete* political thinking' (from *Sir Thomas More* and *Coriolanus*) are situations where common people with a genuine grievance challenge the authority of aristocrats who assert the principle of 'order'. Shakespeare is, Knights argues, revealing 'the class basis . . . of patrician "honour"'. From our perspective, it is somewhat odd to see him describe the apparently complacent decade of the 1950s as 'this age of confusion which also shows signs of being an age of radical re-thinking of old problems', a timely reminder that every age has its 'radical' edge.

Knights did not write in a vacuum, since other critics, especially ones like E. E. Stoll and L. L. Schücking, also stressed historical knowledge in interpreting Shakespeare, and they have been followed by Robert Weimann. They anticipated, or opened up, a very rich vein of criticism which dominated the 1980s and '90s, the cross-fertilization of literature and history conceived as a study of the politics of the personal issuing into public conflict and dispute. The line leads through Boris Ford's historically focused and populist *Pelican Guide to English Literature*, and up to Marxists like Margot Heinemann, Terry Eagleton, and Walter Cohen; and to new historicists and cultural materialists.

Psychoanalytical criticism

Literary criticism has always been open to suggestion and ideas from other disciplines such as history, and another fruitful interaction has been with the field of psychoanalysis. This is not surprising since they share a curiosity about human behaviour, identity, and language. Psychoanalysis is another broad approach to Shakespeare which earlier had seemed eccentric and peripheral but which has emerged as an important underpinning of criticism at the end of the century. It is impossible to draw a line between what the plays give to psychologists and what psychologists bring to the plays, since amongst the latter some have generated theories from Shakespeare and then applied them to 'real' people. This is especially true of the founder of modern psychoanalysis, Sigmund Freud.

Freud's central distinction, which has been immensely influential over twentieth-century thought, is between the conscious and controlling mind (the ego) and the normally repressed unconscious (id) driven by desires, fears, and fantasies. The simplest example is the relation of wakeful reality to dream, the subject of Freud's *The Interpretation of Dreams* (1900). Freud concluded that the boundaries between sleep and waking are blurred and that at all times behaviour is governed by the tension between the conscious and unconscious in the mind. Shakespeare is pivotal to the distinction, and it is hard to say whether

Shakespeare created Freud or Freud recreated Shakespeare. There are references to dreams in many plays, from *Richard III* to *The Tempest*, the most sustained obviously being *A Midsummer Night's Dream*, which is not only ripe for
Freudian analysis but may have suggested itself to Freud in formulating his
theory. The so-called oedipal conflict seems to have been observed most clearly
by Freud not in the Greek drama of Oedipus (who killed his father and unwit-
tingly married his mother) but in *Hamlet*. In turn, this approach to Hamlet's
behaviour has become a critical commonplace, proposed by a Freudian critic,
Ernest Jones, in an article first published in *American Journal of Psychology*
(1910) and then popularized by Laurence Olivier's filmed performance (1948).
The so-called Medusa complex was derived from *Macbeth*.[15] Freud is also an
interesting commentator on the myth underlying Bassanio's choice in the trial of
the three caskets in *The Merchant of Venice*. His analysis of humour as a temporary release of normally repressed mental processes informs (and once again may
be influenced by) Shakespearian comedy in general, and such dramatic events as
Titania's love for Bottom metamorphosed into an ass in particular.

Some Freudian critics used the theory to try to psychoanalyse the author.
Edward A. Armstrong in *Shakespeare's Imagination* (1946) studied what is
revealed of Shakespeare's unconscious mind by associations of images which
appear recurrently in clusters, an enterprise anticipated rather crudely by
Caroline Spurgeon in *Shakespeare's Imagery and What it Tells Us* (1935).
Imagery studies as a form of explication began in the Romantic age with a commentary by Walter Whiter who, in 1794, drew on the contemporary theory of
mind, association of ideas. It was most thoroughly explored (not from a psycho-
analytical direction) by Wolfgang Clemen in *The Development of Shakespeare's
Imagery* (1951). C. L. Barber, best known for *Shakespeare's Festive Comedy*
(1959) with its idea that the comedies enact a carnivalesque release of saturnalian, 'holiday' feelings normally repressed,[16] went on to develop a sustained
Freudian approach in *The Whole Journey: Shakespeare's Power of Development*
(co-authored by Richard P. Wheeler, 1986). This subject is by no means closed,
since in 1989 a dozen distinguished Shakespearian critics psychoanalysed many
aspects of Shakespeare's psyche in *Shakespeare's Personality*.[17]

But since the 1950s it has become dubious to commit the 'intentional fallacy'
(make inferences about the author from his works), and a different use of
Freudianism has developed. It suggests that plays are like the human mind, in
having a conscious structure and an unconscious level. The aim is to explicate
the 'hidden content' behind the 'manifest content', just as dreams can be interpreted as stories that reveal some usually repressed meaning: see, for example,
Ruth Nevo, *Shakespeare's Other Language* (1987). It is worth noting that, once
again, William Empson was interested in Freudian theory, and it seems clear that
he was attracted by its reliance on the coexistence of equal and antithetical meanings (conscious and unconscious). In psychoanalysis 'ambivalence' is in fact a

specialist term, indicating an oscillation between desiring one thing and its opposite, or simultaneous attraction and repulsion.

Carl Jung, Freud's most famous colleague who eventually broke away from his mentor, also had an influence on Shakespeare studies in the 1950s and '60s. His ideas about archetypes stemming from a 'collective unconscious' in Western culture made an impact on criticism in general and Shakespearian criticism in particular. Although one would be hard pressed to find a significant Jungian critic, the mythic theories of Northrop Frye, developed for example in *A Natural Perspective* (1955), and which especially allowed the comedies and late romances to be taken in full seriousness, owe a great indirect debt to this school of psycho-analytical thought.

More recently, literary criticism has been significantly influenced by two post-Freudian theorists. Jacques Lacan decided that the unconscious mind is not anarchically random in its desires, but that it has an intrinsic structure, and he also argues that it has a language – that, in fact, thought is largely constructed from language rather than 'reality'. Lacan was followed by Michel Foucault, whose work on sexuality, madness, and imprisonment took even further the argument that we know ourselves and others through language or 'discourse' alone. These writers do not talk directly about Shakespeare but, judging from the many references in critical books during the 1980s, they have significantly influenced criticism of the plays. This is not surprising in the light of Shakespeare's uncanny and comprehensive creation of imagined worlds, simply through language.

'Materialist' Shakespeare

Having suggested some lines that link earlier with later criticism, it is time now to acknowledge the differences. The 'snapshot' I provided at the beginning of this chapter emphasized the current plurality of Shakespearian criticism, traced some assaults on the Shakespearian citadel, and stressed the tendency of recent critics to draw explicitly on some theoretical model. The general tendency has been to adopt a 'materialist' approach to literature in general.[18] This means that imaginative works are thought to issue not from universals or individual genius, but from material circumstances and from the economic, political, and gender attitudes that pervaded society when the work was written or when it is read and performed. Where Bradleyans and new critics thought art transcends life, and formalists separated art from life, materialists embed art in the concrete circumstances of political and economic life. This approach stresses that readers and critics also work in their own social circumstances which means they unavoidably imprint their own underlying ideologies onto the text, and even appropriate it for their own purposes. The general assumption is that the plays are not 'universal' but that they can be analysed in terms of historical circumstances, gender,

class, and other material conditions. This approach opens up new interpretations, but it is fair to say that it risks losing some of the strengths of earlier modes
like new criticism, which focused attention on textual details, and formalism,
which illuminates dramatic structure in ways that explain theatrical effect. It also
tends to bypass that mainstay of earlier criticism, 'character', in favour of ideas.

The movement which calls itself 'cultural materialism' is largely British in
origin, and builds on Marxism as practised, for example, by Raymond Williams
and social scientists. The best-known exponents are Jonathan Dollimore and
Terence Hawkes. Dollimore's *Radical Tragedy: Religion, Ideology and Power in
the Drama of Shakespeare and his Contemporaries* (1984) argues that tragedies by
Shakespeare and his contemporaries reveal power struggles between vested
interests that have their ideological counterparts in the profession of
Shakespeare criticism today. Hawkes in *That Shakespeherian Rag: Essays on a
Critical Process* (1986) is more concerned with scrutinizing the different ways in
which Shakespeare's words have been reconstructed by successive generations,
particularly in the twentieth century. He irreverently dismantles the institutions
of English education and criticism to explain the ways in which 'the canon' and
'bardolatry' have traditionally been used to give legitimacy to social attitudes
which are implacably conservative. Whether consciously or not, bureaucracies
through educational systems have used 'great literature' to emphasize traditional
values that ensure a docile and uncritical electorate, and Shakespeare has been
centrally used in this process. One might argue that the 1980s and 1990s have
seen a comparable reappropriation of Shakespeare to more libertarian views, a
move from right to left.

As one would expect, voices of resistance have been raised against what might
be seen as an overemphasis on politics, narrowly defined, in the work of materialists: Graham Bradshaw's and Brian Vickers's, for example. Others, such as R.
S. White in *Innocent Victims* (1982, 1986) and Derek Cohen in *Shakespeare's
Culture of Violence* (1993) tend to redefine politics in ethical terms, probing
Shakespeare's moral presentation of cruelty and victimization, with a special
sensitivity to gender issues. They adumbrate G. K. Hunter's creation of a niche
genre which he calls 'victim tragedy', and follow the lead of Harriett Hawkins
who wrote on 'The Victim's Side' in *Poetic Freedom and Poetic Truth* (1976).

Others have taken the materialist approach from outside the immediate
British context but with an eye to the culturally indoctrinating nature of British
imperialism. Michael Bristol in *Shakespeare's America / America's Shakespeare*
(1990) argues that the very profession of Shakespeare studies in America was a
kind of empire in itself, adopting and 'naturalizing' the conservative attitudes
absorbed from their former colonial masters in England. Post-colonial critics
examine the 'hegemony' of the imperial model in changing irrevocably local cultures and political assumptions. Ania Loomba in *Gender, Race, Renaissance
Drama* (1989) writes as both a woman and a product of the English-inspired
Indian educational system, seeking to expose the reactionary assumptions which

that system inherited. To her, as to other post-colonials, *The Tempest* is a crucial text about the nature of colonial rule and its cultural consequences. Martin Orkin takes an ambivalent approach to the same problem, suggesting that in South Africa Shakespeare has been used not only by white conservatives but also by black radicals. In his book *Shakespeare Against Apartheid* (1987) Orkin examines *Othello* in terms of race relations, *King Lear* in terms of property law. His book was published before the dismantling of apartheid in South Africa. In retrospect it demonstrates a prophetic insight that Shakespeare, no matter how central to the white enterprise, has also played a part in critiquing it from a black point of view.

Another materialist approach to Shakespeare is that practised by new historicists, mainly working from the United States. Stephen Greenblatt is their leading light, and he announces his central motivation in the haunting phrase 'a desire to speak with the dead'. Seeking to retrieve underlying attitudes and preoccupations held in Shakespeare's times, he examines political tracts, diaries, and other extra-literary documents, then reads Shakespeare's plays in their light. *Shakespearean Negotiations* (1988) argues that theatre was a part in a chain of commodities and a circulation of money and (more significantly) power, and that dramatists were writing within this economy. He sees the plays as embodying or reflecting two views, one which rulers sought to impose, sanctifying order and class differentiation, keeping subjects in perpetual 'anxiety'; and radical criticism of these attitudes, amounting to subversion. To many, Greenblatt is the most important critic writing today, first because he grapples with the local details of plays in their historical context rather than pursuing a new 'grand narrative' of theory, secondly because he honours the rich diversity and subtlety of views expressed in Shakespeare's plays, and thirdly because he writes with eloquence and passion. Among other practitioners of new historicism are Louis Montrose, Leah Marcus, Jonathan Goldberg, and Jean Howard.

Feminism and gender studies

A critical movement that is steadily and radically changing the field of Shakespeare studies is feminism, and it is one where Grady's claim of a paradigm shift is apt. Antecedents lie not in literary criticism but in the social and political demands for equality voiced by Mary Wollstonecraft and Simone de Beauvoir, and most systematically developed by women in the 1970s. A convenient bridge was built by Germaine Greer, whose Cambridge PhD was on Shakespeare's comedies, and who went on to write the influential *The Female Eunuch* (1971). The degree to which feminism has been assimilated into Shakespeare criticism is illustrated by the fact that the two books which stand out as important pioneers now seem rather tame and mild in their claims. Juliet Dusinberre in *Shakespeare and the Nature of Women* (1975) is more confident than others that there is such a thing as 'the nature of women', while the collaborative *The Woman's Part* (1980) assembles a set of essays (itself a sign of the collaborative ethic of feminism) which, generally speaking, reinterpret Shakespeare's plays either by highlighting the role of women or reading resistantly, 'against the grain', to demonstrate the pervasiveness of patriarchal ideas. Perhaps most importantly, this book included an extensive bibliography which indicates that earlier critics had anticipated strands of feminist thought.

As the women's movement (or more properly movements) has over the last thirty years addressed new issues, so these changes are reflected in Shakespeare studies. One direction was an assault on Shakespeare's plays as repositories of male, heterosexual attitudes which have harmed subsequent generations of women and gay men (Jacqueline Rose, Lisa Jardine, Dympna Callaghan). Another strand emphasized the centrality of female agency, female friendships, family relationships, and companionate love in Shakespeare's plays, arguing that although Shakespeare could not be a feminist yet he laid down the lines of thought that would lead to feminism. Some go further in claiming Shakespeare as a feminist thinker (Constance Jordan), indeed, 'the noblest feminist of them all'. Some analyse Shakespeare's construction of differing models of gender based on sexual identity, and the nature of intersexual erotic relationships (Marilyn French, Coppélia Khan). Still others, following the lead of the openly homosexual Derek Jarman, who made two filmed versions of Shakespeare's works (*The Tempest* (1979) and the Sonnets in a film called *The Angelic Conversation* (1985)), are interested in the proto-gay elements. They include Joseph Pequigney (*Such is My Love: A Study of Shakespeare's Sonnets* (1985)), Jonathan Goldberg (*Sodometries: Renaissance Texts, Modern Sexualities* (1992)), and Kate Chedgzoy (*Shakespeare's Queer Children: Sexual Politics and Contemporary Culture* (1995)). Obviously these approaches at certain points contradict each other, which leads us back to Empson's perception of radical ambiguity in Shakespeare's texts, and the best of gender critics tacitly work on this principle. It is perhaps not surprising that the heterogeneous movement has most systematically claimed the romantic comedies and romances as its main fields, which is welcome since these plays were relatively neglected by critics, if not in the theatre, throughout the twentieth century. But so comprehensive and all-embracing is the construction of gender in Shakespeare, that it has also made possible advances in criticism of the tragedies (Catherine Belsey's *The Subject of Tragedy: Identity and Difference in Renaissance Drama* (1985)) and history plays (Jean E. Howard and Phyllis Rackin, *Engendering a Nation: a Feminist Account of Shakespeare's English Histories* (1997)).

Intertextuality and reception

There used to be a branch of Shakespeare scholarship called 'sources and influences'. As with other areas, these are now underpinned by more theoretical and critical rigour, and accordingly they tend to be renamed 'intertextuality', 'reception theory', and 'reader response'. The new names subtly indicate once again the primacy of context over text, and the constructed rather than 'given' status of literature and theatre. The focus is no longer on Shakespeare as singular icon, with critics scanning what led up to his works and what came after, but rather on Shakespeare as one writer among a multitude of others, all building upon a host of earlier writers, in something like a conversation across centuries. On this view any work is a patchwork quilt of echoes importing other contexts, but like any good quilt something new is made in the creative assembling.

There is a corresponding recognition that Shakespeare's work has been creatively reconstructed in ever new historical moments by directors, actors, and audiences; and by readers and writers. In no other area is textuality so central: all the world's no longer a stage but a text, and all the men and women merely readers. Reception theory, the analysis of recorded readers' responses, and cultural study of theatre practices are potentially endless as shown, for example, in the wide-ranging approaches taken by Jonathan Bate in *Shakespeare and the English Romantic Imagination* (1986) and *Shakespearian Constitutions: Politics, Theatre, Criticism 1730–1830* (1992), R. S. White's detailed study, *Keats as a Reader of Shakespeare* (1986), and Marianne Novy's (ed.) *Women's Re-Visions of Shakespeare: On Responses of Dickinson, Woolf, Rich, H.D., George Eliot, and Others* (1990). The field is inexhaustible enough to keep scholars and critics happily occupied into the twenty-first century, and like Tristram Shandy's fictional autobiography, we can never quite catch up with the present.

Taken together, all these approaches suggest an infinitude of 'new readings' stretching to the crack of doom, so long as there occurs no paradigm shift that somehow writes Shakespeare out of international culture altogether. To this writer in 2000, such an event seems unlikely.

Notes

1. *Representations* 21 (1988), 1–26.
2. See, for example, Kenneth S. Rothwell and Annabelle Henkin Melzer, *Shakespeare on Screen: An International Filmography and Videography* (New York and London: Neal Schuman, 1990), which can be updated from the Internet Movie Database; and see Kenneth S. Rothwell, *A History of Shakespeare on Screen* (Cambridge: Cambridge University Press, 1999), Anthony Davies, ed., *Filming Shakespeare's Plays* (Cambridge University Press, 1988), Anthony Davies and Stanley Wells, eds., *Shakespeare and the Moving Image* (Cambridge University Press, 1994), Lynda E. Boose and Richard Burt, eds., *Shakespeare, The Movie* (London: Routledge, 1997), and Robert Shaughnessy, *Shakespeare on Film: Contemporary Critical Essays* (London: Macmillan, 1998).
3. See Margot Heinemann, 'How Brecht Read Shakespeare' in *Political Shakespeare*, ed. Jonathan Dollimore and Alan Sinfield (Manchester University Press, 1985), pp. 202–30.
4. See Jonathan Bate, *The Romantics on Shakespeare* (Penguin Books: Harmondsworth, 1992).

5. Bradley did have his own predecessors. An interesting, neglected work is Richard G. Moulton's *Shakespeare as a Dramatic Artist: A Popular Illustration of the Principles of Scientific Criticism* (Oxford: Clarendon Press, 1885).

6. See G. K. Hunter, 'A. C. Bradley's *Shakespearian Tragedy*', first published in *Essays and Studies* 21 (1968); rpt in Hunter's *Dramatic Identities and Cultural Tradition* (Liverpool University Press, 1978), pp. 270–85.

7. See R. S. White, 'Marx and Shakespeare', *Shakespeare Survey* 45 (1993), 89–100.

8. Quotations from *The Wheel of Fire: Interpretations of Shakespearian Tragedy* (London: Methuen, 1930, rev. edn 1949), pp. 14–15.

9. See R. S. White, *Hazlitt's Criticism of Shakespeare: A Selection* (Lampeter: Edwin Mellen Press, 1996).

10. *Some Versions of Pastoral* (London: Chatto and Windus, 1935), p. 89.

11. 'Falstaff', in *Essays on Shakespeare* (Cambridge University Press, 1986), p. 37.

12. *Ibid.*, p. 35.

13. *Ibid.*, p. 111.

14. Christopher Norris and Nigel Mapp, eds., *William Empson: The Critical Achievement* (Cambridge University Press, 1993), p. 115: 'Indeed it is remarkable – unless one invokes some collective "anxiety of influence" – that Greenblatt and his colleagues have managed to reinvent so many of Empson's arguments in the *Essays on Shakespeare* without even a token acknowledgment. For there is hardly a page in that volume where he doesn't anticipate the new historicists by asserting – as against the myth-mongers like Traversi – that we can best make sense of the plays by putting them firmly back in their historical context, by drawing on the widest possible range of relevant source-materials, and ceasing to regard them as timeless monuments to some transcendental "truth" enshrined beyond the reach of such mundane secular interests.'

15. See Marjorie Garber, *Shakespeare's Ghost Writers: Literature as Uncanny Causality* (New York: Methuen, 1987), esp. pp. 74–86 and 96–123.

16. Many recent critics emphasize in this area the work by Mikhail Bakhtin in its English translation by Hélène Iswolsky, *Rabelais and His World* (Cambridge, Mass.: MIT Press, 1968).

17. Edited by Norman Holland, Sidney Homan, and Bernard J. Paris (Berkeley: University of California Press, 1989).

18. See Ivo Kamps, ed., *Materialist Shakespeare: A History* (London: Verso, 1995), for essays by different writers, including Fredric Jameson.

Reading list

Bate, Jonathan, ed., *The Romantics on Shakespeare* (Harmondsworth: Penguin, 1992).

Bristol, Michael, *Shakespeare's America / America's Shakespeare* (London: Routledge, 1990).

Eastman, Arthur M., *A Short History of Shakespearian Criticism* (New York: Random House, 1968).

Grady, Hugh, *The Modernist Shakespeare* (Oxford: Clarendon Press, 1991).

Kolin, Philip C., ed., *Shakespeare and Feminist Criticism: An Annotated Bibliography and Commentary* (New York and London: Garland Publishing, 1991).

Rothwell, Kenneth S. and Annabelle Henkin Melzer, eds., *Shakespeare on Screen: An International Filmography and Videography* (New York: Neal Schuman, 1992).

Taylor, Gary, *Reinventing Shakespeare: A Cultural History from the Restoration to the Present* (London: The Hogarth Press, 1989).

Vickers, Brian, *Appropriating Shakespeare: Contemporary Critical Quarrels* (New Haven: Yale University Press, 1994).
Wells, Stanley, ed., *Shakespeare: A Bibliographical Guide* (Oxford: Clarendon Press, 1990).

Some useful websites
Arden Net: The Critical Resource for Shakespeare Studies
  http://www.ardenshakespeare.com/main/ardennet/
Folger Shakespeare Library
  http://www.folger.edu/welcome.htm
Shakespeare Resources on the Internet
  http://www-tech.mit.edu/Shakespeare/other.html
The Internet Movie Database (Shakespeare filmography)
  http://us.imdb.com/Name?Shakespeare,+William
World Shakespeare Online
  http://www-english.tamu.edu/wsb/

19

DIETER MEHL

Shakespeare reference books

Bibliographies

THE reader who wants a more or less complete list of writings on Shakespeare up to 1958 will have to work through four volumes that attempt to provide a comprehensive and systematic record of everything written on the poet and his works. William Jaggard's *Shakespeare Bibliography* (1911) is not very reliable or systematic, but still useful for the information it contains on early Shakespeare criticism. Its continuation by W. Ebisch and L. L. Schücking, *A Shakespeare Bibliography* (1931) and *Supplement for the Years 1930–35* (1937), is more professional and easier to use, whereas the fourth volume, Gordon Ross Smith's *A Classified Shakespeare-Bibliography, 1936–1958* (1963), is rather too complicated in its classification.

An intelligently discriminating list is given in volume one of *The New Cambridge Bibliography of English Literature*, edited by George Watson (1974), and there are a number of helpful shorter bibliographies. A survey of important titles is provided by *A Selective Bibliography of Shakespeare: Editions, Textual Studies*, edited by James G. McManaway and Jeanne Addison Roberts (1975); published for the Folger Shakespeare Library, it lists 4,519 items, mainly from 1930 to about 1973. David Bevington's *Shakespeare* (1978) in the series Goldentree Bibliographies in Language and Literature gives an excellent selection of roughly the same scope. A useful guide of a more discursive kind is provided by *Shakespeare: A Bibliographical Guide*, edited by Stanley Wells (1990), extensively revised from his *Shakespeare: Select Bibliographical Guides* (1973). Its nineteen chapters are written by different scholars, and concise bibliographies are given at the end of each chapter. Other useful tools are David Bergeron and Geraldo U. de Sousa, *Shakespeare: A Study and Research Guide*, in its revised third edition (1995), an up-to-date annotated bibliography, and Larry S. Champion, *The Essential Shakespeare* (1986). More ambitious, but limited in scope, is the compilation edited by Bruce T. Sajdak, *Shakespeare Index: An Annotated Bibliography of Critical Articles on the Plays 1959–1983*, vol. I: *Citations and Author Index*, vol. II: *Character, Scene and Subject Index* (1992). A useful critical survey of editions is provided by *Which Shakespeare? A User's Guide to Editions*, edited by Ann Thompson and others (1992).

For more recent books and other contributions to Shakespeare studies the reader may consult either the *Annual Bibliography of English Language and Literature*, published by the Modern Humanities Research Association, or the annual bibliography published as part of the *Publications of the Modern Language Association of America*. The most complete and up-to-date annual bibliography is that in *Shakespeare Quarterly*, briefly annotated and available as a separate volume as well as on CD-ROM. Between 1971 and 1983 the *Jahrbuch* of the 'Deutsche Shakespeare-Gesellschaft West' included an annual bibliography of works on Shakespeare published in German-speaking countries.

Also useful for most purposes are the annual reviews of the most significant contributions in *The Year's Work in English Studies* (usually about two or three years behind) and, generally more up to date, in *Shakespeare Survey*, with sections on 'Life, Times, and Stage', 'Critical Studies', and 'Textual Studies and Editions'.

More selective and uneven in scope are the volumes of the Garland Shakespeare Bibliographies series, of which several volumes on individual plays have so far appeared, e.g. *'King John': An Annotated Bibliography*, edited by Deborah T. Curren-Aquino (1994), covering the years 1940–91. These volumes include useful digests of the works discussed.

There are also extensive bibliographies in many of the reference books mentioned below, especially the *Shakespeare Encyclopaedia*, the *Shakespeare-Handbuch*, and Geoffrey Bullough's *Narrative and Dramatic Sources of Shakespeare*.

A comprehensive and more easily accessible electronic bibliography was launched in 1995, *The World Shakespeare Bibliography* on CD-ROM 1900–Present, edited by James L. Harner and published by The Arden Shakespeare in association with the Folger Shakespeare Library. It is based on the bibliographies in *Shakespeare Quarterly*. The update of 1999, covering the years 1980–96, includes some 50,000 records; each entry is annotated and provides information on content, reviews, productions, films, and recordings. The bibliography will gradually list every relevant item from 1900 to the present and will be updated annually.

Periodicals

There are several periodicals devoted to the study of Shakespeare.

Shakespeare Quarterly, started in 1950, includes reports on Shakespeare productions all over the world and reviews of important books as well as critical essays. Each volume of the annual *Shakespeare Survey* (from 1948) has a particular theme, but also includes articles on other topics. Several volumes begin with helpful surveys of critical writings on the theme of the volume (e.g. *Hamlet* in 1956 and 1965, *Othello* in 1968, *King Lear* in 1980, and 'Shakespeare in the Eighteenth Century' in 1998). The American *Shakespeare Studies* (from 1965) is another annual collection of essays and reviews.

The oldest periodical is the *Shakespeare Jahrbuch*, first published in 1864 by the Deutsche Shakespeare-Gesellschaft.[1] It has essays in English and German, extensive sections on Shakespeare productions in Germany, Austria, and Switzerland, and reviews of new publications as well as reports of the annual meetings and of other Shakespearian activities. *Shakespearian Research and Opportunities* (from 1965) reports on the annual Modern Language Association conference and provides checklists, reviews, and selected papers as well as a section 'Research in Progress'. *Cahiers Élisabéthains: Late Medieval and Renaissance English Studies*, published by the Centre d'Études et de Recherches Élisabéthaines de l'Université Paul Valéry, Montpellier, also includes articles, reviews, and reports of conferences and other scholarly activities.

Dictionaries, encyclopaedias, handbooks

There are a number of good reference books on Shakespeare's plays and their background. F. E. Halliday's *A Shakespeare Companion, 1564–1964* (1964), a dictionary with entries on a great variety of topics, is surprisingly comprehensive for its size, though by now badly out of date. *A Dictionary of Shakespeare* by Stanley Wells (1998) is thoroughly reliable and pleasant to use though necessarily selective. More ambitious and comprehensive, but less up to date is the splendid *A Shakespeare Encyclopaedia*, edited by Oscar James Campbell and Edward G. Quinn (1966). Many of its articles are written by well-known experts. There are plenty of illustrations and long sections on each play, discussing dates, textual evidence, stage history, and interpretation, and concluding with brief excerpts from influential critics. *William Shakespeare: His World, His Work, His Influence*, edited by John F. Andrews (three volumes, 1985), contains essays by numerous scholars on nearly every aspect of Shakespeare's society, his works and his impact on modern criticism and contemporary theatre. *A Companion to Shakespeare*, edited by David Scott Kastan (1999), is more strictly historical in scope. It has 28 new essays on Shakespeare and his theatrical, literary, and historical background. It is particularly helpful on the conditions of playwriting in Elizabethan and Jacobean London and England. Another useful tool, mainly for its inclusion of documents from the period, is *The Bedford Companion to Shakespeare: An Introduction with Documents*, by Russ McDonald (1996).

The German *Shakespeare-Handbuch: Die Zeit, Der Mensch, Das Werk, Die Nachwelt*, edited by Ina Schabert (fourth edition, completely revised, 2000), is a volume of nearly a thousand pages covering every aspect of Shakespeare studies, from the historical background to the history of Shakespeare criticism and adaptation, with detailed bibliographies at the end of each section. It is perhaps the most comprehensive reference book of its kind.

Among reference books proper, the indispensable *Annals of English Drama, 975–1700* should be mentioned. It was first edited by Alfred Harbage and completely revised by S. Schoenbaum (1964, with supplements in 1966 and 1970). It provides, as the subtitle specifies, *An Analytical Record of all Plays, Extant or Lost, Chronologically Arranged and Indexed by Authors, Titles, Dramatic Companies etc.*

Concordances

John Bartlett's *A New and Complete Concordance or Verbal Index to Words, Phrases, and Passages in the Dramatic Works of Shakespeare with a Supplementary Concordance to the Poems* (1894) was the standard work of its kind until the appearance of Marvin Spevack's *The Harvard Concordance to Shakespeare* (1973), which is based on the monumental, computerized *A Complete and Systematic Concordance to the Works of Shakespeare* in eight volumes (1968–75) by the same editor, classified by plays, characters, and stage directions and providing statistical information on Shakespeare's vocabulary, the language of each character, and the linguistic peculiarities of each play. Both works are keyed to the *Riverside Shakespeare*. Since several complete editions of Shakespeare's works are now available on CD-ROM, various kinds of searches and concordance work can be performed by personal computer. See below under 'Shakespeare on the Internet'.

Language

E. A. Abbott's *A Shakespearian Grammar: An Attempt to Illustrate Some of the Differences between Elizabethan and Modern English* (1869, reprinted 1966) remains useful; so is the more systematic and comprehensive *Die Sprache Shakespeares in Vers und Prosa* (1939, revised and enlarged edition of *Shakespeare-Grammatik*, 1898–1900) by W. Franz. A good modern survey is G. L. Brook's *The Language of Shakespeare* (1976); another stimulating introduction to many aspects of Shakespeare's language is provided by N. F. Blake, *Shakespeare's Language: An Introduction* (1983). Hilda M. Hulme's *Explorations in Shakespeare's Language: Some Problems of Lexical Meaning in the Dramatic Text* (1962) is good on selected aspects (use of proverbs, spelling, pronunciation, meaning).

On the more practical level C. T. Onions's *A Shakespeare Glossary* (1911, extensively revised by R. D. Eagleson, 1986) is an invaluable little dictionary of Shakespearian meanings. Another still indispensable tool is Alexander Schmidt (rev. by Gregor Sarrazin), *Shakespeare-Lexicon and Quotation Dictionary* (1902; repr. 1971). On matters of pronunciation Helge Kökeritz's *Shakespeare's Pronunciation* (1953) has become a classic; it has been only partly superseded by the more systematic and comprehensive accounts of E. J. Dobson, *English Pronunciation, 1500–1700*, two volumes (1957), and Fausto Cercignani, *Shakespeare's Works and Elizabethan Pronunciation* (1981). Dobson's work is, of course, not confined to Shakespeare and Cercignani is rather narrowly phono-logical in method and less concerned with literary aspects. There is also a useful little dictionary by Kökeritz on the pronunciation of names, *Shakespeare's Names: A Pronouncing Dictionary* (1959). Eric Partridge's dictionary of *Shakespeare's Bawdy* (1947, second edition 1968) makes entertaining reading, but sometimes presses connotations too far. More useful is *A Glossary of Shakespeare's Sexual Language* by Gordon Williams (1997). For a different aspect of Shakespeare's language, the comprehensive collection by R. W. Dent, *Shakespeare's Proverbial Language: An Index* (1981) should be consulted. It expands on the important compilation by M. P. Tilley, *A Dictionary of the Proverbs in England in the Sixteenth and Seventeenth Centuries* (1950), by concen-trating on Shakespeare. It lists 4,684 proverbial expressions in Shakespeare's work. Richmond Noble's *Shakespeare's Biblical Knowledge and Use of the Book of Common Prayer* (1935) is a useful inventory of two of the most important influ-ences on Shakespeare's language. More up to date and comprehensive is Naseeb Shaheen's *Biblical References in Shakespeare's Plays* (1999).

Editions

Serious students of Shakespeare will, sooner or later, need a complete edition of the plays and poems, and there are several good one-volume editions to choose from. The most frequently quoted was for a long time Peter Alexander's edition (*The Complete Works*, 1951, revised, with new introductions, 1994); it has a sound text and a brief glossary, but not much in the way of background information or interpretation. A number of American editions are more generous with glosses and commentary. Two paperback single-play series (see below) have been gath-ered into one volume each, the Pelican edition (*The Complete Works*, edited by Alfred Harbage, 1969) and the Signet edition (*The Complete Signet Classic Shakespeare*, edited by Sylvan Barnet, 1972). More expensive and bulky but much more informative and useful for the student is *The Riverside Shakespeare*, edited by G. Blakemore Evans (1974, new edition 1997); it includes background information, illustrations, and some excellent critical essays. David Bevington's *The Complete Works of Shakespeare* (fourth edition, 1992, updated 1997) offers a reliable text and concise introductions to each play and the poems as well as val-uable information about the text and the poet's world. Textually more adventur-ous is the new Oxford volume, edited by Stanley Wells and Gary Taylor, with John Jowett and William Montgomery: *William Shakespeare: The Complete Works* (1986). There is a modern spelling edition, also available in paperback, and a fully edited 'Original Spelling Edition'. The plays are arranged in chronologi-cal order and the texts have been more thoroughly examined and reconsidered than perhaps in any edition since the appearance of the First Folio. The two ver-sions of *King Lear* are both given in full. There are brief introductions to each play, but no annotation. Extensive commentary on textual issues and the individual texts is provided in the companion volume to the edition, *William Shakespeare: A Textual Companion*, by Stanley Wells and Gary Taylor, with John Jowett and William Montgomery (1987); this is easily the best and most comprehensive guide to all textual and editorial problems of Shakespeare's texts. The Oxford text is also, with a few significant modifications, used for the *Norton Shakespeare, based on the Oxford Edition*, General Editor Stephen Greenblatt (1997), with generous critical, illustrative, and bibliographical material, compiled by four American scholars. The edition includes not only the full quarto and Folio versions of *King Lear*, but also a specially edited conflated version. Altogether this is probably the most fully annotated one-volume edition of Shakespeare, handsomely printed, if a little unwieldy, and available in paperback.

For more intensive study of individual works, most readers will prefer single-play editions or separate editions of the poems, perhaps in addition to a one-volume edition. There is an almost embarrassing but also very helpful choice of single-play editions at various levels of sophistication and thoroughness.

The most formidable and the oldest of the series is A New Variorum Edition of Shakespeare, begun more than a century ago by H. H. Furness (1871) and still in progress. It offers not only an old-spelling text with generous glosses, but also selected criticism. The older volumes are invaluable inventories of early Shakespeare criticism and several have been reprinted in paperback form (1963). The more recent volumes are, in a way, less satisfactory, because modern criticism has grown to such an extent that it seems virtually impossible to represent it adequately within a single volume and the editors have to resort to mere bibliographical surveys or listings.

The New Shakespeare, edited almost single-handed by John Dover Wilson between 1921 and 1966, was an influential landmark of textual criticism, but is now largely outdated. The new Arden Shakespeare began as a revision of the 'old' Arden edition (from 1899) in 1951 under the editorship of Una Ellis-Fermor. It soon changed its policy, however, and almost all the later volumes present a new text and commentary, together with full introductions, attempting to cover every important aspect of the play, though mostly with little to say about performance and stage history. Some of the later volumes, especially those by the general editors, e.g. *A Midsummer Night's Dream*, edited by Harold Brooks (1979), and *Hamlet*, edited by Harold Jenkins (1982), are among the most thorough and comprehensive single-volume editions. A complete revision of the new Arden Shakespeare (Third Series), under the general editorship of Richard Proudfoot, Ann Thompson, and David Scott Kastan, began to appear in 1995 and is now steadily progressing. All the plays will eventually be newly edited; text and commentary take account of recent critical developments and, in particular, of performance history and, in some cases, modern adaptations. There are also often helpful illustrations. Some volumes (e.g. *Henry V*) include complete facsimiles of early quarto editions. All the Arden texts currently in print have been gathered into a single volume (1999), with brief new introductions. The some-what uneven collection combines side by side recently revised texts (e.g. *King Lear*) and unrevised editions or editions revised too late to be included (*Love's Labour's Lost*).

The American Signet Classic Shakespeare, edited by Sylvan Barnet (1963–70), is a useful paperback edition. The individual volumes are edited by different scholars. The same applies to the Pelican Shakespeare, edited by Alfred Harbage (1956–67). It is, on the whole, more thorough and original than the Signet edition and the commentary is more scholarly. A complete revision under the general editorship of A. R. Braunmuller and Stephen Orgel is in progress.

The New Penguin Shakespeare (General Editor T. J. B. Spencer; Associate Editor Stanley Wells), begun in 1967 and still not quite complete, is the most widely used paperback edition in England. A number of the editors are the same as those for the Arden, the Oxford and New Cambridge editions, but the Penguin seeks to appeal to a wider audience. The volumes are, nevertheless, based on orig-inal scholarship and include information about text, date, sources, and previous scholarship. There is a fairly long introduction to the play and a critical commen-tary following the text, explaining unfamiliar meanings, but also, in many cases, illuminating construction, style, and staging.

The Oxford Shakespeare (General Editor Stanley Wells) and the New Cambridge Shakespeare (founding editor Philip Brockbank, present General Editor Brian Gibbons), begun in 1982 and 1984 respectively, have progressed steadily and should be complete within a few years. The two series are in many ways similar and, together with the Arden Shakespeare, provide the most useful single editions of many plays. A supplementary Cambridge series gives critical editions of early quartos (e.g. *King Lear*, *Hamlet*, *Richard III*). All the texts are freshly edited, sometimes with surprising results, as in the case of *Henry V*, edited by Gary Taylor (Oxford, 1984); the Oxford Shakespeare is generally more innovative in its textual decisions, though each text is edited independently from the *Complete Works*. The commentary is particularly full on lexical matters (with an index for the Arden and the Oxford volumes) and on staging. Stage history (often with illustrations) plays a much larger part than in most previous editions, and the critical introductions frequently pay as much attention to the theatrical qualities of the text as to its literary aspects. In both series, the principles of arrangement and the style of the commentary are very similar, especially since some editors have edited volumes for both series. In each case the typographical design of the page is particularly successful and makes the texts a pleasure to use. The Cambridge edition perhaps has an even more pronounced emphasis on problems of staging, with, for all the earlier volumes, appealing drawings by C. Walter Hodges, illustrating possible reconstructions of Elizabethan staging. All three series are available in paperback.

The more general reader is well served by The New Folger Library Shakespeare (1992–), edited by Barbara Mowat and Paul Werstine. The volumes are illustrated with material in the Folger Library collections; there are brief, up-to-date critical introductions and helpful material on sources, stage history, and critical problems.

Another new series, only in its initial stages, is the Bedford Shakespeare Series, edited by Jean Howard. The volumes include, apart from the critically edited text, usually by David Bevington, a great number of historical and cultural documents, putting the play in a wider contemporary context. The first volume, E. Frances Dolan's edition of *The Taming of the Shrew* (1996), is a valuable compilation, as is *A Midsummer Night's Dream*, edited by Gail Paster and Skiles Howard (1999).

Mention should also be made of the Cambridge School Shakespeare (Series Editor Rex Gibson, 1992–). It has the complete New Cambridge text, with plenty of helpful annotation of a more basic kind, some supporting material and useful questions and exercises for the classroom.

Many of these recent editions are or will soon be also available on CD-ROM.

Facsimile editions are a special case; they are illuminating not just for the textual scholar, but for anyone wanting to see what the original page of a Shakespeare text looked like. This can provide a very good idea of the complex problems of modernization, emendation, and glossing that the modern editor has to face. The most sophisticated facsimile edition of the First Folio is the Norton Facsimile (*The First Folio of Shakespeare*, edited by Charlton Hinman, 1968; new edition, with an introduction by Peter Blayney, 1996); it is based on the best of the seventy-nine copies of the First Folio in the Folger Shakespeare Library and reproduces each page in its final and most perfect state. Most of the quartos have also been published in facsimile editions (Shakespeare Quarto Facsimiles, edited by W. W. Greg and Charlton Hinman, from 1939), and, in one volume, *Shakespeare's Plays in Quarto*, ed. Michel J. B. Allen and Kenneth Muir (1981).

Textual problems

The best introduction to the textual problems posed by individual plays is in most cases provided by the textual commentary of such critical editions as the Arden, the Oxford, or the New Cambridge. On a number of the problems which confront a modern editor Stanley Wells and Gary Taylor offer challenging and well-considered new ideas in *Modernizing Shakespeare's Spelling, with Three Studies in the Text of 'Henry V'* (1979); more general and wider in scope is Stanley Wells's *Re-Editing Shakespeare for the Modern Reader* (1984). F. P. Wilson's *Shakespeare and the New Bibliography* (revised and edited by Helen Gardner, 1970) is an expert introduction to the principles and the history of modern textual studies. A variety of textual and editorial problems are considered in E. A. J. Honigmann's *The Stability of Shakespeare's Text* (1965). Fredson Bowers, one of the most influential textual scholars of his generation, wrote a useful survey *On Editing Shakespeare* (1966). One of the most thorough and sophisticated demonstrations of modern textual methods (with a touch of Sherlock Holmes, but not quite his finality) is Charlton Hinman's monumental study, *The Printing and Proof-reading of the First Folio of Shakespeare* (two volumes, 1963); it supplements, but does not in all respects supersede, W. W. Greg's *The Shakespeare First Folio: Its Bibliographical and Textual History* (1955). Among new studies of textual issues Grace Ioppolo's *Revising Shakespeare* (1991) and John Jones's *Shakespeare at Work* (1995) will be found helpful, as well as Paul Werstine's survey, 'Shakespeare' in *Scholarly Editing: A Guide to Research*, edited by D. C. Greetham for the Modern Language Association of America (1995).

Shakespeare's life and time

Shakespeare's life has attracted all kinds of biographers and fact has often become inextricably confused with fiction and legend. One of the soundest and most useful works of reference is still E. K. Chambers's authoritative collection of all the surviving evidence relating to Shakespeare's life and his plays: *William Shakespeare: A Study of Facts and Problems* (two volumes, 1930). The condensed version, *A Short Life of Shakespeare with the Sources*, abridged by Charles Williams (1933), is a useful little compendium, even though some of the information is out of date. A good brief survey is G. E. Bentley's *Shakespeare: A Biographical Handbook* (1961), which provides a reliable assessment of the evidence. There are a number of attractive pictorial volumes on Shakespeare's life, such as F. E. Halliday, *Shakespeare: A Pictorial Biography* (1953), and Anthony Burgess, *Shakespeare* (1970), and, of course, many more or less popular biographies, such as the sound, reliable, and lively account by Stanley Wells, *Shakespeare: A Dramatic Life* (1994); paperback title: *Shakespeare: The Poet and his Plays* (1997), or Dennis Kay's informative and useful *Shakespeare: His Life, Work and Era* (1992).

E. I. Fripp's *Shakespeare: Man and Artist* (1938), in two volumes, is a useful quarry for miscellaneous information, particularly on the Stratford and Warwickshire background, but not always very reliable or easy to read. More factual and trustworthy, though more limited in scope, is Mark Eccles's *Shakespeare in Warwickshire* (1961). Recently, there has been a new interest in the subject of Shakespeare's biography. A very reliable, factual, and up-to-date account of Shakespeare's life and historical background, incorporating the latest scholarship, is P. Honan, *Shakespeare: A Life* (1998).

Some of the most authoritative and up-to-date books on Shakespeare's life are by S. Schoenbaum. His monumental *Shakespeare's Lives* (1970) is not a biography in the usual sense, but a fascinating and entertaining history of Shakespeare biographers, biographies, the search for reliable information, and the invention of colourful legends. It is a book *about* biography rather than a straightforward account of Shakespeare's life and yet it leaves the reader with a more substantial and trustworthy image of its subject than most of the traditional biographies. A shortened and revised edition appeared in 1991. Richard Dutton's *William Shakespeare: A Literary Life* (1989) offers a concise account of Shakespeare's life as an author and a man of the theatre. Peter Thomson's *Shakespeare's Professional Career* (1992) is particularly valuable as an account of the dramatist within his theatrical environment. An interesting, though largely undocumented period of Shakespeare's career is investigated in E. A. J. Honigmann's stimulating *Shakespeare: The 'Lost Years'* (1985).

For those who wish to look at all the documentary evidence for themselves Schoenbaum's sumptuously produced collection of photographic facsimiles, *William Shakespeare: A Documentary Life* (1975), provides expert commentary and a wealth of information. The narrative and many of the documents are included in the much cheaper and handier volume, *William Shakespeare: A Compact Documentary Life* (1977; paperback edition 1978). This is easily the most reliable and best-documented concise biography of Shakespeare.

Shakespeare: The Globe and the World (1977) is the catalogue of an exhibition arranged by the Folger Shakespeare Library. It is a wonderful picture-book, with an excellent commentary by S. Schoenbaum, covering a wide range of subjects related to Shakespeare's life and work. The last volume, another splendidly illustrated and attractively produced book, completes the series of biographical documentation and illustration: *William Shakespeare: Records and Images* (1981), again by S. Schoenbaum. It is an invaluable supplement to the earlier works, illustrating and discussing Shakespeare's involvement in various legal disputes, his handwriting, and his portraits.

On Shakespeare's time and background there are, of course, a great number of historical reference books and general studies that fall outside the scope of this brief survey. *Shakespeare's England: An Account of the Life and Manners of his Age*, edited by Sidney Lee and C. T. Onions (two volumes, 1916), is a still very useful collection of essays by various authors on many aspects of English culture in the age of Elizabeth. *Shakespeare Survey 17* (1964) forms a kind of supplement to it as well as an attempt to bring some of it up to date. *Shakespeare Survey 29* (1976) has a good review article by J. W. Lever on 'Shakespeare and the Ideas of His Time'. J. Dover Wilson's *Life in Shakespeare's England* (1911) is an informative and entertaining anthology of contemporary texts, deservedly popular and frequently reprinted.

Several earlier books attempt to describe the Elizabethan world picture as a necessary introduction to the study of Shakespeare's works. Some of the classic studies are still worth considering: Hardin Craig, *The Enchanted Glass: The Elizabethan Mind in Literature* (1935), and the same author's *New Lamps for Old: A Sequel to the Enchanted Glass* (1960), are helpful introductions to crucial Renaissance concepts, as is A. O. Lovejoy's influential study, *The Great Chain of Being* (1936). E. M. W. Tillyard's *The Elizabethan World Picture* (1943), frequently reprinted and quoted, offers perhaps rather too neat a view of a complex subject, but it is still very readable. J. B. Bamborough, *The Little World of Man* (1952), is informative on Elizabethan ideas on psychology. Madeleine Doran's *Endeavors of Art: A Study of Form in Elizabethan Drama* (1954) is one of the most influential accounts of literary conventions of the Renaissance. Such models, however, no longer play a significant part in discussions of the period. Two volumes of essays, significantly called *Alternative Shakespeares*, edited by John Drakakis (1985) and Terence Hawkes (1996) are representative of changing approaches.

Literary sources and influences

The most comprehensive account of Shakespeare's sources, together with all the more important texts, is to be found in Geoffrey Bullough's indispensable collection, *Narrative and Dramatic Sources of Shakespeare* (eight volumes, 1957–75). There is a section on each play, with a substantial introduction and many complete texts or excerpts from sources and analogues. Foreign texts are given in translation. Kenneth Muir's *The Sources of Shakespeare's Plays* (1977) is a briefer survey of the same subject, without the texts.

Most critical editions of the plays give an account of the sources and (as in many volumes of the Arden edition) a selection of texts. More general questions of literary influence are raised in T. W. Baldwin's *Shakspere's Smalle Latine and Lesse Greeke* (two volumes, 1947) which discusses the texts available in Shakespeare's time and in Elizabethan schools. John Velz, *Shakespeare and the Classical Tradition: A Critical Guide to Commentary, 1660–1960* (1968), is a comprehensive bibliography of studies on the subject (2,487 items), with brief comments. More recent studies of Shakespeare's classical world are R. S. Miola, *Shakespeare and Classical Tragedy: The Influence of Seneca* (1992), the same author's *Shakespeare and Classical Comedy: The Influence of Plautus and Terence* (1994), and Jonathan Bate, *Shakespeare's Ovid* (1993).

There are many books on particular influences. V. K. Whitaker, *Shakespeare's Use of Learning* (1953), is stimulating, if rather general. R. A. Brower, *Hero and Saint: Shakespeare and the Graeco-Roman Heroic Tradition* (1972), discusses the tragedies in the light of classical influences. An extremely helpful account of the traditions of comedy and their impact on Shakespeare is to be found in Leo Salingar, *Shakespeare and the Traditions of Comedy* (1974), which covers classical, medieval, and Italian influences. Emrys L. Jones, *The Origins of Shakespeare* (1976), is useful on dramatic influences on the early Shakespeare, especially the combination of popular and classical material. A wide-ranging and influential reassessment of popular traditions and their impact on Shakespeare is offered in Robert Weimann's study, *Shakespeare and the Popular Tradition in the Theater: Studies in the Social Dimension of Dramatic Form and Function*, edited by Robert Schwartz (1978), first published in German (1967). On related themes, François Laroque, *Shakespeare's Festive World: Elizabethan Seasonal Entertainment and the Professional Stage* (1991), first published in French (1988), should also be consulted. More limited, but of seminal importance, is Bernard Spivack, *Shakespeare and the Allegory of Evil* (1958). A different area of influences is discussed in Carol Gesner, *Shakespeare and the Greek Romance* (1970).

Shakespeare's stage

Most of the documents relating to Shakespeare's theatre and his company are collected in Chambers's *William Shakespeare: A Study of Facts and Problems* (two volumes, 1930) and in his equally indispensable *The Elizabethan Stage* (four volumes, 1923). The whole theatrical context is presented and discussed in Glynne Wickham's stimulating and richly documented *Early English Stages 1300 to 1660*, particularly volume II, parts 1 (1963) and 2 (1972). David Bradley, *From Text to Performance in the Elizabethan Theatre: Preparing the Play for the Stage* (1992), is very useful on Elizabethan stage conditions, as is Thomas James King, *Casting Shakespeare's Plays. London Actors and Their Roles, 1590–1642* (1992). More comprehensive, with a wealth of new material, is Andrew Gurr, *The Shakespearian Playing Companies* (1996). An important aspect of Stuart theatre history is covered in Leeds Barroll, *Politics, Plague, and Shakespeare's Theatre: The Stuart Years* (1991). A useful new reference work for the study of stage technique and performance practice is *A Dictionary of Stage Directions in English Drama, 1580–1642* by Alan C. Dessen and Leslie Thomson (1999).

The two most important playhouses are elaborately reconstructed by I. Smith in *Shakespeare's Globe Playhouse* (1956) and *Shakespeare's Blackfriars Playhouse: Its History and Design* (1964); C. W. Hodges's *The Globe Restored* (1953, second edition 1968) is an important and beautifully illustrated book. John Orrell's *The Quest for Shakespeare's Globe* (1983) is a fascinating reconstruction of the structure and the dimensions of Shakespeare's Globe, mainly on the basis of Hollar's 'Long View of London' and related evidence. A balanced introduction to the whole subject and perhaps the best general introduction is Andrew Gurr's *The Shakespearian Stage, 1574–1642* (1970); the third revised edition (1992) includes a discussion of recent developments and discoveries.

Much work has been done in recent years on Shakespeare's theatre and the staging of his plays. On the actual performances at the Globe B. Beckerman's *Shakespeare at the Globe 1599–1609* (1962) is most helpful; Beckerman discusses questions of production, dramaturgy, and stage conditions while T. J. King, *Shakespearian Staging, 1599–1642* (1972), gives useful information about the plays performed and the conclusions we can draw regarding staging and playhouse design. Peter Thomson's *Shakespeare's Theatre* (1983) is a sound and stimulating study of Shakespeare's company, its activities and its stage as well as the way in which these theatrical conditions can influence our reading of the texts. There are many interesting hints about possible ways of staging particular scenes in the new volumes of the Oxford Shakespeare and the New Cambridge

Shakespeare (illustrated by C. W. Hodges). On Elizabethan acting Bertram Joseph's *Elizabethan Acting* (1951, revised edition 1964) is worth consulting. The best and most fully documented study of the audience and of actual visits to the theatre is Andrew Gurr's *Playgoing in Shakespeare's London* (1987, new edition, 1999). An interesting new view of the building and first opening of the Globe in 1599 is offered by S. Sohmer's *Shakespeare's Mystery Play* (1999). The reconstruction of Shakespeare's Globe has been described in a number of books. A particularly useful account of the earlier stages is Andrew Gurr's *Rebuilding Shakespeare's Globe*, with John Orrell (1989). The more recent developments, including the 'Prologue season' (1996), are included in *Shakespeare's Globe Rebuilt*, edited by J. R. Mulryne and Margaret Shewring (1997).

Stage history

Perhaps the most accessible overall account is *Shakespeare: An Illustrated Stage History*, edited by Jonathan Bate and Russell Jackson (1996); it offers an exciting survey of theatrical fashions and highlights from Edward Alleyn to modern experimental theatre. There are good and detailed sections on stage history in the volumes of the Oxford, the New Cambridge, and the 'Third' Arden Shakespeare. G. C. D. Odell's *Shakespeare from Betterton to Irving* (two volumes, 1920) and C. B. Hogan's *Shakespeare in the Theatre* (two volumes, 1952–7) contain valuable material. Robert Speaight, *Shakespeare on the Stage: An illustrated History of Shakespearian Performance* (1973), provides a spirited survey from Richard Burbage to Laurence Olivier. J. C. Trewin's *Shakespeare on the English Stage 1900–1964* (1964) will also be found useful. A colourful anthology of performance criticism is provided by Stanley Wells in *Shakespeare in the Theatre: An Anthology of Criticism* (1997). Michael Mullin's *Theatre at Stratford-upon-Avon* (two volumes, 1980) is a computerized index to performances at Stratford 1879–1978, listing productions, plays, and theatre personnel. William Halstead's *Shakespeare as Spoken* (twelve volumes, 1977–80) collates some 2,500 printed acting editions and prompt-books with the Globe text.

Some modern productions are also discussed in J. R. Brown, *Shakespeare's Plays in Performance* (1966), in J. L. Styan, *The Shakespearian Revolution: Criticism and Performance in the 20th Century* (1977), in Richard David, *Shakespeare in the Theatre* (1978), and in Peter Holland's *English Shakespeares: Shakespeare on the English Stage in the 1990s* (1997). More general and particularly stimulating is Dennis Kennedy, *Looking at Shakespeare: A Visual History of Twentieth-Century Performance* (1993). Wilhelm Hortmann's *Shakespeare on the German Stage: The Twentieth Century* (1998) is a well-documented account of an important non-English stage history of this century. The earlier period is treated, though more summarily, in Simon Williams, *Shakespeare on the German Stage*, volume 1: 1586–1914 (1990). A very different tradition of Shakespearian performance is discussed in *Shakespeare and the Japanese Stage*, edited by

Takashi Sasayama, J. R. Mulryne, and Margaret Shewring (1999). A useful selection of approaches is given in *Foreign Shakespeare: Contemporary Performance*, edited by Dennis Kennedy (1993).

The annual reviews of performances in *Shakespeare Survey* (mainly London and Stratford) and *Shakespeare Quarterly* (more international) are important sources of information. The most detailed studies of the stage history are devoted to individual plays; particularly thorough and informative are books by Marvin Rosenberg on four of the great tragedies: *The Masks of Othello* (1961), *The Masks of King Lear* (1972), *The Masks of Macbeth* (1978), and *The Masks of Hamlet* (1992). Rosenberg's approach is a fascinating combination of stage history and close study of the text. Some series are devoted especially to production histories and accounts of important productions of individual plays, like 'Shakespeare in Performance' (General Editors J. R. Mulryne and J. C. Bulman) and 'Shakespeare in Production' (General Editors J. S. Bratton and Julie Hankey). A particularly stimulating specimen of this kind of work is Gary Jay Williams, *Our Moonlight Revels: 'A Midsummer Night's Dream' in the Theatre* (1997); another, not strictly confined to stage history, is V. Mason Vaughan, *Othello: A Contextual History* (1994). A most welcome addition to scholarly stage histories is provided by the series 'Players on Shakespeare', variously edited by Philip Brockbank, Russell Jackson, and Robert Smallwood (1985–), in which actors with the Royal Shakespeare Company write about some of their Shakespeare parts.

A new and steadily growing area of Shakespearian peformance history is covered in Jack J. Jorgens, *Shakespeare on Film* (1977), *Shakespeare and the Moving Image*, edited by Anthony Davies and Stanley Wells (1994), *Shakespeare on Film*, edited by R. Shaughnessy (1998), and the important reference work, *Shakespeare on Screen: An International Filmography and Videography*, by Kenneth S. Rothwell and Annabelle Henkin Melzer (1990). Rothwell's *A History of Shakespeare on Screen* (1999) is an excellent survey.

Shakespeare's impact and changing reputation

On Shakespeare's immediate impact and his contemporary reputation, E. A. J. Honigmann's *Shakespeare's Impact on His Contemporaries* (1982) is well documented as well as boldly original in some of its conclusions. A different aspect is discussed by David L. Frost, *The School of Shakespeare: The Influence of Shakespeare on English Drama 1600–1642* (1968), which is more strictly confined to literary questions. On early Shakespeare criticism, by far the most important source is the collection by Brian Vickers, *Shakespeare: The Critical Heritage* (six volumes, 1974–81), with long excerpts from critics up to 1801 and excellent introductions. The growth of Shakespeare's reputation in a wider context is well described in Michael Dobson, *The Making of the National Poet: Shakespeare, Adaptation and Authorship, 1660–1769* (1992). A useful anthology is *The Romantics on Shakespeare*, ed. Jonathan Bate (1992), with a substantial introduction. Augustus Ralli, *A History of Shakespeare Criticism* (two volumes, 1932), discusses each critic in sequence and is a mine of useful information. The German *Shakespeare-Handbuch*, edited by Ina Schabert, has a long and intelligent chapter on the development of Shakespeare criticism. A. M. Eastman, *A Short History of Shakespeare Criticism* (1968), provides a useful sketch of the whole subject and there is a judicious brief study of twentieth-century criticism up to 1950 by Kenneth Muir, 'Fifty Years of Shakespearian Criticism: 1900–1950', in *Shakespeare Survey 4* (1951). Many of the reference works mentioned above also give information about the history of Shakespeare criticism; a generous selection from earlier critics will be found in the volumes of the New Variorum edition. A good collection of perceptive criticism is *Women Reading Shakespeare, 1660–1900: An Anthology of Criticism*, ed. Ann Thompson and Sasha Roberts (1997). Useful anthologies of criticism on particular plays, often with good critical introductions, have appeared in the Casebook series (from 1968), supplemented by the New Casebook series. More comprehensive are the volumes in the series 'Shakespeare, the Critical Tradition', ed. Brian Vickers (1996–). Perhaps the fullest collection of excerpts from earlier criticism is *Shakespearian Criticism: Excerpts from the Criticism of William Shakespeare's Plays and Poetry, from the First Published Appraisals to Current Evaluations*, edited by Sandra L. Williamson and James E. Person (twelve volumes so far, 1991–). The second part of the series, from volume 11 onwards, deals with stage history and collects valuable material on past productions. A lively and informative, provocatively polemical account is Brian Vickers, *Appropriating Shakespeare: Contemporary Critical Quarrels* (1994).

Music and the visual arts

Many critics have commented on the important part played by music in Shakespeare's plays. Edward W. Naylor's *Shakespeare and Music* (1896, revised edition 1931) is a classic survey of the subject. More detailed and specialized studies are F. W. Sternfeld's *Music in Shakespearian Tragedy* (second edition 1967) and Peter J. Seng's *The Vocal Songs in the Plays of Shakespeare: A Critical History* (1967). Sternfeld's book is as readable as it is learned and discusses many different aspects of its topic. It takes account of previous scholarship and gives transcriptions of early musical settings. Seng's work is a kind of Variorum edition of the songs, with much useful information on musical settings. Three books by John H. Long attempt a comprehensive survey of the available material: *Shakespeare's Use of Music: A Study of the Music and its Performance in the Original Production of Seven Comedies* (1955), *Shakespeare's Use of Music: The Final Comedies* (1961), and *Shakespeare's Use of Music: The Histories and Tragedies* (1971). *Shakespeare in Music*, edited by Phyllis Hartnoll (1964), is a particularly useful collection of essays on music in Shakespeare and Shakespeare in music. It includes a long and rewarding essay by Winton Dean on 'Shakespeare and Opera' and a seventy-eight page 'Catalogue of Musical Works Based on the Plays and Poetry on Shakespeare'. The *Shakespeare Music Catalogue*, edited by Bryan N. S. Gooch and David S. Thatcher (1991), in five volumes, offers an almost complete inventory of all music connected with Shakespeare, including incidental music in Shakespeare productions. It is an indispensable tool for any further research on Shakespearian music. An interesting, more specialized study is R. L. Neighbarger, *An Outward Show: Music for Shakespeare on the London Stage, 1660–1830* (1992). Gary Schmidgall, *Shakespeare and Opera* (1990), is full of valuable material and stimulating observations, though somewhat loquacious.

Shakespeare in the visual arts (illustration, stage design, and paintings inspired by the plays) has been most imaginatively studied by W. Moelwyn Merchant, whose *Shakespeare and the Artist* (1959) remains the most important book on the subject. *Shakespeare and Pictorial Art*, edited by Charles Holme, with a text by Malcolm C. Salaman (1971), is an instructive picture-book, with 130 plates. Geoffrey Ashton's *Shakespeare and British Art* (1981) is the scholarly catalogue of an important exhibition. Another valuable catalogue of an exhibition shown in Germany, Britain, and the USA is *The Boydell Shakespeare Gallery*, edited by Walter Pape and Frederick Burwick (1996), with important essays including several by art historians.

Shakespeare on the Internet

With the arrival of electronic word processing and the Internet, a completely new set of tools and a steadily growing amount of material of surprisingly large scope has become available to the Shakespeare scholar, and countless databases and other collections can be accessed from the researcher's own desk. Necessarily, only a limited number can be listed here as a first introduction to a rapidly increasing virtual library.

The best up-to-date introduction to Shakespeare resources on the web is through the sites 'Shakespeare Web Links', ed. Ken Bugajski, under the World Shakespeare Bibliography, Electronic Edition (http://www-english.tamu.edu/wsb/links.html). It lists sites on Shakespeare's works, criticism, journals, institutions, festivals and acting companies. Another very convenient gateway to web sites in most areas of Shakespeare and Renaissance literature is 'A Selected Guide to Shakespeare on the Internet' ed. Christa Jansohn (http://www.shakespeare-gesellschaft.de/deutsch/textlinks.html). All the other sites suggested below are listed here.

A useful introduction is through the general Shakespeare site 'Mr. William Shakespeare and the Internet' http://daphne.palomar.edu/shakespeare/, organized by Terry Gray at Palomar College in California. The site provides information on Shakespeare's works, life, and times, the early modern stage, lesson-plans for teachers, a large listing of Shakespeare festivals around the USA and Canada, and much more, including links to many other Shakespeare sites.

Complete texts of Shakespeare's plays and poems are available at the following sites: MIT: http://tech-two.mit.edu/Shakespeare/works.html; and The Works of the Bard (Matty Farrow, Australia): http://www.gh.u.syd.edu.au/~matty/Shakespeare//Shakespeare.html. Michael Best at the University of Victoria offers transcripts of a number of quarto and Folio texts on the Internet Shakespeare Editions: http://castle.uvic.ca/shakespeare/index.html. Excellent digitized reproductions of early editions of *King Lear*, *Henry V*, and *Hamlet*, and of Holinshed's *Chronicles* and Foxe's *Acts and Monuments*, as well as other sources may be found on the Furness Library site at the University of Pennsylvania: http://www.library.upenn.edu/etext/furness/.

Several Shakespeare institutions offer helpful sites. 'Shakespeare's Globe' (Chantal Miller-Schütz at the University of Reading): http://www.reading.ac.uk/globe/ provides information about both the original Globe Theatre and the recently rebuilt Globe, along with a timeline. The website of the Folger Shakespeare Library in Washington, D.C., http://www.folger.edu offers information on their educational programmes as well as a collection of lesson-plans for teaching Shakespeare in school. Their online catalogue, containing about 100,000 records of books in the collection, is also accessible through the Folger website. The Shakespeare Birthplace Trust in Stratford-upon-Avon provides basic information on their properties, tours, and educational events: http://www.shakespeare.org.uk/.

'Shakespeare Illustrated', a site developed by Harry Rusche at Emory University in Georgia, 'explores nineteenth-century paintings, criticism and productions of Shakespeare's plays and their influences on one another': http://www.cc.emory.edu / ENGLISH / classes / Shakespeare_Illustrated / Shakespeare.html.

Notes

1. When this association split up in 1964, the Shakespeare-Gesellschaft West renamed its annual volume *Deutsche Shakespeare-Gesellschaft West. Jahrbuch*, though editors and publisher remained the same, whereas the Shakespeare-Gesellschaft with its seat in Weimar started its own annual volume under the old name. When, in 1993, the two societies reunited, the yearbooks also merged. The volumes for 1993 and 1994 bear the title *Deutsche Shakespeare-Gesellschaft. Jahrbuch*; from 1995 (now volume 131) the publication once more appears with its traditional title and numbering.

INDEX

Page numbers for illustrations are given in italics. Works by Shakespeare appear under title; works by others under author's name.